T0233752

Lecture Notes in Computer Science 8951

Commenced Publication in 1973
Founding and Former Series Editors:
Gerhard Goos, Juris Hartmanis, and Jan van Leeuwen

Editorial Board

David Hutchison
Lancaster University, Lancaster, UK
Takeo Kanade
Carnegie Mellon University, Pittsburgh, PA, USA
Josef Kittler
University of Surrey, Guildford, UK
Jon M. Kleinberg
Cornell University, Ithaca, NY, USA
Friedemann Mattern
ETH Zurich, Zürich, Switzerland
John C. Mitchell
Stanford University, Stanford, CA, USA
Moni Naor
Weizmann Institute of Science, Rehovot, Israel
C. Pandu Rangan
Indian Institute of Technology, Madras, India
Bernhard Steffen
TU Dortmund University, Dortmund, Germany
Demetri Terzopoulos
University of California, Los Angeles, CA, USA
Doug Tygar
University of California, Berkeley, CA, USA
Gerhard Weikum
Max Planck Institute for Informatics, Saarbrücken, Germany

More information about this series at http://www.springer.com/series/7407

Harald Atmanspacher · Claudia Bergomi
Thomas Filk · Kirsty Kitto (Eds.)

Quantum Interaction

8th International Conference, QI 2014
Filzbach, Switzerland, June 30 – July 3, 2014
Revised Selected Papers

 Springer

Editors
Harald Atmanspacher
ETH Zürich
Zürich
Switzerland

Claudia Bergomi
Universitätsspital Bern
Bern
Switzerland

Thomas Filk
University of Freiburg
Freiburg
Germany

Kirsty Kitto
Queensland University of Technology
Brisbane, QLD
Australia

ISSN 0302-9743 ISSN 1611-3349 (electronic)
Lecture Notes in Computer Science
ISBN 978-3-319-15930-0 ISBN 978-3-319-15931-7 (eBook)
DOI 10.1007/978-3-319-15931-7

Library of Congress Control Number: 2015932682

LNCS Sublibrary: SL1 – Theoretical Computer Science and General Issues

Springer Cham Heidelberg New York Dordrecht London
© Springer International Publishing Switzerland 2015
This work is subject to copyright. All rights are reserved by the Publisher, whether the whole or part of the material is concerned, specifically the rights of translation, reprinting, reuse of illustrations, recitation, broadcasting, reproduction on microfilms or in any other physical way, and transmission or information storage and retrieval, electronic adaptation, computer software, or by similar or dissimilar methodology now known or hereafter developed.
The use of general descriptive names, registered names, trademarks, service marks, etc. in this publication does not imply, even in the absence of a specific statement, that such names are exempt from the relevant protective laws and regulations and therefore free for general use.
The publisher, the authors and the editors are safe to assume that the advice and information in this book are believed to be true and accurate at the date of publication. Neither the publisher nor the authors or the editors give a warranty, express or implied, with respect to the material contained herein or for any errors or omissions that may have been made.

Printed on acid-free paper

Springer International Publishing AG Switzerland is part of Springer Science+Business Media
(www.springer.com)

Preface

Since its inception in 2007, the conference series on Quantum Interaction is by now a tradition of its own. The eighth meeting within the series took place at the Conferene Center Lihn (Filzbach, Switzerland), in an exciting environment close to Lake Walensee and the Glarner Alps, from June 30 to July 3, 2014. It was co-hosted by Collegium Helveticum, an interdisciplinary research institute jointly operated by the University of Zurich and the Swiss Federal Institute of Technology (ETH) at Zurich, and by the International Society for Mind-Matter Research.

For the uninitiated, the term Quantum Interaction may need a bit of commentary. It is important to emphasize that it does not refer to interactions between particles or fields in quantum physics. Rather, it addresses areas of research in which – for good reasons – mathematical tools of quantum physics (non-commutative operations, Bell-type inequalities, Hilbert space models, etc.) are applied to a variety of topics outside the natural remit of physics.

The Quantum Interaction conferences have provided a debating ground for such applications and have developed into an emerging interdisciplinary area of science, combining research topics in mathematics, physics, psychology, economics, cognitive, and computer science. The breadth reflected in this list of disciplines remains a challenge for a coherent framework in which all the different approaches find their systematic place.

The presentations at the Quantum Interaction conference covered essentially five thematic fields: (1) fundamental issues, (2) semantics and memory, (3) decision making, (4) games, politics, and social aspects, and (5) nonlocality and entanglement. Three distinguished keynote speakers, Michael Turvey (University of Connecticut), Paavo Pylkkänen (Universities of Skövde and Helsinki), and Günter Mahler (University of Stuttgart) added exciting novel perspectives to these fields.

The 21 papers included in this volume are based on the contributions to the conference. Each one of them was assessed by three referees and revised according to their comments. We are grateful to all members of the Program Committee for their hard work and for due delivery of reports. In an interdisciplinary area like this careful and accurate reviews are certainly not a matter of course.

We are grateful for the splendid hospitality we experienced at the Lihn and thank Hannes Hochuli and his staff for their sensitive cooperation in matters large and small, ensuring the success of the conference. Alfred Hofmann and Anna Kramer at Springer International Publishing provided helpful advice for the smooth and speedy publication of the proceedings in the Springer Series Lecture Notes in Computer Science. And, last but not least, we thank Gerd Folkers, director at Collegium Helveticum, for his invaluable support.

December 2014

Harald Atmanspacher
Claudia Bergomi
Thomas Filk
Kirsty Kitto

Organization

Steering Committee

Peter Bruza — Queensland University of Technology, Brisbane, Australia

Trevor Cohen — University of Texas at Houston, USA

Bob Coecke — Oxford University, UK

Ariane Lambert-Mogiliansky — Paris School of Economics, France

Dominic Widdows — Microsoft Inc., Seattle, USA

General Chairs

Harald Atmanspacher — Collegium Helveticum Zurich, Switzerland

Claudia Bergomi — University Hospital of Psychiatry, Bern, Switzerland

Program Chairs

Thomas Filk — University of Freiburg, Germany

Kirsty Kitto — Queensland University of Technology, Brisbane, Australia

Program Committee

Harald Atmanspacher — Collegium Helveticum Zurich, Switzerland

Reinhard Blutner — University of Amsterdam, The Netherlands

Peter Bruza — Queensland University of Technology, Brisbane, Australia

Trevor Cohen — University of Texas at Houston, USA

Thomas Filk — University of Freiburg, Germany

Peter beim Graben — Humboldt University, Berlin, Germany

Emmanuel Haven — University of Leicester, UK

Andrei Khrennikov — Linnaeus University, Växjö, Sweden

Kirsty Kitto — Queensland University of Technology, Brisbane, Australia

Ariane Lambert-Mogiliansky — Paris School of Economics, France

Bill Lawless — Paine College, Augusta, USA

Massimo Melucci — University of Padova, Italy

Jian-Yun Nie — University of Montreal, Canada

Emmanuel Pothos — City University London, UK

Mehrnoosh Sadrzadeh — Oxford University, UK

Sonja Smets   University of Amsterdam, The Netherlands
Sandro Sozzo   University of Leicester, UK
Jennifer Trueblood   University of California at Irvine, USA
Giuseppe Vitiello   University of Salerno, Italy
Joyce Wang   Ohio State University, Columbus, USA
Dominic Widdows   Microsoft Inc., Seattle, USA
Guido Zuccon   Queensland University of Technology, Brisbane,
                               Australia

Website

Claudia Bergomi   University Hospital of Psychiatry, Bern,
                              Switzerland

Contents

Fundamentals

Fundamental Physics and the Mind –
Is There a Connection?

Paavo Pylkkänen[1,2(✉)]

[1] Department of Cognitive Neuroscience and Philosophy, University of Skövde,
P.O. Box 408, 541 28 Skövde, Sweden
[2] Department of Philosophy, History, Culture and Art Studies,
The Finnish Center of Excellence in the Philosophy of the Social
Sciences (TINT), University of Helsinki, P.O. Box 24, 00014 Helsinki, Finland
paavo.pylkkanen@his.se

Abstract. Recent advances in the field of quantum cognition (Pothos and
Busemeyer 2013; Wang et al. 2013) suggest a puzzling connection between
fundamental physics and the mind. Many researchers see quantum ideas and
formalisms merely as useful pragmatic tools, and do not look for deeper
underlying explanations for why they work. However, others are tempted to
seek for an intelligible explanation for why quantum ideas work to model
cognition. This paper first draws attention to how the physicist David Bohm
already in 1951 suggested that thought and quantum processes are analogous,
adding that this could be explained if some neural processes underlying thought
involved non-negligible quantum effects. The paper next points out that the idea
that there is a connection between fundamental physics and the mind is not
unique to quantum theory, but was there already when Newtonian physics was
assumed to be fundamental physics, advocated most notably by Kant. Kant
emphasized the unique intelligibility of a Newtonian notion of experience, and
this historical background prompts us to ask in the final part of the paper
whether we can really make sense of any quantum-like experience (whether
experience of the empirical phenomena in the "external world" or the "inner
world" of psychological phenomena). It is proposed that intelligibility is a relative notion and that, regardless of initial difficulties, quantum approaches to
cognition and consciousness are likely to provide valuable new ways of
understanding the mind.

1 Introduction

Recent advances in the field of quantum cognition (see e.g. Pothos and Busemeyer
2013; Wang et al. 2013) suggest a connection between fundamental physics and the
mind that some may find puzzling. Perhaps to alleviate the puzzle, many quantum
cognition researchers are keen to distance themselves from the more speculative
research programs of "quantum mind" or "quantum consciousness". Broadly speaking,
these latter programs involve the hypothesis that mind and/or consciousness are in
some more or less literal sense quantum phenomena, e.g. in the underlying (sub)
neuronal processes. The situation reminds us of the field of artificial intelligence (AI),
as characterized by Searle (1980), where "strong AI" refers to a claim that a suitably

© Springer International Publishing Switzerland 2015
H. Atmanspacher et al. (Eds.): QI 2014, LNCS 8951, pp. 3–11, 2015.
DOI: 10.1007/978-3-319-15931-7_1

programmed computer literally has intelligence and consciousness, while "weak AI" refers to much more modest claims to the effect that computer programs provide useful models of intelligent cognition. So, analogously we could say that there is "weak quantum cognition" (WQC, cognitive processes can be modeled by quantum concepts and formalisms; cf. Atmanspacher et al. 2002) and "strong quantum cognition" (SQC, cognitive processes have literally quantum mechanical aspects); see Pylkkänen 2015.

Suppose that a broad consensus develops that certain principles and mathematical tools of quantum theory (such as quantum probability, entanglement, non-commutativity, non-Boolean logic and complementarity) provide a good way of modeling many significant cognitive phenomena (such as decision processes, ambiguous perception, meaning in natural languages, probability judgments, order effects and memory; see Wang et al. 2013). In such a situation many researchers may still be happy to see quantum ideas and formalisms merely as useful pragmatic tools, and not worry about looking for deeper underlying explanations for why they work. However, it is likely that others, especially philosophers of mind, would be tempted to seek for an *intelligible explanation* for *why* quantum ideas work to model cognition. Just think of the philosophical debates about conscious experience during recent decades. There a major focus of research has been the "hard problem" - the challenge of providing an intelligible explanation of how conscious experience might possibly arise from underlying (e.g. physical, biological, computational or non-conscious mental) processes. Analogously, *the hard problem of quantum cognition* would be to provide an intelligible explanation for *why* various principles and formalisms of the quantum theory seem to work so well to model cognitive phenomena and predict behavioral outcomes. And here, it seems, the most obvious thing to do, at least in the beginning, is to consider the various suggestions within the stronger quantum mind/consciousness programs (for a critical review of these, see Atmanspacher 2011).

This strategy should make sense for, say, a reductive materialist, who believes that mental states are identical with some neurophysiological states. According to physics the constituents of neural states obey the rules of quantum mechanics. So, if some mental states, too, obey quantum principles, perhaps the explanation for this is that the dynamics of those mental states reflects in some way the dynamics of the quantum mechanical aspects of the neural states that underlie or even constitute those mental states. Further, even someone who is a functionalist in philosophy of mind might be tempted to consider the role of quantum effects in the underlying dynamical structures that implement cognition. If some aspects of cognitive processes turn out to be radically quantum-like, perhaps their implementation requires some quantum mechanical structures and dynamics in the processes that realize them (regardless of whether these processes are neurophysiological or, say, silicon based).

In this paper I will first consider how the physicist David Bohm already in his 1951 discussion was engaged with both WQC and SQC. I will then briefly consider how Bohm's discussion connects with contemporary philosophy of mind and cognitive science. I next point out that the idea that there is a connection between fundamental physics and the mind is not unique to quantum theory, but was there already when Newtonian physics was assumed to be fundamental physics, advocated most notably by Kant. Kant emphasized the unique intelligibility of a Newtonian notion of experience, and this historical background prompts us to ask in the concluding section whether we can really make sense of any quantum-like experience (whether inner or outer experience).

2 Weak and Strong Quantum Cognition in 1951: Bohm's Early Discussion

The idea that mental phenomena and quantum processes are analogous to each other goes back to the founding architects of the quantum theory. For example, Niels Bohr had become familiar with the idea of complementarity in the field of psychology, and was led to propose that complementarity is a key feature of quantum phenomena (Wang et al. 2013, p. 678). Influenced by Bohr's ideas, the physicist David Bohm included a discussion of "analogies between thought and quantum processes" in his acclaimed 1951 textbook *Quantum theory* (Bohm 1951, pp. 168–172). Note that this book was written while Bohm was still a supporter of the standard interpretation of quantum theory; more precisely (as Bohm himself realized only later), the book's approach is close to Wolfgang Pauli's variant of the "Copenhagen interpretation". I have discussed these analogies elsewhere at some length (Pylkkänen 2014), so will here provide only a brief summary and some further reflection. I want to emphasize here that in his discussion Bohm not only pointed to various analogies between cognitive processes and quantum processes (in the spirit of WQC), he also moved on to consider (in the spirit of SQC) whether these analogies could be explained if there were non-negligible quantum effects in the neural processes underlying cognition.

Bohm drew attention to three analogies between human thought process and quantum processes, which can be denoted as follows:

- Effects of observation
- Unanalyzability
- Both have a "classical limit".

Let us consider these briefly in turn.

Effects of observation. Bohm first considered the fact that introspective observation of thought (say, an attempt to define the content of thought) typically introduces unpredictable and uncontrollable changes in the way thought proceeds thereafter. Analogously, in the quantum domain, the observation of the position of a particle introduces unpredictable and uncontrollable changes in the particle's momentum. So in both cases it may be difficult to measure properties of interest without profoundly influencing them. Thus "measurement" in both the introspective psychological domain and in the quantum domain cannot necessarily be assumed to be revelation of well-defined pre-existing properties (cf. Wang et al. 2013, p. 674). In quantum theory it is typical that the measurement influences the system under observation, and it seems that such influences are also characteristic of introspection. Note in particular that this analogy concerns *empirical* phenomena – on the one hand our attempts to empirically study the contents of the mind in introspection, and on the other hand our attempts to empirically study the properties of quantum systems. In this sense this analogy is not mere metaphysical speculation. It actually has to do with our empirical attempts to connect with the domains under interest.

Note also that partly due to these kinds of features of introspection, already Kant thought that empirical psychology (insofar as it relies on introspection) cannot be a science (Brook 1994, pp. 9–10). In contemporary discussions, while some have tried to rehabilitate introspection as a respectable method in psychological research (e.g., Jack and Roepstorff 2003), others have focused on bringing out its various biases and limitations (e.g., Pronin and Kugler 2007). Bohm's suggestion that introspection and quantum measurement are analogous suggests, at least in principle, the possibility of improving the status of introspection as a scientific method. One way to do this is to see how far the principles and formal tools of quantum measurement theory could be applied (*mutatis mutandis*) to characterize observation in introspection (cf. Wang et al. 2013, p. 674).

Unanalyzability. Bohm next suggests that a part of the significance of each element of thought process (and language) originates in its indivisible and incompletely controllable connections with other elements. He notes that if we try to analyze a thought into smaller and smaller elements we eventually come to a point where further analysis seems impossible. Analogously, some of the essential properties of a quantum system (e.g. whether it is a wave or a particle) depend on its indivisible and incompletely controllable connections with surrounding objects. This suggests that both thought and quantum phenomena are characteristic of a radical type of wholeness, unanalyzability and context-dependence. Again such wholeness can be considered a challenge for any informative scientific analysis of the holistic phenomenon. However, quantum theory (and its various interpretations) involve novel ways of tackling radically holistic phenomena both mathematically and conceptually. Indeed, quantum cognition researchers have made use of such ways when modeling holistic cognitive phenomena, such as the holistic features of concepts. For example, Gabora and Aerts (2002) have described the context-dependence of concepts in generalized quantum terms, while Bruza et al. (2009) have explored meaning relations in terms of the quantum-like concept of entanglement.

Both thought and quantum processes have a "classical limit". Bohm then moves on to suggest that the logical process corresponds to the most general type of thought process as the classical limit corresponds to the most general quantum process. The idea is that the rules of logic are analogous to the causal laws of classical physics, while concepts are analogous to objects, in the sense that logically definable concepts play the same fundamental role in abstract and precise thinking as do separable objects and phenomena in our customary description of the world. At the same time, he notes that there is also an analogy between pre-logical thinking and quantum process. He suggests that the basic thinking process probably cannot be described as logical. For example, a sudden emergence of a new idea seems analogous to a "quantum jump".

The classical limit analogy implies that we have "two physical worlds" - i.e., the general quantum world which contains as its part the special case of a classical world. But it also suggests that we have "two minds", i.e. the mind in the sense of a general alogical and aconceptual thinking process, which in some conditions gives rise to the special case of the mind as logical thinking process with logically definable concepts. So there are, in a sense, two levels of thought. This is similar to e.g. Smolensky's (1988) view of the relation between connectionist and symbolic cognition (see below); it also anticipates Aerts's (2009) notion of two modes of human thought.

From weak to strong quantum cognition. Bohm finally raises the question of whether these analogies between quantum processes and thought are just a co-incidence, or whether they instead might be a sign of a deeper connection between the two domains. He acknowledges that they could be a mere co-incidence, but goes on to consider an alternative, namely the possibility that the physical aspect of thought might involve quantum processes in some important way. This, he suggests, would explain in a qualitative way many features of our thinking. For example, if the physical aspect of thought involved quantum processes in a non-negligible way, this would enable us to develop a qualitative account of why the direction ("momentum") of thought is disturbed by an attempt to define its content ("position"). Similarly, if the physical aspect of thought and language involved quantum processes (e.g. indivisible links), it might be possible to develop a qualitative naturalistic explanation of some holistic features of language and meaning. Further, the "classical limit analogy" might be explainable if the physical aspect of the general (alogical, aconceptual) thought process involved quantum processes (with inseparability, discontinuity etc.), while the physical aspect of the logical and conceptual thought process involved classical processes (e.g. classically describable, separable neural "activation patterns" governed by the classical laws of physics).

3   Comparison with Contemporary Philosophy of Mind and Cognitive Science

A fair amount of recent philosophy of mind and cognitive science has emphasized the non-conceptual or aconceptual aspect of the human mind (see e.g. Bermúdez and Cahen 2012 and the references therein; Pylkkö 1998). For a physicalist it is natural to ask what the proposed physical or computational concomitants of such aconceptual mental processes might be. Connectionist models are one candidate for the computational concomitants. But, as e.g. Pylkkö (1998) has pointed out, these are (mostly) mechanically computable and thus deterministic. They are thus an implausible candidate to be the physical aspect of a truly non-mechanical level of aconceptual mental processes.

More plausibly, one could propose that ideas and perceptions about classical objects supervene on some classically describable neural processes. Then, just as it is possible for the body to manipulate external objects, so it might be possible in the mind to "manipulate" representations, symbols etc., which latter are assumed to supervene on classical neural patterns. But let us then further assume that there is another kind of (i.e., aconceptual) activity of the mind which supervenes on some neurophysiological process in which quantum effects play a non-negligible role. Now, just as classical and quantum levels are related in physical reality, so the classical and quantum-like mental processes (and their classical and quantum mechanical neural correlates, respectively), might be related via particular types of mutual influences, amplifications, etc. (cf. Smolensky 1988).

The above implies that the explanation for the possibility of quantum-like cognition experience is that the matter we are composed of has quantum properties. The problem here is, of course, that it is currently very difficult to test hypotheses about, say, non-negligible quantum effects in neural processes. However there is currently a growing body of promising theoretical and empirical work on the role of quantum effects in biological systems, which might make the above speculations more plausible - or at any rate more testable – in the future (see Ball 2011; Craddock et al. 2014; see also Atmanspacher 2011 for a critical review of a number of quantum approaches to consciousness).

4   Fundamental Physics and the Mind in Kant's Critical Philosophy

We started off by noting that many researchers may find puzzling the connection between fundamental physics and the human mind that seems implied by recent advances in quantum cognition, not to mention the speculations in the quantum mind/consciousness programs. However, the idea that there is a connection between fundamental physics and the mind is not new in Western science and philosophy. Most notably, Kant's critical philosophy suggested that there is a strong connection between the principles of Newtonian physics and experience. Toulmin (2003) points out that Kant attempted to give a philosophical justification for Newton's results by claiming that a scientist can arrive at a coherent, rational system of empirically applicable explanations only by constructing her theories around Euclidean and Newtonian concepts. In other words, Kant assumed that Newton had hit on a uniquely adequate system of physics. But even more radically, Kant held that these principles are necessarily a part of human every-day experience of the world, and not just scientific experience. More precisely, he thought that the presuppositions of Newtonian physics are part of the *necessary conditions of the possibility of experience in general* (Strawson 1966).

   To get a better idea of Kant's thoughts on this difficult issue it is useful to consider the opening words of Peter Strawson's acclaimed 1966 book *Bounds of Sense: An Essay on Kant's Critique of Pure Reason*:

> "It is possible to imagine kinds of world very different from the world as we know it. It is possible to describe types of experience very different from the experience we actually have. But not any purported or grammatically permissible description of a possible kind of experience would be a truly intelligible description. There are limits to what we can conceive of, or make intelligible to ourselves, as a possible general structure of experience. The investigation of these limits, the investigation of the set of ideas which forms the limiting framework of all our thought about the world and experience of the world, is, evidently, an important and interesting philosophical undertaking. No philosopher has made a more strenuous attempt on it than Kant." (1966, p. 15).

So, according to Strawson, Kant was centrally concerned with the "bounds of sense" – with the "...limits to what we can conceive of, or make intelligible to ourselves, as a possible general structure of experience" (1966, p. 15). Kant's own view of these limits was closely tied with Newtonian physics. For as we already mentioned, Kant thought that the presuppositions of Newtonian physics are part of the necessary conditions of the possibility of experience in general. So in this sense it is fair to say that Kant's view of the general structure of experience is Newtonian. Indeed, when we consider the main general theses of what Strawson (1966, p. 24) calls Kant's "metaphysics of experience", we find in them a strong emphasis upon features of Euclidian geometry and Newtonian physics. For example, according to Strawson Kant argues that "…there must be one unified (spatio-temporal) framework of empirical reality embracing all experience and its objects" and that "…certain principles of permanence and causality must be satisfied in the physical or objective world of things in space." (1966, p. 24). Kant (1787) himself wrote:

> "Other forms of intuition besides those of space and time, other forms of understanding besides the discursive forms of thought, or of cognition by means of conceptions, we can neither imagine nor make intelligible to ourselves; and even if we could, they would still not belong to experience, which is the only mode of cognition by which objects are presented to us." (B263).

In retrospect we can say that Kant was, even by his own standards, mistaken in assuming that Newton had discovered a uniquely adequate system of physics. For, as Toulmin (2003) points out,

> "…20th-century astrophysics and quantum mechanics have succeeded in giving non-Euclidean and post-Newtonian concepts an entirely coherent empirical application in the scientific explanation of natural phenomena - and this was something that Kant was not prepared to contemplate."

However, does the fact that Newtonian physics fails to account for natural phenomena in the quantum and relativistic domains imply that Kant was wrong in claiming that the principles of Newtonian physics are part of the necessary conditions of human every-day experience? And what is the relation of Kant's view of the connection between experience and physics to the quantum view of experience sketched earlier in the paper?

5 Concluding Remarks: Extending or Traversing the Bounds of Sense?

In the previous section we considered an idea that has been a key part of Western philosophy since Kant, namely that philosophy should be concerned with investigating the "bounds of sense" – i.e. the limits to "…what we can conceive of, or make intelligible to ourselves, as a possible general structure of experience" (Strawson 1966). We noted that Kant himself thought that Newtonian physics played a key role in defining these limits. According to this view, our experience typically consists of a self-conscious subject perceiving a law-governed world of objects. However, our discussion in the earlier sections explored the possibility that quantum rather than Newtonian principles might play a key role in human cognition and experience.

So, what should we make of the Newtonian, classical character of Kant's view of experience? Note that in our sketches of a more general, quantum view of experience described earlier in this article, we were not denying the validity of the Kantian view altogether. We were rather implying that Kant was describing the "classical limit" of human experience. Note also that an aconceptual view of the mind is typically asub-jectivist (e.g. Pylkkö 1998). It is assumed that a fully self-conscious subject is typically not present or dominant in the more general, aconceptual experience. Rather, such a subject is something that only emerges in the classical limit of experience, i.e., when aconceptual experience in some typical circumstances divides and crystallizes into concepts and objects. So a quantum view of human experience need not deny altogether the role that Kant gives to the self-conscious subject. However, such a subject is no longer seen as a fundamental aspect of human experience. Of course, as Pylkkö (1998) has emphasized, asubjectivist views have also – independently of any quantum considerations - been proposed in the "post-phenomenological" approaches of e.g. the late Heidegger, Merleau-Ponty, Bataille and Patocka.

There is a potential difficulty that any quantum view of experience needs to face. Note that Strawson gives great weight to *intelligibility* as a criterion. For the challenge, according to him, is to find the limits to *what we can make intelligible to ourselves*, as a possible general structure of experience. Now, quantum theory is notoriously difficult to understand, so much so that some philosophers, like G.H. von Wright (1986) have indeed spoken about a "crisis of intelligibility" in connection to it. The obvious risk is that any attempt to develop a quantum view of experience (whether experience of the empirical phenomena in the "external world" or the "inner world" of psychological phenomena) will inherit the lack of intelligibility characteristic of quantum theory. Such a view would then traverse, rather than extend, the bounds of sense and risk leading to descriptions empty of meaning.

However, it is here important to bear in mind that intelligibility is a relative notion. In recent years this has been particularly vividly brought out by Ladyman and Ross, e.g. in their provocative and ground-breaking 2007 book *Every Thing Must Go: Metaphysics Naturalized* where they, among other things, discuss the role of intuitions and common sense in metaphysics. For example, they point out that "[w]hat counts as intuitive depends partly on our ontogenetic cognitive makeup and partly on culturally specific learning" (2007, p. 10). Surely the same applies for intelligibility. From time to time scientific research involves encountering puzzling empirical phenomena (e.g. the experimental results that necessitated the development of quantum theory) and making sense of these puzzles often requires us to develop new concepts or even whole new conceptual frameworks (e.g. Bohr's complementarity or Bohm's implicate order). Often such new concepts and frameworks are very difficult to grasp at first, but they justify their existence by the light they are able throw upon the puzzling phenomena that prompted their development in the first place. In line with this, Wang et al. (2013, p. 681) are optimistic about the intelligibility and explanatory power of the quantum cognition approach:

> "Perhaps in contrast to the common impression of being mysterious, quantum theory is inherently consistent with deeply rooted psychological conceptions and intuitions. It offers a fresh conceptual framework for explaining empirical puzzles of cognition and provides a rich new source of alternative formal tools for cognitive modeling."

To be sure, in the course of ground-breaking scientific research (whether in physics or in cognitive science) there are times when some may feel that others have traversed rather than extended the bounds of sense. And, of course, the very notion of aconceptual experience (Pylkkö 1998) that a quantum view of experience may involve suggests that our possibilities to give intelligible conceptual descriptions of the aconceptual aspects of experience are likely to be limited. But, if one is allowed to indulge in a bit of anachronistic speculation, given Kant's aspirations to develop a *scientific metaphysics*, he himself might well have attempted to incorporate quantum principles into his view of experience – both "outer" and "inner" - had he been aware of the empirical results that led to the development of quantum theory.

Literature

Atmanspacher, H.: Quantum approaches to consciousness. In: Zalta, E.N. (ed.) The Stanford Encyclopedia of Philosophy (2011). http://plato.stanford.edu/archives/sum2011/entries/qt-consciousness/

Atmanspacher, H., Römer, H., Walach, H.: Weak quantum theory: complementarity and entanglement in physics and beyond. Found. Phys. **32**, 379–406 (2002)

Atmanspacher, H.: At home in the quantum world. Behav. Brain Sci. **36**, 276–277 (2013)

Ball, P.: The dawn of quantum biology. Nature **474**, 272–274 (2011)

Bermúdez, J., Cahen, A.: Nonconceptual mental content. In: Zalta, E.N. (ed.) The Stanford Encyclopedia of Philosophy (2012). http://plato.stanford.edu/archives/spr2012/entries/content-nonconceptual/

Brook, A.: Kant and the Mind. Cambridge University Press, Cambridge (1994)

Bruza, P.D., Kitto, K., Nelson, D., McEvoy, C.: Is there something quantum like in the human mental lexicon? J. Math. Psychol. **53**, 362–377 (2009)

Bohm, D.: Quantum Theory. Prentice Hall, New York (1951). Republished by Dover (1989)

Craddock, T.J.A., Friesen, D., Mane, J., Hameroff, S., Tuszynski, J.A.: The feasibility of coherent energy transfer in microtubules. J. R. Soc. Interface **11**, 20140677 (2014). http://dx.doi.org/10.1098/rsif.2014.0677

Gabora, L., Aerts, D.: Contextualizing concepts using a mathematical generalization of the quantum formalism. J. Exp. Theor. Artif. Intell. **14**, 327–358 (2002)

Jack, A., Roepstorff, A. (eds.): Trusting the Subject?: The Use of Introspective Evidence in Cognitive Science. Imprint Academic, Thorverton (2003)

Kant, I.: Critique of Pure Reason, 2nd edn. J.M. Dent & Sons Ktd, London (1991). Originally published in German in 1787

Ladyman, J., Ross, D.: Every Thing Must Go: Metaphysics Naturalized. Oxford University Press, Oxford (2007)

Pronin, E., Kugler, M.B.: Valuing thoughts, ignoring behavior: the introspection illusion as a source of the bias blind spot. J. Exp. Soc. Psychol. **43**(4), 565–578 (2007)

Pylkkänen, P.: Can quantum analogies help us to understand the process of thought? Mind Matter **12**(1), 61–91 (2014)

Pylkkänen, P.: Weak vs. strong quantum cognition. In: Liljenström, H. (ed.) Advances in Cognitive Neurodynamics (IV). Springer, Dordrecht (2015)

Pylkkö, P.: The Aconceptual Mind: Heideggerian Themes in Holistic Naturalism. John Benjamins, Amsterdam and Philadelphia (1998)

Searle, John: Minds, Brains and Programs. Behav. Brain Sci. **3**(3), 417–457 (1980)

Smolensky, P.: On the proper treatment of connectionism. Behav. Brain Sci. **11**, 1–74 (1988)

Strawson, P.F.: The Bounds of Sense: An Essay on Kant's Critique of Pure Reason. Routledge, London (1966)

Toulmin, S.: Philosophy of science. In: Encyclopedia Britannica (2003)

Wang, Z., Busemeyer, J.R., Atmanspacher, H., Pothos, E.M.: The potential of using quantum theory to build models of cognition. Top. Cogn. Sci. **5**, 672–688 (2013)

von Wright, G.H.: Vetenskapen och förnuftet. Ett försök till orientering. Söderströms, Helsinki (1986)

What is Quantum? Unifying Its Micro-physical and Structural Appearance

Diederik Aerts[1] and Sandro Sozzo[1,2]([✉])

[1] Center Leo Apostel (Clea), Brussels Free University (VUB),
Pleinlaan 2, 1050 Brussel, Belgium
{diraerts,ssozzo}@vub.ac.be
[2] School of Management and IQSCS, University of Leicester,
University Road, Leicester LE1 7RH, UK
ss831@le.ac.uk

Abstract. We can recognize two modes in which 'quantum appears' in macro domains: (i) a *micro-physical appearance*, where quantum laws are assumed to be universal and they are transferred from the micro to the macro level if suitable *quantum coherence* conditions (e.g., very low temperatures) are realized, (ii) a *structural appearance*, where no hypothesis is made on the validity of quantum laws at a micro level, while genuine quantum aspects are detected at a structural-modeling level. In this paper, we inquire into the connections between the two appearances. We put forward the explanatory hypothesis that, 'the appearance of quantum in both cases' is due to 'the existence of a specific form of organisation, which has the capacity to cope with random perturbations that would destroy this organisation when not coped with'. We analyse how 'organisation of matter', 'organisation of life', and 'organisation of culture', play this role each in their specific domain of application, point out the importance of evolution in this respect, and put forward how our analysis sheds new light on 'what quantum is'.

Keywords: Micro-physical quantum appearance · Structural quantum appearance · Coherence · Evolution

1 Introduction

The strange quantum world unveils every day more its mysterious aspects to us. On one hand, increasing evidence confirms that, whenever entities on large scales are pushed in delicate and specific ways to show quantum effects, such as entanglement, nonlocality, interference, and Bose or Fermi identity, they reveal aspects of this quantum behavior [1–11]. Such experiments have reached the astonishing scales of distances of 18 km in the case of entanglement, sizes of large macro- and bio-molecules in the case of interference [9,10], and room temperature realisations of Bose-Einstein condensates [11]. On the other hand different aspects of the structure of quantum theory are identified, its probability model, but also the structure of interference and entanglement, and the Bose and Fermi

© Springer International Publishing Switzerland 2015
H. Atmanspacher et al. (Eds.): QI 2014, LNCS 8951, pp. 12–23, 2015.
DOI: 10.1007/978-3-319-15931-7_2

behavior of identity, in situations with entities that are part of the macroscopical world surrounding us. More specifically in human cognition and human decision processes, and in cultural entities such as languages, but also in situations in biology, economics and computer science, such typical quantum structures have been found [12–25, 28–31].

These two ways in which 'quantum appears' are looked upon differently, and even give rise to different thought about 'what quantum is'. We will call these two appearances 'micro-physical' and 'structural', respectively.

The 'micro-physical appearance' of quantum is always accompanied by an explanation which links it with 'quantum in the micro-world', assuming that quantum laws hold universally in this micro-world. Quantum effects can then be detected also in the macroscopic world if suitable conditions of control are verified, these conditions being of different types. The conditions can range from the construction of an interferometer capable of creating interference on the macro level to the cooling down of a gas of bosonic quantum particles making them join into one quantum state, a so called 'Bose-Einstein condensate'. This tenet constitutes the basis of the research which flourishes in many areas, namely, quantum computation and information [32], Bose-Einstein condensation [6], superconductivity [3], superfluidity [1, 2], and ever more macroscopic realisations of double slit interference and entanglement [9, 10].

The 'structural appearance' of quantum is identified by the criterion that the considered situation can be modeled by using a quantum-theoretic formalism, without a necessary connection with the quantum nature of particles at a microscopic level. This approach has recently produced important achievements in the study of cognitive processes, in the domain of concept research [15, 16, 20, 23], human decision making [24, 25], but also by modeling situations in economics [21, 22, 30], biology and ecology [31], and computer science, i.e. for information retrieval and natural language processing [13, 14, 17, 18].

Since our research activity has touched both quantum appearances, we are naturally led to wonder whether and how they can be connected. In the present paper, we try to answer this question. We put forward an explanatory hypothesis which makes it possible to understand the two quantum appearances as being manifestations of one underlying specific organisational state of reality. Our hypothesis leads also to a challenging view on 'what quantum is'.

The hypothesis that we put forward, first here in short, and in the following more explored in detail, is the following. "That 'quantum appears' is connected with the presence of a specific type of organisation, with the property of being able to cope with the intrinsic destructive aspects of random influences of change perturbing the organisation". We will call this organisation a 'quantum organisation'. Hence, it is an organisation able to save itself from destruction due to random influences of change. Concretely, and for the two quantum appearances that we have mentioned, the micro-physical appearance and the structural appearance, we think of 'organisations of matter', 'organisations of life', and 'organisations of culture', and will explain more in detail in the following how these are good examples illustrating our general explanatory hypothesis.

2 The Micro-physical Quantum Appearance

The identification of what we have called 'micro-physical appearance of quantum' has been historically associated with wave-particle interpretations, and so was the identification of the emergence of quantum effects in the macroscopic physical world. More concretely, it is the original formula by Louis de Broglie $\lambda = h/p$, where λ is the de Broglie wave length of an entity with momentum p, and $h = 6.62 \cdot 10^{-34} J \cdot s$ is Planck's constant [33] which is customarily used – certainly by experimentalists – to reason about the micro-physical appearance of quantum also if this happens in the macro world. The idea is that quantum behavior within a collection of entities appears when the de Broglie waves of these entities can overlap, i.e. when the wavelengths are bigger than the typical distance between the entities. The mechanism imagined within the wave-particle interpretations is that with overlapping de Broglie waves, the waves can vibrate in phase, join together to (more or less) form a single wave. For a gas of particles, such a situation can only occur at very low temperatures, since with increasing temperature, heat adds energy and hence momentum to each of the particles, so that their de Broglie wave lengths will become smaller and smaller, to the extent that the waves no longer overlap. We stress that the pure effect of becoming smaller is not what makes quantum behavior disappear. It is the non-globally structured way in which the wavelength decreases that destroys the quantum coherence. Indeed, heat is intrinsically a non-structured random way of adding energy, which is why "it is a process profoundly disturbing the quantum coherence'. The particles of the gas, that at low temperatures were united into one macroscopically sized de Broglie quantum wave, start to get disconnected, their de Broglie waves being pushed out of phase as a consequence of the collisions with random packets of heat energy. This means that with rising temperature the gas starts to become a collection of separated particles, behaving classically with respect to each other. Considering our explanatory hypothesis, the quantum organisation here is correlated with the temperature of the environment, if this temperature is low enough, the micro-quantum realm is able to cope with the random disturbance of bombarding energy packets. Hence, the appearance of quantum behavior at a macroscopic scale for gases at very low temperatures, and disappearance of this quantum behavior, being substituted by classical behavior if temperature rises, is a good example of what we have called 'quantum organisation'.

Let us give a short overview of these macroscopic quantum entities that constitute a micro-physical appearance of quantum. In 1917 Einstein proposed the microscopic description for the quantum-mechanical mechanism of the 'laser' [34]. This was definitely the first macroscopic quantum entity, and no cooling is needed here. The reason is that only photons are involved, and the random bombarding of heat packets existing at room temperature also consists of photons. Photons scatter only extremely rarely with other photons, which is the reason that the laser does not suffer under heat [35]. Next to the laser, Bose-Einstein condensates are the entities that have brought the micro-quantum behavior to the macroscopic level, but they need heavy cooling, since they exists of atoms or molecules in a gas. And atoms or molecules are highly disturbed by bombardment of random packets of energy, which means that only when cooling down the gas, and in this way shielding of the bombardment, what we have called a quantum organisation becomes possible. The experimental realisation of a Bose-Einstein condensate came about after a long exciting history of cooling gases to temperatures close to the absolute zero. The phenomena of superfluidity and superconductivity, both already observed more than a century ago by Kamerlingh Onnes in Leiden, and later studied in more detail by Kapitsa, Meissner, London, Landau, Ginzburg and others, were only stepwise identified as being caused by the quantum 'Bose-Einstein condensation' phenomenon, and lead in 1995 finally to a first conscious and identified realisation of such a condensate [6].

3   The Structural Quantum Appearance

The attention for the structural appearance of quantum was originally rooted in the investigation of the structure of the theory of quantum physics itself from its axiomatic to its operational aspects [36–38]. An essential step took place in identifying similar types of structures in situations of entities in the macroscopic world surrounding us, without the appearance of this structure being connected in any way to micro-physical aspects of quantum [38–40]. A new important step took place when structural quantum aspects started to get identified in aspects of human thought, more specifically in how the human mind makes decisions [12], developing further to the fruitful use of the mathematical formalism of quantum theory in Hilbert space to model complex situations of decision making [25,29,41]. Parallel a successful quantum-theoretic modeling was elaborated for how the human mind uses conceptual entities, like in a language [15,16,20,28,43], and genuine quantum aspects, such as 'contextuality', 'emergence', 'entanglement', 'interference', 'superposition' were identified as responsible of the observed deviations from classical (fuzzy set) logic and probability theory [44]. Quantum modeling approaches have also been employed in information retrieval and natural language processing to integrate and generalize latent semantic analysis methods [13,14,17,18]. The domain of research that followed from this has now been called 'quantum cognition', it concerns the use of the theoretical framework of quantum theory to model situations in human cognition and is now emerging as a flourishing domain of research [12,15,16,20,23–25,28,29,40–43].

The detection of quantum structures occurs at the level of the modeling of cognitive and decision phenomena, which involves the Hilbert space framework of quantum theory. More explicitly, one describes the situations mentioned above by introducing conceptual entities, their states, measurements and the corresponding probabilities of outcomes, and then represents them by using the standard Hilbert space representation of entities, states, measurements and probabilities of outcomes in quantum theory. This means that such a modeling does not presuppose the validity of quantum laws at a microscopic level. And, further, there is no need to suppose that the structural quantum appearance would be due to the existence of microscopic quantum processes occurring in the human brain, although such an hypothesis is no a priori rejected. Due to the specific situations that have been investigated, it has meanwhile been possible to go deeper in the identification of the structural appearance of 'quantum' than just the detection of a Hilbert space structure for a fruitful model. Indeed, mechanisms have been identified that make it possible to put forward operational structural definitions for entanglement, interference and Bose or Fermi identity.

Let us specify these operational mechanisms.

With respect to entanglement,[1] we investigated its structural appearance when concepts combine to form a new concept. We considered the concepts *Animal* and *Acts* and their combination *The Animal Acts*. Then we measured in an experiment the relative frequencies of changes of this combined concept to more concrete states, i.e. exemplars, of it [23,28]. One set of four exemplars that we considered for the concept combination *The Animal Acts* are, *The Horse Growls*, *The Horse Whinnies*, *The Bear Growls*, and *The Bear Whinnies*. Of the 81 persons that participated in the experiment, there were 4, hence a fraction of 0.05, which chose *The Horse Growls* as the 'their preferred good example of *The Animals Acts*', and there were 51, hence a fraction of 0.63, who chose *The Horse Whinnies*, 21, hence a fraction of 0.26, who chose *The Bear Growls*, and 5, hence a fraction of 0.06, who chose *The Bear Whinnies*. This means that the two exemplars *The Horse Whinnies* and *The Bear Growls* were considered to be the preferred good examples of the concept combination *The Animal Acts*, which is what we would expect taken into account the 'meaning' of the sentence *The Animal Acts*. However, if we asked the same participants in the experiment to elect their 'preferred good example of *Animal* and of *Acts*, as separated concept', resulted that 43 of the 81 chose *Horse* and 38 chose *Bear*, hence respectively fractions 0.53 and 0.47, for the concept *Animal*, while 39 chose *Growls* and 42 chose *Whinnies*, respectively fractions 0.48 and 0.52, for the concept *Acts*. If we consider these fractions as estimates of the probabilities of change or collapse, our experiment shows that the combination *The Animal Acts* collapses respectively with probabilities 0.05, 0.63, 0.26 and 0.06, to the more concrete states or exemplars of it, namely *The Horse Growls*, *The Horse Whinnies*, *The Bear Growls*, *The Bear Whinnies*, within the human minds of the participants of the experiments. However the concepts apart, *Animal* and *Acts* collapse respectively with probabilities 0.53 and 0.47 to *Horse* or *Bear*, and with probabilities 0.48 and 0.52 to *Growls* or *Whinnies*. If both, the collapse mechanism of the combined concept *The Animals Acts* to one of the collapsed states and the collapse mechanism of the single concepts *Animal* and *Acts* to a combination of the collapsed states would be the same, we would need the four joint probabilities, 0.05, 0.63,

---

[1] Some authors [45] have recently observed that our example *The Animal Acts* does not satisfy the marginal law, which would entail that Bell's inequalities are not informative in this case. In this respect, we have also elaborated an explicit quantum model for *The Animal Acts* situation, showing that entanglement is present in both states and measurements [46]. This result supports our claim that the violation of Bell's inequalities is due to the entanglement between the considered concepts.

0.26 and 0.06, to be the products of the single probabilities, 0.53 and 0.47, and 0.48 and 0.52. Let us see that this is not the case. We have 'just combining without involving meaning' $\leftrightarrow$ (*Horse, Growls*) $\leftrightarrow$ $0.53 \cdot 0.48 = 0.25 \neq 0.05$ $\leftrightarrow$ (*The Horse Growls*) $\leftrightarrow$ 'meaningfully combining'. Also, 'just combining without involving meaning' $\leftrightarrow$ (*Horse, Whinnies*) $\leftrightarrow$ $0.53 \cdot 0.52 = 0.28 \neq 0.63$ $\leftrightarrow$ (*The Horse Whinnies*) $\leftrightarrow$ 'meaningfully combining'. The same reasoning can be repeated for (*Bear, Growls*) with respect to (*The Bear Growls*), and for (*Bear, Whinnies*) with respect to (*The Bear Whinnies*), and results again in the joint probabilities not being products of the single one.

We understand very well why these joint probabilities are not equal to the products of the combined probabilities: it is because the sentence *The Animal Acts* carries 'meaning', and the minds of the humans participating in the experiment carry also this meaning, which makes the collapses in their minds to more concrete exemplars be guided by this meaning of the combination, and not just be a combination of the collapses that their minds provoke with the single concepts. We have proved [23] that the way these joint probabilities deviate from being products of the single probabilities makes them violate Bell's inequalities [47]. We do not dwell on this here, but we only mention that such a violation of Bell's inequalities proves that the joint probabilities cannot be products of probabilities related to the single component concepts, and cannot be fit into a classical probability structure, which is what entanglement means when it appears in quantum physics. Hence *Animal* and *Acts* are entangled through meaning in the combination *The Animal Acts*.

We also have understood how the structural appearance of interference takes place. We have studied the combination of concepts *Fruits* and *Vegetables* in the disjunction *Fruits or Vegetables*. This time however participants in a test are asked to choose amongst exemplars that are all concrete states of the three concepts, the two single ones, and the combined one. Interference effects results in this experiment. For example, an exemplar such a *Olive*, will be chosen much more often for the combination *Fruits or Vegetables* than a 'logical disjunction analysis' of the data allows, even if we apply quantum logic. The reason is that next to the disjunction *Fruits* or *Vegetables*, the combination *Fruits or Vegetables* is also a new emergent concepts, that gives special weight to the exemplars for which one can doubt whether they are fruits or whether they are vegetables, and *Olive* is such an exemplar. It is quite amazing that this effect is captured in a complete way by interference of the type encountered in quantum theory. And the complex numbers in quantum theory, which make interference much more expressive as compared to how it appears with waves and real numbers, plays a crucial role in the faithful modeling of the data [19, 20, 28].

We believe that, in the structural appearance of quantum, even more unique quantum aspects manifest, such as 'how identical quantum entities behave'. Indeed, although we have demonstrated above entanglement and interference by means of concepts and how they combine, these effects can also appear structurally at the level of physical matter, without the need to consider the cognitive realm where the human mind interacts. We have, e.g., presented examples of entanglement by connected vessels of water [40], and interference is well known to take place with physical waves in matter. But, the weird way in which identical quantum entities behave, we have only structurally found back in how concepts behave within the realm of human cognition [19, 48, 49], and we have good reasons to believe that it only there appears. Indeed, we have an explanation, although speculative, for why it appears in human cognition structurally in the way identified in [19, 48, 49]. Our explanation rests on a theory about the evolution of human concepts, where these come into existence when humans develop the capacity to create states of minds for shared intentions during collaborations [50]. Although the identification of objects, and the communication about these objects, which usually is thought to be at the origin of concepts, certainly has played an important role in the primitive stages of human conceptuality, recent research indicates that 'shared intentionality' would be the major aspect giving rise to the specifics of this human conceptuality. Following this research, the crucial difference between human cognition and that of other species would be the ability to participate with others in collaborative activities with shared goals and intentions, where participation in such activities would require a unique motivation to share psychological states with others and unique forms of cognitive representation for doing so. This results in a species-unique form of cultural cognition including the use of linguistic symbols, construction of social norms and individual beliefs [50]. Hence, 'shared intentionality' would be the driving force behind human cognition along this scenario, resulting in 'a human mind with increasing capacity to create internal states representing such shared intentions'. We believe that the conceptual representations resulting from such shared intentions carry within them the paradoxical aspects also to be found in the behavior of identical quantum entities. To explain what we mean, let us imagine eleven of our ancestors to be collaborating in hunting. The collaboration will only be successful in case all eleven are able to create a conceptual representation of the hunting scene which is 'identical' on the conceptual level – it represents the same unique hunting scene – but of course will be (at least slightly) different for each of the eleven minds – for example, they all will have a different role in the hunting activity. The equivalent in quantum theory are eleven fermionic identical quantum entities, being identical, but when actualised within a piece of matter – the equivalent of the hunting scene actualised in each of the eleven minds – will always appear in different states, due to the Pauli exclusion principle. In a further stage of development of human language, also the bosonic version of quantum identify appears, namely when communicated about 'eleven hunting events'. Indeed, within the communication itself, hence the exchange of concepts, these concepts are identical and can also be in the same state. It is indeed not necessary for eleven minds to be involved to communicate about eleven hunting events, two minds is enough. This is the way we have analysed the concept 'eleven animals' and found it to obey a Bose-Einstein statistics [19]. We are investigating actually these identity aspects of human concepts including the data of an experiment on human subjects [51].

The analysis above and in the first section illustrates that in both situations, the one of micro-physical appearance and the one of structural appearance of quantum, this 'quantum' is destroyed in case random perturbations are allowed to take place, at least if the perturbations are able to provoke a change in the quantum state of the entities involved. On the contrary, quantum persists in case such perturbations are able to be avoided, which can be by shielding of or in other ways, for example by the nature of the organisation itself. In Sect. 4 we analyse our explanatory hypothesis in additional detail.

4   Unifying Micro-physical and Structural Appearance

Let us mention, to initiate the reasoning we will develop in this section, that a Bose-Einstein condensate has recently been fabricated at room temperature – lasting for a few picoseconds – by using a thin non-crystalline polymer film of approximately 35 nanometers thick [11]. Also important for our analysis is that genuine quantum effects of the micro-physical appearance type have been identified in biology, more specifically a quantum tunneling phenomenon in the process of photo-synthesis. Also the effect discovered in biology occurs at room temperature or, better, at earth crust temperature [52]. Since the size of the random bombardment of energy packets of any entity in our surroundings depends crucially on the temperature both cases mentioned above are again good illustrations for our explanatory hypothesis. Indeed, it is plausible that a plant, in the processes that enable it to use photo-synthesis, has managed to be less disturbed by this bombardment of random heat packets of energy due to the mechanism of biological evolution that has played a fundamental role in what the plant is, and how photo-synthesis works. And what about the appearance of quantum effect in human laboratories at room temperature? Human culture is also an evolutionary process, albeit not Darwinian. It has not only managed resistance against the random bombardment of heat energy packets, but also evolved to use this heat energy and make it into non-random energy. Humans' energy-harvesting from heat started with the first steam engine, which literally is the transformation of random energy into structured energy. Does this gives rise to quantum structure? Not always, and not automatically, but this is certainly the case for the energy used in those laboratories that have produced quantum effect at room temperature. What about the vessels of water and other macroscopic situations we invented to violate Bell's inequalities [40], and the identification of quantum structure in cognition [12,15,16,20,23,43]? Well, the vessels of water and the other entities violating Bell's inequalities are realized within human culture, so that they can be said to have been specially devised to violate Bell's inequalities, albeit not in explicit laboratory situations. In doing so, they make use of all knowledge available to achieve this. As regards the presence of quantum structure in human cognition, we note that human cognition is a product of human culture, and hence profits from the mechanism of cultural evolution to fight the destructive effect of random perturbations in case these perturbations invoke changes that are destructive for cognition. A simple example, we avoid to have too much noise in the environment in case we want to have a conversation with someone. Hence, not only for plants, but more generally, the capacity of living matter to manage destructive effects of bombardments of random energy packets is the product of evolution. For plants and photo-synthesis it is the consequence of biological evolution, and it takes place even on a semi-microscopic level. For animals, and humans, which materially speaking are made of living matter, but additionally have a nervous system, and brains, the interaction with the environment contains primitive and less primitive aspects of conceptuality. For primitive animals, with primitive nervous systems, these interactions create coordinations and/or competitions or collaborations and hence give rise to situations where entanglement and interference appear on the macroscopic level. One could state that a nervous system is an amplifier for quantum from the micro-level to the macro-level, because it allows the entity with the nervous system to develop complicated strategies of defence against random perturbations with changes that are destructive for the evolved organisation. In the case of human beings, this capacity of defence has evolved to a very sophisticated level, fully exploring the amplifying effect of the nervous system, and giving rise to cultural cognition, with languages and other cultural items as manifestations of it. This is in our opinion the essence of cultural evolution. These effects manifest in the macroscopic world in the two ways we have discussed in Sects. 2 and 3. We can even classify the ability of experimentally controlling random bombardments of heat energy packets for the construction of suitable experimental situations which allow the emergence of quantum in the macro world, as a fruit of cultural evolution. Equally so, the appearance of quantum structures in human cognition, decision making and language is a consequence of humans being able to organize, transfer and communicate language in a coherent way, without it being destroyed by 'random perturbations'.

Consider the situation where you go to a big garbage belt, like the ones one typically finds in a metropolis, and you collect the words belonging to pieces of texts, newspapers, scrambled books, etc., that you find there, and put them in a huge basket. These words are not connected by meaning, they are completely random. This situation of a 'bag of words' can be modeled by using the known classicalities (set theory, Boolean logic, Kolmogorovian product probabilities). Consider instead the situation where you go to a library. This is completely different, because meaning is keeping purposefully all the words in the books on their one and unique place, as an exemplar consequence of human cultural evolution. We now know that quantum aspects will occur in this case, if one collects experimental data on the words belonging to the books in that library. Now, take one of these books and cut it in several pieces of paper, corresponding to single words in the book, repeat the operation for all the books and mix together the pieces of paper so obtained. The library has in this way taken the form of a 'bag of words' which is very similar to a garbage belt, hence one expects that the situation is classical. To demonstrate this concretely, let us perform the experiment on the conceptual combination *The Animal Acts* considered in Sect. 3 [23, 28, 46], and ask a subject to report the first combination among *The Horse Growls*, *The Bear Whinnies*, etc. that he/she finds at random in the pieces of paper in the library. This situation is obviously classical, the joint probabilities for the different exemplars of the combined concepts *The Animal Acts*, will all be neatly product probabilities of the exemplars related to the single concepts *Animal* and *Acts*, because the 'bag of words' only contains single words, and not any meaning is left to connect these single words, which means that Bell's inequalities will not be violated, in this case.

In a garbage belt, the quantum organisation of human culture is destroyed, exactly as in a bombardment of random packets of energy at room temperature, the quantum organisation occurring at the microscopic level is destroyed. Analogously, the situation of two persons who talk with each other communicating and exchanging meaning, preserves the quantum organisation that is identified within human conceptuality and language.

Our unification of the two ways that 'quantum appear' should not make us forget that also still differences exists between the two ways. In particular, it seems that the entire technical apparatus of Hilbert space is fully represented for its micro-physical appearance – although 'separated quantum entities' might cause of problem in this respect [49] –, while only particular aspects of it – although the major ones – can be identified for its structural appearance. Of course, this difference is also fundamentally due to the structural appearance being defined as 'allowing structure to be identified step by step', which means that the existence of this difference should not be seen as a flaw in the analysis we put forward in the present article. It does mean however that some quantum effects notably present in its micro-physical appearance do not find their counterpart – at least not till now – in its structural appearance. We only mention the role played by 'spin', and its connection to Bose or Fermi identity behavior for what concerns the micro-physical appearance of quantum. This means that, although we believe that in the present article we reveal a crucial new aspect of 'what quantum is' with our unification of its micro-physical appearance and its structural appearance, and our explanatory hypothesis of why this unification is possible, still other aspects of 'what quantum is' remain open as challenging questions for future research.

References

1. Kapitza, P.: Viscosity of liquid helium below the l-point. Nature **141**, 74–75 (1938)
2. London, F.: The λ-phenomenon of liquid Helium and the Bose-Einstein degeneracy. Nature **141**, 643–644 (1938)
3. Bardeen, J., Cooper, L.N., Schrieffer, J.R.: Theory of superconductivity. Phy. Rev. **108**, 1175–1205 (1957)
4. Rauch, H., Zeilinger, A., Badurek, G., Wilfing, A., Bauspiess, W., Bonse, U.: Verification of coherent spinor rotation of fermions. Phys. Lett. A **54**, 425–427 (1975)
5. Aspect, A., Grangier, P., Roger, G.: Experimental realization of Einstein-Podolsky-Rosen-Bohm Gedankenexperiment. A new Violation of Bell's Inequalities. Phys. Rev. Lett. **49**, 91 (1982)

6. Anderson, M.H., Ensher, J.R., Matthews, M.R., Wieman, C.E., Cornell, E.A.: Observation of Bose-Einstein condensation in a dilute atomic vapor. Science **269**, 198–201 (1995)
7. Tittel, W., Brendel, J., Gisin, B., Herzog, T., Zbinden, H., Gisin, N.: Experimental demonstration of quantum correlations over more than 10 km. Phys. Rev. A **57**, 3229–3232 (1998)
8. Arndt, M., Nairz, O., Vos-Andreae, J., Keller, C., van der Zouw, G., Zeilinger, A.: Wave-particle duality of C 60 molecules. Nature **401**, 680–682 (1999)
9. Salart, D., Baas, A., van Houwelingen, J.A.W., Gisin, N., Zbinden, H.: Spacelike separation in a Bell test assuming gravitationally induced collapses. Phys. Rev. Lett. **100**, 220404 (2008)
10. Gerlich, S., Eibenberger, S., Tomandl, M., Nimmrichter, S., Hornberger, K., Fagan, P.J., Tüxen, J., Mayor, M., Arndt, M.: Quantum interference of large organic molecules. Nature Commun. **2**, 263 (2011)
11. Plumhof, J.D., Stöferle, T., Mai, L., Scherf, U., Mahrt, R.F.: Room-temperature Bose-Einstein condensation of cavity exciton-polaritons in a polymer. Nat. Mater. **13**, 247–252 (2013)
12. Aerts, D., Aerts, S.: Applications of quantum statistics in psychological studies of decision processes. Found. Sci. **1**, 85–97 (1995)
13. Van Rijsbergen, K.: The Geometry of Information Retrieval. Cambridge University Press, Cambridge (2004)
14. Aerts, D., Czachor, M.: Quantum aspects of semantic analysis and symbolic artificial intelligence. J. Phys. A: Math. Theor. **37**, L123–L132 (2004)
15. Aerts, D., Gabora, L.: A theory of concepts and their combinations I. The structure of the sets of contexts and properties. Kybernetes **34**, 167–191 (2005)
16. Aerts, D., Gabora, L.: A theory of concepts and their combinations II. A Hilbert space representation. Kybernetes **34**, 192–221 (2005)
17. Widdows, D.: Geometry And Meaning. CSLI Publications, University of Chicago Press, Stanford, Chicago (2006)
18. Melucci, M.: A basis for information retrieval in context. ACM Trans. Inf. Syst. **26**, 1–41 (2008)
19. Aerts, D.: Quantum particles as conceptual entities: a possible explanatory framework for quantum theory. Found. Sci. **14**, 361–411 (2009)
20. Aerts, D.: Quantum structure in cognition. J. Math. Psychol. **53**, 314–348 (2009)
21. Khrennikov, A., Haven, E.: Quantum mechanics and violations of the sure-thing principle: the use of probability interference and other concepts. J. Math. Psychol. **53**, 378–388 (2009)
22. Aerts, D., D'Hooghe, B., Haven, E.: Quantum experimental data in psychology and economics. Int. J. Theor. Phys. **49**, 2971–2990 (2010)
23. Aerts, D., Sozzo, S.: Quantum structures in cogniton: Why and how concepts are entangled. In: Song, D., Melucci, M., Frommholz, I., Zhang, P., Wang, L., Arafat, S. (eds.) QI 2011. LNCS, vol. 7052, pp. 116–127. Springer, Heidelberg (2011)
24. Busemeyer, J.R., Pothos, E., Franco, R., Trueblood, J.S.: A quantum theoretical explanation for probability judgment 'errors'. Psycholical Rev. **118**, 193–218 (2011)
25. Busemeyer, J.R., Bruza, P.D.: Quantum Models of Cognition and Decision. Cambridge University Press, Cambridge (2012)
26. Busemeyer, J.R., Dubois, F., Lambert-Mogiliansky, A., Melucci, M. (eds.): QI 2012. LNCS, vol. 7620. Springer, Heidelberg (2012)
27. Aerts, D., Broekaert, J., Gabora, L., Sozzo, S.: Quantum structure and human thought. Behav. Brain Sci. **36**, 274–276 (2013)

28. Aerts, D., Gabora, L., Sozzo, S.: Concepts and their dynamics: A quantum-theoretic modeling of human thought. Top. Cogn. Sci. **5**, 737–772 (2013)
29. Pothos, E.M., Busemeyer, J.R.: Can quantum probability provide a new direction for cognitive modeling? Behav. Brain Sci. **36**, 255–274 (2013)
30. Haven, E., Khrennikov, A.: Quantum Social Science. Cambridge University Press, Cambridge (2013)
31. Aerts, D., Czachor, M., Kuna, M., Sinervo, B., Sozzo, S.: Quantum probabilistic structures in competing lizard communities. Ecol. Model. **281**, 38–51 (2014)
32. Nielsen, M.A., Chuang, I.L.: Quantum Computation and Quantum Information. Cambridge University Press, Cambridge (2000)
33. de Broglie, L.: Ondes et Quanta. C. R. **177**, 507–510 (1923)
34. Einstein, A.: Zur quantentheorie der strahlung. Physikalische Zeitschrift **18**, 121–128 (1917)
35. d'Enterria, D., da Silveira, G.G.: Observing light-by-light scattering at the Large Hadron Collider. Phys. Rev. Lett. **111**, 080405 (2013)
36. Mackey, G.W.: Mathematical Foundations of Quantum Mechanics. W. A. Benjamin, New York (1963)
37. Piron, C.: Foundations of Quantum Physics. Benjamin, Reading (1976)
38. Aerts, D.: A possible explanation for the probabilities of quantum mechanics. J. Math. Phys. **27**, 202–210 (1986)
39. Aerts, D., Durt, T., Grib, A., Van Bogaert, B., Zapatrin, A.: Quantum structures in macroscopical reality. Int. J. Theor. Phys. **32**, 489–498 (1993)
40. Aerts, D., Aerts, S., Broekaert, J., Gabora, L.: The violation of Bell inequalities in the macroworld. Found. Phys. **30**, 1387–1414 (2000)
41. Khrennikov, A.Y.: Ubiquitous Quantum Structure. Springer, Berlin (2010)
42. Wang, Z., Busemeyer, J.R., Atmanspacher, H., Pothos, E.M.: The potential of using quantum theory to build models of cognition. Top. Cogn. Sci. **5**, 672–688 (2013)
43. Sozzo, S.: A quantum probability model in Fock space for borderline contradictions. J. Math. Psychol. **58**, 1–12 (2014)
44. Hampton, J.A.: Disjunction of natural concepts. Mem. Cogn. **16**, 579–591 (1988)
45. Dzhafarov, E.N., Kujala, J.V.: On selective influences, marginal selectivity, and Bell/CHSH inequalities. Top. Cogn. Sci. **6**, 121–128 (2014)
46. Aerts, D., Sozzo, S.: Quantum entanglement in concept combinations. International Journal of Theoretical Physics (2014). doi:10.1007/s10773-013-1946-z. In press
47. Bell, J.S.: On the Einstein-Podolsky-Rosen paradox. Physics **1**, 195–200 (1964)
48. Aerts, D.: A potentiality and conceptuality interpretation of quantum physics. Philosophica **83**, 15–52 (2010)
49. Aerts, D.: Quantum theory and human perception of the macro-world. To appear in Frontiers in Perception Science (2014). arXiv:1403.4307
50. Tomasello, M., Carpenter, M., Call, J., Behne, T., Moll, H.: Understanding and sharing intentions: the origins of cultural cognition. Behav. Brain Sci. **28**, 675–691 (2005)
51. Aerts, D., Sozzo, S., Veloz T.: The quantum nature of identity and Bose-Einstein statistics in human concepts (2014) (in preparation)
52. Sarovar, M., Ishizaki, A., Fleming, G.R., Whaley, K.B.: Quantum entanglement in photosynthetic light-harvesting complexes. Nat. Phys. **6**, 462–467 (2010)

Feedback Loops: A Fundamental Ingredient of Information Processing

Paul Baird[✉]

Laboratoire de Mathématiques de Bretagne Atlantique,
Université de Bretagne Occidentale, Brest, France
paul.baird@univ-brest.fr

Abstract. In order to acquire meaning, information has to be processed. But how do we define meaning and what does processing consist of? Examples show that information processing involves feedback, and that this is a fundamental driver of change. Change is the physical quality of information, whereas meaning comes from observer-participancy. Furthermore, change can come about by the processing of *potential information*, whose realization reflects quantum behaviour at a macroscopic level.

1 Introduction

In nature, we often observe hierarchies of structure: galaxies, clusters of galaxies...; fractal shorelines; scale-free networks; or temporal hierarchies: the frequency of electron transitions ($\sim 10^{-14}$ s), of acoustical solar waves (about two hours), of solar cycles (about eleven years). In seeking some fundamental principle that drives the world, "Law without law," as J. A. Wheeler wrote [23] (p. 11), we can perhaps take note of phenomena that surround us, that drive, for example biological evolution, the development of language, our assimilation of data, the structure of social networks, and entertain the possibility that here lies a hierarchy that goes deep down to a fundamental level. Order comes from disorder via feedback, an exploration of possibilities that leads to a conclusion.

Wheeler described the world of existences as a "system self-sythesized by quantum networking". To illustrate this idea, he took the example of telecommunications [23] (p. 13): "Beginning with a single telegraph line connecting a single sender and a single receiver and expanding to a global multi-mode network, telecommunications constitute today an industry ever more immense in its extent. However, that growth is no machine. It is an immensity of demands and responses.... The telecommunications industry is telecommunication plus life. Only so could telecommunications become what it is today, a self-synthesizing system."

Paul Baird: The author would like to thank the three referees whose input has significantly improved this paper, as well as Thomas Filk for useful conversations and Kirsty Kitto for pointing out the importance of semantic information.

© Springer International Publishing Switzerland 2015
H. Atmanspacher et al. (Eds.): QI 2014, LNCS 8951, pp. 24–38, 2015.
DOI: 10.1007/978-3-319-15931-7_3

The drawback of such an example in explaining both the order and complexity of the world, as Wheeler noted, is that it had pre-existing foundations on which to build itself. However, in this article, I wish to revisit the idea that *change* and *choice* are two ingredients that drive the world, from the most fundamental structures to the most encompasing and complex. Furthermore, change at a "meaningful" level is achieved by feedback loops.

Consider for example, the sound produced by a guitar string. A local disturbance of the string results in two waves propagating along its length in opposite directions. As these bounce back and forth between the ends, interference produces a standing wave whose resonance frequency depends on the length of the string and its tension. This in turn disturbs air molecules resulting in the sound wave which reaches our ears. What we interpret as an orderly conclusion–a well-defined sound–has come about by a local disturbance reacting with its global environment through feedback. In this example, the local disturbance was determined, say, by my decision to pluck the string. However, if we trace the event far enough back in the causal chain, one can hypothesize that at some point an indeterministic event took place, a quantum event, whose resolution also came about by feedback.

The idea is not new, that a quantum event be amplified and decoherence occurs. Where I take a radical view is in the concept of *state*, which I consider to be contextual, determined by feedback and far more encompasing than an "elementary quantum state". A state may be considered as "potential information" and can be realized over an extended time period. Examples are the spin, position or momentum of a particle as elicited by some measuring apparatus; potential mutations of a DNA molecule; geometric states as we discuss in Sect. 5; causal sequences of a complex system; one of the many worlds of Everett.

After reviewing notions of information, highlighting its relational nature, I consider five fundamental examples of feedback mechanisms that apparently lead from disorder to order. These occur on widely differing time scales. The examples are based on computation, cognitive assimilation, biological systems and the anthropic cosmological principle. With reference to these examples, I consider how information acquires meaning. In the following section (Sect. 5), I discuss a geometric model based on combinatorial structure that was introduced in [2,3]. This model highlights the way in which *state* can have a broad interpretation, in this case as distinct visualizations of 3–dimensional objects. To conclude, I consider the puzzle of how a universal system can bring about its own change.

2   Types of Information

The *mathematical* theory of information relies on the notion of *bit*. The term was used by Shannon in his 1948 paper "A mathematical theory of communication" [19], although apparently, Tukey first coined the term in a Bell Laboratories memorandum [21]. Szilard used the notion if not the term in 1929 when linking entropy and information in respect of Maxwell's demon [20]. A *bit* is the information obtained from the answer to a yes/no question. It can be quantified as follows [1].

Given a probability space $(S, \mathcal{B}, p)$ consisting of a sample space S, a Boolean algebra $\mathcal{B}$ of events and a probability measure p, then the *information content* of an event $E \in \mathcal{B}$ is defined to be

$$I(E) := -\log_2(p(E)).$$

If $X : S \to R$ is a random variable taking values in some space R, then by definition, $p(X = a)$ is equal to $p(A)$, where $A = X^{-1}(\{a\})$. For example, given a symmetric Bernoulli random variable X taking values 0 and 1; then

$$I(X = 0) = I(X = 1) = -\log_2(1/2) = 1,$$

so we gain one bit of information when we choose between two equally likely alternatives. The definition is based on the desirable property that for independent events E_1 and E_2 we should have

$$I(E_1 \cap E_2) = I(E_1) + I(E_2)$$

and that $I(E) \geq 0$ for all $E \in \mathcal{B}$. The information content of a low probability event is high.

This definition of information is convenient in communication theory, where we have a source, a channel across which information is transmitted and a receiver to pick up the information. For example, DNA directs protein synthesis by "informing" a cell which amino acids to produce, by sending out a message (involving a procedure far more complex than suggested here) consisting of codewords of length three in an alphabet of four symbols. In this case there is a high redundancy, since 4^3 possible codewords are available for the 20 amino acids. Each codeword, say CAC, can be considered as made up of bits of information.

Given these definitions, we can quantify precisely concepts such as noise, transmission rate, error. But this doesn't give us the quality of information, its *meaning*, as we perceive it.

The theory of *semantic information* attempts to attach *meaning* to the notion, as well as taking a wider view as to what constitutes information, even in a context that is not necessarily linguistic [12]. First one needs a sufficiently general definition of *data*. The Diaphoric Definition emphasizes difference: *a datum is a putative fact regarding some difference or lack of uniformity within some context*. In particular, data can be determined by *absence* [11]. Note also that data is contextual. Given this definition, an instance σ of information, understood as semantic content, is characterized by the following three properties:

(i) σ consists of one or more data;
(ii) the data in σ are well-formed;
(iii) the well-formed data in σ are meaningful.

Here, "meaningful" requires that the data must comply with the meanings (semantics) of the chosen system, code or language, although the term is fraught with difficulties of interpretation [13]. As such, we would like to dispense with questions of "meaning" and instead lay emphasis on "change" as the quality of information.

3   Potential Information; Change of State

Landauer writes [16]: "Information is not a disembodied abstract entity; it is always tied to a physical representation. It is represented by engraving on a stone tablet, a spin, a charge, a hole in a punched card, a mark on paper, or some other equivalent. This ties the handling of information to all the possibilities and restrictions of our real physical world, its laws of physics and its storehouse of available parts."

I take a different view: that information is synonymous with *change*. We don't actually see a bit, but rather its effect. This is the lesson of quantum theory. The measurement process consists of the preparation of a quantum state and that of a test. A birefringent plate can be used to prepare a photon polarized along a particular axis, say the $0x$–axis. If we associate the bit value 0 with such a photon and the bit value 1 with a photon polarized along the $0y$–axis, then we can transmit information along an optical fibre as a series of binary bits [17]. In this context information appears physical. It is tied in with the binary sequence transmitted along the fibre. However, the binary sequence as such doesn't contain information, only potential information, that is realized when it is interpreted. But interpretation requires a change in the state of the receiver. Information is *relational*; its realization corresponds to a change of state.

It would seem possible to associate information with anything we wish. For example, the sequence 1111111... does not appear to contain much information, but if we write it as

$$11111111111111 \ldots = 1000111011011 \ldots + 0111000100100 \ldots$$

and associate bases of DNA as follows: $00 = A$, $01 = T$, $10 = C$, $11 = G$, then one of the terms on the RHS, if it goes on long enough and in the right context, may contain a great deal of information; enough to construct a complex living organism.

To split the sequence in this way has required some external input, or, to put it another way, *correlation has occurred*. Something happens to a composite system to form a new system. In this sense, as underscored in [2], information is *relational*; it has no absolute status. Furthermore, its relational character, or "meaning", has come about by correlation between systems.

What is correlation but *change* of a composite system, consisting say, of the sequence of 1 s on the paper and my brain (together with all the surrounding sources of communication: photons, retinae, neural network, ...). The combined system has changed, resulting in a decomposition of the sequence and a transcription of terms into DNA code.

But then the question arises: what has caused this change to come about? What rule dictated change and its nature? As suggested by Wheeler [23], the laws of the world could be part of a "self-synthezising" system, and do not exist "out there" somewhere, or are handed down from a divine entity. If we accept this view, the rules that determine change must be part of the (extraordinarily complex) system consisting of my brain and its immediate surroundings (and possibly far distant surroundings, if we consider the entangled nature of quantum states).

In the language of artificial intelligence, systems which contain the rules for their own change are called *universal machines*, for example, a universal Turing machine, or a universal cellular automaton. However, such a machine still requires an outside entity to interpret its data, such as a conscious being. In [2], I propose that consciousness exploits *potential information*, rather than the hardware of a binary sequence, or some other such alphabet, to enact change. Whatever the nature of consciouness, meaning must come about as a product of change.

Semantic information emphasizes *difference* in some context, whereas mathematical information concerns physical data. Potential information (PI) on the other hand, concerns the possible states of a system. These may be the spin states of an elementary particle, geometric states as we discuss in Sect. 5, possible mutations of a DNA molecule,..... PI is defined by its relevance in some context and so in that sense may be considered to fall under the umbrella of semantic information. However, it is to be understood that states are realized upon correlation between systems and in this sense PI is inextricably linked with change. Prior to measurement, a spin-$\frac{1}{2}$ particle is not in any state. Its possible states are potential information that we may find convenient to formalize with mathematical symbols, and that is all. A correlation takes place between a measuring apparatus and the particle with the result that a spin is revealed based on a probabilistic formula.

How should we view the realization of PI in respect of the 2nd Law of Thermodynamics, which requires that the total entropy of a system isolated from its environment will not decrease. It is well known that even though physical information corresponds to a local decrease in entropy, work has been done to produce it, so that the total entropy has not decreased. PI on the other hand seems to be a rather ethereal concept requiring no work to produce it. However, PI is contextual and cannot be taken in isolation; it is part of a greater whole to which the 2nd Law should apply. For PI to be realized, correlation must take place and in general work will have been done to achieve this. On a cautionary note, I take the view that a causal chain of events (or time sequence) is also the realization of PI and since the 2nd Law is inextricably linked to time, until the nature of time is understood, so the 2nd Law will remain a mystery.

4   Feedback: Five Examples

Physical data may be considered as information; states that derive from this data as potential information. The realization of a state is synonymous with information processing: by definition, correlation between systems, whether between a measuring apparatus and a particle, or between a biological organism and its environment, requires the respective systems to fall into states, for example a spin state, or a brain state (the latter term left as undefined). The viability, or "fitness" of a state is established through feedback loops. Here, fitness is a relational concept dictated by the surrounding environment.

What we might loosely term *order* tends to flow from such a process. Living systems have a capacity for self-organization that keeps them far from equilibrium so as to maintain an evolutionary advantage. An ant colony can achieve a highly sophisticated societal structure, in spite of the fact that each individual ant does not have the blueprint for the global scheme ingrained into its brain. Why is this?

As cited from Wheeler in the Introduction: "[The telecommunications industry] is an immensity of demands and responses". There is no a priori law which governs evolution; it just happens. As chance would have it, ever more sophisticated structures appear with self-contained regulatory processes such as the immune system and administrative centres such as the brain. What we interpret as order is relational; in terms of semantic information, it may be viewed simply as *difference*. The following examples should be considered in the light of these remarks.

1. *Computation.* In the formal theory of computation, a calculation has a precise meaning as an operation performed by a *recursive function* [7]. Such an operation is given by an algorithm which often contains loops. For example, Euclidean division performs the calculation: *given two natural numbers a and b with b non-zero, then find q and r such that* $a = qb + r$. In programming language the algorithm can be written:

> *Input* : a, b natural numbers with b non-zero
> *Output* : q and r such that $a = qb + r$ with $0 \leq r < b$
> *Initialization* : $a_0 = a$
> *if* $a_i \geq b$ *return*
> $a_i := a_i - b$
> *end when*
> $a_i < b$ *give output* $q = ib$ *et* $r = a - ib$
> *end*

The loop in this case involves subtracting b from a; evaluating the sign of the result; if it is positive, subtract b once more, and so on, until there is a negative result. Feedback in this case is an entirely deterministic procedure.

In the science of artificial intelligence, a *genetic algorithm* is a search heuristic that mimics the process of natural selection. For a given input, one seeks an algorithm to produce a particular output. One begins with a collection of randomly generated algorithms and tests each of them on different inputs. The fitness of the algorithm is the fraction of times it produces the correct output. If one only retains algorithms that pass a certain fitness level, then eventually one may home in on a viable algorithm. A loop occurs, whereby one tests all (suitable) algorithms, evaluates the results, refines the search, repeats the process. *Order*, in the form of a viable algorithm, arises from a random collection of algorithms by the requirement of a result. An element of chance occurs here, since the algorithms are *randomly generated* (in practice a randomly generated number is produced by some deterministic process, but we can imagine in principle how this could come about by quantum events, say in a quantum computer).

2. *Cognitive assimilation.* The following example, with variants, has been doing the rounds of social networks [10]:

```
7H15 M3554G3
53RV35 7O PR0V3
H0W 0UR M1ND5 C4N
D0 4M4Z1NG 7H1NG5!
1MPR3551V3 7H1NG5!
1 N 7H3 B3G1NN1NG
17 WA5 H4RD BU7
N0W, 0N 7H15 LIN3
Y0UR M1ND 1S
R34D1NG 17
4U70M471C4LLY
W17H0U7 3V3N
7H1NK1NG 4B0U7 17.
```

This provides an instance of what I suggest is a back-and-forth process, or feedback loop, involving comparison and error correction, until resolution is achieved. Our mind is confused at first, but rapidly grasps the "code" and adapts. A state has been realized (a correct interpretation of the text) by feedback. The state was present as potential information, but required the right context to be achieved. A further example based on visual perception is discussed in Sect. 5.

3. *Learning.* The idea that feedback mechanisms may be an essential ingredient in the function of learning has its origins in the work of D. O. Hebb. His cell assembly theory concerns reverbatory activity in the brain which induces lasting cellular change [15].

H. J. Briegel and G. De las Cuevas propose a model of a learning agent whose "interaction with the environment is governed by a *simulation-based projection*, which allows the agent to project itself into future situations before it takes real action." Their model is made up of a network of *clips* which correspond to stored episodes of experience. An excited clip calls, with certain probabilities, another, neighbouring clip.... [5] (p. 3): "A call of the episodic memory triggers a random walk through this memory space (network). In this sense, the agent jumps through the space of clips, invoking patchwork-like sequences of virtual experience."

This model is suggestive of the way our own brains function as we explore possibilities to evalutate a situation, or indeed as we dream during sleep (see Sect. 6 below).

4. *Evolution of language and species.* Evolution illustrates how feedback can produce change over time scales that can range from months to hundreds of thousands of years. Inside the nucleus of each living cell is the molecule DNA, with its characteristic shape of a double helix. Along each DNA strand are embedded the molecular bases adenine (A), thymine (T), cytosine (C) and guanine (G). The bases occur in pairs on opposite strands of the helix and there are approximately 10^9 such pairs in the DNA of a mammal. These bases form the alphabet

$\{A, T, C, G\}$ for the genetic code. A key ingredient for evolution is the occurrence of small random errors in the DNA replication process. Genes replicate and their survival depends on their capacity to adapt to the surrounding environment. There is a feedback loop, whereby successful adaptation encourages replication, replication modifies the environment and change occurs.

A similar process occurs in the evolution of language: a new word is produced, or an existing word modified; the new form is either reinforced by users of the language, or else it is abandoned and eventually dies out. Feedback once more occurs, whereby acceptance encourages transmission which ultimately reinforces change.

5. *Physical laws in a participatory universe.* One of Wheeler's more radical ideas was that of a feedback loop involving the whole universe, illustrated with the well-known image of a eye at one end of a large U looking at the tailend [25] (opening page). He considered us to be participants in the universe and that our very observations today may influence the laws that govern us. This is perhaps the ultimate feedback loop based on observer participancy.

Wheeler writes [23] (p. 13): "The past has no existence except as it is contained in the records, near and far, of the present.... Quantum theory denies all meaning to the concepts of "before" and "after" in the world of the very small...".

Wheeler gives an instructive example to illustrate observer participancy [24] (pp. 13–14): "The photon that we are going to register tonight from that four billion-year-old quasar cannot be said to have had an existence "out there" three billion years ago, or two (when it passed an intervening gravitational lens) or one, or even a day ago. Not until we have fixed arrangements at our telescope do we register tonight's quantum as having passed to the left (or right) of the lens or by *both* routes (as in the double-slit experiment). This registration, like every delayed choice experiment, reminds us that no elementary quantum phenomenon is a phenomenon until, in Bohr's words [6], "It has been brought to a close" by an "irreversible act of amplification."

Wheeler objected to "law without law". He rejected the concept of "universe" because one has to "postulate explicitly or implicitly, a supermachine, a scheme, a device, a miracle, which will turn out universes in infinite variety and infinite number." Rather the world is "self-synthesized". For this he proposed a loop, whereby physics gives rise to light, sound and pressure - tools to communicate, as well as chemistry and biology, and through them observer-participators [23] (p. 5): "by the way of devices they employ, the questions they ask, and the registrations that they communicate, put into action quantum-mechanical probability amplitudes and thus they develop all they know or ever can know about the world... Fields and particle give physics and close the loop." Wheeler called this loop the *meaning circuit* [23] (p. 4).

S. Hawking and T. Herzog take up the theme [14]: "The... histories of the universe thus depend on what is being observed, contrary to the usual idea that the universe has a unique, observer independent history." In Wheeler's delayed choice experiment, the observer has the choice of deciding which of two complementary experiments shall be done, one that reveals the photon as a particle, the other as a wave. By deciding particle, the experiment determines that the photon was a particle even before the decision was made. As P. Davies writes [8] (p. 136, see also [9]): "In principle, this entanglement between present and past can stretch right back to the origin of the universe."

5   Potential Information as a Quantum State: Quantum Interaction

The different perceptions of the Necker Cube are strikingly analogous to states of a spin-$\frac{1}{2}$ particle. Whatever position the cube, that is, whatever axis we use to project it to the plane, we see one of two possible 3-dimensional realizations,

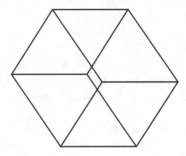

aside from the exceptional positions illustrated in the pictures below (ignoring perspective effects).

We may formalize the visualizations of the Necker Cube with elementary linear algebra. Specifically, if we fix attention on a particular vertex which we suppose located at the origin, then the three edges of the cube emanating from that vertex can be described by three vectors in Euclidean space $\mathbb{R}^3$ which are orthogonal and of the same length. Equivalently, the (3×3)–matrix whose columns are the endpoints of these vectors:

$$A := \begin{pmatrix} x_1 & x_2 & x_3 \\ y_1 & y_2 & y_3 \\ z_1 & z_2 & z_3 \end{pmatrix}$$

is proportional to an orthogonal matrix: $AA^t = \rho I_3$, where A^t is the transpose matrix, I_3 is the (3×3)–identity matrix and ρ is a positive scalar. In particular the rows of A are also orthogonal and of the same length. If we now project the endpoints of the vectors to the complex plane $\mathbb{C}$ via the orthogonal projection $(x, y, z) \mapsto x + iy$ and set $w_j = x_j + iy_j$ $(j = 1, 2, 3)$, then the orthogonality and identical lengths of the first two rows imply:

$$w_1{}^2 + w_2{}^2 + w_3{}^2 = 0 \,.$$

Conversely, given three such complex numbers not all zero, there are precisely two vectors $\pm(z_1, z_2, z_3)$ differing by a sign, orthogonal to the two rows (x_1, x_2, x_3) and (y_1, y_2, y_3) of A. This is essentially the Theorem of Axonometry of Gauss and the two choices of sign correspond to the two visualizations of the the Necker Cube. In fact, one has two-valuedness at each vertex, but the combinatorial structure of the cube requires that for a global realization, these difference choices be compatible.

In a similar way, when we measure the spin of a spin-$\frac{1}{2}$ particle along *any* axis, there are two possible outcomes: spin up, or spin down. This is solely a quantum phenomenon which has no analogue in classical mechanics. In general, we represent the state as a unit vector $|\Phi\rangle = \lambda|+\rangle + \mu|-\rangle$ $(\lambda, \mu \in \mathbb{C}, |\lambda|^2 + |\mu|^2 = 1)$ in a two dimensional complex vector space with basis $\{|+\rangle, |-\rangle\}$; then the orthogonal spin states

$$|\Phi\rangle_+ = e^{-i\phi/2} \cos\frac{\theta}{2}|+\rangle + e^{i\phi/2} \sin\frac{\theta}{2}|-\rangle \quad \text{and}$$

$$|\Phi\rangle_- = e^{-i\phi/2} \sin\frac{\theta}{2}|+\rangle - e^{i\phi/2} \cos\frac{\theta}{2}|-\rangle$$

are eigenvectors of the Hermitian operator

$$\begin{pmatrix} \cos\theta & e^{-i\phi}\sin\theta \\ e^{i\phi}\sin\theta & -\cos\theta \end{pmatrix}$$

with eigenvalues $+1$ and -1, respectively. In a different state, we must take into account transition amplitudes to determine the probability of measuring spin up or spin down. But what is the analogue of the state vector and the Hermitian operator for the Necker Cube?

Consider any orthogonal projection $\Phi : \mathbb{R}^3 \to \mathbb{C}$ from Euclidean 3-space to the complex plane. A *framework* in $\mathbb{R}^3$ is a graph embedded in $\mathbb{R}^3$ with edges straight line segments joining the vertices. So, for example, when we visualize the Necker Cube, we see rather the framework which is made up of the vertices and edges of the cube (its 1-*skeleton*). We use the notation $\mathcal{F} = (V, E)$ to denote a framework with vertex set V and edge set E. For a given *real*-valued function $\gamma : V \to \mathbb{R}$, we introduce the quadratic difference equation

$$\gamma(\Delta\Phi)^2 = (\nabla\Phi)^2 \tag{1}$$

for $\Phi : V \to \mathbb{C}$. The equation should be interpreted at each vertex $x \in V$ as:

$$\gamma(x)\left(\frac{1}{n(x)}\sum_{y \sim x}(\Phi(y) - \Phi(x))\right)^2 = \frac{1}{n(x)}\sum_{y \sim x}(\Phi(y) - \Phi(x))^2 \,,$$

where the sum is taken over all vertices y connected to x by an edge ($y \sim x$) and $n(x)$ is the degree at x (the number of edges incident with x). We are interested in frameworks in $\mathbb{R}^3$, called *invariant*, which by definition satisfy equation (1) for some given function γ, with Φ an orthogonal projection to the complex plane, *independently of any similarity transformation of the framework*. For example, the 1-skeleton of the cube is an invariant framework with γ identically zero.

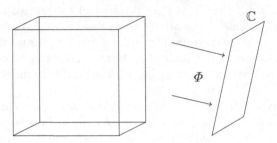

The 1-skeletons of all regular polytopes, as well as other striking configurations are also invariant with γ now taking on different values [4].

The motivation for introducing this equation is discussed in [3] as a way of understanding how geometry may emerge from combinatorial structure. An abstract graph carries around with it an admissible collection of functions γ for which (1) has non-trivial solutions. Call this the *geometric spectrum of the graph*. For each non-trivial solution Φ there is a local geometric realization of a vertex and its neighbours as an invariant framework with Φ an orthogonal projection to $\mathbb{C}$. We think of these realizations as *geometric states*. By analogy with quantum mechanics, in order to correlate, graphs must fall into geometric states and so geometry emerges, just as a cube emerges when the sketch on paper correlates with the system of our brain. The invariance by similarity transformation is fundamental in order that the geometry is intrinsic to the graph and does not depend on the way it is embedded as a framework in Euclidean space.

When we are presented with the sketch of the cube on a flat piece of paper, we are given the projections of the vertices $\Phi(x)$ ($x \in V$) and the edges joining them. As above, for a particular vertex $x = (x_j, y_j, z_j)$, if we take its projection to be $w_j = x_j + iy_j$, we are effectively required to deduce the third coordinate z_j ($j = 1, \ldots, 8$) to obtain a *lift* into Euclidean 3–space. There are precisely two choices of lift up to translation along the axis of projection which give an invariant framework satisfying (1) with $\gamma \equiv 0$. These two different lifts are obtained, one from the other, by reflection in a plane orthogonal to the axis of projection (the xy–plane with our particular choice of projection). There are different ways to interpolate between the two lifts, but the most appropriate would seem to be to allow complexification of the coordinates. In the notation above, setting the coordinates of the eight vertices of the cube as column vectors of a matrix, for a given projection $w_1 = x_1 + iy_1, \ldots, w_8 = x_8 + iy_8$, the general state of the Necker Cube would have an expression:

$$\begin{pmatrix} x_1 & x_2 & \cdots & x_8 \\ y_1 & y_2 & \cdots & y_8 \\ e^{i\theta}z_1 & e^{i\theta}z_2 & \cdots & e^{i\theta}z_8 \end{pmatrix}$$

where $(z_1, \ldots, z_8)$ is one of the lifts and θ is an arbitrary real number. In general, (1) is satisfied invariantly (that is after an arbitrary similarity transformation)[1], only when $e^{2i\theta} = 1$, giving as two "eigenstates" the real visualizations of the cube.

For a large collections of particles that have been put into the same pure quantum state via a Stern-Gerlach apparatus, then the spin has a well-defined experimental meaning. Specifically, it specifies the direction in space in which a subsequent detector must be oriented in order to achieve the maximum probability (100 %) of detecting the particles.

If we now return to the Necker Cube and attach one to another, then one can observe similar phenomena.

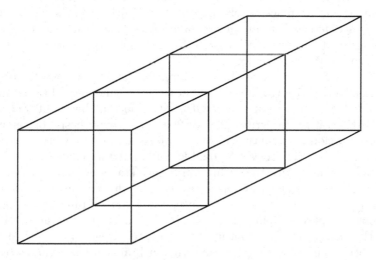

We find it almost impossible to mix a visualization of one cube together with its reflected counterpart in the same ensemble; a choice regarding one cube becomes deterministic for the rest. Feedback occurs (we refer to the discussion of Example 2 of Sect. 4), so that a choice of lift for one cube dictates the choice for the others. We conjecture that this is analogous to similar phenomena at a quantum level: given a statistically large collection of spin-$\frac{1}{2}$ particles say, once a significant number have taken a predominant "direction" (spin up, or spin down) along an axis as a result of correlation with another system, feedback dictates that this should be the universal choice and hence decoherence. This may also explain the apparent deterministic nature of information processing.

---

[1] This requires an involved computation which we omit.

6   The Brain, The Universe

A hierarchy too far, perhaps; the brain as a microcosm of the whole universe. The perspective of this article, is that of a universe as an information processing machine, in which feedback loops produce meaning. One tries to understand how a complex system can evolve without laws imposed upon it from outside. As for evolution, if change occurs then a feedback loop can validate this change or not over the long term - long term here, may refer to nanoseconds or a million years. However, for "change to occur", we seem to be back at an impass in respect of time.

Time is one of the problems highlighted by Wheeler in his list of four puzzles [23] (p. 13): "How to derive time without presupposing time". However, as Wheeler notes [23] (p. 13): "The very word [time] is a human invention, and the problems that come with it are of human origin."

At the quantum level, time seems to have a very shaky existence. I took up this issue in [2] and proposed that time is *relational*, specifically, in the context of this article, it is information about an ordering of states that has been given meaning via feedback involving a system which includes the brain. The process: *change–feedback–meaning–information–change* seems the only way to kick-start a world without invoking law from outside. But how can something change without outside influence?

H. Rolston III describes the human brain as "the most complex object in the known universe" [18] (p. 224). However we are to understand the term "conscious", the idea that the universe itself is conscious has been put forward, for example by K. Ward, who writes [22] (p. 290): "... a hypothesis consonant with many interpretations of quantum physics is to see the actual world as rooted in a consciousness that conceives all possible states, and actualizes some of them for a reason connected with the evaluation of such states by that consciousness." Once more, *feedback* is suggested as a prompter of change (an evaluation).

When we sleep, in an idealized sense, the human brain functions as an autonomous complex system. True, our bodily functions guarantee that the machine that keeps us alive continues to operate: oxygen is absorbed by the lungs, the heart pumps at a regular rhythm, our brains are maintained by blood flow in a state that allows information to be transmitted and processed via chemical reactions in neurons. But our sense organs have ceased to be the major directing influence on our thought processes. As we dream, our minds roam. Indeed, the model proposed by Briegel and De la Cuevas [5], is suggestive as to the exploratory process involved, whereby episodes of memory are resurrected "invoking patchwork-like sequences of virtual experience" (p. 3). Whatever else, change occurs. The complex system of our brain is changing and the rules for that change are somehow encoded by the system itself. To understand this process–the way the brain changes using its own resources–may give some clue as to the workings of the greater whole.

References

1. Applebaum, D.: Probability and Information, 2nd edn. Cambridge University Press, Cambridge (2008)
2. Baird, P.: Information, universality and consciousness: a relational perspective. Mind Matter **11**(1), 21–44 (2013)
3. Baird, P.: Emergence of geometry in a combinatorial universe. J. Geom. Phys. **74**, 185–195 (2013)
4. Baird, P.: An invariance property for frameworks in Euclidean space. Linear Algebra Appl. **440**, 243–265 (2014)
5. Briegel, H., De las Cuevas, G.: Projective simulation for artificial intelligence, Scientific Reports **2**, 400. doi:10.1038/srep00400
6. Bohr, N.: Can quantum-mechanical desription of physical reality be considered complete? Phys. Rev. **48**, 696–702 (1935)
7. Cohen, P.J.: Set Theory and the Continuum Hypothesis. Benjamin, Amsterdam (1966)
8. Davies, P.: The nature of the laws of physics and their mysterious biofriendliness. Euresis J. **5**, 117–138 (2013)
9. Davies, P.: Does consciousness lead to God: http://www.closertotruth.com/video-profile/Does-Consciousness-Lead-to-God-Paul-Davies-/1614. For transcript, see: http://biocentricity.blogspot.fr/
10. Davis, M.: Medical Research Council, Cognition and Brain Sciences Unit, Cambridge, WEB publication. http://www.mrc-cbu.cam.ac.uk/people/matt.davis/cmabridge/
11. Deacon, T.: What is missing from theories of information? In: Davies, P., Henrik, N. (eds.) Gregersen Information and the Nature of Reality: From Physics to Metaphysics, pp. 146–169. Cambridge University Press, New York (2010)
12. Floridi, L.: Semantic conceptions of information, Stanford Encyclopedia of Philosophy, WEB publication
13. Floridi, L.: Is semantic information meaningful data. Philos. Phenomenological Res. **70**, 351–370 (2005)
14. Hawking, S., Herzog, T.: Populating the landscape: a top down approach. Phys. Rev. D **73**, 123527 (2006)
15. Hebb, D.O.: The organization of Behaviour: A Neuropsychological Theory. Wiley, New York (1949)
16. Landauer, R.: The physical nature of information. Phys. Lett. A **217**, 188–193 (1996)
17. Le Bellac, M.: A Short Introduction to Quantum Information and Quantum Computing. Cambridge University Press, Cambridge (2006)
18. Rolston III, H.: Care on earth: generating informed concern. In: Davies, P., Gregersen, N.H. (eds.) Information and the Nature of Reality: From Physics to Metaphysics, pp. 205–245. Cambridge University Press, New York (2010)
19. Shannon, C.E.: A mathematical theory of communication. Bell Syst. Tech. J. **27**, pp. 379–423, 623–656 (1948)
20. Szilard, L.: On the decrease of entropy in a therodynamic system by the intervention of intelligent beings. Zeitschrift fuer Physik **53**, 840–856 (1929)
21. Tukey, J.W.: Sequential conversion of continuous data to digital data, Bell Laboratories memorandum of Sept. 1, 1947. Reprinted in Tropp, H.S.: Origin of the term bit. Annals Hist. Comput. **6**, 152–155 (1984)

22. Ward, K.: God as the ultimate informational principle. In: Davies, P., Gregersen, N.H. (eds.)Information and the Nature of Reality: From Physics to Metaphysics, pp. 282–300. Cambridge University Press (2010)

23. Wheeler, J.A.: World as system self-synthsized by quantum networking. IBM J. Res. Develop. **32**(1), 4–15 (1988)

24. Wheeler, J.A.: Information, physics, quantum: The search for links. In: Zurek, W.H. (ed.) Complexity, Entropy and the Physics of Information, Santa Fe Institute Studies in the Sciences of Complexity, pp. 3–28 (1990)

25. Zurek, H. (ed.): Complexity. Entropy and the Physics of Information, Santa Fe Institute Studies in the Sciences of Complexity (1990)

Semantics and Memory

Semantic Composition Inspired by Quantum Measurement

William Blacoe[(✉)]

School of Informatics, University of Edinburgh, Edinburgh, Scotland
`w.b.blacoe@sms.ed.ac.uk`

Abstract. We represent the meaning of words with density operators learned from a large corpus of dependency-parsed English sentences in an unsupervised way. This generalizes vector-space semantics in a straightforward manner by allowing an arbitrary number of subspaces. Our lexical density operators encode syntactic and semantic information. These structures allow us to compose the meaning of a sentence from the meaning of its words, again without any supervision. This model is able to detect whether a pair of sentences constitutes a paraphrase. We also analyse the entanglement among syntactic relations within linguistic density operators.

1 Introduction

Finding an accurate way to represent meaning in natural language has proven to be a difficult problem. Varying formalisms and models have been suggested in the literature, the main two camps originating from logics, the other from statistics. The former is known for its straightforward compositionality. The latter commonly uses vectors to encode distributions over linguistic contexts to express a word's meaning, lending lexical representations a geometric interpretation (e.g. [18]). Despite the usefulness of distributional semantics on the word level, it is difficult to scale its applicability to the sentence level. Promising models in the literature include [8] and [19]. They learn vector, matrix or tensor representations for words and operators to combine word meanings to sentence meanings.

In this work we take a similar approach to compositional distributional semantics by identifying and testing interesting mathematical analogies with quantum mechanics. Quantum states are used to express meanings of words and sentences, quantum measurement can be reinterpreted to serve as an algorithm to compose the meaning of words, and entropy measures are instrumental in evaluating the ambiguity and entanglement of the senses of words and sentences.

One typical entanglement detection method is to test for a violation of the CHSH inequality [6]. The typical CHSH test requires two subsystems (subspaces) A, B with two possible values (dimensions) each ($\{a_1, a_2\}$ and $\{b_1, b_2\}$). In this work we are dealing with multipartite operators with more than two subspaces each with hundreds of dimensions. Therefore we resort to another entanglement detection method, in this case an entanglement inequality based on von Neumann entropy.

© Springer International Publishing Switzerland 2015
H. Atmanspacher et al. (Eds.): QI 2014, LNCS 8951, pp. 41–53, 2015.
DOI: 10.1007/978-3-319-15931-7_4

Our contributions in this paper are as follows: We design a composition algorithm for creating sentence representations, given the representations of the containing words. An experiment on paraphrase detection will aid to determine the efficacy of the composition algorithm and quality of the resulting representations. Secondly, we show that many of the density operators at word and sentence level contain entanglement among their subsystems. This is discovered by means of an entropy inequality from the literature. Sections 2, 3 and 4 reiterate the math of density operators as quantum states, their measurement and their entropy, and explain our application of them to this linguistics. The experiments we perform are explained in Sect. 5. Their results and consequences are discussed in Sect. 6.

2   States

Just as quantum states are commonly represented using kets, distributional semantics is known to use vectors to represent the meaning of words. However, as has been done in quantum physics we here use density operators which can be thought of as a probability distribution over orthonormal (eigen) kets. This is an expressive generalization of vectors.

Our linguistic use can be thought of as an extension of [4] who captured co-occurences of words in a basic matrix using the Hyperspace Analogue of Language (HAL) [10]. Just as they uncovered word senses by applying singular value decomposition to their matrices, we assume that eigen-decomposing a word's density operator renders that word's senses.

Section 2.1 details relevant formalities and properties of density operators. Section 2.2 then outlines our method for learning lexical density operators from a dependency-parsed corpus.

2.1   Density Operators

Subspaces. A density operator ρ is an Hermitian matrix over kets $|s\rangle \in \mathcal{H}$ residing in a Hilbert space $\mathcal{H}$. This space is the tensor product of an arbitrary number of subspaces: $\mathcal{H} = \mathcal{H}_1 \otimes \ldots \otimes \mathcal{H}_M$. Each subspace $\mathcal{H}_m$ has arbitrary dimensionality D_m. The base kets of $\mathcal{H}$ result from all possible tensor products of the subspaces' base kets:

$$base(\mathcal{H}) = \{|b_1\rangle \otimes \ldots \otimes |b_M\rangle \mid |b_i\rangle \in \mathcal{H}_i, i = 1, \ldots, M\} \tag{1}$$

Thus, ρ is a weighted sum of outer products of $\mathcal{H}$'s base kets:

$$\rho = \sum_{i_1,\ldots,i_M,j_1,\ldots,j_M} w_{i_1,\ldots,i_M,j_1,\ldots,j_M}(|b_{i_1}\rangle \otimes \ldots \otimes |b_{i_M}\rangle)(\langle b_{j_1}| \otimes \ldots \otimes \langle b_{j_M}|) \tag{2}$$

If a matrix can be illustrated as a two-dimensional array of weights, then ρ can be thought of as a hypercube as an M-dimensional array of weights.

Eigen Spectrum. The spectral theorem tells us that there is an eigen decomposition for ρ. This means that ρ can also be expressed as the weighted sum of outer products of eigen kets $|e\rangle$: $\rho = \sum_i \lambda_i |e_i\rangle\langle e_i|$.

For a Hermitian matrix to be a density operator all of its eigen values must be nonnegative. Therefore, after normalization the λ_i constitute a probability distribution over eigen kets $|e_i\rangle$. Each eigen ket can be thought of as representing a syntactico-semantic sense of *word*.

An operator's eigen decomposition is extremely useful to know for many different problems. However, we find that explicitly computing eigen kets and values is prohibitive, given the order and dimensionality of the operators we employ. In the following sections we describe the ways in which we manage to circumvent this problem.

Similarity Function. A common similarity function for vectors is the cosine of the angle they enclose. This is simply their normalized inner product. For words w_1, w_2 which are respectively represented by density operators ρ_{w_1}, ρ_{w_2} their similarity is defined as $\text{sim}(w_1, w_2) = \text{Tr}(\rho_{w_1}\rho_{w_2})$ which can be considered a multilinear extension of the vector similarity function.

Marginalization. Analogous to a joint probability distribution, subsystems of a density operator can be marginalized out via the partial trace function. We write

$$\text{Tr}_{\{S_1,\ldots,S_N\}}(\rho) = \sum_{|b\rangle \in base(\mathcal{H}_{S_1} \otimes \ldots \otimes \mathcal{H}_{S_N})} \langle b|\rho|b\rangle \tag{3}$$

to denote that a proper subset of ρ's subsystems $S_1, \ldots, S_N$ gets traced out by multiplying ρ on both sides with all base kets from $\mathcal{H}_{S_1} \otimes \ldots \otimes \mathcal{H}_{S_N}$. This results in a density operator of lower order. This will prove useful when partially tracing over linguistic density operators in order to extract information specific to some syntactic relation. More about this application in Sect. 3.2.

Entanglement. A multipartite ket $|s\rangle$ describes an entangled system if there are no subkets $|s_1\rangle, |s_2\rangle$ such that $|s\rangle = |s_1\rangle \otimes |s_2\rangle$. One way of extending this notion to a density operator is through its eigen kets: If there is at least one eigen ket whose subsystems are entangled then the entire density operator is entangled.

2.2 Learning Lexical Density Operators

When a physical system contains more than one subsystem each is modeled with a subspace as described above. The multipartite space $\mathcal{H}$ is then able to accomodate joint probability distributions over subsystems. In our linguistic implementation a lexical density operator's subsystems come from the syntactic relations used by the parser. These are the labels found, for example, on the arcs

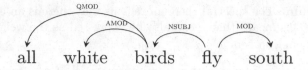

Fig. 1. Dependency parse tree of "all white birds fly south".

of the parse tree in Fig. 1. In this example the neighborhood nbh of "birds" is $nbh = \{\text{QMOD:all}, \text{AMOD:white}, \text{NSUBJ}^{-1}\text{:fly}\}$. This is translated into a ket in a straightforwad manor: $|nbh\rangle = |b_{all}\rangle_{\text{QMOD}} \otimes |b_{white}\rangle_{\text{AMOD}} \otimes |b_{fly}\rangle_{\text{NSUBJ}^{-1}} \otimes |\emptyset\rangle_{\text{MOD}} \otimes \ldots$ where, for instance, $|b_{all}\rangle_{\text{QMOD}}$ is the base ket in subspace $\mathcal{H}_{\text{QMOD}}$ corresponding to the context word "all". Any syntactic relation R which does not appear in the target word's immediate dependency neighborhood is realized by a dummy ket $|\emptyset\rangle_{\text{R}}$, rather than a base ket. This is a unit length ket in a uniform superposition over all context words (dimensions) in the respective subspace.

We summarize the entire learning process with the following simplified formula. For lack of space we refer the reader to Blacoe et al. [3] for further details.

$$\rho_w = \frac{\sum_{doc \in corpus} |doc_w\rangle\langle doc_w|}{Tr\left(\sum_{doc \in corpus} |doc_w\rangle\langle doc_w|\right)}, \text{ where } |doc_w\rangle = \sum_{tr \in trees_{doc}} |nbh_{w,tr}\rangle \quad (4)$$

It describes how the lexical density operator ρ_w for word w is learned from the corpus which is divided into documents doc. Every occurence of w within the same document is assumed to be used in the same sense. Hence the "grouping" of document kets $|doc_w\rangle$. Since the corpus is parsed, each document is a set of parse trees t. By $|nbh_{w,t}\rangle$ we mean the ket which is the tensor product of certain base kets and dummy kets in the subspaces.

Following Blacoe et al. [3], we make use of a corpus of 88.2M sentences in 2.7M documents in British English, the ukWaC corpus [2]. They created dependency parse trees for all sentences in the corpus using the MaltParser [14].

3   Composition via Measurement

Quantum measurement lies at the foundation of quantum mechanics. It is the description of what happens when a system is observed by a measuring device. In general, an observation changes the system's state. What the system's state is after measurement depends on its state before and on the design of the measuring device. In Sect. 3.1 we reiterate the math for two well-known formalisms of measurement. Then we introduce custom variants thereof which proved useful in our computational experiments. Section 3.2 then explains how semantic composition can be modeled by means of quantum measurement.

3.1   Formalisms

Projector-Valued Measurement. In a PVM a state ρ is measured by a device which is represented by an observable A which is also an Hermitian operator. Let the eigen decomposition of A be $A = \sum_i a_i |a_i\rangle\langle a_i|$. The eigen values $a_i \in \mathbb{R}$ can be negative or positive. The eigen kets encode a collection of projectors $A_i = |a_i\rangle\langle a_i|$ which serve as measures in the PVM. When ρ is measured by device A its outcome is i with probability $p_i = \text{Tr}(A_i\rho)$. That is, its outcome state is

$$\rho_i' = \frac{|a_i\rangle\langle a_i|\rho|a_i\rangle\langle a_i|}{\text{Tr}(A_i\rho)} = |a_i\rangle\langle a_i|\frac{\text{Tr}(A_i\rho)}{\text{Tr}(A_i\rho)} = A_i \tag{5}$$

with probability p_i. ρ and all A_i have trace 1, but $|a_i\rangle\langle a_i|\rho|a_i\rangle\langle a_i|$ does not necessarily. The denominator $\text{Tr}(A_i\rho)$ in Eq. 5 serves to normalize the outcome state to trace 1.

The statistical outcome state of a PVM is:

$$\rho' = \sum_i p_i\rho_i' = \sum_i |a_i\rangle\langle a_i|\rho|a_i\rangle\langle a_i| = \sum_i \text{Tr}(A_i\rho)A_i \tag{6}$$

which is already normalized.

Positive Operator-Valued Measurement. The PVM is a special case of the more general form of measurement, the positive operator-valued measurement (POVM). Here not just projectors but any positive operators can serve as measures. They need not be mutually orthogonal. The only restriction on a POVM's measures is that they sum to the identity operator I. Let the positive operators be π_i. Then a POVM measurement of state ρ has outcome i with probability $p_i = \text{Tr}(\pi_i\rho)$. The i-th outcome stateis given as:

$$\rho_i' = \frac{M_i\rho M_i^\dagger}{\text{Tr}(M_i^\dagger M_i\rho)} = \frac{M_i\rho M_i^\dagger}{\text{Tr}(\pi_i\rho)} \tag{7}$$

where $M_i = \sqrt{\pi_i}$ is a root operator of π_i. Again, the normalisation ρ_i' is guaranteed by the denominator $\text{Tr}(\pi_i\rho)$.

The state that encodes all possible outcomes with their respective possibilities is the statistical state

$$\rho' = \sum_i p_i\rho_i' = \sum_i M_i\rho M_i^\dagger \tag{8}$$

Thus this state contains the contribution that all measures π_i make after interacting with ρ.

Partial POVM. We define a partial POVM to be a measurement where not all provided measures are used. Therefore $\sum_i \pi_i \neq I$. This is important in cases where we only wish for a subset of measures π_i to interact with the system ρ. Only these chosen measures will contribute to the final statistical outcome state:

$$\rho' = \frac{\sum_i p_i\rho_i'}{\sum_i p_i} = \frac{\sum_i M_i\rho M_i^\dagger}{\sum_i \text{Tr}(\pi_i\rho)} \tag{9}$$

Here division by $\sum_i \mathrm{Tr}(\pi_i\rho)$ is required for ρ' to be normalized because the probability mass from the omitted positive operators is missing. If the sum of the omitted positive operators is π_{omitted} (that is, $\pi_{\mathrm{omitted}} + \sum_i \pi_i = I$) then the missing probability mass is $p_{\mathrm{missing}} = \mathrm{Tr}(\pi_{\mathrm{omitted}}\rho)$ (that is, $p_{\mathrm{missing}} + \sum_i \mathrm{Tr}(\pi_i\rho) = 1$). The smaller the summed trace of the missing positive operators is, the smaller p_{missing} is and the closer the outcome state of the partial POVM is to the one the full POVM would have produced.

Approximated Partial POVM. We consider one more alternative measurement scheme. It approximates partial POVM and is interesting because it is computationally more efficient. As before, we require a finite set of positive operators π_i which need not sum to the identity operator. Again, measuring results in the $i - th$ possible outcome $\rho_i = \mathrm{Tr}(\pi_i\rho)\pi_i$ with probability $p_i = \mathrm{Tr}(\pi_i\rho)$. Thus,

$$\rho' = \frac{\sum_i \mathrm{Tr}(\pi_i\rho)\pi_i}{\sum_i \mathrm{Tr}(\pi_i\rho)} \tag{10}$$

is the normalized statistical outcome state which is inspired by the definition of the PVM's statistical post-measurement state.

3.2   Semantic Composition

Extracting Selectional Preferences. A simple way of extracting the information of how a linguistic object (words, phrases, sentences) connects to others is to trace out all except one subspace (see Eq. 3). If we wish to know what subjects a verb goes with, for example, we simply trace out all subspaces except for the one which encodes the subject relation. This results in a density operator in only the subject subspace. Now we can simply read the probability for each context word (one each dimension) off its diagonal.

Recursive Modification. When we compose the meaning of a sentence from the meaning of its words we first obtain the dependency parse tree of the sentence and then proceed from the leaves all the way to the root node x_{root}. The only other objects we need are the lexical density operators learned from corpus. The following algorithm then directs the composition.

In the sentence "all white birds fly south" (see Fig. 1 for its dependency parse tree) "birds" is modified by the leaf nodes "all" via the relation QMOD (quantor modification) and by "white" via the relation AMOD (adjectival modification). Subsequently, "fly" is modified by "south" and the (now modified) "birds". Each modification is made by a POVM measurement. In this quantum analogy the head's density operator acts as the state of the system being observed. The modifying dependent induces a POVM which serves for the measurement.

Since a head and its dependent are on different syntactic levels they will not be comparable directly. For example, $sim(white, birds) = 0$ with virtual certainty. However, we can make use of the knowledge that AMOD is the relation which connects "white" with "birds". We use the method described in the foregoing paragraph to extract a probability distribution p_i over neighboring words w_i that "white" usually occurs with via the relation AMOD.

The words w_i are now on the same syntactic level as "birds" which makes them comparable. This comparability is necessary for the measurement to work, because the lexical density operators serve as the positive operators in the current POVM. That is, the state ρ_{birds} gets measured by the POVM $\{p_i\rho_{w_i}\}$. A similar measurement is performed when modifying "birds" with "all" via the relation QMOD. Now that all dependents of "birds" have caused a measurement, all (in this case 2) post-measurement states are summed together with another copy of ρ_{birds} and normalized to represent the subtree for "all white birds".

The resulting subtree representation is a density operator in the same space as all lexical density operators. Therefore it is amenable to the same process recursively as were the leaf nodes in the last step. This is convenient, as it is now the dependent of "fly", together with "south". The representation of the subtree headed by "fly" is the result of measuring "fly" in the context of "all white birds" and "south", summing the outcome states together with ρ_{fly} and normalizing. Since the root node has been reached, the recursion terminates and the resulting density operator at this point represents the entire tree.

4   Entropy

As is typical in natural languages, many words have multiple senses. They can, for example, vary in their syntactic category and their semantic applicability. Here we use the joint entropy of a density operator ρ_w to quantify the ambiguity of word w. We assume that ρ_w's eigen kets represent w's senses. By computing the joint entropy we determine how (un)biased the probability distribution over eigen kets is.

What is more, we explain how a measure of conditional entropy can serve to detect entanglement in density operators. This is of linguistic interest, as it will show correlations between syntactic relations in the mental lexicon. As mentioned in Sect. 2.1, entanglement in a density operator ρ_w indicates entanglement in at least one of its eigen kets. That is, for at least one sense of word w its joint distribution over context words under different syntactic relations cannot be expressed as a product of separate distributions. Examples include verbs whose selectional preferences of subjects and objects are not independent. In general, the more a word's meaning is defined by specific syntactic combinations of context words, the lower its conditional entropy.

Renyi Entropy. A generalization of the Shannon entropy measure H is the Renyi entropy H_α [17]. It comes with a parameter α, thus making it a family of measures. Let X be a random variable with n possibles outcomes $x_1, x_2, \ldots, x_n$ and corresponding probabilities $p_{x_1}, p_{x_2}, \ldots, p_{x_n}$. Then the Renyi entropy is defined as

$$H_\alpha(X) = \frac{1}{1-\alpha} \log \left(\sum_x p_x^\alpha \right) \tag{11}$$

Interesting special cases include $\alpha = 1$ and $\alpha = 2$. $H_1(X) = -\sum_x p_x \log p_x$ is the regular Shannon entropy. But in this work $H_2(X) = -\log \sum_x p_x^2$ will be of interest for reasons of computational convenience (see next paragraph).

Entropy of Density Operators. Von Neumann [12] generalized the Shannon entropy to apply to density operators. That is, the eigen values λ_i of a (normalized) density operator are interpreted as the probabilities of a distribution whose entropy is:

$$S_1(\rho) = -\mathrm{Tr}(\rho \log \rho) = -\sum_i \lambda_i \log \lambda_i \tag{12}$$

Computing this requires knowing the eigen values λ_i. The von Neumann entropy S can also be generalized using Renyi's family of entropy measures. For $\alpha = 2$ this is:

$$S_2(\rho) = -\log \mathrm{Tr}(\rho^2) = -\log \sum_i \lambda_i^2 \tag{13}$$

As eigen decomposition is prohibitive for computational reasons, we take advantage of the possibility to compute the S_2 entropy of a density operator without knowing its eigen values.

Conditional Entropy. We repeat pertinent knowledge from Sect. 11.2 in [13] here for convenience. The following paragraph includes the defininition of joint entropy and conditional entropy with regards to Shannon entropy. Entropies of regular probability distributions are subject to entropy inequalities. When generalizing to von Neumann entropy, it is possible for a certain class of density operators to violate this inequality. In such cases we know that there is entanglement among subspaces of the density operator.

Let X, Y be two random variables with out comes x_i and y_j, respectively. The joint probability $p(x_i, y_j)$ tells us how likely it is that the outcomes x_i and y_j happen together. The joint entropy of the two variables is defined as

$$H(X,Y) = -\sum_{i,j} p(x_i, y_j) \log p(x_i, y_j) \tag{14}$$

The conditional entropy $H(Y|X)$ is defined as the entropy that is "left over" from the joint entropy after knowing the outcome of X:

$$H(Y|X) = -\sum_{i,j} p(x_i, y_j) \log \frac{p(x_i, y_j)}{p(x)} = H(X,Y) - H(X) \tag{15}$$

Entropy Inequality. The conditional entropy is always non-negative in the classical Shannon paradigm. That is, the joint distribution of X and Y always contains at least as much entropy as any of its separate distributions:

$$H(X,Y) \geq \max\{H(X), H(Y)\} \tag{16}$$

Horodecki et al. [15] survey many entanglement criteria, among them Bell inequalities, distillation of states, positive partial transpose, and entropy inequalities. Horodecki et al. [16] examine the latter: When we substitute probability distributions with density operators it is possible for the conditional entropy $S(\rho_{X,Y}|\rho_X)$ to be negative. This violation of the entropy inequality in Eq. 16 indicates an entangled state. One simple application is to take some multi-partite density operator $\rho_{A,B}$ with subsystems A and B. Next, we trace out one of the subsystems: $\rho_A = \text{Tr}_B(\rho_{A,B})$. If $S(\rho_A)$ exceeds $S(\rho_{A,B})$ then the subspaces A and B are entangled in $\rho_{A,B}$. The same can be done with the other subsystem: $\rho_B = \text{Tr}_A(\rho_{A,B})$. Horodecki et al. [16] point out that the converse is not guaranteed: Not every entangled state violates the inequality.

Mean Conditional Entropy. What can be done when a density operator has more than two subspaces? We propose considering all possible two-way partitions. In the case of a tripartite density operator $\rho_{A,B,C}$ we can partition the set of three subspaces in 3 different ways making 6 conditional entropies computable:

1. $S(\rho_{A,B,C}|\rho_A)$ 2. $S(\rho_{A,B,C}|\rho_B)$ 3. $S(\rho_{A,B,C}|\rho_C)$
4. $S(\rho_{A,B,C}|\rho_{B,C})$ 5. $S(\rho_{A,B,C}|\rho_{A,C})$ 6. $S(\rho_{A,B,C}|\rho_{A,B})$

Here we leave out the two trivial variants where no or all subsystems are traced out. If, say, the first variant is negative, then we know that the subsystem A is entangled with the subsystem $B \otimes C$ in $\rho_{A,B,C}$. The number of variants is exponential in the amount of subsystems. To get a better overview of the entropy inequality violations in each density operator we introduce the mean conditional entropy which is simply the average of all non-trivial conditional entropies. If this value is still negative, then we have a significant amount of variants which violate the inequality.

5   Experiments

In this section we describe two experiments that examine the effects of composing lexical density operators to sentential ones in the manor outlined in Sect. 3.2. Experiment 1 evaluates how useful the information which ist propagated from the word to the sentence level is for detecting paraphrases. In Experiment 2 can detect whether lexical and sentential density operators contain entanglement by violating the entropy inequality in Eq. 16.

Experiment 1: Paraphrase Detection. The Microsoft Research paraphrase corpus (MSRPC) [7] contains 4076 training and 1724 test sentence pairs with an average sentence length of 25.5 tokens. The task is to predict which sentence pairs have the same meaning and which do not by comparing human judgments with model predictions. 67.5 % of the training pairs are paraphrases, whereas 66.5 % of the test pairs are paraphrases. Once all sentence density operators are computed we predict the similarity of two sentences s_1, s_2 using the same similarity measure as with words: $\text{sim}(s_1, s_2) = \text{Tr}(\rho_{s_1}\rho_{s_2})$.

This value and others, such as the sentence lengths and how many unigrams and bigrams they have in common, are collected in a feature vector. The feature vectors obtained from the instances in the training set are fed to a logistic regression classifier which in turn is applied to the instances in the test set in order to predict which sentence pairs are paraphrases and which are not. Section 6 presents the results from this procedure when using partial POVM and approximated partial POVM measurement.

We compare the quantum model to two unsupervised vector space models: $\text{SDS}(\odot)$ [11] is a simple distributional space whose vectors contain co-occurence statistics also learned from the ukWaC. It takes no syntax into account, as its co-occurences are based on a context window of 5 words to the left and right of each target word. $\text{DM}(+)$ [1] stands for distributional memory and comes originally in the form of a third-order tensor which encodes co-occurence statistics about word pairs and their syntactic relation. We reinterpreted the DM tensor as a set of vectors whose dimensions encode context word-neighbor word tuples. Whereas $\text{SDS}(\odot)$ composes word vectors to sentence vectors using pointwise multiplication, $\text{DM}(+)$ does so by summing them.

Experiment 2: Entanglement Detection. We use the density operators created by the partial POVM model in Experiment 1 to examine their conditional entropy. The higher ρ_w's joint entropy is, the more syntactico-semantically ambiguous w is. ρ_w's conditional entropy additionally quantifies how interdependent w's neighboring words of different syntactic contexts are. One would expect a full sentence to have little remaining ambiguity after being created from its words, since context serves to determine which senses of the involved words apply in the given sentence. Since a sentence representation is the result of mixing many lexical ones together its joint entropy should be higher than that of lexical density operators. However, we expect its conditional entropy to be lower than that of lexical ones, as typically many syntactic parts come together in an interdependent fashion to create the whole entangled sentence.

6   Results and Conclusions

The quantum composition algorithm manages to accurately predict whether a sentence pair is paraphrastic in 71.5% and 75.2% of all test instances, respectively without and with an approximation of the partial POVM composition (see Table 1). Hence, the latter is not only more efficient computationally, but also creates more useful sentence representations. The $\text{DM}(+)$ model does slightly better than the $\text{SDS}(\odot)$ model, which might be ascribed to its taking syntax into account. Surprisingly, both outperform the first quantum model. The second quantum model, however seems to employ a better way of capturing and mixing lexical meanings to form sentence meanings. We should mention here that many supervised models have been applied to the same task, several of

Table 1. Classification accuracy for paraphrase detection on the Microsoft Research paraphrase corpus (MSRPC). SDS and DM are comparative unsupervised vector-space models for distributional compositional semantics. Two quantum models are "partial POVM" and "approximated partial POVM" (see Sect. 3). The baseline comes about when predicting all test instances to be paraphrases.

Model	Accuracy (%)	F1 score (%)
Baseline	66.5	80.0
Partial POVM	71.5	80.2
SDS(⊙)	73.0	82.3
DM(+)	73.5	82.2
approx. part. POVM	75.2	82.8

which achieve still higher accuracies. To our knowledge the state of the art is a syntax-oblivious vector-based model which achieves 80.4 % accuracy with an F1 score of 86.0 % [9].

Table 2. Hand-picked words from the MSRPC dataset whose density operators have a particularly negative or positive mean conditional entropy (MCE). This is computed as the joint entropy (JE) minus the mean entropy (ME). The rightmost column is the standard deviation of entropy values for all 2^{10} possible subsets of subspaces. The lower a negative MCE value is, the more entanglement there is among syntactic relations in the word's syntactico-semantic representation.

word	MCE	JE	ME	SD_{ME}
simply	-1.95	5.40	7.35	2.45
merely	-1.74	5.62	7.37	2.02
mainly	-1.68	5.53	7.22	1.98
really	-1.40	4.36	5.77	3.34
both	-1.39	5.71	7.11	1.90
estimated	-1.33	4.43	5.77	1.73
selected	-1.28	5.07	6.35	1.43
there	-1.25	5.15	6.40	1.793
such	-1.21	4.68	5.89	2.60
...				

word	MCE	JE	ME	SD_{ME}
...				
yrs	1.83	3.94	2.10	1.86
magdalene	1.87	3.98	2.11	2.23
oct	1.88	2.75	0.86	1.94
pennsylvania	1.92	4.46	2.53	1.85
jul	2.03	2.46	0.42	2.02
wallace	2.10	3.95	1.85	1.10
could	2.15	4.31	2.15	2.15
must	2.16	4.32	2.16	2.16
would	2.16	4.33	2.16	2.16

Table 2 shows some hand-picked words from the MSRPC dataset. Among the very negative mean conditional entropy (MCE) values are many adverbs (e.g. mainly, really, merely, simply). This can be attributed to the versatile applicability of adverbs: They can modify verbs, adjectives and other adverbs. The verb phrases they modify can be anything from a single word to an entire clause. Another interesting class of words is participles (e.g. selected, estimated) since they are often considered to adjectives, too. There are many other syntactioc-semantically ambiguous words (e.g. both, there, such) that can be in more than one syntactic relation with other words and can change meaning significantly depending on the context.

On the very positive end of the spectrum modal verbs (e.g. would, must, could) stand out. They are linked to verb phrases with a wide variety of meaning, but always under the same syntactic relation. We find several proper nouns here (e.g. magdalene, wallace, pennsylvania), perhaps because they only ever attach to one other word at a time since they have no dependents and are leaves, thus making correlation among subspaces unlikely. Verbs such as coincide, wring, tamper, fend are verbs that only appear in fairly specific contexts. Abbreviations (e.g. mb, jul, oct, nov, yrs) are found to have positive MCE values because there is a syntactic relation specifically provided for them by the dependency parser.

As for the sentence density operators, it is difficult to give an interpretation of their eigen components, but we can make some broad statements about their MCE values: 91.1 % of all sentences have a negative MCE, where the mean is -0.58985 with a standard deviation of 0.590663. Hence, sentences generally have a lower conditional entropy where syntactic relations are somewhat entangled. This harmonizes with the intuition that lower entropy means more correlation among internal components: The interaction of words in a sentence provide context and disambiguate each other's usages, rendering a sentence with a precise meaning.

Conclusion. Using Blacoe et al.'s [3] method for learning density operators from a dependency-parsed corpus, we expanded upon their model to scale to full sentences. It turns out that their density operators contained enough structural information for semantic composition. In fact, the sentences can be arbitrarily long. The compositional algorithm sums over lexical density operators to create phrasal and sentential ones. Thus, this method is essentially an additive composition. The longer the sentence is, the more information is collected in the data structure representing it which improves its quality. As is intuitive, more context helps to make the meaning of a sentence more precise. Since lexical, phrasal and sentential density operators are all in the same Hilbert space, they are amenable to the same similarity and composition function. That is, words, phrases and sentences can be compared to each other and can serve to extract syntactico-semantic selectional preferences.

An intriguing consequence of our mathematical design of representing and composing meaning is the limitation to a closed area of the overall Hilbert space. Since every composed density operator is a convex combination of lexical density operators, all sentence operators must reside inside the convex hull delimited by the lexicon. This is somewhat reminiscent of the Whorf-Sapir hypothesis that the content of one's mental lexicon influences how one conceptualizes one's surroundings [5].

References

1. Baroni, M., Lenci, A.: Distributional memory: a general framework for corpus-based semantics. Comput. Linguist. **36**(4), 673–721 (2010)
2. Baroni, M., Bernardini, S., Ferraresi, A., Zanchetta, E.: The wacky wide web: a collection of very large linguistically processed web-crawled corpora. Lang. Resour. Eval. **43**(3), 209–226 (2009)

3. Blacoe, W., Kashefi, E., Lapata, M.: A quantum-theoretic approach to distributional semantics. In: Proceedings of the 2013 Conference of the North American Chapter of the Association for Computational Linguistics: Human Language Technologies, pp. 847–857 (2013)

4. Bruza, P.D., Cole, R.J.: Quantum logic of semantic space: an exploratory investigation of context effects in practical reasoning. In: Artemov, S., Barringer, H., d'Avila Garcez, S.A., Lamb, L.C., Woods, J. (eds.) We Will Show Them: Essays in Honour of Dov Gabbay, vol. 1, pp. 339–361. College Publications, London (2005)

5. Carroll, J.B. (ed.): Language, Thought, and Reality: Selected Writings of Benjamin Lee Whorf. MIT Press, Cambridge (1956)

6. Clauser, J.F., Horne, M.A., Shimony, A., Holt, R.A.: Proposed experiment to test local hidden-variable theories. Phys. Rev. Lett. **23**, 880–884 (1969)

7. Dolan, B., Quirk, C., Brockett, C.: Unsupervised construction of large paraphrase corpora: exploiting massively parallel news sources. In: Proceedings of the 17th International Conference on Computational Linguistics, pp. 350–356 (2004)

8. Grefenstette, E., Sadrzadeh, M.: Experimental support for a categorical compositional distributional model of meaning. In: Proceedings of the 2011 Conference on Empirical Methods in Natural Language Processing, pp. 1394–1404 (2011)

9. Ji, Y., Eisenstein, J.: Discriminative improvements to distributional sentence similarity. In: Proceedings of the 2013 Conference on Empirical Methods in Natural Language Processing, pp. 891–896 (2013)

10. Lund, K., Burgess, C.: Producing high-dimensional semantic spaces from lexical co-occurrence. Behav. Res. Methods Instrum. Comput. **28**(2), 203–208 (1996)

11. Mitchell, J., Lapata, M.: Composition in distributional models of semantics. Cogn. Sci. **38**(8), 1388–1429 (2010)

12. von Neumann, J.: Mathematische Grundlagen der Quantenmechanik. Springer, Berlin (1932)

13. Nielsen, M.A., Chuang, I.L.: Quantum Computation and Information Theory. Cambridge University Press, Cambridge (2010)

14. Nivre, J., Hall, J., Nilsson, J., Chanev, A., Eryigit, G., Kübler, S., Marinov, S., Marsi, E.: Maltparser: a language independent system for data-driven dependency parsing. Nat. Lang. Eng. **13**(2), 95–135 (2007)

15. Horodecki, R., Horodecki, P., Horodecki, M., Horodecki, K.: Quantum entanglement. Rev. Mod. Phys. **81**, 865–942 (2009)

16. Horodecki, R., Horodecki, P., Horodecki, M.: Quantum α-entropy inequalities: independent condition for local realism? Phys. Lett. A **210**, 377–381 (1996)

17. Renyi, A.: On measures of entropy and information. In: Proceedings of the Fourth Berkeley Symposium on Mathematical Statistics and Probability, vol. 1, pp. 547–561. University of California Press, Berkeley (1961)

18. van Rijsbergen, K.: The Geometry of Information Retrieval. Cambridge University Press, Cambridge (2014)

19. Socher, R., Huval, B., Manning, C.D., Ng, A.Y.: Semantic compositionality through recursive matrix-vector spaces. In: Proceedings of the 2012 Joint Conference on Empirical Methods in Natural Language Processing and Computational Natural Language Learning, pp. 1201–1211 (2012)

Expansion-by-Analogy: A Vector Symbolic Approach to Semantic Search

Trevor Cohen[1]([⊠]), Dominic Widdows[2], and Thomas Rindflesch[3]

[1] University of Texas School of Biomedical Informatics at Houston, Houston, USA
trevor.cohen@uth.tmc.edu
[2] Microsoft Bing, Redmond, WA, USA
[3] National Library of Medicine, Bethesda, MD, USA

Abstract. In this paper, we develop an approach to semantic search that utilizes high-dimensional vector representations to infer the nature of the relationship between query concepts and other concepts in relevant documents. We do so by incorporating outside knowledge drawn from tens of millions of concept-relation-concept triplets, known as *semantic predications*, extracted from the biomedical literature using a Natural Language Processing (NLP) system called SemRep. Inference is accomplished in high-dimensional space using Expansion-by-Analogy, a novel analogical approach to pseudo-relevance feedback, in which the relationships between query concepts and other concepts in documents they occur in guide the query expansion process. The semantic vector based approaches developed in this work show improvements in performance over a baseline bag-of-concepts model, and these improvements are most pronounced on queries that are not conducive to keyword-based search.

Keywords: Distributional semantics · Information retrieval · Vector symbolic architectures

1 Introduction

Within the biomedical research community, considerable effort has been invested in the development of structured knowledge resources [1]. Efforts have been made to leverage these resources to improve the performance on information retrieval tasks [2–6]. The emphasis of this work has been on the application of controlled terminologies and thesauri as a means to map between variant expressions of the same concept (which has proven especially useful in the genomics domain), at times with the utilizaton of taxonomic (ISA) relationships existing within structured knowledge resources to further elaborate upon query concepts [6]. The utilization of outside resources in order to elaborate upon a stated query is referred to as *query expansion*. In this paper, we attempt to leverage a different sort of knowledge resource for query expansion.

Specifically, we utilize SemMedDB [7], a publicly available database of concept-predicate-concept triplets (such as haloperidol TREATS schizophrenia),

© Springer International Publishing Switzerland 2015
H. Atmanspacher et al. (Eds.): QI 2014, LNCS 8951, pp. 54–66, 2015.
DOI: 10.1007/978-3-319-15931-7_5

or *semantic predications*, that have been extracted from the biomedical literature using a Natural Language Processing system known as SemRep [8]. SemRep extracts predications from biomedical text using domain knowledge in the Unified Medical Language System [9]. For example, the predication "fluoxetine TREATS Major Depressive Disorder" (MDD) is extracted from the phrase "patients who have been successfully treated with fluoxetine for major depression." SemMedDB differs from the human-curated resources that have been utilized in previous work in several ways. Firstly, it contains a richer set of semantic relationships than the "ISA" relationships provided by a taxonomy. SemRep extracts a total of 31 predicate types, of which many relate to clinical medicine (e.g. TREATS, DIAGNOSES) and interactions between substances and biological entities (e.g. INHIBITS, STIMULATES). Therefore an inference mechanism of some sort is required in order to determine which of these possible pathways for query expansion is relevant for a particular concept. Secondly, it cannot be assumed to be perfectly accurate, on account of the difficulties inherent in the automated processing of biomedical language. In a recent evaluation of SemRep, Kilicoglu et al. report .75 precision and .64 recall (.69 f-score) [10]. Finally, it consists of a large number of assertions (more than 50 million) in predication form, and these assertions are not unique - they carry distributional information describing the number of times each predication has been extracted from the corpus of biomedical literature to which SemRep has been applied.

To model this extracted knowledge we use a method called Predication-based Semantic Indexing (PSI) [11], leveraging vector-based approaches to reasoning we have developed during the course of research documented in our prior Quantum Interaction contributions [12–14]. PSI is well suited to modeling the information contained in SemMedDB as it captures both distributional information, in the manner of conventional distributional semantic models (for recent reviews see [15] and [16]), and logical relations between concepts. Therefore, it allows for weighting of the relationships between concepts in accordance with their relative frequency. As PSI is based on the Random Indexing paradigm [17], it provides a computationally convenient way to generate a reduced-dimensional approximation of the information in SemMedDB, which can then be retained in RAM for efficient inference. In this paper, we describe a new approach to query expansion we term Expansion-by-Analogy, in which we infer the significant relationships between query concepts and other concepts in documents they occur in. These inferences are drawn from PSI concept vectors, and the document vectors derived from them, without the need to identify co-occurring concepts explicitly.

2   Expansion-by-Analogy

In previous research, we have developed methods to draw inference from SemMedDB in order to recover held-out therapeutic relationships using a process of analogical reasoning [12–14,18]. This process occurs in a high-dimensional space in which concepts are represented as vectors that encode the nature and distribution of the relationships they occur in. Sets of predicates that link one

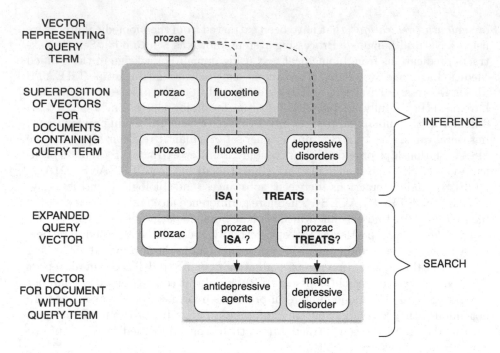

VECTOR
REPRESENTING
QUERY
TERM

SUPERPOSITION
OF VECTORS
FOR
DOCUMENTS
CONTAINING
QUERY TERM

EXPANDED
QUERY
VECTOR

VECTOR
FOR DOCUMENT
WITHOUT
QUERY TERM

INFERENCE

SEARCH

Fig. 1. Inferring predicates from related documents. The solid line indicates direct co-occurrence. The dashed lines indicate inferred predicate paths, which are used to expand the term "prozac" so as to retrieve related documents that do not contain it directly.

concept to another can be inferred from their vector representations by reversing the vector transformations used during encoding. Once inferred, vector representations of these predicate pathways can be used to find concepts that relate to some other concept in a similar way. As distributional models can derive document representations from concept vector representations, it seems reasonable that one might infer the predicates that connect a query concept to related concepts in a document from a document vector in a similar manner. Figure 1 illustrates this process schematically. Documents containing the query concept "prozac" are retrieved, and the types of relationships (or predicates) between prozac and other concepts in these documents are inferred. It is not necessary to decompose the vector representations of the concepts or the documents to draw these inferences: the connecting predicates are inferred from these representations directly. Vector representations of these predicates can then be used to generate an expanded query vector, which will be similar to vectors representing documents containing concepts that relate to prozac in accordance with the inferred predicates. We refer to this process as Expansion-by-Analogy as it involves applying a relational structure inferred from one set of documents to retrieve others. Such alignment of relational structure is a defining characteristic of analogical reasoning [19]. In the section that follows we will describe the methods through which the vectors and inferences concerned are generated.

3 Mathematical Structure and Methods

3.1 Circular Holographic Reduced Representations

To accomplish the encoding of predicate types within a vector space representation of concepts, we draw upon the capabilities of a family of representational approaches collectively known as Vector Symbolic Architectures (VSAs) [20]. In our experiments the VSA we will employ is Plate's Circular Holographic Reduced Representation (CHRR) [21], which uses complex vectors each of whose coordinates is a number on the unit circle in the complex plane, generated using the implementation developed in [22]. We will refer to such a complex vector as a *circular vector*. The use of complex vectors is standard in physics, particularly quantum theory, but remains comparatively unexplored in artificial intelligence and machine learning [23]. However, the approach we have developed is readily applicable to other VSAs, such as the Binary Spatter Code (BSC) [24]. Though the BSC offers more storage capacity on a bit-for-bit basis [25], this is not required for the modestly sized document collection we employ here. Furthermore, the simplicity of the circular binding operation (which unlike real-valued HRR, involves simple addition of phase angles) and superposition (which unlike the BSC, requires no random tie-breaking) make the complex vectors more agile for experimentation.

VSAs share with other distributed vector representations the ability to generate composite vector representations of terms or concepts, which we will refer to as *semantic vectors*, by superposing randomly generated *elemental vectors*. For example, the semantic vector representation of a term might be composed from the elemental vectors of terms that surround it. In this way, two terms surrounded by similar other terms will obtain similar vector representations, providing a convenient way to estimate semantic relatedness [26]. In addition to the standard superposition operator $(+)$, VSAs introduce a compositional operator known as *binding*, which we will represent with the symbol $\otimes$. Binding is a multiplication-like operator through which two vectors are combined to form a third vector C that is *dissimilar from* either of its component vectors A and B. Binding has an inverse, which we will represent with the symbol $\oslash$. If C = A $\otimes$ B, then A $\oslash$ C = A $\oslash$ (A $\otimes$ B) $\approx$ B. This recovery may be approximate, but the robust nature of the representation guarantees that A $\oslash$ C is similar enough to B that B can be recognized as the best candidate for A $\oslash$ C in the original set of concepts. Thus the invertible nature of this operator facilitates retrieval of the information it encodes.

In CHRR, binding through circular convolution is accomplished by pairwise multiplication: $X \otimes Y = \{X_1Y_1, X_2Y_2, \ldots X_{n-1}Y_{n-1}, X_nY_n\}$, which is equivalent to addition of the phase angles of the circular vectors concerned. Binding is inverted by binding to the inverse of the vector concerned: $X \oslash Y = X \otimes Y^{-1}$, where the inverse of a vector is its complex conjugate. Elemental vectors are initialized by randomly assigning a phase angle to each dimension (dimensionality is user-defined). Superposition is accomplished by pairwise addition of the unit circle vectors, and normalization of the result for each circular component. In the implementation used in our experiments, normalization occurs after training concludes, so the sequence in which superposition occurs is not relevant. Also, the "random" initiation of elemental vectors is rendered deterministic by seeding the random number generator with a hash value derived from a string or character of interest following the approach developed in [25], ensuring that incidental overlap between elemental vectors is consistent across experiments.

3.2 Predication-Based Semantic Indexing (PSI)

PSI derives vector representations of concepts by superposing obound products representing concept-predicate pairs. Elemental vectors are generated for each concept $E(\text{concept})$, and each relation type $E(\text{PREDICATE})$ and its inverse $E(\text{PREDICATE-INV})$. Semantic vectors are learned gradually by superposing the bound products of elemental vectors representing related items: thus, to encode a predication xRy, the semantic vector for x, written $S(x)$, is incremented by the bound product $E(R) \otimes E(y)$. The same process is applied in reverse to $S(y)$. For example, encoding a single instance of the predication "prozac ISA fluoxetine" is accomplished as follows:

$$S(\text{prozac}) \mathrel{+}= E(\text{ISA}) \otimes E(\text{fluoxetine})$$
$$S(\text{fluoxetine}) \mathrel{+}= E(\text{ISA-INV}) \otimes E(\text{prozac})$$

Thus, the semantic vector for prozac encodes the assertion that it is (a trade name for) fluoxetine, and the semantic vector for fluoxetine encodes the assertion that it has the hyponym prozac. As the same predication may be extracted from many documents, it is advantageous to apply weighting metrics to temper the effect of repeated predications, and increase the influence of infrequently occurring concepts. In our experiments we applied local (LW) and global weighting (GW) metrics as follows:

$$S(\text{concept}_1) \mathrel{+}= E(\text{PREDICATE}) \otimes E(\text{concept}_2) \times \text{LW} \times \text{GW}$$
$$\text{LW} = \log(1 + \text{total occurrences of predication})$$
$$\text{GW} = IDF(\text{concept}_2)$$
$$IDF(\text{concept}_2) = \log \frac{\text{number of predications}}{\text{predications containing concept}_2}$$

The net result is a set of concept vectors derived from the set of predications each concept occurs in. On account of the reversible nature of the binding operator, this information can be retrieved. So one would anticipate:

$$S(\text{fluoxetine}) \oslash E(\text{ISA-INV}) \approx E(\text{prozac})$$
$$S(\text{fluoxetine}) \oslash E(\text{prozac}) \approx E(\text{ISA-INV})$$

This process results in three sets of vector representations, collectively containing a semantic and elemental vector for each concept, as well as an elemental predicate vector for each predicate and its inverse.

3.3 Document Vector Construction

Document vectors are constructed by superposition of the PSI semantic vectors representing concepts (C_1 to C_n) extracted from this document, as follows:

$$S(\text{document D}) = \sum_{i=1}^{n} S(C_i) \times TF(C_i) \times IDF(C_i)$$

$$TF(C) = \text{frequency concept C in document D}$$

$$IDF(C) = \log \frac{\text{number of documents}}{\text{documents containing C}}$$

3.4 Pseudo-Relevance Feedback

Pseudo-relevance feedback is an automated technique based on the assumption that the nearest neighboring documents retrieved using standard methods are relevant, and that their contents can therefore be used to expand the original query. In our experiments we implement a form of pseudo-relevance feedback as follows. For each concept that was extracted from a query, we retrieve ten related documents by finding the ten nearest neighboring semantic document vectors to the semantic vector for this concept. These semantic document vectors representations are then superposed, and the predicates that connect them to the concept in question are inferred by finding the nearest neighboring predicate vectors to the composite query $S(\text{superposed document vectors}) \oslash E(\text{concept})$, as illustrated schematically earlier in Fig. 1. Consider for example the concept "prozac", which was extracted from the query "relationship between prozac and liver disease". First we find the ten-nearest neighboring *semantic* document vectors to the semantic vector for the concept "prozac". Then we superpose those vectors to generate the vector $S(\text{prozac}_{NN})$, and retrieve the nearest neighboring predicate vectors to the bound product $S(\text{prozac}_{NN}) \oslash E(\text{prozac})$, which are shown in Table 1.

Table 1. Nearest Neighboring Predicate Vectors to $S(\text{prozac}_{NN}) \oslash E(\text{prozac})$

Score	Predicate	STD above mean
0.072	ISA-INV	3.83
0.043	LOCATION_OF-INV	2.24
0.040	PREVENTS-INV	2.11
0.039	NEG_STIMULATES	2.06
0.038	SAME_AS	1.99

Predicates with a similarity to $S(\text{prozac}_{NN}) \oslash E(\text{prozac})$ of more than 2.5 standard deviations above the mean across all predicates are retained. In our case, this applies to ISA-INV. For the concept "liver_disease" (LD) only COEX-ISTS_WITH met this threshold, and no predicate met the threshold for concept "relationships". So the query vector for "relationship between prozac and liver disease" is constructed as follows:

$$QV(\text{prozac}_{\text{ISA-INV}}) = S(\text{prozac}) + E(\text{ISA-INV}) \otimes E(\text{prozac})$$
$$QV(\text{LD}_{\text{COEXISTS\_WITH}}) = S(\text{LD}) + E(\text{COEXISTS\_WITH}) \otimes E(\text{liver\_disease})$$
$$QV(\text{entire query}) = QV(\text{prozac}) \times IDF(\text{prozac}) + QV(\text{LD}) \times IDF(\text{LD})$$
$$+ S(\text{relationships}) \times IDF(\text{relationships})$$

Documents are then ranked in order of the relatedness between their vector representations and this composite query.

4   Evaluation

4.1   Methods and Materials

We evaluate Expansion-by-Analogy (EbA) using OHSUMED, a widely-used information retrieval evaluation set [27]. OHSUMED consists of 348,566 clinically-oriented abstracts and titles extracted from 270 medical journals over a five year period, and 106 clinically-oriented queries, with background information. For each query, a set of documents have been annotated as probably relevant, definitely relevant or irrelevant. This annotation is not exhaustive, but does include all relevant articles discovered by a set of human annotators and a base-line information retrieval system. For the purpose of our evaluation, we consider any document annotated as probably or definitely relevant to a query to be relevant. Background information was not utilized - we restricted our evaluation to the query text only. Two queries were excluded from the evaluation - query 8 as no documents are annotated as possibly relevant, and query 68 as this maps to a single concept, "mesenteric_vasculitis", which was not extracted from any document in the OHSUMED corpus resulting in an empty query vector in concept-based models. Both the queries and documents were processed by SemRep. Rather than attempting to extract predications from these documents, SemRep was configured to extract and normalize concepts recognized in the text. This step would usually precede the extraction of predications, and is accomplished within SemRep by the widely-used MetaMap concept extraction and normalization system [28]. Concepts occurring in more than 100,000 documents were excluded. The concepts extracted from queries and documents are then used in place of the original terms following [29, 30], an approach that has been referred to as "bag-of-concepts" (BoC). Our PSI space was derived from the June 2013 release of SemMedDB [7], which contains 65,465,536 predications extracted from 13,537,476 MEDLINE citations. From this, we created a 2000-dimensional complex-valued PSI space using the open source Semantic Vectors package [23, 31]. Concepts occurring in more than 500,000 predications were excluded, in order to eliminate uninformative frequently-occurring concepts. The purpose of our evaluation was to determine whether query expansion improved the performance of the BoC approach, and the extent to which both of these approaches were able to address queries that are difficult to address using a conventional keyword-based, or "bag-of-words" (BoW), approach. To do so, we evaluate the performance of six models, summarized in Table 2.

Table 2. Evaluated models

BoC_L	Bag-of-concepts implemented using Apache Lucene [32]
BoC_E	Vector space implementation of bag-of-concepts, using E(concept)
BoC_S	Semantically enriched bag-of-concepts, using S(concept)
EbA	Expansion-by-Analogy
BoW_L	Bag-of-terms implemented using Apache Lucene
BoW_E	Vector space implementation of bag-of-terms, using E(term)

All models use Term-frequency Inverse Document Frequency (TF-IDF) weighting for the generation of both query and document vector representations, and terms occurring in more than 100,000 documents were excluded from term-based models. In addition to representing the full document-by-term matrix (BoC_L), we generate a reduced-dimensional approximation of this space by deriving document vectors from the elemental vector representations of concepts they contain (BoC_E). We do so in order to evaluate the extent to which information loss on account of dimension reduction affects performance. We also generate document vectors using the PSI semantic vectors for concepts (BoC_S), so we can identify improvements in performance on account of the enriched nature of these vector representations, and improvements due to inference by analogy. Finally, we evaluate the performance of two bag-of-words based models, one using the full document-by-term matrix (BoW_L), and the other using a reduced-dimensional approximation of this space derived from elemental term vector representations, also in an effort to evaluate the effects of information loss during dimension reduction. For each of these models we report the Mean Average Precision (MAP) and the precision at k=10 and 100 ($P^{k=10|100}$), estimated using trec_eval [33].

4.2   Results and Discussion

It is apparent upon review of the results in Table 3 that unlike the case with other test sets such as the TREC Medical Records collection (see for example

Table 3. Cumulative results. Best in class (BoC vs. BoW) and overall are shown in boldface.

	BoC_L	BoC_E	BoC_S	EbA	BoW_L	BoW_E	μSIM
MAP	0.1212	0.1261	0.1530	**0.1574**	**0.1748**	0.1456	**0.1996**
$P^{k=10}$	**0.2615**	0.2394	0.2587	0.2529	**0.3212**	0.2394	**0.3250**
$P^{k=100}$	0.1019	0.1158	0.1347	**0.1388**	**0.1397**	0.1232	**0.1589**

[34]), concept extraction has a detrimental effect on overall performance, as compared with BoW approaches. Nonetheless, the baseline performance of BoC is improved considerably by the application of semantic vector based approaches for all metrics shown other than $P^k = 10$. For example, there is a 26% and 30% improvement in MAP over BoC_L for BoC_S and EbA respectively. These improvements are still not adequate to improve performance beyond a term-based baseline (BoW_L), unless the document-by-term matrix is subjected to the same representational constraints as the reduced-dimensional vector representations (BoW_E). In addition to the results for individual models, we report those obtained by combining the best-performing models in each category (concept-based: EbA, keyword-based: BoW_L) by assigning the mean of the scores from these models to each query document pair (μSIM). These results exceed those obtained by any individual model, as the performance gains of semantic vector based approaches often occur on queries where keyword-based approaches perform poorly.

Figure 2 shows the average precision for each query, with queries ordered in accordance with the performance of BoW_L, represented by the grey shaded area of the graph. When BoC_L (—•), BoC_S (- -+) or EbA (· · · ∗) perform better than the baseline, their respective demarcator appears above the shaded area. It is evident from this figure that in many cases the semantic vector approaches lead to considerable improvements on queries in which the average precision of the term-based baseline was relatively poor (≤ 0.2). In many of these cases, concept extraction alone (—•) had less effect than retrieval based on PSI semantic vector representations (- -+), with further improvements obtained when using EbA to accomplish inference (· · · ∗) on a number of queries. These queries provide insight into where EbA offers advantages over conventional approaches. Table 4 shows

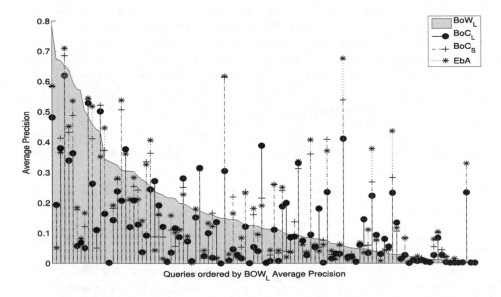

Fig. 2. Comparison of concept-based methods with bag-of-words.

those queries in which the AP of EbA was at least double that of BoW_L. Two characteristics of these queries stand out, though these are not universal. Firstly, many of the queries concern rare clinical entities. However, we were not able to identify a consistent pattern relating the document frequency of query concepts to EbA performance. Secondly, the degree to which many of these queries were expanded (P↑) is often greater than the average across all queries ($\mu = 5.2$, $\sigma = 3.4$) suggesting that identification of further pathways for expansion may be advantageous.

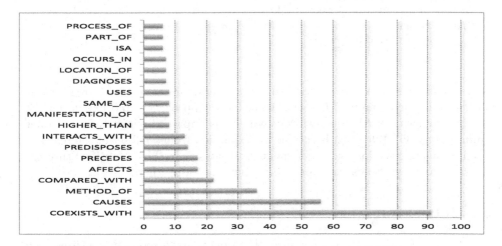

Fig. 3. Frequently-utilized predicates. The X axis shows the number of times this predicate was utilized for expansion across all queries.

Figure 3 shows all predicates that were used more than five times to expand queries in the set, with counts of the number of times they were employed. These counts are aggregated with respect to direction (such that counts of ISA and ISA-INV are aggregated) and include negated forms of the predicates (e.g. NEG_TREATS), which made up approximately 13 % of the 384 expansions that occurred. It is apparent from this figure that EbA uses a much broader range of semantic relations than the ISA relationships that predominate in taxonomy-based query expansion. In fact "ISA" expansions made up a small proportion (<2 %) of the total number only, and were not utilized for expansion of any of the queries in Table 4. This may be an artifact of our method. EbA is likely to infer paths for expansion from documents that contain an exact match for the query concept concerned. So inferring an ISA pathway would require that both this concept and its taxonomic relative appear in the same document, which may not always be the case. Nonetheless, it is clear that EbA makes extensive use of a wide range of the predicate types represented in SemMedDB.

Though these results do suggest that EbA may be complementary to BoW and BoC approaches, our evaluation has limitations - we have evaluated our method on a single test set only, and have made no attempt to optimize parameters such as statistical weighting metrics, dimensionality or underlying VSA.

Table 4. Queries with EbA > 100 % improvement in AP over BoW_L and AP > MAP(BoW). P↑ = no. predicates added. %↑ = % improvement.

Query	P↑	%↑
"review article on cholesterol emboli"	1	315
"spontaneous unilateral galactorrhea differential diagnosis and workup"	5	1386
"keratoconus treatment options"	3	260
"indications for and success of pericardial windows and pericardectomies"	15	1081
"diverticulitis differential diagnosis and management"	10	383
"surgery vs percutaneous drainage for lung abscess"	12	141
"infiltrative small bowel processes information about small bowel lymphoma and heavy alpha chain disease"	10	793

Nonetheless, the current evaluation suggests several directions for future research. These include combining EbA with term-based approaches, and extending the length of inferred predicate pathways which has improved performance in other applications [35]. Inferring directions for expansion from a subset of the relevant results may also lead to more pertinent predicates than those identified through the pseudo-relevance based approach we have developed here.

5 Conclusion

This paper describes EbA, an approach to query expansion that utilizes as a knowledge source a reduced-dimensional vector space approximation of tens of millions of semantic predications extracted from the biomedical literature. In addition to document vector representations, expanded vector representations of query concepts are derived from the vectors in this space using a vector-symbolic model of analogical reasoning, and used to construct query vectors. Evaluation on a standard information retrieval test set shows improvements over the aggregate performance of bag-of-concepts vector space approaches, and that the method performs well on a number of queries that are not conducive to standard keyword-based approaches. To do so, EbA utilizes a broader range of semantic relations than is possible with taxonomy-based approaches.

Acknowledgments. This research was supported by US National Library of Medicine grants R21 LM010826 and R01 LM011563. It was also supported in part by the Intramural Research Program of the US National Institutes of Health, National Library of Medicine. We would like to thank Lance DeVine, for contributing the CHRR implementation that was used in this research.

References

1. Bodenreider, O., Stevens, R.: Bio-ontologies: current trends and future directions. Briefings Bioinform. **7**, 256–274 (2006). PMID: 16899495 PMCID: PMC1847325

2. Zhou, W., Yu, C., Smalheiser, N., Torvik, V., Hong, J.: Knowledge-intensive conceptual retrieval and passage extraction of biomedical literature. In: Proceedings of the 30th Annual International ACM SIGIR Conference on Research and Development in Information Retrieval, pp. 655–662. ACM (2007)
3. Hersh, W.R.: Report on the TREC 2004 genomics track. In: ACM SIGIR Forum, vol. 39, pp. 21–24. ACM (2005)
4. Hersh, W.R., Cohen, A.M., Roberts, P.M., Rekapalli, H.K.: TREC 2006 genomics track overview. In: TREC (2006)
5. Koopman, B., Zuccon, G., Bruza, P., Sitbon, L., Lawley, M.: An evaluation of corpus-driven measures of medical concept similarity for information retrieval. In: Proceedings of the 21st ACM International Conference on Information and Knowledge Management, pp. 2439–2442. ACM (2012)
6. Zuccon, G., Koopman, B., Nguyen, A., Vickers, D., Butt, L.: Exploiting medical hierarchies for concept-based information retrieval. In: Proceedings of the Seventeenth Australasian Document Computing Symposium, pp. 111–114. ACM (2012)
7. Kilicoglu, H., Shin, D., Fiszman, M., Rosemblat, G., Rindflesch, T.C.: SemMedDB: a PubMed-scale repository of biomedical semantic predications. Bioinformatics 28(23), 3158–3160 (2012)
8. Rindflesch, T.C., Fiszman, M.: The interaction of domain knowledge and linguistic structure in natural language processing: interpreting hypernymic propositions in biomedical text. J. Biomed. Inf. 36, 462–477 (2003)
9. Bodenreider, O.: The unified medical language system (UMLS): integrating biomedical terminology. Nucleic Acids Res. 32(Database Issue), D267 (2004)
10. Kilicoglu, H., Fiszman, M., Rosemblat, G., Marimpietri, S., Rindflesch, T.C.: Arguments of nominals in semantic interpretation of biomedical text. In: Proceedings of the 2010 Workshop on Biomedical Natural Language Processing, pp. 46–54 (2010)
11. Cohen, T., Schvaneveldt, R., Rindflesch, T.: Predication-based semantic indexing: permutations as a means to encode predications in semantic space. AMIA Annu. Symp. Proc., 114–118 (2009)
12. Cohen, T., Widdows, D., Schvaneveldt, R., Rindflesch, T.C.: Finding Schizophrenia's prozac emergent relational similarity in predication space. In: Song, D., Melucci, M., Frommholz, I., Zhang, P., Wang, L., Arafat, S. (eds.) QI 2011. LNCS, vol. 7052, pp. 48–59. Springer, Heidelberg (2011)
13. Cohen, T., Widdows, D., Schvaneveldt, R.W., Rindflesch, T.C.: Logical leaps and quantum connectives: forging paths through predication space. In: Proceedings of AAAI Fall Symposium on Quantum Informatics for Cognitive, Social, and Semantic Processes, pp. 11–13 (2010)
14. Cohen, T., Widdows, D., De Vine, L., Schvaneveldt, R., Rindflesch, T.C.: Many paths lead to discovery: analogical retrieval of cancer therapies. In: Busemeyer, J.R., Dubois, F., Lambert-Mogiliansky, A., Melucci, M. (eds.) QI 2012. LNCS, vol. 7620, pp. 90–101. Springer, Heidelberg (2012)
15. Cohen, T., Widdows, D.: Empirical distributional semantics: methods and biomedical applications. J. Biomed. Inf. 42, 390–405 (2009)
16. Turney, P.D., Pantel, P.: From frequency to meaning: vector space models of semantics. J. Artif. Intell. Res. 37(1), 141–188 (2010)
17. Kanerva, P., Kristofersson, J., Holst, A.: Random indexing of text samples for latent semantic analysis. In: Proceedings of the 22nd Annual Conference of the Cognitive Science Society, vol. 1036 (2000)
18. Cohen, T., Widdows, D., Schvaneveldt, R., Davies, P., Rindflesch, T.: Discovering discovery patterns with predication-based semantic indexing. J. Biomed. Inf. 45, 1049–1065 (2012)

19. Gentner, D., Markman, A.B.: Structure mapping in analogy and similarity. Am. psychol. **52**(1), 45 (1997)
20. Gayler, R.W.: Vector symbolic architectures answer jackendoff's challenges for cognitive neuroscience. In: Slezak, P. (ed.), ICCS/ASCS International Conference on Cognitive Science, (Sydney, Australia. University of New South Wales.), pp. 133–138 (2004)
21. Plate, T.A.: Holographic Reduced Representation: Distributed Representation for Cognitive Structures. CSLI Publications, Stanford (2003)
22. De Vine, L., Bruza, P.: Semantic oscillations: encoding context and structure in complex valued holographic vectors. Proceedings of AAAI Fall Symposium on Quantum Informatics for Cognitive Social, and Semantic Processes (2010)
23. Widdows, D., Cohen, T.: Real, complex, and binary semantic vectors. In: Busemeyer, J.R., Dubois, F., Lambert-Mogiliansky, A., Melucci, M. (eds.) QI 2012. LNCS, vol. 7620, pp. 24–35. Springer, Heidelberg (2012)
24. Kanerva, P.: Binary spatter-coding of ordered k-tuples. In: von der Malsburg, C., von Seelen, W., Vorbrüggen, J.C., Sendhoff, B. (eds.) Artificial Neural Networks — ICANN 1996. LNCS, vol. 1112, pp. 869–873. Springer, Heidelberg (1996)
25. Wahle, M., Widdows, D., Herskovic, J.R., Bernstam, E.V., Cohen, T.: Deterministic binary vectors for efficient automated indexing of MEDLINE/PubMed abstracts. AMIA Annu. Symp. Proc., 940–949 (2012)
26. Karlgren, J., Sahlgren, M.: From Words to Understanding, Foundations of Real-World Intelligence, pp. 294–308. CSLI Publications, Stanford (2001)
27. Hersh, W., Buckley, C., Leone, T.J., Hickam, D.: OHSUMED: an interactive retrieval evaluation and new large test collection for research. In: Proceedings of the 17th Annual International ACM SIGIR Conference on Research and Development in Information Retrieval, pp. 192–201 (1994)
28. Aronson, A.R., Lang, F.: An overview of MetaMap: historical perspective and recent advances. J. Am. Med. Inf. Assoc. **17**, 229–236 (2010)
29. Hersh, W.R., Hickam, D.H., Haynes, R.B., McKibbon, K.A.: A performance and failure analysis of SAPHIRE with a MEDLINE test collection. J. Am. Med. Inf. Assoc. **1**, 51–60 (1994)
30. Aronson, A.R., Rindflesch, T.C., Browne, A.C.: Exploiting a large thesaurus for information retrieval. RIAO **94**, 197–216 (1994)
31. Widdows, D., Cohen, T.: The semantic vectors package: new algorithms and public tools for distributional semantics. In: Fourth IEEE International Conference on Semantic Computing (ICSC) (2010)
32. Apache lucene. https://lucene.apache.org
33. trec-eval. http://trec.nist.gov/trec_eval/
34. Koopman, B., Zuccon, G., Bruza, P., Sitbon, L., Lawley, M.: Graph-based concept weighting for medical information retrieval. In: Proceedings of the Seventeenth Australasian Document Computing Symposium, ADCS 2012, pp. 80–87. ACM, New York, NY, USA (2012)
35. Cohen, T., Widdows, D., Schvaneveldt, R., Rindflesch, T.: Discovery at a distance: farther journey's in predication space. In: Proceedings of the First International Workshop on the role of Semantic Web in Literature-Based Discovery (SWLBD2012), The IEEE International Conference on Bioinformatics and Biomedicine (BIBM 2012). Philadelphia, PA, USA, 4–7 October 2012

Subadditivity of Episodic Memory States: A Complementarity Approach

Jacob Denolf[✉]

Department of Data Analysis, Ghent University,
H. Dunantlaan 1, 9000 Ghent, Belgium
jacob.denolf@ugent.be

Abstract. We will comment on a paper by Brainerd, C., Wang, Z. and Reyna, V. [1] in which they introduce the quantum episodic memory (QEM) model which models the subadditivity in the classical disjunction rule that the human episodic memory exhibits in an experiment concerning word remembrance, also described in their paper. After listing and generalizing some issues we have with their use of quantum techniques in this approach and showing that the QEM model actually yields classical probabilities, we will propose an alternative quantum technical model, in which we see different memory types as incompatible measurements on an agent. Next to subadditivity, we will discuss other quantum features such as order effects of our model and propose a new experiment to observe these. We will use this example to argue that quantum models with all relevant vectors orthogonal always have classical equivalents and that non-orthogonality is the most important distinction between classical and quantum models.

1 Introduction

In this paper we will comment on a recent paper by Brainerd et al. [1], where a memory analogue of the superposition principle, borrowed from quantum physics is used to model episodic subadditivity, a phenomenon where the human episodic memory exhibits violations of the rules of classical probability when memorizing word lists. They also compare this quantum approach with an overdistribution model, which uses classical mathematics. This article can be placed within the large growing field in which the non-classical mathematics behind quantum mechanics are used in Social Sciences (for an overview see [3]). Quantum approaches are an elegant way to deal with non-classical probabilities (e.g. [4]), but the use goes deeper, specifically in the way it deals with the impact of measurement. Brainerd et al. draw in their paper an analogue between the human memory and the double-slit experiment. While in the double-slit experiment, particles pass through two different slits to create an interference pattern (for more, see [2]), here, the human mind is said to have two types of memory trace slits, through which word recognition passes. One of these memory trace types/slits is linked with the verbatim memorization of words, the other of these memory trace types is linked with gist memorization of words. We will start this

© Springer International Publishing Switzerland 2015
H. Atmanspacher et al. (Eds.): QI 2014, LNCS 8951, pp. 67–77, 2015.
DOI: 10.1007/978-3-319-15931-7_6

paper by giving an overview of the experiment in which the human mind exhibits the above mentioned subadditivity and show how the double-slit analogue is used to explain and model the observed violations of classical probability.

After this, we will point out some problems with this approach and propose an alternative quantum technique to solve our issues, elaborating on the points raised by Lambert-Mogiliansky in [6]. Instead of drawing a parallel to the two slits of the double-slit experiment, we will see these two types of memory traces as two incompatible representations of the same memory system, in the vein of Bohr complementarity. This complementarity view has already been implemented successfully in Social Sciences in e.g. [5]. The elicitation of these two memory types can be seen as two incompatible measurements on the agent. An analogue phenomenon of this incompatible measurements approach in Physics is the Stern-Gerlach experiment, in which it is impossible to measure spins of a particle in different directions at the same time. This approach will not only give a clearer picture of the interaction between these different memory traces and the outside world, but will still give rise to the violation of the classical probability.

We will also use this example to discuss the more general question of when, where, why and how to use these quantum techniques in Human Cognition. While in Physics the choice of appropriate techniques (e.g. entanglement, complementarity,...) stems relatively easily from the description of the problem (e.g. from the number of particles described), the situation in Human Cognition is less clear. Using this discussion we will try to give a more formal idea of when a system can be considered non-classical and when the quantum formalism truly gives a modeling advantage.

2   Episodic Subadditivity

In the experiment described in [1], each participant was asked to remember three distinct word lists (list 1, list 2 and list 3). Words across the three lists were possibly related but different. After these lists were remembered, agents were presented with a target word together with a recognition statement, which they accepted or rejected. The four types of target words that were presented, were words from list 1, list 2, list 3 or were unrelated distractor words, not appearing on any list. The four possible recognition statements were, (a) the target is on list 1, (b) the target is on list 2, (c) the target is on list 3 or (d) the target is on list 1, list 2 or list 3.

From these answers, the following proportions were calculated, for each type of target word: p_1, p_2, p_3 which were the proportions of accepted statements of resp. type (a), type (b) and type (c) and p_{123} which was the proportion of accepted statements of type (d). These proportions are seen as the probability of the event that an agent thinks that the target word is on a certain list, for proportions p_i or the probability of the event that the agent thinks that the target word is on any of the lists. Because of the structure of the recognition statements, the event associated with p_{123} can be seen as the disjunction of the events associated with p_i.

The above defined proportions exhibited a disjunction fallacy in the experiment of Brainerd et al.. A disjunction fallacy is a situation where the classical disjunction rule, $p(A \cup B) = p(A) + p(B) - p(A \cap B)$, does not hold. We will show that in the cases considered here, we have that $p(A \cap B) = 0$. Since this fallacy will allow for subadditivity, the resulting proportions exhibited:

$$p(A \cup B) \leq p(A) + p(B)$$

or

$$p(A) + p(B) - p(A \cup B) \geq 0$$

We shall now apply this disjunction rule to the proportions from the above described experiment. If agents would follow the classical set theory rules, the calculated proportions should exhibit:

$$S = p_1 + p_2 + p_3 - p_{123} = 0$$

We can set the conjunction part of the disjunction rule to zero, since no agent would accept a recognition statement of the type 'the target word was on list i and j'. The data collected in the above described experiment, however, yield $S = 0.38$, a highly reliable difference. So the human episodic memory clearly exhibits subadditivity.

3   The Quantum Episodic Model

To model this violation of the disjunction rule in the human episodic memory, it is proposed in [1] to use a quantum approach. It is assumed that agents use two types of memory traces in parallel: verbatim and gist. Verbatim traces store the exact form content of the remembered word, their spelling and phonology, next to contextual information, while gist traces are a representation of the semantic content of a word. In terms of the experiment, when agents are asked to accept or decline statements, they call upon both verbatim and gist traces. The difference between these two types of traces is the reason the agent exhibits subadditivity. The link to the quantum formalism is found in the fact that the agent is in superposition between these verbatim and gist traces: the remembered words are stored in two ways.

The QEM model is built in three steps. Firstly, the model is constructed in a 5 dimensional Hilbert space $\mathbb{H}^5$, spanned by the base $\{|V_1\rangle, |V_2\rangle, |V_3\rangle, |G\rangle, |U\rangle\}$. The vectors named $|V_i\rangle$ correspond with the verbatim traces of list i, the vector $|G\rangle$ corresponds to the gist traces and the vector $|U\rangle$ with the agent rejecting a statement. Agents are represented by a normalized state vector $|S\rangle$ in this Hilbert space:

$$|S\rangle = v_1|V_1\rangle + v_2|V_2\rangle + v_3|V_3\rangle + g|G\rangle + u|U\rangle$$

Secondly, when a target word from list 1 is given, the state vector is set to $|S_1\rangle$, with $v_2 = v_3$. Similarly, for a list 2 target word, the state vector is set to $|S_2\rangle$, with $v_1 = v_3$, for a list 3 target word, the state vector is set to $|S_3\rangle$, with $v_1 = v_2$ and for a distractor target word, the state vector is set to $|S_4\rangle$, with $v_1 = v_2 = v_3$.

Lastly, from these possible state vectors $|S_1\rangle, \ldots, |S_4\rangle$, using associated projectors in $\mathbb{H}_5$, the associated probabilities of accepting or declining a statement are calculated. The projector associated with accepting a statement of type (a) is defined as $M_1 = \mathrm{diag}(1, 0, 0, 1, 0)$, since both the verbatim traces of list 1 and the gist traces lead to accepting the statements. Similarly, the projector associated with accepting statements of type (b) and (c) are $M_2 = \mathrm{diag}(1, 0, 0, 1, 0)$ and $M_3 = \mathrm{diag}(1, 0, 0, 1, 0)$ respectively. The resulting probability of accepting a statement of type (a) is: $p_1 = ||M_1.S_i||^2 = v_1^2 + g^2$. Likewise we get a probability of $p_2 = ||M_2.S_i||^2 = v_2^2 + g^2$ for accepting a statement of type (b) and a probability of $p_3 = ||M_3.S_i||^2 = v_3^2 + g^2$ for accepting a statement of type (c). The probability of accepting a statement of type (d) is not defined by a projection of the state vector with an own associated projector, but as $p_{123} = 1 - ||(I - M_3)(I - M_2)(I - M_1).S_i||^2 = 1 - u^2 = v_1^2 + v_2^2 + v_3^2 + g^2$. This can be seen as the probability of the complement of the agent thinking the target word is not on list 1, 2 or 3. These probabilities clearly exhibit the previous described subadditivity:

$$p_1 + p_2 + p_3 = v_1^2 + v_2^2 + v_3^2 + 3g^2 \geq v_1^2 + v_2^2 + v_3^2 + g^2 = p_{123}$$

We will now lay out some issues we have with the QEM model itself and the choice of using a quantumlike formalism in this particular memory paradigm. The reasoning behind using quantumlike formalisms in Social Sciences seems, in our opinion, twofold. Firstly, there might be interpretational arguments who favor using a superposition construct. In the field of cognitive psychology this might, for example, model that an agent is an indefinite state between two beliefs. Secondly, there might be mathematical and/or statistical proporties of a system which can not be modeled using classic mathematics/statistics. We will point out some questions we have in light of the aforementioned two reasons when constructing the QEM model. On the interpretational side we will discuss some issues concerning the meaning of the vectors in the Hilbert space that is used. On the mathematical side, we will construct a non-quantum model, which will yield the same probabilities as the QEM model.

As is said in [1], the geometrical relation between vectors associated with events define the statistical relations between these events. Specifically, when two vectors are orthogonal, their associated events are mutually exclusive. Applying these notions to the QEM model, the event of the agent exhibiting both definite verbatim and gist traces is impossible. Take e.g. the limit case of an easy task were the agent(s) was/were able to memorize list 1 perfectly. When presented with a list 1 target word, the resulting state vector should be $(1, 0, 0, 0, 0)$, to obtain a probability of 1 to accept statements of type (a) and (d). However, the gist-coordinate being 0, seems to imply that this agent does not exhibit gist traces. This seem counterintuitive.

Next to interpretational arguments, there might be mathematical proporties that make the QEM model a strong use of the quantum formalism. However, we argue that a classical non-quantum model can yield the same probabilities. Consider for each of the four types j of target words the following 5 mutual exclusive events: V_1^j, V_2^j, V_3^j, G^j and U^j, each with respective probabilities v_1^j, v_2^j, v_3^j, g^j and u^j, which sum up to one. Define event V_i^j as the agent, using verbatim traces, remembering the target word being on list i, define event G^j as the agent remembering gist traces of the target word and define event U as the agent remembering the word as an unrelated distractor. Define now the event of the agent accepting a statement of type (a), (b) or (c) as the union of the associated event V_i^j and G^j, each with a probability of p_i^j and define the event of the agent accepting a statement of type (d) as the disjunction of V_1^j, V_2^j, V_3^j and G^j, with a probability of p_{123}^j. Straightforward calculation shows that this classical distribution yields the same probabilities as the QEM model, with $v_i^j = v_i^2$ and $g^j = g^2$.

The fact that there is an equivalent classical model might seem surprising, since the use of quantum techniques was justified by the violation of the classical disjunction rule. However, this violation stems here from the fact that the conjunction of the events of accepting statements is not empty, not because of non-classical statistics within the QEM model.

The previous reasoning can be generalized and applied to all quantumlike systems, where all relevant vectors are orthogonal. When only one measurement is considered, the normalization of the state vector puts constraints on its coordinates, such that the associated probabilities are classical. When two or more measurements are being done, with all relevant vectors still orthogonal, the associated matrices are commuting. This way, each of these measurements can be considered as being done first, resulting in classical probabilities. This way, no order effects are possible. The formal proofs of these claims can be found in the appendix. So even more complex systems than the here considered QEM model, such as doing multiple measurements or entangling systems with all relevant vectors orthogonal, will have a classical equivalent. It seems that non-orthogonality of vectors is the driving force behind the non-classicality of quantumlike systems.

4   The Complementarity Model

We will now propose an alternative quantum approach to this model, expanding on ideas from Chap. 6 of [3] and investigate again both reasons of using these techniques. Since we have shown that constructing the space with only orthogonal vectors, produces classical probabilities, we will now construct a space in which not all vectors are orthogonal. To do this, we will view the verbatim and gist traces as two different incompatible measurements. So we will have a base associated with the verbatim traces: $\{|V_1\rangle, |V_2\rangle, |V_3\rangle, |U\rangle\}$ and within this 4 dimensional vector space $\mathbb{H}^4$, we will have a second base associated with the gist traces: $\{|U_i'\rangle, |G'\rangle\}$, where $|U_i'\rangle$ represents 3 orthogonal vectors in the space orthogonal to $|G'\rangle$. When gist traces are observed, the state vector will be projected on $|G'\rangle$, when no gist traces are measured, the state vector will be projected on the hyperplane spanned by $\{|U_i'\rangle\}$. Since this space is completely determined by $|G'\rangle$, the choice of $|U_i'\rangle$ is arbitrary. Since, when measuring the gist traces, none of the lists plays a special role, we define the vector associated with the gist traces as:

$$|G'\rangle = \frac{1}{\sqrt{3}}|V_1\rangle + \frac{1}{\sqrt{3}}|V_2\rangle + \frac{1}{\sqrt{3}}|V_3\rangle$$

The assumption that none of three lists plays a special role could be false. There is a possibility that e.g. the first remembered list leaves stronger gist traces than the following. We will, however, continue to work under this assumption to construct an example of the complementarity model. Changing the definition of $|G'\rangle$ would retain the exhibited mathematical proporties. Note that $|G'\rangle$, the vector associated with the gist trace, is not orthogonal to $|V_1\rangle, |V_2\rangle$ or $|V_3\rangle$, the vectors associated with the verbatim trace and that this is the only difference between this model and the QEM model. This way we can investigate the impact of non-orthogonality.

The agent is now considered to be in a superposition between the possible verbatim traces and, at the same time, in superposition between the presence or absence of gist traces. This way, the event of exhibiting verbatim traces and the event of exhibiting gist traces, while being correlated, are not exclusive, as was the case in the QEM model.

While this model seems more in line with the interpretation that is given traditionally to quantumlike systems, we might have lost the mathematically property which made the QEM model interesting in the first place, namely subadditivity. To show that the complementarity model still allows for subadditivity, we will explicitly calculate the resulting probabilities. Accepting a statement of type (a), (b) or (c) should project the state vector on the plane spanned by the relevant $|V_i\rangle$ and $|G'\rangle$. Straightforward calculations give us the associated projector matrices:

$$M_1' = \begin{pmatrix} 1 & 0 & 0 & 0 \\ 0 & \frac{1}{2} & \frac{1}{2} & 0 \\ 0 & \frac{1}{2} & \frac{1}{2} & 0 \\ 0 & 0 & 0 & 0 \end{pmatrix} \qquad M_2' = \begin{pmatrix} \frac{1}{2} & 0 & \frac{1}{2} & 0 \\ 0 & 1 & 0 & 0 \\ \frac{1}{2} & 0 & \frac{1}{2} & 0 \\ 0 & 0 & 0 & 0 \end{pmatrix} \qquad M_3' = \begin{pmatrix} \frac{1}{2} & \frac{1}{2} & 0 & 0 \\ \frac{1}{2} & \frac{1}{2} & 0 & 0 \\ 0 & 0 & 1 & 0 \\ 0 & 0 & 0 & 0 \end{pmatrix}.$$

Using these projectors, we get for the probability of an agent accepting a statement of type (a) $p_1' = ||M_1'.S_i||^2 = v_1^2 + (v_2 + v_3)^2/2$. Likewise, we get respectively $p_2' = v_2^2 + (v_1 + v_3)^2/2$ and $p_3' = v_3^2 + (v_1 + v_2)^2/2$ as probabilities for the agent accepting statements of type (b) or (c). We keep the notion that the probability of an agent accepting a statement of type (d) is the complement of the agent thinking that the target word is not on any of the lists: $p_{123}' = 1 - u^2 = v_1^2 + v_2^2 + v_3^2$. These probabilities lead to:

$$p_1' + p_2' + p_3' = v_1^2 + v_2^2 + v_3^2 + (v_2 + v_3)^2/2 + (v_1 + v_3)^2/2 + (v_1 + v_2)^2/2 \quad (1)$$
$$= 2v_1^2 + 2v_2^2 + 2v_3^2 + v_1 v_2 + v_1 v_3 + v_1 v_2 \quad (2)$$
$$\geq v_1^2 + v_2^2 + v_3^2 \quad (3)$$
$$= p_{123}', \quad (4)$$

showing clearly the subadditivity which was the reason for constructing the QEM model. Note that it is not possible to define equivalent events with a classical distribution leading to these probabilities.

Next to subadditivity, we would like to point out another quantum mechanical mathematical property our complementarity model naturally exhibits, but the QEM model does not have. When, in our model, the state vector is forced to leave superposition, because the agent resolves his indeterminacy concerning one of the two types of memory traces, the state vector does not leave the superposition between the possible outcomes of the measurement that was not done. The agent is therefore still indetermined for the other type of memory trace. The action of leaving one superposition, however, impacts the other superposition, since the state vector fundamentally changes, by getting projected and normalized. This way, by seeing the verbatim and gist traces as two incompatible measurements, our model will allow interference effects to be modeled. These effects are the result of the non-commutativity of the gist and verbatim trace measurements. Using these notions, we can model the effect the measuring of the gist trace has on the verbatim trace and vice versa. This type of order effects can also not be modeled using classical probability.

To be able to see these effects, the original experiment should be extended into an experiment where both types of traces are measured on the same agent. We will illustrate this with a fictive example, to show the non-classical nature of the complementarity model, but the proposed experiment might open up the view concerning human memory. The idea that an agent first uses verbatim traces before gist traces is suggested by Brainerd, C., Wang, Z. and Reyna, V. in their Overdistribution Model, which is used as a classical alternative to the QEM model in [1].

Suppose, after being presented with a target word form list 1, the agent is in the following superposition:

$$|S\rangle = \frac{8}{10}|V_1\rangle + \frac{1}{10}|V_2\rangle + \frac{1}{10}|V_3\rangle + \sqrt{0.34}|U\rangle$$

This would mean that the agent has a probability of $\langle S||V_1\rangle\langle V_1||S\rangle = 0.64$ of exhibiting verbatim list 1 traces. Likewise, the agent has a probability of $\langle S||G'\rangle\langle G'||S\rangle = 0.4$ of exhibiting gist traces. Suppose we measured the verbatim list 1 traces before measuring the gist traces. Measuring the agent exhibiting these verbatim traces, forces a collapse of the state vector on $|S_{L1}\rangle = (1, 0, 0, 0)$. The agent now has a conditional probability of $\langle S_{L1}||G'\rangle\langle G'||S_{L1}\rangle = 0.33$ of exhibiting gist traces. Likewise, an agent not exhibiting these verbatim traces forces a collapse on $|S_{\neg L1}\rangle = (0, 1/\sqrt{2}, 1/\sqrt{2}, 0)$, leading to a conditional probability of $\langle S_{\neg L1}||G'\rangle\langle G'||S_{\neg L1}\rangle = 0.66$. Therefore the probability of the agent exhibiting gist traces, after measuring the presence of verbatim list 1 traces (without specifying the outcome) is $0.64 \cdot 0.33 + 0.36 \cdot 0.66 = 0.45$, which does not equal the probability 0.4 of exhibiting gist traces, without first measuring the presence of verbatim list 1 traces.

This shows clearly the order effect of first measuring the gist traces before measuring the verbatim traces. So the act of resolving indeterminacy with respect to one memory type, will impact the other memory type. They are both distinct, but closely related and interfering, representations of the agents word remembrance. It seems possible that, e.g., measuring the more literal verbatim traces, makes the agent doubt or forget the more intuitive gist traces. If the proposed experiment with two measurements on each agent would yield these types of results, the quantum nature of the human episodic memory would become very clear. These interference effects are what separates quantum models using the complementarity notion, from the classical models or quantum models using only orthogonal vectors, as these interference effects exhibit non-classical probabilities.

5   Conclusion

While we strongly believe that the quantum formalism is a very fitting way to model human behavior and beliefs, we pointed out some flaws in the QEM model for the subadditivity disjunction fallacy that the human episodic memory exhibits. These flaws were twofold. There were flaws on an interpretational level, where in the QEM model the agent was supposed to exhibit behavior that did not seem to make sense, since the orthogonality of the verbatim and gist traces implied that these were associated with exclusive events. There were also flaws on a mathematical level, since the QEM model only uses orthogonal vectors for possible outcomes, which actually resulted in classical probabilities.

Instead of viewing the human mind in a superposition between verbatim and gist traces, we argued that these different traces are actually incompatible representations of the remembered word lists. We implemented this idea by giving the two types of memory traces each a different base within the same vector space. Since we described the 'gist basis' in terms of the 'verbatim basis', we got a view of how these two traces relate to each other. They are not two completely distinct possible outcomes of a measurement, but two closely related measurements, which influence each other. This seems more in line with how human recollection works: the two traces are parallel and distinct, but not independent. Next to being more appropriate to deal with this distinction between types of memory traces on an interpretational level, we also showed that this model still retains the possibility to exhibit subaddivity. Next to subadditivity, our model also allowed for other quantum effects, such as interference effects. These are the result of the impact the verbatim measurement has on the gist measurement and vice versa. To illustrate this, we produced an example of a proposed extension of the original experiment, where agents could exhibit this quantum effect.

We also generalized these ideas for all quantum model with only orthogonal vectors, by proving that these always have classical equivalents even when considering multiple measurements or entanglement. Since, by making just one relevant vector non-orthogonal, we built a model which was clearly non-classical and allowed for modeling more complex phenomena (e.g. order effects), we argue that non-orthogonality is the most important distinction between classical and quantum models and the driving force behind the power of the use of the quantum formalism in Social Sciences. We believe that this approach of viewing the agent as switching between different representations/measurements, shows that it would be able to deal with a lot of other human behavior modeling, next to the here described episodic subadditivity.

We did not yet try to fit the data of the word remembrance experiment to our model, since our main goal was to use this example as a case study of when, where, why and how to use the quantum formalism effectively in Social Sciences. The question if our proposed model is empirically better than the QEM model is, however, an interesting one. There are therefore future plans of a statistical comparison between the two. If our proposed model does not fit the data better than the QEM model (and therefore a classical model), it seems that a quantum approach was not suited for this particular problem. A better fit for our model, however, would open up this view of memory modeling and allow for more complex memory situations to be tackled with this complementarity approach.

Appendix

Lemma 1. *The product of two diagonal matrices A and B is commuting.*

Proof. Easily proven with standard algebra.   □

Lemma 2. *All projector matrices associated with a set of orthogonal vectors $\{|V_i\rangle\}$ are diagonal.*

Proof. A set of orthogonal vectors are linear independent and can always be extended into a base of the relevant Hilbert space. This way, we can construct a base in which the vectors $|V_i\rangle$ have a 0 on all coordinates, except a 1 on the coordinate i. The projector matrix $|V_i\rangle\langle V_i|$ has therefore a 0 on all positions, except a 1 on (i,i).

To illustrate this, we will list the projectors associated with the possible outcomes of the verbatim and gist measurements in the QEM model.

$$
|V_1\rangle\langle V_1| = \begin{pmatrix} 1 & 0 & 0 & 0 & 0 \\ 0 & 0 & 0 & 0 & 0 \\ 0 & 0 & 0 & 0 & 0 \\ 0 & 0 & 0 & 0 & 0 \\ 0 & 0 & 0 & 0 & 0 \end{pmatrix} \quad |V_2\rangle\langle V_2| = \begin{pmatrix} 0 & 0 & 0 & 0 & 0 \\ 0 & 1 & 0 & 0 & 0 \\ 0 & 0 & 0 & 0 & 0 \\ 0 & 0 & 0 & 0 & 0 \\ 0 & 0 & 0 & 0 & 0 \end{pmatrix}
$$

$$
|V_3\rangle\langle V_3| = \begin{pmatrix} 0 & 0 & 0 & 0 & 0 \\ 0 & 0 & 0 & 0 & 0 \\ 0 & 0 & 1 & 0 & 0 \\ 0 & 0 & 0 & 0 & 0 \\ 0 & 0 & 0 & 0 & 0 \end{pmatrix} \quad |G\rangle\langle G| = \begin{pmatrix} 0 & 0 & 0 & 0 & 0 \\ 0 & 0 & 0 & 0 & 0 \\ 0 & 0 & 0 & 0 & 0 \\ 0 & 0 & 0 & 1 & 0 \\ 0 & 0 & 0 & 0 & 0 \end{pmatrix}
$$

$$
|U\rangle\langle U| = \begin{pmatrix} 0 & 0 & 0 & 0 & 0 \\ 0 & 0 & 0 & 0 & 0 \\ 0 & 0 & 0 & 0 & 0 \\ 0 & 0 & 0 & 0 & 0 \\ 0 & 0 & 0 & 0 & 1 \end{pmatrix}
$$

These are clearly all diagonal. We can generalize this result. Suppose we also consider measurements in which logical combinations of the here considered possible outcomes are also possible outcomes. This would e.g. mean that an agent exhibits both verbatim and gist traces, such as is done in [1]. Observations of this type have an associated projector matrix which is the sum of the diagonal matrices $|V_i\rangle\langle V_i|$, for all relevant i's. The resulting matrix is still diagonal. $\quad\square$

Theorem 3. *When only one measurement is done, the resulting probabilities are classical.*

Proof. Consider a measurement with n possible outcomes A_i, with associated vectors $|A_1\rangle, \ldots |A_n\rangle$, which form a base of the Hilbert Space $\mathbb{H}^n$. Define the state vector as $|S\rangle = a_1|A_1\rangle + \ldots + a_n|A_n\rangle$. Since the state vector is normalized, the sum of the probabilities a_i^2 of the possible outcomes is 1, with no other restrictions. These are identical to the classical probabilities.

We will now suppose that logical combinations of the possible outcomes are also considered as possible outcomes. We get for the negation of outcome A_i:

$$p(\neg A_i) = \langle S| \left(\mathbf{1}_n - |A_i\rangle\langle A_i|\right) |S\rangle \tag{5}$$
$$= \langle S||S\rangle - \langle S||A_i\rangle\langle A_i||S\rangle \tag{6}$$
$$= 1 - p(A_i) \tag{7}$$

and for the conjunction of two distinct outcomes A_i and A_j:

$$p(A_i \cup A_j) = \langle S| \left(|A_i\rangle\langle A_i| + |A_j\rangle\langle A_j|\right) |S\rangle \tag{8}$$
$$= \langle S||A_i\rangle\langle A_i||S\rangle + \langle S||A_j\rangle\langle A_j||S\rangle \tag{9}$$
$$= p(A_i) + p(A_j). \tag{10}$$

These resulting probabilities are also identical to the classical probabilities. All other logical operators and related probabilities can be derived from the negation and disjunction. $\quad\square$

Theorem 4. *Suppose we have two measurements A and B with respective outcomes A_i and B_j, with respective vectors $|A_i\rangle$ and $|B_j\rangle$. When all relevant vectors are orthogonal, the resulting probabilities are classical and there are no order effects.*

Proof. Since all of the relevant matrices commute, both of the measurements can be seen as being done first. The resulting probabilities $p(A_i)$ and $p(B_j)$ are therefore identical to the classical probabilities. The outcomes of the two measurements A and B therefore have a classical joint distribution. $\quad\square$

Theorem 5. *Suppose we have two distinct Hilbert spaces $\mathbb{H}_A$ and $\mathbb{H}_B$, with respective base vectors $|A_i\rangle$ and $|B_j\rangle$, representing outcomes A_i and B_j of measurements A and B. All probabilities associated with possible measurements in the entangled space $\mathbb{H}_{AB} = \mathbb{H}_A \otimes \mathbb{H}_B$ are classical.*

Proof. All relevant vectors $|A_iB_j\rangle = |A_i\rangle \otimes |B_j\rangle$ are orthogonal. $\quad\square$

References

1. Brainerd, C.J., Wang, Z., Reyna, V.F.: Superposition of episodic memories: overdistribution and quantum models. Top. Cogn. Sci. **5**, 773–799 (2013)
2. Feynman, R.P., Leighton, R.B., Sands, M.: The Feynman Lectures on Physics, vol. 3. Addison-Wesley, Reading (1965)
3. Busemeyer, J.R., Bruza, P.: Quantum Models of Cognition and Decision Making. Cambridge University Press, New York (2012)
4. Franco, R.: The inverse fallacy and quantum formalism. In: Proceedings of the Quantum Interaction Symposium 2008, pp. 94–98 (2008)
5. Lambert-Mogiliansky, A., Zamir, S., Zwirn, H.: Type indeterminacy - a model of the KT (Khaneman Tversky)-man. J. Math. Psychol. **53**(5), 349–361 (2009)
6. Lambert-Mogiliansky, A.: Comments on episodic superposition of memory states. Top. Cogn. Sci. **6**(1), 63–66 (2014)

A Vector Field Approach to Lexical Semantics

Peter Wittek[1], Sándor Darányi[1]([✉]), and Ying-Hsang Liu[2]

[1] University of Borås, Borås, Sweden
sandor.daranyi@hb.se
[2] Charles Sturt University, Wagga Wagga, Australia

Abstract. We report work in progress on measuring "forces" underlying the semantic drift by comparing it with plate tectonics in geology. Based on a brief survey of energy as a key concept in machine learning, and the Aristotelian concept of potentiality vs. actuality allowing for the study of energy and dynamics in language, we propose a field approach to lexical analysis. Until evidence to the contrary, it was assumed that a classical field in physics is appropriate to model word semantics. The approach used the distributional hypothesis to statistically model word meaning. We do not address the modelling of sentence meaning here. The computability of a vector field for the indexing vocabulary of the Reuters-21578 test collection by an emergent self-organizing map suggests that energy minima as learnables in machine learning presuppose concepts as energy minima in cognition. Our finding needs to be confirmed by a systematic evaluation.

1 Introduction

In the context of Semantic Web dynamics [1], there is a growing body of literature about the semantic drift [2,3], the language-related version of abrupt parameter value changes in data mining called concept drifts [4–7]. By semantic drift we mean how the features of ontology concepts gradually change as their knowledge domain evolves. In what follows, we briefly outline a synoptic approach to the modeling of such a process from a QI perspective which departs from Aristotle and results in a vector field of word meaning. The evolution of this observable structure goes back to the underlying non-observable dynamics of concepts.

In the second section of this paper, we discuss how, in several disciplines, researchers have come up with more or less the same model over time, the combination of a continuous and a discrete plane to describe "fluid" content or experience being shaped into recognizable form for communication. The hidden layer of this construct is always field-like, sampled to build the discrete observable part. This biplanar construct can be compared to Aristotle's stance about potentiality versus actuality, including a distinction between dynamics and energy. Such a distinction, on the other hand, helps to spell out our working hypothesis.

In Sect. 3, we look at how machine learning uses energy minima on a potential surface to model both the goal state of learning, and concepts to be learnt for

© Springer International Publishing Switzerland 2015
H. Atmanspacher et al. (Eds.): QI 2014, LNCS 8951, pp. 78–89, 2015.
DOI: 10.1007/978-3-319-15931-7_7

document categorization. Based on our past work, in Sect. 4 these ideas are combined to convert the vocabulary of a test collection of economic news into a vector field. After the experiment design, Sect. 5 describes the results and sets the scene for a systematic evaluation, not dealt with here. Section 6 brings us to our conclusions and refers to future work.

2 A Tale of Two Planes

We find the tradition of using a combination of two planes to describe a phenomenon in several disciplines. Our first example is the general practice of evaluating the effectiveness of information retrieval and text categorization models by measures like recall, precision, accuracy, and many more [8]. For example there is ongoing work to build semantic spaces from distributional vs. compositional semantics [9,10], representing both word and sentence meaning as locations in high-dimensional space where for phrase or sentence component binding, recursive matrix-vector spaces [11], the tensor product [12–14], or circular holographic reduced representation are used [15]. In these models, the representation of semantic content in documents is compared to an ideal state of language use, provided by the human standards of interpretation inherent in the evaluation method [16]. Using geometry or probability as a vehicle of meaning, i.e. building a new medium of language, aims at maximizing similarity between the human standard and its statistical reconstruction. This hypothetic original, a correlate of spoken language called a mental state or internal state in neuroscience [17], recalls the "language of thought hypothesis" in philosophy [18], also called *mentalese*. What we can observe as a joint element in the above is that whereas language as a mental phenomenon is assumed to be continuous, its uttered or mathematically modelled representations are discrete.

The same duplicity returns as "hidden metaphysics" in traditional mentalist and more recent generalist-universalist theories about language: language is but a tool operated by something deeper – thought, reason, logic, cognition – which functions in line with biological-neurological mechanisms common to all human beings [19]. Moreover, a linguistic school of thought orthogonal to the above theories, called Neo-Humboldtian field theories of word meaning, goes back to the same dual model where discrete distributions of related content called lexical or semantic fields, based on language use, are underpinned by the assumption of conceptual fields in the mind. Then, the lexical field of related words is only an outward manifestation of the underlying conceptual field so that the sum total of conceptual fields describes one's world view [20]. In yet another unrelated school of thought, Saussure's structural linguistics, language (*langue*) is a mental grammar with a rule set specifying ideal content pronunciation, whereas speech (*parole*) stands for the exemplification of those rules [21].

An important symptom of lexical fields is that regions of related content are separated by lexical gaps. These are nonexistent names for things where one could exist by rules of a particular language, and indicate possible conceptual distinctions not mapped to actual language use, such as mother's father (Swedish *morfar*) vs. father's father (Swedish *farfar*), both called *grandfather* in English, or father's brother (Swedish *farbror*) not distinguished from mother's brother (Swedish *morbror*), both called *uncle*. Such discontinuities of content play a prominent role in our working hypothesis.

2.1   Aristotle and QI

Apparently the assumption that products of the mind are continuous while their mapping to spoken language is discrete goes back ultimately to Aristotle's *Metaphysics*. In this, existence or reality is described as the sum total of two components, conceivable potentiality (*dynamis*) plus observable-measurable actuality (*energeia*). These are names for the latent vs. manifest capacity of existents to induce change.

As reviewed by Koznjak, (2007) [22], the first ones to link Aristotle and quantum mechanics were Bohm, (1951) [23] and Heisenberg, (1958) [24]. In the QI frame of thought, Aerts and Gabora, (2005) used the same insight [25]: a context-dependent property of a concept lends graded existence to it by weights spanning potential to actual existence because certain feature combinations are "less real", i.e. less typical for assessors. Therefore in our current thinking, existence consists of two layers, potentiality (a continuum) and actuality (a discrete distribution sampling the former). Importantly, one ascribes a field nature to mental experience because of the potentiality layer which we indirectly perceive by the actualized values of events.

The above have familiar repercussions in QI. For localized entities, the state of actuality correponds to one particular position of an observed particle (or a particular configuration of many particles), whereas potentiality means all possible locations or configurations in superposition. Moreover reality is in the state of potentiality before and after observation, something that can be speculated about but not observed. On the other hand, actuality and the constant collapse of the wave function are the same. Phenomena pop in and out of existence: anything in the present is in the overlap between the last moment of the future and first moment of the past while being observed, but returns to uncertainty thereafter. This also means a link between potentiality as a continuous experience vs. actuality as its discrete mapping to real, objective existence. Last but not least, expanding on the implications, energy manifest in observed events (such as *parole*) must go back to dynamics latent in fields (here, *langue*).

2.2   Working Hypothesis

In what follows, our working hypothesis will be that word meaning can be expressed as "energy" [26,27], because semantic content located in vector space generates a potential with energy minima on a potential surface. Such content constitutes regions with different semantic density [28] so that both concepts and categories as their combinations are modelled by the above minima. More importantly, using the concept of kinds [29], one can look into the dynamic "origins" of distributions of related content. To this end, one must add interpolation between located items of meaning such as by Gaussian blurring [30] – its role is to approximate a previous state of potentiality from observation as actuality. The result will show lexical gaps as metaphoric fault lines in plate tectonics, with new semantic content about to protrude.

3   Word Semantics as a Vector Field: Experiment Design

Mathematical "energy" and machine learning (ML) are related, the latter often being based on minimizing a constrained multivariate function such as a loss function. Concepts in feature space "sit" at global energy minima, representing the cost of a classification decision as an energy minimizing process. This suggests that ML must identify concepts with such minima, and since potential energy in physics is carried by a field or a respective topological mapping, concepts naturally have something to do with energy as work capacity.

Our research problem below will be to model this "energetic" nature of language on a vector field, and relate the results to theoretical constraints set by distributional semantics. The novelty of this approach is that we integrate the energetic implications of ML algorithms with the like nature of the raw material they process (Sect. 3.1). The solution we propose here is to use emergent self-organizing maps to generate an artificial semantic field. The space in this regard is a two dimensional surface, and the vector field associated with the points on the surface is a high-dimensional one. Each term in the corpus is associated with a neuron in the map, and additional neurons interpolate nearby terms; thus there are approximately five neurons per term (Sect. 4). We expect both lexical fields of meaning and lexical gaps between them to emerge in this model, making it useful for linguistic analysis (Sect. 5). Further we hope that combining this approach with earlier semantic models using the Hamiltonian of a quantum system, we will be able to come up with a dynamic model of language change (Sect. 6).

3.1   Energy-Like Objectives in Machine Learning

To underpin our working hypothesis, first we overview the metaphoric use of the energy concept in ML.

Supervised learning algorithms measure the difference between target labels and the predictions of the model being trained. The goal is to minimize the difference: in such a scenario, we may regard the objective as 'energy', and we look for a global minimum. This is not always the case, as error on the training sample does not necessarily imply a good generalization performance on unseen examples, as we know it from the theory of structural risk minimization. Hence, for instance, support vector machines do not fit this paradigm, but feedforward neural networks and certain types of boosting algorithms do.

Some unsupervised algorithms also seek a minimum on a high-dimensional surface, which, again, we may treat as a metaphor of energy. Examples include Hopfield networks, which map to an Ising Hamiltonian, or dynamic quantum clustering, where data instances are rolled along a potential surface to local minima.

Dynamic quantum clustering is more direct in using energy as a metaphor [31]. It takes ψ as the ground solution for the generic Hamiltonian of the Schrödinger equation:

$$H\psi = (T + V(x))\psi = E_0\psi, \tag{1}$$

where H is the Hamiltonian, T is the kinetic energy, V is the potential energy, and E_0 is the ground energy level. The algorithm evolves the Hamiltonian to identify the clustering structure by tracking the expectation values of the position operator X: $\langle\psi(t)|x|\psi(t)\rangle = \int \psi(x,t)^* x\psi(x,t)dx$. The expectation values of the position operator obey their corresponding classical equations of motion, that is, the centre of each wave packet rolls towards the nearest minimum of the potential, according to Newton's law of motion.

These energy-type objective functions find a good fit with physical implementations of quantum optimization. For instance, adiabatic quantum computing finds the ground state of an Ising Hamiltonian, and small-scale demonstrations with boosting are promising [32]. The quantum analogue of Hopfield networks, quantum associative memories, define a Hamiltonian to retrieve elements from memory, albeit storage and optimization is unrelated to the energy function [33].

3.2   Implementing a Potential Field with Lexical Gaps

We are now in a position to return to our above working hypothesis with the following observations: in ML, the only reason why gradient descent and – in a more approximative fashion – simulated annealing algorithms work is that minima as learning goal states overlap with minima as concepts, that is, the nature of the learning algorithm and the phenomenon are identical. Put another way, the learning function is isomorphic with the semantic substratum it is supposed to identify, both belonging in function space. Hence we regard concepts as attractors in a conceptual field, with lexemes as lexical attractors in its respective lexical field mapping [34,35]. This view is supported by neurosemantics where concrete noun representations are stored in a spectral fashion [36].

It is immediately clear that such a view can be generalized to features and feature agglomerations as attractors. On the other hand, it is no less evident that the dynamics of language cannot be conceived without the linguistic parallels of force, work and energy.

Let us revisit the Schrödinger equation in Eq. 1. Taking the spectrum of the Hamilton operator H in a finite dimensional space, Wittek and Darányi (2011) conjectured that index terms are associated with a set of eigenvalues, giving them a spectral signature [26]. The eigenvalues corresponded to the different senses of the word, where a higher level energy state was more unlikely to be occupied.

Following a different train of thought, Darányi and Wittek (2012) studied the kinetic term of the Hamiltonian, T, to identify words with weights, and derive dynamics through Ehrenfest's theorem [27].

What has been missing so far is the potential term in the Hamiltonian, which is also the most complex one. We venture a step towards defining a potential field by interpolating the distributional semantic description of term vectors.

4   Emergent Self-organizing Maps for Semantic Interpolation

The vectors of the term space in a distributional vector space model point to disjoint locations in a high-dimensional space. A field, on the other hand, is defined at all points in a space. To bridge this problem, we work on a two-dimensional surface. Some points on this surface correspond to terms; the corresponding term vector is the value of the vector field in that point. We interpolate the vector field in all the other points of the surface.

The mapping between points on the surface and the term vectors is done by training a self-organizing map. A self-organizing map is a two-dimensional grid of artificial neurons. Each neuron is associated with a weight vector that matches the dimension of the training data. We take an instance of the training data, find the closest weight vector, and pull it closer to the data instance. We also pull the weight vectors of nearby neurons closer to the data instance, with decreasing weight as we get further from the best matching unit. We repeat this procedure with every training instance. This consists one epoch. We repeat the same process in the second epoch, but with a smaller neighbourhood radius, and a lower learning rate when adjusting the weight vectors. We continue training several epochs, until the network remains stationary. The resulting network reflects the local topology of the high-dimensional space [37].

An important condition for us is that the total number of neurons, N_n, is much larger than the number of terms, N_t. For instance, given 12,000 terms, we expect to train a map with 60,000 neurons or more. The superfluous neurons will be the interpolation in the points which are not directly associated with a term (Fig. 1). Such maps are called emergent self-organizing maps [38], and they require highly parallel computational models [39]. Five times more neurons than data instances is a typical choice for an emergent map, allowing a small neighbourhood for each point.

By default, the weight vectors of the self-organizing maps are initialized by random vectors. We train the map until updates slow down. There is at least one matching neuron for each data point, but, since this is an emergent map, most neurons do not have a corresponding data point. What does the weight vector of such a neuron mean?

This weight vector is a form of interpolation. The weight vector was formed during the training as it was pulled by best matching neurons in its neighborhood. The weight vector is closest to its most nearby neuron that has a matching data point, but it is also somewhat similar to more remote but still close neurons with matching data points. This weight vector fills the lexical gap between two data points, and corresponds to a gradually decreasing potential.

The grid is discrete, but the weight vectors in between neurons are easy to calculate by, for instance, a simple linear interpolation. Thus we can assign a high-dimensional weight vector to any point in the plane: we create a field.

Using a toroid map is advantageous as it avoids edge effects. The field is continuous in nature – a planar map would introduce an artificial discrete cut-off at the edges.

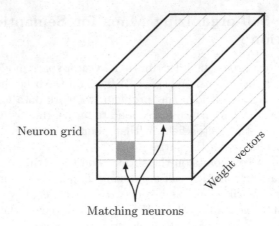

Neuron grid

Matching neurons

Fig. 1. A section of the two-dimensional surface of an emergent self-organizing map. At the end of the training, some neurons will correspond to index terms; these are shaded in the figure. Their corresponding weight vectors define the high-dimensional vector field at that point. Other neurons will interpolate the vector field between neurons that are associated with terms.

5   Results and Evaluation

We used the vocabulary of the Reuters-21578 ML test collection of economic newswire items to generate an artificial lexical field. To measure lexical semantic relatedness, researchers typically compare the scores of words based on a taxonomic structure such as WordNet or Wikipedia with a gold standard as determined by correlations with human judgment [40,41]. For instance, an evaluation of topic coh erence in topic modelling recruited users to score the topics with respect to their usefulness [42,43]. In this study, we resorted to a first evaluation of lexical gaps based on the structure of an emergent self-organizing map by "cherry picking" [44].

We used Lucene 3.6.2 to create an inverted index of the document collection. Terms were stemmed by the Porter stemmer, with those discarded that occurred less than three times or were in the top ten per cent of the most frequent ones. Thus we had 12,347 index terms, lying in an approximately twenty-thousand dimensional space.

We trained a toroid emergent self-organizing map of 336×205 dimensions using Somoclu [39]. The initial learning rate was 1.0, which decreased linearly over ten epochs to 0.1. The initial radius for the neighbourhood was a hundred neurons, and it also decreased linearly to one. The neighbourhood function was a noncompact Gaussian.

We studied the U-matrix of the map which depicts the Euclidean distance between the codebook vectors of neighbouring neurons, using the Databionics ESOM Tools for their visualization [38]. The global structure of the map is shown in Fig. 2.

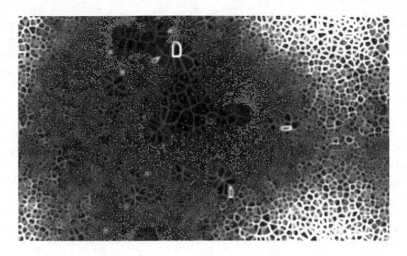

Fig. 2. U-matrix of the toroid emergent self-organizing map after ten epochs of training on the term space of Reuters-21578. The individual dots are neurons with a weight vector that match a term vector. All other neurons are interpolating the field. Dark areas reflect neurons that are close to each other, whereas bright areas indicate large distances between neighbouring neurons.

An important limitation of self-organizing maps is that they preserve the local topology but do not necessarily reflect the global topology of the high-dimensional space. If the initial weight vectors are not random but are primed with the global topology, then this problem is less severe. We trained the map starting with random weights, hence local regions are topologically meaningful, but neighbouring regions in the map may be entirely unrelated.

Figure 3(a) shows a tightly bundled group of terms. The gap between these words, based on the corpus, is small. The terms in this group, including ones that are not plotted in the figure, are: *bongard, consign, ita, louisvill, occupi, reafffirm* (with this misspelling), *stabil, stabilis, strength, temporao, tight*. Some are clearly related, for others, we need to look at the corpus for justification. The expression Bongard appears in two senses: the corrupt head of a bank, and as the name of a brokerage firm. ITA always refers to the International Tin Association, which was debating a pact extension at the time. *Temporao* is a

(a) A tight cluster of words.   (b) Large gaps between words.

Fig. 3. Cropped sections of the U-matrix with best matching units. Some labels are not displayed as they overlapped with others.

kind of cocoa, firms trading it were listed on stock exchanges. Louisville as a location appeared frequently in the economic news typical in this test collection. The gaps are small between these words, which does not necessarily rule out the insertion of new words in the gaps, but based on the limited vocabulary a newswire, the lexical field represented by these expression appears to be covered.

Large gaps are also interesting to look at. Take these examples (Fig. 3(b)): *energet, exploit, garrison, nato, petroleo*. Apart from *energet* and *garrison*, these words are frequent, with over twenty occurrences in the collection each. The reason for their isolation is not because their corresponding term vectors do not contain entries. These words are related, but their best matching units were pulled in other directions, creating a tension in the lexical field. Over time, words labelling new content could be expected to emerge in such "red hot" topic zones where metaphoric fault lines separate cells containing terms displayed as white dots. Such fault lines manifest lexical gaps, indicating content discontinuities in the observable field.

6   Conclusions and Future Work

Based on a brief survey of energy as a key concept in machine learning, and the Aristotelian concept of potentiality vs. actuality allowing for the study of energy and dynamics in language, we proposed a field approach to lexical analysis. Until evidence to the contrary, it was assumed that a classical field in physics is appropriate to model word semantics. The approach used the distributional hypothesis to statistically model word meaning. We did not address the modelling of sentence meaning here. The computability of a vector field for the indexing vocabulary of the Reuters-21578 test collection by an emergent self-organizing map proved that energy minima as learnables in machine learning presuppose concepts as energy minima in cognition.

Next we plan a detailed evaluation of vector fields as vehicles of word meaning. This will focus on two things: a genuine lexical corpus instead of Reuters for the measurement of semantic and concept drifts, and the analysis of different field modification scenarios, including the context-dependent change of meaning of specific words; the dislocation of such terms and how their positions evolve over time ("drifts"); and the emergence of new words ("lexical gap studies").

In other words, we plan to look at the dynamics (i.e. the tensions) underlying semantic and concept drifts by specifically looking at:

- Distributional similarity studies [45,46], generalized to an algebraic form [47], also applied to image content [48];
- New studies of word meaning in context [16];
- Neural models of lexical semantics, e.g. Ursino et al. 2010 who suggest that during processing [49], it is regions and not single locations that become activated in the brain.

We also intend to combine earlier efforts to use the Hamiltonian of a quantum system to model linguistic changes.

Acknowledgement. The authors are grateful for the comments of three anonymous reviewers. Numerous suggestions from the audience of QI-14 helped to link our work to ongoing parallel research in the field. The current development phase of Somoclu was supported by the European Commission Seventh Framework Programme under Grant Agreement Number FP7-601138 PERICLES.

References

1. Antoniou, G., d'Aquin, M., Pan, J.Z.: Semantic web dynamics. Web Seman. Sci. Serv. Agents World Wide Web **9**, 245–246 (2011)
2. Lauriston, A.: Criteria for measuring term recognition. In: Proceedings of EACL-95, 7th Conference of the European Chapter of the Association for Computational Linguistics, pp. 17–22 (1995)
3. Gulla, J.A., Solskinnsbakk, G., Myrseth, P., Haderlein, V., Cerrato, O.: Concept signatures and semantic drift. In: Filipe, J., Cordeiro, J. (eds.) WEBIST 2010. LNBIP, vol. 75, pp. 101–113. Springer, Berlin (2011)
4. Delany, S.J., Cunningham, P., Tsymbal, A., Coyle, L.: A case-based technique for tracking concept drift in spam filtering. Knowl. Based Syst. **18**, 187–195 (2005)
5. Wang, S., Schlobach, S., Klein, M.: Concept drift and how to identify it. Web Seman. Sci. Serv. Agents World Wide Web **9**, 247–265 (2011)
6. Ross, G.J., Adams, N.M., Tasoulis, D.K., Hand, D.J.: Exponentially weighted moving average charts for detecting concept drift. Pattern Recogn. Lett. **33**, 191–198 (2012)
7. Gonçalves Jr., P.M., Barros, R.S.M.: Rcd: A recurring concept drift framework. Pattern Recogn. Lett. **34**, 1018–1025 (2013)
8. Turney, P.D., Pantel, P.: From frequency to meaning: vector space models of semantics. J. Artif. Intell. Res. **37**, 141–188 (2010)
9. Padó, S., Lapata, M.: Dependency-based construction of semantic space models. Comput. Linguist. **33**, 161–199 (2007)
10. Erk, K., Padó, S.: A structured vector space model for word meaning in context. In: Proceedings of EMNLP-08, 13th Conference on Empirical Methods in Natural Language Processing, pp. 897–906. (2008)
11. Socher, R., Huval, B., Manning, C.D., Ng, A.Y.: Semantic compositionality through recursive matrix-vector spaces. In: Proceedings of EMNLP-CoNLL-12, Joint Conference on Empirical Methods in Natural Language Processing and Computational Natural Language Learning, pp. 1201–1211 (2012)
12. Baroni, M., Lenci, A.: Distributional memory: a general framework for corpus-based semantics. Comput. Linguist. **36**, 673–721 (2010)
13. Blacoe, W., Kashefi, E., Lapata, M.: A quantum-theoretic approach to distributional semantics. In: Proceedings of NAACL-HLT-13, Conference of the North American Chapter of the Association for Computational Linguistics: Human Language Technologies, pp. 847–857 (2013)
14. Grefenstette, E., Dinu, G., Zhang, Y.Z., Sadrzadeh, M., Baroni, M.: Multi-step regression learning for compositional distributional semantics (2013). arXiv:1301.6939
15. Cohen, T., Widdows, D., Schvaneveldt, R.W., Rindflesch, T.C.: Discovery at a distance: farther journeys in predication space. In: Proceedings of BIBMW-12, IEEE International Conference on Bioinformatics and Biomedicine Workshops, pp. 218–225 (2012)

16. Erk, K., McCarthy, D., Gaylord, N.: Measuring word meaning in context. Comput. Linguist. **39**, 511–554 (2013)
17. Elman, J.L.: An alternative view of the mental lexicon. Trends Cogn. Sci. **8**, 301–306 (2004)
18. Fodor, J.A.: The Language of Thought, vol. 5. Harvard University Press, Massachusetts (1975)
19. House, J.: Linguistic relativity and translation. Amsterdam Stud. Theory Hist. Linguist. Sci. **4**, 69–88 (2000)
20. Trier, J.: Das sprachliche feld. Neue Jahrbucher fur Wissenschaft und Jugendbildung **10**, 428–449 (1934)
21. De Saussure, F.: Course in General Linguistics. Columbia University Press, New York (2011)
22. Kožnjak, B.: Möglichkeit, wirklichkeit und quantenmechanik. Prolegomena **6**, 223–252 (2007)
23. Bohm, D.: Quantum Theory. Dover Publications, New York (1989)
24. Heisenberg, W.: Physics and Philosophy: The Revolution of Modern Science. Harper & Row, New York (1958)
25. Aerts, D., Gabora, L.: A theory of concepts and their combinations I: the structure of the sets of contexts and properties. Kybernetes **34**, 151–175 (2005)
26. Wittek, P., Darányi, S.: Spectral composition of semantic spaces. In: Song, D., Melucci, M., Frommholz, I., Zhang, P., Wang, L., Arafat, S. (eds.) QI 2011. LNCS, vol. 7052, pp. 60–70. Springer, Heidelberg (2011)
27. Darányi, S., Wittek, P.: Connecting the dots: mass, energy, word meaning, and particle-wave duality. In: Busemeyer, J.R., Dubois, F., Lambert-Mogiliansky, A., Melucci, M. (eds.) QI 2012. LNCS, vol. 7620, pp. 207–217. Springer, Heidelberg (2012)
28. Mihalcea, R., Moldovan, D.I.: Word sense disambiguation based on semantic density. In: Proceedings of COLING-ACL, 36th Annual Meeting of the Association for Computational Linguistics and 17th International Conference on Computational Linguistics (1998)
29. Melucci, M.: Initial specifications for the design of information retrieval systems based on quantum detector using kinds. In: Atmanspacher, H., Haven, E., Kitto, K., Raine, D. (eds.) QI 2013. LNCS, pp. 59–70. Springer, Berlin (2013)
30. Darányi, S., Wittek, P.: Demonstrating conceptual dynamics in an evolving text collection. J. Am. Soc. Inf. Sci. Technol. **64**, 2564–2572 (2013)
31. Weinstein, M., Horn, D.: Dynamic quantum clustering: a method for visual exploration of structures in data. Phys. Rev. E **80**, 066117 (2009)
32. Neven, H., Denchev, V.S., Drew-Brook, M., Zhang, J., Macready, W.G., Rose, G.: Binary classification using hardware implementation of quantum annealing. In: Demonstrations at NIPS-09, 24th Annual Conference on Neural Information Processing Systems, pp. 1–17 (2009)
33. Trugenberger, C.A.: Probabilistic quantum memories. Phys. Rev. Lett. **87**, 067901 (2001)
34. Amit, D.J.: Modeling Brain Function: The World of Attractor Neural Networks. Cambridge University Press, Cambridge (1992)
35. Falissard, B.: A thought experiment reconciling neuroscience and psychoanalysis. J. Physiol Paris **105**, 201–206 (2011)
36. Just, M.A., Cherkassky, V.L., Aryal, S., Mitchell, T.M.: A neurosemantic theory of concrete noun representation based on the underlying brain codes. PLoS ONE **5**, e8622 (2010)

37. Kohonen, T.: Self-Organizing Maps. Springer, Heidelberg (2001)
38. Ultsch, A., Mörchen, F.: ESOM-maps: tools for clustering, visualization, and classification with emergent SOM. Technical report. Data Bionics Research Group, University of Marburg (2005)
39. Wittek, P.: Somoclu: an efficient distributed library for self-organizing maps (2013). arXiv:1305.1422
40. Budanitsky, A., Hirst, G.: Evaluating WordNet-based measures of lexical semantic relatedness. Comput. Linguist. **32**, 13–47 (2006)
41. Zhang, Z., Gentile, A.L., Ciravegna, F.: Recent advances in methods of lexical semantic relatedness-a survey. Nat. Lang. Eng. **19**, 411–479 (2013)
42. Newman, D., Lau, J.H., Grieser, K., Baldwin, T.: Automatic evaluation of topic coherence. In: Proceedings of NAACL-HLT-10, Conference of the North American Chapter of the Association for Computational Linguistics: Human Language Technologies, Association for Computational Linguistics, pp. 100–108 (2010)
43. Wittek, P., Ravenek, W.: Supporting the exploration of a corpus of 17th-century scholarly correspondences by topic modeling. In: Proceedings of SDH-11, Supporting Digital Humanities: Answering the Unaskable (2011)
44. Kievit-Kylar, B., Jones, M.N.: Visualizing multiple word similarity measures. Behav. Res. Meth. **44**, 656–674 (2012)
45. Weeds, J., Weir, D.: Co-occurrence retrieval: a flexible framework for lexical distributional similarity. Comput. Linguist. **31**, 439–475 (2005)
46. Rohde, D.L., Gonnerman, L.M., Plaut, D.C.: An improved model of semantic similarity based on lexical co-occurrence. Commun. ACM **8**, 627–633 (2006)
47. Clarke, D.: A context-theoretic framework for compositionality in distributional semantics. Comput. Linguist. **38**, 41–71 (2012)
48. Bruni, E., Uijlings, J., Baroni, M., Sebe, N.: Distributional semantics with eyes: using image analysis to improve computational representations of word meaning. In: Proceedings of MM-12, 20th ACM International Conference on Multimedia, pp. 1219–1228 (2012)
49. Ursino, M., Cuppini, C., Magosso, E.: A computational model of the lexical-semantic system based on a grounded cognition approach. Embodied and Grounded Cognition 1 (2010)

Decision Making

Quantum(-like) Formalization of Common Knowledge: Binmore-Brandenburger Operator Approach

Irina Basieva[1,2] and Andrei Khrennikov[1]($\boxtimes$)

[1] International Center for Mathematical Modeling in Physics
and Cognitive Sciences, Linnaeus University, Växjö-Kalmar, Sweden
Andrei.Khrennikov@lnu.se
[2] Prokhorov General Physics Institute of Russian
Academy of Science, Moscow, Russia

Abstract. We present the detailed account of the quantum(-like) viewpoint to common knowledge. The Binmore-Brandenburger operator approach to the notion of common knowledge is extended to the quantum case. We develop a special quantum(-like) model of common knowledge based on information representations of agents which can be operationally represented by Hermitian operators. For simplicity, we assume that each agent constructs her/his information representation by using just one operator. However, different agents use in general representations based on noncommuting operators, i.e., incompatible representations. The quantum analog of basic system of common knowledge features $\mathcal{K}1 - \mathcal{K}5$ is derived.

Keywords: Common knowledge · Binmore-Brandenburger operator approach · Quantum(-like) decision making

1 Introduction

Common knowledge plays the crucial role in establishing of social conventions (as was firstly pointed out at the scientific level by David Hume in 1740). And the last 50 years were characterized by development of numerous formal (sometimes mathematical, but sometimes not) models of common knowledge and operating with it. One of the most useful mathematical formalizations is due to Binmore-Brandenburger [1]. Starting with classical measure-theoretic model of probability theory (Kolmogorov, 1933) they elaborated the formal approaches to the notion of common knowledge. The operator approach Binmore-Brandenburger is based on the notion of agents' knowledge operators K_i.

Common knowledge models play an important role in decision making theory, game theory, and cognitive psychology leading, in particular, to the Aumann theorem on the impossibility to agree on disagree in the presence of nontrivial common knowledge and the common prior [2,3]. Recently the quantum(-like)

© Springer International Publishing Switzerland 2015
H. Atmanspacher et al. (Eds.): QI 2014, LNCS 8951, pp. 93–104, 2015.
DOI: 10.1007/978-3-319-15931-7_8

decision theory flourished as the result of the fruitful cooperation of the psychological and quantum probability communities, see, e.g., the monographs [4–7]. Therefore it is a good time to present quantum(-like) formalization of the notion of common knowledge and to extend Aumann's argument on "(dis)agree on disagree" to the quantum case. The latter is discussed in another paper of the authors presented to QI2014 [8] (see also this paper for extended bibliography on quantum cognition). And in this note we present the detailed account of the quantum(-like) approach to common knowledge. We start with a quantum analog of Aumann's definition of knowing of an event E for the fixed state of the world $\omega \in \Omega$. Then we introduce the knowledge operator corresponding to such a notion of knowing. We show that this quantum (super)operator satisfies the system of axioms $\mathcal{K}1 - \mathcal{K}2$ for the Binmore-Brandenburger [1] knowledge operators. Thus the quantum knowledge operator can be considered as a natural generalization of the classical knowledge operator. One of possible interpretations of such generalization is that the collection of possible information representations of the world by agents is extended. Such nonclassical information representations are mathematically given by spectral families of Hermitian operators ("questions about the world" stated by the agents). In this operator framework we introduce hierarchically defined common knowledge (which was used to formulate the quantum(-like) analog of the (anti-)Aumann theorem [8]).

In classical theory the operator definition of common knowledge matches with the heuristic viewpoint on common knowledge; for two agents $i = 1, 2$.

COM$_K$N. An event E is common knowledge at the state of the world ω if 1 knows E, 2 knows E, 1 knows 2 knows E, 2 knows 1 knows E, and so on...

Our quantum(-like) notion of operator common knowledge matches with human intuition as well. (The difference is mathematical formalization of knowing.)

To simplify mathematics, we proceed with *finite dimensional state spaces*. Generalization to the infinite dimensional case is evident, but it will be based on more advanced mathematics.

We also remark that our model of quantum(-like) formalization of common knowledge can be generalized by using the formalism of open quantum systems leading to questions represented by positive operator valued measures, cf. [5, 9, 10], or even more general operator valued measures [11]. (In principle, there is no reason to expect that the operational description of cognitive phenomena, psychology, and economics would be based on the exactly the same mathematical formalism as the operational description of physical phenomena. Therefore we cannot exclude that some generalizations will be involved, see again [11].) However, at the very beginning we would like to separate the mathematical difficulties from the formalism by itself; therefore we proceed with quantum observables of the Dirac-von Neumann class, Hermitian operators and projector valued operator measures.

2   Set-Theoretic Model of Common Knowledge

In the classical set-theoretic model events (propositions) are represented by subsets of some set Ω. Elements of this set represent all possible states of the world (or at least states possible for some context). In some applications, e.g., in sociology and economics, Ω represents possible states of affairs. Typically considerations are reduced to finite (or countable) state spaces. In the general case, one has to proceed as it common in classical (Kolmogorov) model of probability theory and consider a fixed σ-algebra of subsets of Ω, say $\mathcal{F}$, representing events (propositions).

There is a group of agents (which are individual or collective cognitive entities); typically the number of agents is finite, call them $i = 1, 2, \ldots, N$. These individuals are about to learn the answers to various multi-choice *questions* about the world (about the state of affairs), to make observations. In the Bayesian model agents assign prior probability distributions for the possible states of the world; in many fundamental considerations such as, e.g., Aumann's theorem, it is assumed that the agents set the common prior distribution p, see [8] for more details. Here one operates with the classical Kolmogorov probability space $(\Omega, \mathcal{F}, p)$. In this note we shall not study the problem of the prior update, see again [8]. Therefore at the classical level our considerations are restricted to set-theoretic operations.

Each agent creates its information representation for possible states of the world based on its own possibilities to perform measurements, "to ask questions to the world." Mathematically these representations are given by partitions of $\Omega : \mathcal{P}^{(i)} = (P_j^{(i)})$, where $\cup_j P_j^{(i)} = \Omega$ and $P_j^{(i)} \cap P_k^{(i)} \emptyset, j \neq k$. Thus an agent cannot get to know the state of the world ω precisely; she can only get to know to which element of its information partition $P_j^{(i)} = P^{(i)}(\omega)$ this ω belongs. The agent i knows an event E in the state of the world ω if

$$P^{(i)}(\omega) \subset E. \tag{1}$$

Let $K_i(E)$ be the event "ith agent knows E":

$$K_i E = \{\omega \in \Omega : P^{(i)}(\omega) \subset E\}. \tag{2}$$

As was shown by Binmore-Brandenburger [1], the *knowledge operator* K_i has the following properties:

$$\mathcal{K}1 : \quad K_i E \subset E$$

$$\mathcal{K}2 : \quad \Omega \subset K_i \Omega$$

$$\mathcal{K}3 : \quad K_i(E \cap F) = K_i E \cap K_i F$$

$$\mathcal{K}4 : \quad K_i E \leq K_i K_i E$$

$$\mathcal{K}5 : \quad \overline{K_i E} \leq K_i \overline{K_i E}$$

Here, for an event E, $\bar{E}$ denotes its complement. We remark that one can proceed another way around [1]: to start with $\mathcal{K}1 - \mathcal{K}5$ as the system of axioms determining the operator of knowledge and then derive that such an operator has the form (2).

The statement $\mathcal{K}1$ has the following meaning: if the ith agent knows E, then E must be the case; the statement $\mathcal{K}2$: the ith agent knows that some possible state of the world in Ω occurs; $\mathcal{K}3$: the ith agent knows a conjunction if, and only if, i knows each conjunct; $\mathcal{K}4$: the ith agent knows E, then she knows that she knows E; $\mathcal{K}5$: if the agent does not know an event, then she knows that she does not know.

3   Quantum(-like) Scheme

Let H be (finite dimensional) complex Hilbert space; denote the scalar product in H as $\langle\cdot|\cdot\rangle$. For an orthogonal projector P, we set $H_P = P(H)$, its image, and vice versa, for subspace L of H, the corresponding orthogonal projector is denoted by the symbol P_L.

In our model the "*states of the world*" are given by pure states (vectors of norm one); events (propositions) are represented by orthogonal projectors. As is well known, these projectors form a lattice ("quantum logic") with the operations corresponding to operations on orthocomplemented subspace lattice of complex Hilbert space H (each projector P is identified with its image-subspace of H_P).

Questions posed by agents are mathematically described by self-adjoint operators, say $A^{(i)}$. Since we proceed with finite-dimensional state spaces, $A^{(i)} = \sum_j a_j^{(i)} P_j^{(i)}$, where $(a_j^{(i)})$ are real numbers, all different eigenvalues of $A^{(i)}$, and $(P_j^{(i)})$ are the orthogonal projectors onto the corresponding eigen-subspaces. Here (a_j) encode possible answers to the question of the ith agent. The system of projectors $\mathcal{P}^{(i)} = (P_j^{(i)})$ is the spectral family of $A^{(i)}$. Hence, for any agent i, it is a "disjoint partition of unity": $\vee_k P_k^{(i)} = I$, $P_k^{(i)} \wedge P_m^{(i)} = 0, k \neq m$, or equivalently $\sum_k P_k^{(i)} = I$, $P_k^{(i)} P_m^{(i)} = 0, k \neq m$. This spectral family can be considered as information representation of the world by the ith agent. In particular, "getting the answer $a_j^{(i)}$" is the event which is mathematically described by the projector $P_j^{(i)}$.

If *the state of the world*[1] is represented by ψ and, for some k_0, $P_\psi \leq P_{k_0}^{(i)}$, then, for the quantum probability distribution corresponding to this state, we have:

$$p_\psi(P_{k_0}^{(i)}) = \mathrm{Tr} P_\psi P_{k_0}^{(i)} = 1 \text{ and, for } k \neq k_0, \ p_\psi(P_k^{(i)}) = \mathrm{Tr} P_\psi P_k^{(i)} = 0.$$

Thus, in this case, the event $P_{k_0}^{(i)}$ happens with the probability one and other events from information representation of the world by the ith agent have zero probability.

However, opposite to the classical case, in general ψ need not belong to any concrete subspace $H_{P_k^{(i)}}$. Nevertheless, for any pure state ψ, there exists the minimal

---

[1] The general discussion on the meaning of the state of the world is presented in our second conference paper [8]. It is important to remark that in models of qunatum cognition states are typically not physical states, but information states. They give the *mental representation* of the state of affairs in human society in general or in a social group of people. In particular, such a ψ can be the mental representation of a real physical phenomenon. However, even in this case ψ is not identified with the corresponding physical state. (By using the terminology invented by H. Atmanspacher and H. Primas, see, e.g., [12], we can consider the physical state as an ontic state and its mental image as an epistemic state.) This interpretation of representation of a state of the world by a pure quantum state matches well with the information interpretation of quantum mechanics (due to Zeilinger and Brukner). Roughly speaking this ψ-function is not in nature, but in heads of people. See Remark 1 for further discussion.

projector $Q_\psi^{(i)}$ of the form $\sum_m P_{j_m}^{(i)}$ such that $P_\psi \le Q_\psi^{(i)}$. Set $O_\psi^{(i)} = \{j : P_j^{(i)} \psi \neq 0\}$. Then $Q_\psi^{(i)} = \sum_{j \in O_\psi^{(i)}} P_j^{(i)}$. The projector $Q_\psi^{(i)}$ represents the ith agent's knowledge about the ψ-world. We remark that $p_\psi(Q_\psi^{(i)}) = 1$.

Consider the system of projectors $\tilde{\mathcal{P}}^{(i)}$ consisting of sums of the projectors from $\mathcal{P}^{(i)}$:

$$\tilde{\mathcal{P}}^{(i)} = \{P = \sum_m P_{j_m}^{(i)}\}. \tag{3}$$

Then

$$Q_\psi^{(i)} = \min\{P \in \tilde{\mathcal{P}}^{(i)} : P_\psi \le P\}. \tag{4}$$

Definition 1. *For the ψ-state of the world and the event E, the ith agent knowns E if*

$$Q_\psi^{(i)} \le E. \tag{5}$$

It is evident that if, for the state of the world ψ, the ith agent knows E, then $\psi \in H_E$. In general the latter does not imply that E is known (for the state ψ), see [8] for a discussion on definitions of knowing an event in the classical set-theoretic and quantum Hilbert space models.

Remark 1. For a single agent i, "quantumness" is encoded in the possibility that the state of the world ψ can be superposition of states belonging to different components of its information representation. In the classical probabilistic framework knowing of an event E means that, although an agent does not know precisely the state of the world ω, she/he knows precisely at least to which component P_j this state belong. For quantum(-like) thinking agent, a superposition state of the world does not give a possibility for "precise orientation" even in her/his information representation.

Example 1. (Boeing MH17) For example, let us consider the case of the crush of Malaysian Boeing MH17 at Ukraine. As was pointed out in footnote 1, the state of the world ψ represents the state of believes in society about possible sources of this crush. Suppose that there are only two possibilities: either the airplane was shut down by Keiv's military forces or by Donetsk's militants. For the illustrative purpose, it is sufficient to consider the two dimensional state space (although the real information state space related to the MH17-crush has a huge dimension depending on variety or political, economic, and military factors). Consider the basis (e_K, e_D) representing the possibilities: e_K : "Kiev is responsible", e_D : "Donetsk is responsible". (We remark that in this model, if Kiev is responsible than Donetsk is not and vise versa.) In our model

$$\psi_{MH17} = c_1 e_K + c_2 e_D, \tag{6}$$

where c_1 and c_2 complex probabilistic amplitudes for Kiev and Donetsk responsibilities, respectively. An agent tries to get know the truth about the MH17 crush by asking experts (say in terrorism).[2] She/he asked about their opinions; so the single question-observable is in the use: "Who is responsible?" In the quantum model this agent operates with the spectral family $\mathcal{P} = \{P_1, P_2\}$, where $P_1 = P_{e_K}$, $P_2 = P_{e_D}$. If both amplitudes in (6) are nonzero (and in the present situation for July 24, 2014, it can be assumed that $c_1 = c_2 = 1/\sqrt{2}$), then, for this state of the world, neither the event E_K represented by P_1 nor the event E_D represented by P_2 is known (to be true) for this agent. In the classical model the state of the world ω has to belong either to the element P_1 of the information partition or to the element P_2. Thus one (and only one) of the events E_K and E_D has to be known.

We now define the *knowledge operator K_i* which applied to any event E, yields the event "ith agent knows that E."

Definition 2. $K_i E = P_{H_{K_i E}}$, *where* $H_{K_i E} = \{\phi : Q^{(i)}_{\phi/\|\phi\|} \leq E\}$.

See [8] for the proof of the following proposition:

Proposition 1. *For any event E, the set $H_{K_i E}$ is a linear subspace of H.*

Thus Definition 2 is consistent. The operator K_i has the properties similar to the properties of the classical knowledge operator:

Proposition 2. *For any event E,*

$$\mathcal{K}1 : \quad K_i E \leq E. \tag{7}$$

Proof. Take nonzero $\phi \in H_{K_i E}$. Then $Q^{(i)}_{\phi/\|\phi\|} \leq E$ and, hence,

$$H_{Q^{(i)}_{\phi/\|\phi\|}} \subset H_E.$$

This implies that $\phi \in H_E$ and that $H_{K_i E} \subset H_E$.

We also remark that trivially

$$\mathcal{K}2 : \quad I \leq K_i I, \tag{8}$$

in fact,

$$I = K_i I.$$

Proposition 3. *For any pair of events E, F,*

$$E \leq F \text{ implies } K_i E \leq K_i F. \tag{9}$$

Proof. Take nonzero $\phi \in H_{K_i E}$. Then $Q^{(i)}_{\phi/\|\phi\|} \leq E \leq F$. Thus $\phi \in K_i F$.

---

[2] The first point is related to the discussion in Footnote 1. The ψ_{MH17} is not the actual physical state! The real physical state of affairs can be (mentally) identified either with e_K or with e_D; the ontic state by the Atmanspacher-Primas terminology. However, one has be careful in putting too much weight to the ontic state. It might happen that it would be never known.

Proposition 4. *For any event pair of events E, F,*

$$\mathcal{K}3: \quad K_i E \wedge K_i F = K_i E \wedge F. \tag{10}$$

Proof. (a) Take nonzero $\phi \in H_{K_i E} \cap H_{K_i F}$. Then $Q^{(i)}_{\phi/\|\phi\|} \leq E$ and $Q^{(i)}_{\phi/\|\phi\|} \leq F$. Hence, $Q^{(i)}_{\phi/\|\phi\|} \leq E \wedge F$ and $\phi \in H_{K_i E \wedge F}$. Therefore $K_i E \wedge K_i F \leq K_i E \wedge F$.

(b) Take nonzero $\phi \in H_{K_i E \wedge F}$. Then $Q^{(i)}_{\phi/\|\phi\|} \leq E \wedge F$ and, hence, $Q^{(i)}_{\phi/\|\phi\|} \leq E$ and $Q^{(i)}_{\phi/\|\phi\|} \leq F$. Therefore $\phi \in H_{K_i E} \cap H_{K_i E} = H_{K_i E \wedge K_i F}$ and $K_i E \wedge F \leq K_i E \wedge K_i F$.

Proposition 5. *For any event E,*

$$K_i E = \sum_{P_j^{(i)} \leq E} P_j^{(i)}. \tag{11}$$

Proof. (a) First we show that $K_i E \leq \sum_{P_j^{(i)} \leq E} P_j^{(i)}$. Take nonzero $\phi \in H_{K_i E}$. Then $Q^{(i)}_{\phi/\|\phi\|} \leq E$ and $\phi = \sum_{j \in O^{(i)}_{\phi/\|\phi\|}} P_j^{(i)} \phi$. Since $\sum_{j \in O^{(i)}_{\phi/\|\phi\|}} P_j^{(i)} \leq E$, then for any $j \in O^{(i)}_{\phi/\|\phi\|}$, $P_j^{(i)} \leq E$. Therefore $\phi = \sum_{P_j^{(i)} \leq E} P_j^{(i)} \phi$.

(b) Now we show that $\sum_{P_j^{(i)} \leq E} P_j^{(i)} \leq K_i E$. Let $\phi = \sum_{P_j^{(i)} \leq E} P_j^{(i)} \phi$. Then $Q^{(i)}_{\phi/\|\phi\|} \leq \sum_{P_j^{(i)} \leq E} P_j^{(i)} \leq E$.

We also remark that

$$E = \sum P_{j_k}^{(i)} \text{ implies } K_i E = E. \tag{12}$$

This immediately implies that

$$K_i E = K_i K_i E \tag{13}$$

and, in particular, we obtain the following result (important for comparison with the classical operator approach to definition of common knowledge):

Proposition 6. *For any event E,*

$$\mathcal{K}4: \quad K_i E \leq K_i K_i E. \tag{14}$$

Finally, we have:

Proposition 7. *For any event E,*

$$(I - K_i E) = K_i (I - K_i E). \tag{15}$$

Proof. Take for simplicity that $K_i E = \sum_{j=1}^m P_j^{(i)}$, see (11). Then $I - K_i E = \sum_{j>m} P_j^{(i)}$. By using (12) we obtain that $K_i (I - K_i E) = (I - K_i E)$.

In particular, we obtained that

$$\mathcal{K}5: \quad (I - K_iE) \leq K_i(I - K_iE). \tag{16}$$

The classical analogs of $\mathcal{K}1 - \mathcal{K}5$ form the axiomatic base of the operator approach to common knowledge [1]. (Therefore we were so detailed in the presentation of $\mathcal{K}1 - \mathcal{K}5$; in particular, this aim, to match closer with the classical case, explains the above transitions from statements in the form of equalities, which are definitely stronger, to statements in the form of inequalities.) We also remark that in the classical approach to the knowledge operator the classical analog of the system $\mathcal{K}1 - \mathcal{K}5$ corresponds to the modal system $S5$ and of the system $\mathcal{K}1 - \mathcal{K}4$ to the modal system $S4$, see [13]. To analyze our quantum system $\mathcal{K}1 - \mathcal{K}5$ from the viewpoint of its logical structure is an interesting and nontrivial problem.

Remark 2. (Quantum truth?) This is a good place to discuss the truth content of quantum logic (which is formally represented as orthocomplemented closed subspace lattice of complex Hilbert space). There are two opposite viewpoints on the truth content of quantum logic, see [14,15] for the detailed discussion. From one viewpoint, quantum logic carries not only the novel formal representation of knowledge about a new class of physical phenomena, but also assigns to statements about these phenomena (at least to some of them) a special truth value, "nonclassical truth". Another viewpoint is that one can proceed even in the quantum case with the classical notion of truth as correspondence, which was explicated rigorously by Tarski's semantic theory, see [14,15]. The same problem states even more urgently in applications of the quantum formalism in cognitive science and psychology: *Does quantum logic express new (nonclassical) truth assignment to propositions?* Opposite to Garola et al. [14,15], the authors of this paper consider quantum formalism as expressing the new type of truth assignment, cf. [16]. However, the problem is extremely complex and it might happen that our position is wrong and the position of Garola [14], see also Garola and Sozzo [15], is right. However, nowadays our approach is more common in discussions on the logical structure of quantum mechanics. It is usual in literature, e.g., [17] to mention the use of different geometries, or probability theories, to uphold the thesis that also different logics could be needed in different physical theories.

Remark 3. (Accessibility of quantum truth) The structures discovered in this paper are the formalization of the specific notion of common knowledge. Thus they do not by themselves formalize a notion of truth, but of a specific access to truth. Therefore, although the problem of whether the "quantum truth" can be reduced to the "classical truth" discussed in Remark 2 is important for clarification of quantum knowledge theory, it has no direct relation to the subject of this paper.

Definition 3. *Agent i's it possibility-projector $\mathcal{H}_\psi^{(i)}$ at the state of the world ψ is defined as*

$$\mathcal{H}_\psi^{(i)} = \bigwedge_{\{\psi \in K_i(E)\}} E.$$

It is easy to see that

$$\mathcal{H}_\psi^{(i)} = Q_\psi^{(i)}. \tag{17}$$

It is interesting to point out that the collection of i-agent's possibility-projectors (for all possible state) does not coincide with her spectral family and that different projectors are not mutually orthogonal. The latter is the crucial difference from the classical case. In the latter any "knowledge-map" K_i defined on the subsets of the set of states of the world, denoted as Ω, and satisfying axioms $\mathcal{K}1 - \mathcal{K}5$ generates possibility sets giving disjoint partition of Ω.

Then, as in the classical case, we define:

$$M_0 E = E, M_1 E = K_1 E \wedge \ldots \wedge K_N E, \ldots, M_{n+1} E = K_1 M_n E \wedge \ldots \wedge K_N M_n E, \ldots$$

As usual, $M_1 E$ is the event "all agents know that E" and so on. We can rewrite this definition by using subspaces, instead of projectors:

$$H_{M_1 E} = H_{K_1 E} \cap \ldots \cap H_{K_N E}, \ldots, H_{M_{n+1} E} = H_{K_1 M_n E} \cap \ldots \cap H_{K_N M_n E}, \ldots$$

Now we define the *"common knowledge"* operator, as mutual knowledge of all finite degrees:

$$\kappa E = \wedge_{n=0}^{\infty} M_n E.$$

Based on such quantum(-like) formalization of common knowledge, the validity of the Aumann theorem was analyzed in [8].

4   Possible Generalization to Multi-question Information Representations

We considered a very special model of knowledge and common knowledge in which information representation of each agent i is based on a *single question-operator* $A^{(i)}$. Of course, it is natural to consider a more general model in which the ith agent can create his information representation based on the state of the world ψ by using a few question-observables, $A_k^{(i)}, k = 1, \ldots, M$. First of all consider the case of compatible observables, i.e., $[A_k^{(i)}, A_s^{(i)}] = 0$. Already in this case generalization of our model is nontrivial and non-unique.

First we recall how joint measurement of compatible observables is treated in quantum mechanics, starting with von Neumann [18]. Consider the case $M = 2$ and omit the agent index i. Thus the information representation is based on two question-observables which are mathematically represented by commuting operators A_1 and A_2. There exists a Hermitian operator R such that both operators can be represented as functions of $R : A_1 = f_1(R), A_2 = f_2(R)$. Then the joint measurement of these operators is reduced to measurement of the observable represented by R and, for its value r, the values $f_1(r)$ and $f_2(r)$ are assigned to compatible question-observables. Introduction of such a "joint measurement operator" R completely washes out the individual spectral families of $A_k, k = 1, 2$, which played the crucial role in the definitions of knowledge/common knowledge. Suppose that the operator R has the spectral decomposition

$$R = \sum_j r_j P_j.$$

Then the corresponding knowledge model is simply based on the projectors $\mathcal{R} = (P_j)$. (Thus we get nothing new comparing with the previous sections.) Consider the system of projectors $\tilde{\mathcal{R}}$ consisting of sums of the projectors from $\mathcal{R}$, see (3) (We work in the finite dimensional case, so all sums are finite). For each state of the world ψ, we introduce the projector

$$Q_\psi = \min\{P \in \tilde{\mathcal{R}} : P_\psi \leq P\}. \tag{18}$$

For the ψ-state of the world and the event E, the agent knowns E if

$$Q_\psi \leq E. \tag{19}$$

We call this model of knowing the von Neumann model.

Although the presented scheme of measurement is the standard for quantum mechanics, it is not self-evident that precisely this scheme have to be used as the basis for the quantum(-like) knowledge model corresponding to an agent operating with a family of questions represented by commuting operators. We propose another scheme which seems to be more natural for the quantum modeling of cognition. The main objection to application of the standard (von Neumann) quantum mechanical scheme of measurement for compatible observables is that in general an agent has not reason to try to construct the single observable such that both compatible question-observables can be expressed as its functions. Even if this is always possible theoretically, practically this process may be complicated and time consuming. An agent can prefer to proceed in testing knowing of an event E by using each question separately. Mathematically this scheme is described as follows.

Consider the spectral families of the question-operators (again we restrict consideration to the case of two operators), $\mathcal{P}_1 = (P_{1j})$ and $\mathcal{P}_2 = (P_{2j})$ (we remind that the upper index corresponding to the agent was omitted). Consider the systems of projectors $\tilde{\mathcal{P}}_k, k = 1, 2$, consisting of sums of the projectors from $\mathcal{P}_k$: $\tilde{\mathcal{P}}_k = \{P = \sum_m P_{kj_m}\}$.

For each state of the world ψ and $k = 1, 2$, we introduce the projectors

$$Q_{k;\psi} = \min\{P \in \tilde{\mathcal{P}}_k : P_\psi \leq P\}. \tag{20}$$

Definition 1A. *For the ψ- state of the world and the event E, the agent knowns E if*

$$\text{either } Q_{1;\psi} \leq E \text{ or } Q_{2;\psi} \leq E. \tag{21}$$

It is clear that such knowing of E implies its "von Neumann knowing" based on (18) and (19). However, the inverse is not true.

Example 2. The state space H of an agent is four dimensional with the orthonormal basis (e_1, e_2, e_3, e_4), the projectors P_{11} and P_{12} project H onto the subspaces with the bases (e_1, e_2) and (e_3, e_4) and the projectors P_{21} and P_{22} project H onto the subspaces with the bases (e_1, e_4) and (e_2, e_3). The spectral family of the operator R is given by one dimensional projectors $P_j = P_{e_j}$. Consider the event E given by the projector onto the subspace with the basis (e_1, e_2, e_3). Take the state of the world $\psi = (e_1 + e_2 + e_3)/\sqrt{3}$. Then $Q_\psi = E$ and the agent operating in the von Neumann scheme, i.e., who spent efforts to prepare the question-observable representing both compatible questions-operators, knows E. However, the agent who produces knowledge by using two question-observables separately does not know E. For him, $Q_{1;\psi} = P_{11} + P_{12} = I$ as well as $Q_{1;\psi} = P_{21} + P_{22} = I$.

One of the advantages of the "either/or" scheme is that it has the straightforward generalization to incompatible observables, the same definition, Definition 1A.

Example 3. The state space H of an agent is two dimensional. Consider in it two orthonormal bases (e_{11}, e_{12}) and (e_{21}, e_{22}) such that $\langle e_{1j}|e_{2m}\rangle \neq 0$ and the one-dimensional projectors corresponding to these bases, $P_{kj} = P_{e_{kj}}$. Here $\mathcal{P}_k = \{P_{k1}, P_{k2}\}$ and $\tilde{\mathcal{P}}_k = \{P_{k1}, P_{k2}, I\}, k = 1, 2$. Consider the event $E_1 = P_{11}$. Then this agent knowns it ("through the question observable with the spectral family $\mathcal{P}_1$".) Consider the event $E_1 = P_{21}$. Then this agent knowns it ("through the question observable with the spectral family $\mathcal{P}_2$"). Since projectors, for different k, do not commute, there is no the "joint measurement possibility" and the operator R does not exists, so the knowing scheme based on (18) and (19) cannot be applied at all.

However, theory of such generalized knowledge operators is really beyond the scope of this paper.

Acknowledgments. The authors would like to thank C. Garola, E. Rosinger, and A. Schumann for resent exchange of ideas about the logical structure of quantum propositions.

References

1. Binmore, K., Brandenburger, A.: Common knowledge and game theory. ST/ICERD Discussion Paper 88/167, London School of Economics (1988)
2. Aumann, R.J.: Agreeing on disagree. Ann. Stat. **4**, 1236–1239 (1976)
3. Aumann, R.J.: Backward induction and common knowledge of rationality. Games Econ. Behav. **8**, 6–19 (1995)
4. Khrennikov, A.: Information Dynamics in Cognitive, Psychological, Social, and Anomalous Phenomena. Fundamental Theories of Physics. Kluwer, Dordreht (2004)
5. Khrennikov, A.: Ubiquitous Quantum Structure: From Psychology to Finances. Springer, Heidelberg (2010)
6. Busemeyer, J.R., Bruza, P.D.: Quantum Models of Cognition and Decision. Cambridge Press, Cambridge (2012)
7. Haven, E., Khrennikov, A.: Quantum Social Science. Cambridge Press, Cambridge (2013)
8. Khrennikov, A., Basieva, I.: Quantum(-like) decision making: on validity of the Aumann theorem. In: Atmanspacher, H., Bergomi, C., Filk, T., Kitto, K. (eds.) QI 2014. LNCS, vol. 8951, pp. 105–118. Springer, Heidelberg (2014)
9. Asano, M., Basieva, I., Khrennikov, A., Ohya, M., Yamato, I.: Non-Kolmogorovian approach to the context-dependent systems breaking the classical probability law. Found. Phys. **43**, 2083–2099 (2013)

10. Khrennikov, A., Basieva, I., Dzhafarov, E.N., Busemeyer, J.R.: Quantum Models for Psychological Measurements: An Unsolved Problem. arXiv:1403.3654 (q-bio.NC), Neurons and Cognition (2014)
11. Basieva, I., Khrennikov, A.: Observables generalizing positive operator valued measures. In: Khrennikov, A., Atmanspacher, H., Migdall, A., Polyakov, S. (eds.) Quantum Theory: Reconsideration of Foundations-6, Conference Proceedings, vol. 1508, pp. 94–83. AIP, Melville (2012)
12. Atmanspacher, H., Primas, H.: Epistemic and ontic quantum realities. In: Adenier, G., Khrennikov, A. (eds.) Foundations of Probability and Physics-3, Conference Proceedings, vol. 750, pp. 49–62. AIP, Melville (2005)
13. Kripke, S.A.: Semantical considerations on modal logic. Acta Philosophica Fennica **16**, 83–94 (1963)
14. Garola, C.: A Pragmatic Interpretation of Quantum Logic. Preprint. arXiv:quant-ph/0507122v2
15. Garola, C., Sozzo, S.: Recovering nonstandard logics within an extended classical framework. Erkenntnis **78**, 399–419 (2013)
16. Khrennikov, A., Schumann, A.: Quantum Non-objectivity from Performativity of Quantum Phenomena. Preprint. arXiv:1404.7077 [physics.gen-ph]. (To be published in Physica Scripta)
17. Khrennikov, A.: Contextual Approach to Quantum Formalism. Springer, Heidelberg (2009)
18. Von Neuman, J.: Mathematical Foundations of Quantum Mechanics. Princeton University Press, Princeton (1955)

Quantum(-Like) Decision Making: On Validity of the Aumann Theorem

Andrei Khrennikov[1](✉) and Irina Basieva[1,2]

[1] International Center for Mathematical Modeling in Physics and Cognitive Sciences, Linnaeus University, Växjö-kalmar, Sweden
Andrei.Khrennikov@lnu.se
[2] Prokhorov General Physics Institute of Russian Academy of Science, Moscow, Russia

Abstract. Through set-theoretic formalization of the notion of common knowledge, Aumann proved that if two agents have the common priors, and their posteriors for a given event are common knowledge, then their posteriors must be equal. In this paper we investigate the problem of validity of this theorem in the framework of quantum(-like) decision making.

Keywords: Aumann theorem · Quantum(-like) decision making · Common knowledge

1 Introduction

We remark that during recent years the mathematical formalism of quantum mechanics was widely applied to problems of decision making and more generally modeling of cognition, see, e.g., the monographs [1–4] as well as the series of articles [5–28]. This project is based on the *quantum-like paradigm* [2]: that information processing by complex cognitive systems (including social systems) taking into account contextual dependence of information and probabilistic reasoning can be mathematically described by quantum information and probability theories.

One can find evidences of violation of laws of classical probability theory, e.g., in violation of the *law of total probability*. Its violation have been found in various sets of statistical data, see, e.g., [2,4,6,9,10,12,13,16,17,22]. The derivation of this law is based on the additivity of classical probability measures and the classical definition of conditional probabilities based on the *Bayes formula*. Thus the law of total probability can be violated as the result of violation of either additivity of classical probability, cf. with Feynman's viewpoint [33], or classical Bayesian rule or both jointly. One can say that this is an integral statistical test of classicality of probability combining its two basic features, additivity and Bayesianity. It is interesting to find cognitive phenomena in which just one of these factors is responsible for deviation from the classical probabilistic predictions.

The role of the Bayesian updating in decision making was analyzed in [25] with application to the problem of *human probability judgment errors*; in [28]

© Springer International Publishing Switzerland 2015
H. Atmanspacher et al. (Eds.): QI 2014, LNCS 8951, pp. 105–118, 2015.
DOI: 10.1007/978-3-319-15931-7_9

this analysis was performed for such an important psychological phenomenon as *cognitive dissonance*. In both studies it was shown that by using quantum probability updating one can present consistent mathematical descriptions of aforementioned problems.

In this paper we show that the quantum generalization of the Bayesian updating leads to violation of the celebrating *Aumann theorem* [29, 30] which states that *if two agents have the common priors, and their posteriors for a given event E are common knowledge*[1]*, then their posteriors must be equal; agents with the same priors cannot agree to disagree.* In this note we show that in *some contexts* agents using quantum(-like) information processing can *agree to disagree* even if they have the common priors, and their posteriors for a given event E are common knowledge. The most interesting problem is to find elements of classical Aumann's model for common knowledge whose quantum generalization induces violation of his theorem, we preset one of sufficient conditions of validity of the Aumann theorem even for agents whose information processing is described by quantum information theory and quantum probability.

We remark that violations of the Aumann theorem in real situations were widely discussed in literature (see, e.g., [29, 31] for discussion). Typically such violations are related to violation of one of the basic assumptions of the Aumann theorem, on the common prior probability and common knowledge about the posterior probabilities: either the agents do not have such a prior probability or the posterior probabilities are not common knowledge. However, sometimes agents agree on disagree even having the common prior and common knowledge. One of the important sources of such violations is the presence of biases contributing to irrational update of probabilities, see appendix 1 on the discussion; in particular, about the agreement on disagree for agents proceeding with the *Self Sampling Assumption.*[2]

---

[1] For readers' convenience, we now present the original Aumann's definition of common knowledge for two agents: "An event E is common knowledge at the state of the world ω if 1 knows E, 2 knows E, 1 knows 2 knows E, 2 knows 1 knows E, and so on." The aforementioned heuristic notion of common knowledge can be formally described by various mathematical models. The classical probabilistic formalization of this notion was presented, e.g., in [29, 30]. (In fact, the problem of common knowledge plays very important role in cognitive science, psychology, philosophy, decision making, economics. There were published numerous papers enlightening various aspects of common knowledge studies. We are not able to review such studies in this paper, see, e.g., easily approachable work [31] for extended bibliography.) In this paper we present a novel formalization of the heuristic notion of common knowledge, namely, based on quantum probability and quantum logics. However, we do not change the cognitive meaning of this notion. Our quantum(-like) model just describe some features of common knowledge which were known by experts in aforementioned areas, but were not covered by the classical probability model.

[2] We also remark that a deep connection between biased decision making and quantum modeling of cognition was established in the framework of theory of open quantum systems, where biases were modeled as components of the "mental environment" [19, 20].

We point out that the Aumann argument is based on usage of classical Boolean logic and quantum violation of his theorem can be interpreted as a consequence of using of nonclassical logic, i.e., consideration of agents processing information by using a nonclassical logical system, see appendix 2 for a discussion. This appendix also contains a brief discussion on the role of the ontic and epistemic descriptions in the (anti-)Aumann argumentaion.

A brief introductions to the classical approach to the problem of agreement on disagree is presented in footnote 3 and appendix 3.

2   Quantum(-Like) Approach to Common Knowledge

Following von Neumann [34] and Birkhoff and von Neumann [32] we represent *events, propositions,* as orthogonal projectors in complex Hilbert space H. Denote the scalar product in H as $\langle \cdot | \cdot \rangle$. For an orthogonal projector P, we set $H_P = P(H)$, its image, and vice versa, for subspace L of H, the corresponding orthogonal projector is denoted by the symbol P_L.

The set of orthogonal projectors is a *lattice* with the order structure: $P \leq Q$ iff $H_P \subset H_Q$ or equivalently, for any $\psi \in H$, $\langle \psi | P\psi \rangle \leq \langle \psi | Q\psi \rangle$. For a pure state $|\psi\rangle$, we set $P_\psi = |\psi\rangle\langle\psi|$, the orthogonal projector on this vector, $P_\psi \phi = \langle \phi | \psi \rangle \psi$.

Aumann's considerations [29,30] are applicable for a finite number of *agents*, call them $i = 1, 2, ..., N$. These individuals are about to learn the answers to various multi-choice *questions*, to make observations.

In our quantum-like model the "*states of the world*" are given by pure states.[3] Questions posed by agents are mathematically described by self-adjoint operators, say $A^{(i)}$. We state again that events (propositions) are identified with orthogonal projectors. For the state of the world ψ, an event P *occurs* (takes place with probability 1) if ψ belongs to H_P.

To simplify considerations, we proceed in the case of the finite dimensional state space of the world, $m = \dim H < \infty$. Here each self-adjoint operator can be represented as a linear combination of orthogonal projectors to its eigensubspaces. In particular, the questions of agents can be expressed as $A^{(i)} = \sum_j a_j^{(i)} P_j^{(i)}$, where $(a_j^{(i)})$ are real numbers, all different eigenvalues of $A^{(i)}$, and

---

[3] The notion of possible worlds is very complex and it has been discussed in hundreds of papers, in philosophy, knowledge theory, modal logics. One can think about states as representing Leibniz's possible worlds or Wittgenstein's possible states of affairs. Of course, by representing the states of world by pure quantum states and saying nothing about a possible interpretation of the wave function, quantum state, we proceed in the purely operational way. What quantum state interpretation does match with the notion of the "possible worlds" used in literature? Suprisingly, it seems that the many worlds interpretation matches best, see also appendix 1. There is a similarity between the state of the world and the wave function of universe. However, since we are not so much excited by the many worlds interpretation, we proceed in the purely operational approach. The information interpretation of the quantum state (A. Zeilinger, C. Brukner) seems to be the most appropriate for our purposes.

$(P_j^{(i)})$ are the orthogonal projectors onto the corresponding eigen-subspaces. Here (a_j) encode possible answers to the question of the ith agent. The system of projectors $\mathcal{P}^{(i)} = (P_j^{(i)})$ is the spectral family of $A^{(i)}$. Hence, for any agent i, it is a "disjoint partition of unity":

$$\bigvee_k P_k^{(i)} = I, \; P_k^{(i)} \wedge P_m^{(i)} = 0, k \neq m. \tag{1}$$

We remark that (1) is simply the lattice-theoretical expression of the following operator equalities:

$$\sum_k P_k^{(i)} = I, \; P_k^{(i)} P_m^{(i)} = 0, k \neq m. \tag{2}$$

This spectral family can be considered as information representation of the world by the ith agent. In particular, "getting the answer $a_j^{(i)}$" is the event which is mathematically described by the projector $P_j^{(i)}$.

If the state of the world is represented by ψ and, for some k_0, $P_\psi \leq P_{k_0}^{(i)}$, then

$$p_\psi(P_{k_0}^{(i)}) = \mathrm{Tr} P_\psi P_{k_0}^{(i)} = 1 \text{ and, for } k \neq k_0, \; p_\psi(P_k^{(i)}) = \mathrm{Tr} P_\psi P_k^{(i)} = 0.$$

Thus, in this case, the event $P_{k_0}^{(i)}$ happens with the probability one and other events from information representation of the world by the ith agent have zero probability.

However, opposite to the classical case, in general ψ need not belong to any concrete subspace $H_{P^{(i)}_k}$. Nevertheless, for any pure state ψ, there exists the minimal projector $Q_\psi^{(i)}$ of the form $\sum_m P_{j_m}^{(i)}$ such that $P_\psi \leq Q_\psi^{(i)}$. Set $O_\psi^{(i)} = \{j : P_j^{(i)} \psi \neq 0\}$. Then $Q_\psi^{(i)} = \sum_{j \in O_\psi^{(i)}} P_j^{(i)}$. The projector $Q_\psi^{(i)}$ represents the ith agent's knowledge about the ψ-world. We remark that $p_\psi(Q_\psi^{(i)}) = 1$.

Consider the system of projectors $\tilde{\mathcal{P}}^{(i)}$ consisting of sums of the projectors from $\mathcal{P}^{(i)}$:

$$\tilde{\mathcal{P}}^{(i)} = \{P = \sum_m P_{j_m}^{(i)}\}. \tag{3}$$

Then

$$Q_\psi^{(i)} = \min\{P \in \tilde{\mathcal{P}}^{(i)} : P_\psi \leq P\}. \tag{4}$$

(We remark that, since we proceed with finite dimensional Hilbert spaces, this minimum is uniquely determined.)

Definition 1. *For the ψ- state of the world and the event E, the ith agent knowns E if*

$$Q_\psi^{(i)} \leq E. \tag{5}$$

It is evident that if, for the state of the world ψ, the ith agent knows E, then $\psi \in H_E$. In general the latter does not imply that E is known (for the state ψ).

However, if $\psi \in E = P_j^{(i)}$, then this event is known for i. The same is valid for any event of the form $E = P_{j_1}^{(i)} \vee \ldots \vee P_{j_k}^{(i)} (= P_{j_1}^{(i)} + \ldots + P_{j_k}^{(i)})$; if $\psi \in H_E$, then such E is known for i.

We remark that the straightforward analog of the classical definition would be based on condition $P_j^{(i)} \leq E$ for $P_\psi \leq P_j^{(i)}$, instead of more general condition (5). However, it would trivialize the class of possible states of the world.

We now define the *knowledge operator* K_i which applied to any event E, yields the event "ith agent knows that E."

Definition 2. $K_i E = P_{H_{K_i E}}$, where $H_{K_i E} = \{\phi : Q_{\phi/\|\phi\|}^{(i)} \leq E\}$.

Proposition 1. *For any event E, the set $H_{K_i E}$ is a linear subspace of H.*

Proof. Take two vectors $\phi_1, \phi_2 \in H_{K_i E}$ and consider their linear combination $\phi = a_1 \phi_1 + a_2 \phi_2$. We consider also the corresponding pure states $\psi_1 = \phi_1/\|\phi_1\|$, $\psi_2 = \phi_2/\|\phi_2\|$ and $\psi = \phi/\|\phi\|$. We have $Q_{\psi_m}^{(i)} \leq E$. Thus $\psi_m = \sum_{j \in O_{\phi_m}^{(i)}} P_j^{(i)} \psi_m$. It is clear that ϕ can be represented in the form $\phi = \sum_{j \in O_{\phi_1}^{(i)} \cup O_{\phi_1}^{(i)}} P_j^{(i)} \psi$. Therefore $O_\psi^{(i)} \subset O_{\psi_1}^{(i)} \cup O_{\psi_2}^{(i)}$ and, hence, $Q_\psi^{(i)} \leq E$.

Thus definition 2 is consistent. Formally the operator K_i has the properties similar to the properties of the classical knowledge operator. However, the real logical situation is not so simple, see appendix 2.

Now, as in the classical case, we define:

$$M_0 E = E, M_1 E = K_1 E \wedge \ldots \wedge K_N E, \ldots, M_{n+1} E = K_1 M_n E \wedge \ldots \wedge K_N M_n E, \ldots$$

As usual, $M_1 E$ is the event "all agents know that E" and so on. We can rewrite this definition by using subspaces, instead of projectors:

$$H_{M_1 E} = H_{K_1 E} \cap \ldots \cap H_{K_N E}, \ldots, H_{M_{n+1} E} = H_{K_1 M_n E} \cap \ldots \cap H_{K_N M_n E}, \ldots$$

Now we define the *"common knowledge"* operator, as mutual knowledge of all finite degrees:

$$\kappa E = \wedge_{n=0}^\infty M_n E.$$

As in the classical case we have that "Where something is common knowledge everybody knows it."

Lemma 1. *If $\kappa E \neq 0$, then, for each i, it can be represented as*

$$\kappa E = \sum_m P_{j_m}^{(i)}. \tag{6}$$

Proof. Take any nonzero vector $\phi \in H_{\kappa E}$. Then it belongs to $H_{K_i M_n E}$ for any n. Thus $Q_{\phi/\|\phi\|}^{(i)} \leq M_n E$ and, hence, $Q_{\phi/\|\phi\|}^{(i)} \leq \wedge_{n=0}^\infty M_n E = \kappa E$. Hence, for each $\phi \in H_{\kappa E}$, we have $\phi = Q_{\phi/\|\phi\|}^{(i)} \phi$. Thus (6) holds.

3   Quantum(-Like) Viewpoint on the Aumann's Theorem

3.1   Common Prior Assumption

Suppose now that both agents assigned to possible states of the world the same quantum probability distribution given by the density operator ρ, a priori state. Thus they do not know exactly the real state of the world (the latter is always a pure state) and a possible state of the world appears for them as a mixed quantum state. A priori probability for possible states of the world is combined with the information pictures used by the agents and given by their partitions of unity.

3.2   Quantum Probability Update

Consider some event E. The agents assign to it probabilities after conditioning ρ on the answers to their questions (on their information representations of the world):

$$q_k^{(i)} = p_\rho(E|P_k^{(i)}) = \frac{\mathrm{Tr}P_k^{(i)}\rho P_k^{(i)}E}{\mathrm{Tr}P_k^{(i)}\rho P_k^{(i)}}. \tag{7}$$

We remark that the agents can assign probabilities conditioned on the results of observations only for the answers $a_k^{(i)}$ such that $\mathrm{Tr}P_k^{(i)}\rho P_k^{(i)} > 0$.

Consider the events

$$C_{q^{(i)}} \equiv \{q_k^{(i)} = q^{(i)}\} = \bigvee_{\{k:q_k^{(i)}=q^{(i)}\}} P_k^{(i)}, \tag{8}$$

$i = 1, ..., N$, and set

$$C_{q^{(1)}...q^{(N)}} = \{q_k^{(1)} = q^{(1)}, , , , q_k^{(N)} = q^{(N)}\} = \bigwedge_i C_{q^{(i)}}.$$

Remark 1. Consider the classical Aumann model [29,30]. Here

$$q^{(i)}(\omega) = p(E|P^{(i)}(\omega)) = \frac{p(E \cap P^{(i)}(\omega))}{p(P^{(i)}(\omega))} \tag{9}$$

and $C_{q^{(i)}} \equiv \{\omega : q_k^{(i)}(\omega) = q^{(i)}\}$. We remark that if for some ω_0 the probability $q^{(i)}(\omega_0) = q^{(i)}$, then, for any $\omega \in P^{(i)}(\omega_0)$, the probability $q^{(i)}(\omega) = q^{(i)}$. Thus

$$C_{q^{(i)}} = \bigcup_{\{k:q_k^{(i)}=q^{(i)}\}} P_k^{(i)}, \tag{10}$$

cf. (8).

Remark 2. So, the quantum definition (8) is a natural generalization of the classical definition (10). The main difference is that the classical definition is based on the Boolean logic and the quantum one on the quantum logic. The quantum operation $\vee$ differs crucially from the classical operation $\cup$. To make the comparison clearer, we consider projection subspaces, instead of projectors. Then, for two subspaces, say H_1 and H_2, the subspace $H_1 \vee H_2$ is not simply the set-theoretic union $H_1 \cup H_2$, but $H_1 \vee H_2$ is the minimal subspaces containing $H_1 \cup H_2$. We emphasize that the quantum logic operation $\vee$ is a nontrivial generalization of the classical operation $\cup$ even in the case of orthogonal subspaces H_1 and H_2. We also point out that quantum logic operations violate some basic laws of the Boolean logic, for example the law of distributivity for the operations $\vee$ and $\wedge$ is violated, i.e., for three projectors P, P_1, P_2, in general $P \wedge (P_1 \vee P_2) \neq (P \wedge P_1) \vee (P \wedge P_2)$. (Even the orthogonality of P_1 and P_2 does not help.)

We remark that, in fact, as a consequence of mutual orthogonality of projectors from the spectral family of any Hermitian operator, the event $C_{q^{(i)}}$ can be represented as

$$C_{q^{(i)}} = \sum_{\{k: q_k^{(i)} = q^{(i)}\}} P_k^{(i)}. \tag{11}$$

Thus the event $C_{q^{(1)}...q^{(N)}}$ has representation:

$$C_{q^{(1)}...q^{(N)}} = \left(\bigvee_{\{k: q_k^{(1)} = q^{(1)}\}} P_k^{(1)} \right) \wedge ... \wedge \left(\bigvee_{\{k: q_k^{(N)} = q^{(N)}\}} P_k^{(N)} \right). \tag{12}$$

By taking into account Remark 2 we know that in general:

$$C_{q^{(1)}...q^{(N)}} \neq \bigvee_{\{k_1: q_{k_1}^{(1)} = q^{(1)}\}} ... \bigvee_{\{k_N: q_{k_N}^{(1)} = q^{(1)}\}} P_{k_1}^{(1)} \wedge ... \wedge P_{k_N}^{(N)}. \tag{13}$$

3.3   Interference Prevents Agreement

Suppose that the possibility of $C_{q^{(1)}...q^{(N)}}$ becoming common knowledge is not ruled out completely, i.e.,

$$p_\rho(\kappa C_{q^{(1)}...q^{(N)}}) > 0. \tag{14}$$

Then the straightforward quantum generalization of the classical Aumann theorem [29,30] would imply that $q^{(1)} = ... = q^{(N)}$. However, this is not the case! (as it may be expected, since the classical Aumann theorem was heavily based on usage of Boolean logics).

By Lemma 1 the common knowledge projector can be represented as $\kappa E = \sum_j P_{k_j}^{(i)}, i = 1, ..., N$. For each such $P_{k_j}^{(1)}, .., P_{k_j}^{(N)}$, we have

$$p_\rho(E|P_{k_j}^{(1)}) = q^{(1)}, ..., p_\rho(E|P_{k_j}^{(N)}) = q^{(N)}.$$

(In particular, for any such projector conditional probabilities are well defined, i.e., $\mathrm{Tr} P_{k_j}^{(i)} \rho P_{k_j}^{(i)} > 0$.) Consider now the conditional probability:

$$p_\rho(E|\kappa C_{q^{(1)}...q^{(N)}}) = \frac{\mathrm{Tr}\kappa C_{q^{(1)}...q^{(N)}} \rho \kappa C_{q^{(1)}...q^{(N)}} E}{\mathrm{Tr}\kappa C_{q^{(1)}...q^{(N)}} \rho \kappa C_{q^{(1)}...q^{(N)}}}.$$

First we remark that, for any projector M, $\mathrm{Tr}M\rho M = \mathrm{Tr}\rho M$. Thus

$$p_\rho(E|\kappa C_{q^{(1)}...q^{(N)}}) = \frac{\mathrm{Tr}\kappa C_{q^{(1)}...q^{(N)}}\rho\kappa C_{q^{(1)}...q^{(N)}}E}{\mathrm{Tr}\rho\kappa C_{q^{(1)}...q^{(N)}}}.$$

By using representation given by Lemma 1 we obtain

$$p_\rho(E|\kappa C_{q^{(1)}...q^{(N)}}) = \frac{1}{\mathrm{Tr}\rho\kappa C_{q^{(1)}...q^{(N)}}}\left(\sum_j \mathrm{Tr}P^{(i)}_{k_j}\rho P^{(i)}_{k_j}E + \sum_{j\neq m}\mathrm{Tr}P^{(i)}_{k_j}\rho P^{(i)}_{k_m}E\right).$$

(15)

The first (diagonal) sum can be written as

$$\frac{1}{\mathrm{Tr}\rho\kappa C_{q^{(1)}...q^{(N)}}}\sum_j\frac{\mathrm{Tr}P^{(i)}_{k_j}\rho P^{(i)}_{k_j}E}{\mathrm{Tr}\rho P^{(i)}_{k_j}}\mathrm{Tr}\rho P^{(i)}_{k_j} = \frac{q_i}{\mathrm{Tr}\rho\kappa C_{q^{(1)}...q^{(N)}}}\mathrm{Tr}\sum\rho P^{(i)}_{k_j} = q^{(i)}.$$

In the absence of the off-diagonal term in (15) we get $q^{(1)} = ... = q^{(N)}$. This corresponds to the classical case. However, in general the off-diagonal term does not vanish – this is *the interference type effect*.

Hence, in general *the Aumann theorem is not valid for "quantum(-like) decision makers*. Thus *agents processing information in the quantum information and probability framework can agree on disagree.*

Form the expression (15) for the interference term, it is clear that it has three main contributions:

– Incompatibility of information representations of agents.
– Incompatibility of an event E under consideration with individual information representations.
– Incompatibility of information representations of agents with the prior state.

3.4   Sufficient Conditions of Validity of the Quantum(-Like) Version of the Aumann Theorem

Now we present a special situation in which even quantumly thinking agents cannot agree on disagree.

Proposition 2. *Let the common a priori state ρ is given by the unity operator normalized by the dimension. If condition (14), the assumption of common prior, holds, then $q^{(1)} = ... = q^{(N)}$.*

To prove this statement, we point to the fact that, for such ρ, the off-diagonal term in (15) equals to zero and the proof can be completed in the same way as in the classical case.

If $\rho = I/\mathrm{dim}H$, then all states of the world are equally possible. Thus, for all agents, the a priori state of the world was gained in the total absence of information about the world. In this case these agents have to come to the same posteriors (if their posteriors are common knowledge), though they may base their posteriors on different information: the information partitions of unity, see (1), can be incompatible, i.e., the projectors $(P_j^{(i)})$ need not commute with the projectors $(P_j^{(s)})$.

We remark that, although in the rigorous mathematical framework a density operator cannot be scaling of the unit operator, formally one can operate with such "generalized density operators", see von Neumann [34]. Thus formally Proposition 2 can be generalized to infinite-dimensional state spaces.

In fact, Proposition 2 is a special case of a more general statement which will be soon formulated. However, we started with Proposition 2, since it has the very clear interpretation. The interpretation of the following statement is not straightforward:

Theorem 1. *Let the common a priori state ρ commutes with the elements of all partitions, i.e., for $i = 1, ..., N$,*

$$[\rho, P_j^{(i)}] = 0 \tag{16}$$

for any j. If condition (14) holds, then $q^{(1)} = ... = q^{(N)}$.

Here we again see that the interference term in (15) equals to zero.

As was mentioned, the interpretation of the basic condition of this theorem is not straightforward. In quantum mechanics, commutativity of observables is interpreted as the condition of joint measuring. However, commutativity of an observable and a quantum state has no direct interpretation.

Lemma 3. *Let ρ have non-degenerate spectrum and let the condition (16) holds. Then the partitions $(P_j^{(1)}), ...(, P_j^{(N)})$ are compatible, i.e., $[P_j^{(i)}, P_m^{(s)}] = 0$ for any pair j, m and i, s.*

Proof. Suppose that ρ has non-degenerate spectrum, i.e., $\rho = \sum_k p_k P_{e_k}$, where $p_k \neq p_m, k \neq m$, and (e_k) is the orthonormal basis consisting of eigenvectors of ρ. Then, for any orthogonal projector P, the condition $[P, \rho] = 0$ implies that there exists a set of indexes O_P such that $P = \sum_{m \in O_P} P_{e_m}$. This is easy to show. We have $\rho P = P\rho$, i.e., for any pair of basis vectors e_t, e_s, we have, on one hand, $\langle e_t | \rho P | e_s \rangle = p_t \langle e_t | P | e_s \rangle$ and, on the other hand $\langle e_t | P\rho | e_s \rangle = p_s \langle e_t | P | e_s \rangle$. Hence, for $t \neq s$, $\langle e_t | P | e_s \rangle = 0$. Thus $P | e_s \rangle = a_s | e_s \rangle$, where $a = 0, 1$. Set $O_P = \{s : a_s = 1\}$. For the projectors $P_j^{(i)}$, such sets will be denoted as $O_j^{(i)}$.

Thus in the non-degenerate case the condition (16) implies that $P_j^{(i)} = \sum_{k \in O_j^{(i)}} P_{e_k}$. Then $P_j^{(i)} P_m^{(s)} = \sum_{k \in O_j^{(i)} \cap O_m^{(s)}} P_{e_k} = P_m^{(s)} P_j^{(i)}$. Thus the (quantum) information partitions are compatible.

However, if the spectrum of the state ρ is degenerate, then the condition (16) does not imply compatibility of partitions of two agents (see Proposition 2).

Corollary 1. *Even in the case of incompatible (quantum) information partitions, it is possible to find such common a priori (quantum) states that it is impossible to agree on disagreeing.*

4   Conclusion

Agents representing and processing information in the quantum(-like) manner can agree on disagree. Thus our quantum(-like) model of probability update in the presence of common knowledge matches better with the real situation.

Typically in classical analysis of sources of violations of the Aumann theorem (and it is often violated in reality) the common a priori probability distribution and the presence of common knowledge are pointed as questionable assumptions in Aumann's argumentation. We show that the validity of these assumptions does not prevent from the possibility that agents agree on disagree.

The main conclusion is that agents can simply use more general rules for processing of information and probability than given by the classical set-measure-theoretic model based on the Kolmogorov axiomatics of probability theory. And this model has its own restricted domain of applications, as any mathematical model, cf. with the Euclidean model of geometry, and departure from it given by Lobachevsky geometry (which plays an important role in special relativity theory).

Acknowledgments. The authors would like to thank J. Acacio de Barros, H. Atmanspacher, J. Busemeyer, E. N. Dzhafarov, E. Haven, E. M. Pothos, for discussions on quantum probabilistic modeling of cognitive phenomena and especially decision making and probability update.

Appendix 1: Biased Decision Making and Violation of the Aumann Theorem

An important source of possible violation of the Aumann theorem is the presence of various biases in the "heads of agents". Roughly speaking any bias may destroy the purity of the Bayesian update.

As a widely discussed example of the anti-Aumann bias, we consider the so called SSA-bias. A *Self Sampling Assumption* (SSA) says you are more likely to be present in worlds where a greater proportion of agents which are like you, see N. Bostrom for the detailed discussion on SSA [35]. Except that "agents" can be any set of things you could have been in some sense, even if you currently know you are not some of them. This group is called a *reference class.* Agents basing their reasoning on the SSA and having different reference classes need not come to the same posterior probabilities, even if the assumptions of the Aumann theorem, about the common prior and common knowledge, hold true. And this is clear why. Such an agent can ignore some of her/his information in forming her/his reference classe, since it asks for the proportion of her/his reference class of whom all of her/his information is true. This can lead to simple ignorance of a part of information presented in common knowledge. It is often argued that the decision making based on the selection of an appropriate reference class is irrational. And we agree with such evaluation of the SSA decision makers. However, we do not assign negative valuation to "irrationality" in the decision making.

As was demonstrated in [35], the SSA-operating is quite common phenomenon. Since this happens and happens in many contexts, such a behavior of agents has to be modeled mathematically. And if in the classical probabilistic framework this is impossible (as signed in the violation of the Aumann theorem which is heavily based on Kolmogorov probability), then it is natural to explore other probabilistic models, e.g., quantum probability. In this short note we are not able to discuss quantum modeling of SSA in more details, it will be done in one of further articles. We finish this discussion on SSA with the following remark on the interpretation of the wave function, quantum state. The SSA approach to decision making matches well with the many world interpretation of the quantum state. A SSA-agent position her/him self as belonging to a few possible reference classes, which play here the roles of the worlds.

Appendix 2: On the Logical Structure of the Aumann Argument

As ia well known, he Aumann argument on the impossibility of agree on disagree is based on the special systems of axioms of the modal logic, the system S5. And, of course, any deviation from this system might lead to a violation of the classical Aumann theorem. In this paper it was shown that the usage of quantum logic can generate a possibility to agree on disagree. This is a good place to point out that our emphasize on similarity between the classical (S5) and quantum knowledge operators is a bit provocative, since this similarity is only formal, operational, and from the logical viewpoint these are very different representations of knowledge.

In fact, understanding of "what quantum logic is from semantic viewpoint" is a complex problem by itself, see, e.g., works of Garola [36] and of Garola and Sozzo [37] and the recent paper of Khrennikov and Schumann [38] for details. One of still debated problems is whether one can really assign to propositions a special "quantum truth" value or it is even possible to proceed with the classical truth value. In [38] it was motivated that the essence of logical nonclassicality is the performative part of quantum mechanics and at the theoretical level one can still proceed with classical logic. Thus it was motivated that even in quantum physics logical nonclassicality is only due to the language representation. Such a discussion is helpful to come closer to understanding the following fundamental problem: whether quantumness is in the world or in the mind. It seems that the argument presented in [38] supports the latter, i.e., that violations of classical logic and "quantum logical effects" are generated by the performative structure used for the interpretation of some natural and mental phenomena.

In this context it may useful to use the scientific methodology in which any scientific representation has two level, the ontic level and the epistemic level, see, e.g., Atmanspacher and Primas [39]. In such an approach violation of classical logic happens at the level of epistemic description.

Appendix 3: Classical Formalization for the Aumann Argument

Aumann's considerations are applicable for a finite number of *agents*, call them $i = 1, 2, ..., N$. These individuals are about to learn the answers to various multi-choice *questions*, to make observations.

Mathematically the situation is represented with the aid of classical probability space (based on the Kolmogorov axiomatics, 1933). Typically it is assumed that the state space Ω representing all possible states of the world is finite. Events are subsets of Ω.

Each agent creates its information representation for possible states of the world based on its own possibilities to perform measurements, "to ask questions to the world." Mathematically these represesetations are given by partitions of $\Omega : \mathcal{P}^{(i)} = (P_j^{(i)})$, where $\cup_j P_j^{(i)} = \Omega$ and $P_j^{(i)} \cap P_k^{(i)} \emptyset, j \neq k$. Thus an agent cannot get to know the state of the world ω precisely; she can only get to know to which element of its information partition $P_j^{(i)} = P_j^{(i)}(\omega)$ this ω belongs. The agent i knows an event E in the state of the world ω if

$$P_j^{(i)}(\omega) \subset E. \tag{17}$$

It is assumed that on Ω there is defined probability p, *the common prior* of all agents. In the accordance with the measure-theoretic model of probability theory (Kolmogorov, 1933) there is given a σ-algebra, say $\mathcal{F}$, of subsets of Ω, its elements represent events ("propositions" in some interpretations), and there is given a probability measure p defined on $\mathcal{F}$. In the knowledge models it is typically assumed that $\mathcal{F}$ is generated by agents' partitions, i.e., this is the minimal σ-algebra containing all systems of set $\mathcal{P}^{(i)}, i = 1, ..., N$.

We consider the systems of sets $\tilde{\mathcal{P}}^{(i)} = \{\cup_m P_{j_m}^{(i)}\}$ consisting of finite unions of the elements of the systems $\mathcal{P}^{(i)}$ and the system $\tilde{\mathcal{P}} = \cap_i \tilde{\mathcal{P}}^{(i)}$. We recall that the *meet* of the partitions $\mathcal{P}^{(i)}$, denoted by the symbol $\wedge_i \mathcal{P}^{(i)}$, is the *finest common coarsening* of $\mathcal{P}^{(i)}$. In particular, $\wedge_i \mathcal{P}^{(i)} \subset \tilde{\mathcal{P}}$.

As was proven in [29], *an event E is common knowledge at ω if E contains that element of $\mathcal{P}^{(1)} \wedge \mathcal{P}^{(2)}$ (the meet) containing ω*. (See footnote 3 on the definition of common knowledge.)

This result implies that, for each i, the set of all states of the world for which E is common knowledge, denoted by the symbol κE, can be represented (in the case $\kappa E \neq \emptyset$) in the form:

$$\kappa E = \cup_m P_{j_m}^{(i)}. \tag{18}$$

References

1. Khrennikov, A.: Information Dynamics in Cognitive, Psychological, Social, and Anomalous Phenomena. Ser.: Fundamental Theories of Physics. Kluwer, Dordreht (2004)

2. Khrennikov, A.: Ubiquitous Quantum Structure: from Psychology to Finances. Springer, Berlin (2010)
3. Busemeyer, J.R., Bruza, P.D.: Quantum Models of Cognition and Decision. Cambridge Press, Cambridge (2012)
4. Haven, E., Khrennikov, A.: Quantum Social Science. Cambridge Press, Cambridge (2013)
5. Khrennikov, A.: On quantum-like probabilistic structure of mental information. Open Syst. Inf. Dyn. **11**(3), 267–275 (2004)
6. Busemeyer, J.R., Wang, Z., Townsend, J.T.: Quantum dynamics of human decision making. J. Math. Psychol. **50**, 220–241 (2006)
7. Khrennikov, A.: Quantum-like formalism for cognitive measurements. Biosystems **70**, 211–233 (2003)
8. Khrennikov, A.: Quantum-like brain: interference of minds. BioSystems **84**, 225–241 (2006)
9. Conte, E., Todarello, O., Federici, A., Vitiello, F., Lopane, M., Khrennikov, A., Zbilut, J.P.: Some remarks on an experiment suggesting quantum-like behavior of cognitive entities and formulation of an abstract quantum mechanical formalism to describe cognitive entity and its dynamics. Chaos Solitons Fractals **31**(5), 1076–1088 (2007)
10. Busemeyer, J.R., Santuy, E., Lambert-Mogiliansky, E.: Comparison of Markov and quantum models of decision making. In: Bruza, P., Lawless, W., van Rijsbergen, K., Sofge, D.A., Coeke, B., Clark, S. (eds.) Quantum interaction: Proceedings of the Second Quantum Interaction Symposium, pp. 68–74. College Publications, London (2008)
11. Conte, E., Khrennikov, A., Todarello, O., Federici, A., Mendolicchio, L., Zbilut, J.P.: Mental state follow quantum mechanics during perception and cognition of ambiguous figures. Open Syst. Inf. Dyn. **16**, 1–17 (2009)
12. Conte, E., Khrennikov, A., Todarello, O., Federici, A., Mendolicchio, L., Zbilut, J.P.: A pre-liminary experimental verification on the possibility of bell inequality violation in mental states. NeuroQuantology **6**(3), 214–221 (2008)
13. Busemeyer, J.R., Wang, Z., Lambert-Mogiliansky, A.: Empirical comparison of Markov and quantum models of decision making. J. Math. Psychol. **53**(5), 423–433 (2009)
14. de Barros, A.J., Suppes, P.: Quantum mechanics, interference, and the brain. J. Math Psychol. **53**, 306–313 (2009)
15. Lambert-Mogiliansky, A., Zamir, S., Zwirn, H.: Type indeterminacy: a model of the KT (Kahneman-Tversky)-man. J. Math. Psychol. **53**(5), 349–361 (2009)
16. Pothos, E.M., Busemeyer, J.R.: A quantum probability explanation for violation of rational decision theory. Proc. Royal. Soc. B **276**, 2171–2178 (2009)
17. Haven, E., Khrennikov, A.: Quantum mechanics and violation of the sure-thing principle: the use of probability interference and other concepts. J. Math. Psychol. **53**, 378–388 (2009)
18. Trueblood, J.S., Busemeyer, J.R.: A quantum probability account of order effects in inference. Cogn. Sci. **35**, 1518–1552 (2011)
19. Asano, M., Ohya, M., Tanaka, Y., Khrennikov, A., Basieva, I.: On application of Gorini-Kossakowski-Sudarshan-Lindblad equation in cognitive psychology. Open Syst. Inf. Dyn. **18**, 55–69 (2011)
20. Asano, M., Ohya, M., Tanaka, Y., Khrennikov, A., Basieva, I.: Dynamics of entropy in quantum-like model of decision making. J. Theor. Biol. **281**, 56–64 (2011)

21. Dzhafarov, E.N., Kujala, J.V.: Quantum entanglement and the issue of selective influences in psychology: an overview. Lect. Notes Comput. Sci. **7620**, 184–195 (2012)
22. Aerts, D., Sozzo, S., Tapia, J.: A quantum model for the Elsberg and Machina paradoxes. Lect. Notes Comput. Sci. **7620**, 48–59 (2012)
23. Atmanspacher, H., Filk, T.: Contra classical causality: violating temporal Bell inequalities in mental systems. J. Conscious. Stud. **19**(5/6), 95–116 (2012)
24. Atmanspacher, H., Römer, H.: Order effects in sequential measurements of noncommuting psychological observables. J. Math. Psychol. **56**, 274–280 (2012)
25. Asano, M., Basieva, I., Khrennikov, A., Ohya, M., Tanaka, Y.: Quantum-like generalization of the Bayesian updating scheme for objective and subjective mental uncertainties. J. Math. Psychol. **56**, 166–175 (2012)
26. Khrennikova, P.: Evolution of quantum-like modeling in decision making processes. aip conf. proc. **1508**, 108 (2012)
27. Asano, M., Basieva, I., Khrennikov, A., Ohya, M., Yamato, I.: Non-kolmogorovian approach to the context-dependent systems breaking the classical probability law. Found. Phys. **43**, 2083–2099 (2013)
28. Khrennikova, P.: A quantum framework for 'sour grapes' in cognitive dissonance. In: Proceedings of Quantum Interaction-13, University of Leicester Press (2013)
29. Aumann, R.J.: Agreeing on disagree. Ann. Stat. **4**, 1236–1239 (1976)
30. Aumann, R.J.: Backward induction and common knowledge of rationality. Game. Econ. Behav. **8**, 619 (1995)
31. Vanderschraaf, P., Sillari, G.: Common Knowledge. In: Zalta, E.N. (ed.) The Stanford Encyclopedia of Philosophy. Continuum Press, New York (2013). http://plato.stanford.edu/archives/fall2013/entries/common-knowledge
32. Birkhoff, J., von Neumann, J.: The logic of quantum mechanics. Ann. Math. **37**, 823–843 (1936)
33. Feynman, R., Hibbs, A.: Quantum Mechanics and Path Integrals. McGraw-Hill, New York (1965)
34. Von Neuman, J.: Mathematical Foundations of Quantum Mechanics. Princeton University Press, Princeton (1955)
35. Bostrom, N.: Anthropic Bias: Observation Selection Effects in Science and Philosophy (Studies in Philosophy). Routledge Publ, New York (2010)
36. Garola, C.: A Pragmatic Interpretation of Quantum Logic. Preprint arXiv:quant-ph/0507122v2
37. Garola, C., Sozzo, S.: Recovering nonstandard logics within an extended classical framework. Erkenntnis **78**, 399–419 (2013)
38. Khrennikov, A., Schumann, A.: Quantum Non-objectivity from Performativity of Quantum Phenomena. arXiv:1404.7077 [physics.gen-ph]. To be published in Physica Scripta
39. Atmanspacher, H., Primas, H.: Epistemic and ontic quantum realities. In: Adenier, G., Khrennikov, A. (eds.), Foundations of Probability and Physics-3, Conf. Proc. Ser. vol. 750, pp. 49–62. AIP, Melville, NY (2005)

Modelling Attitudes to Climate Change — An Order Effect and a Test Between Alternatives

Kirsty Kitto[1]([✉]), Luke Sonnenburg[1,2,3], Fabio Boschetti[2,3], and Iain Walker[2]

[1] Queensland University of Technology, Brisbane 4000, Australia
kirsty.kitto@qut.edu.au
[2] Commonwealth Scientific and Industrial Research Organisation (CSIRO),
Floreat, Australia
[3] The University of Western Australia, Wembley 6913, Australia

Abstract. Quantum-like models can be fruitfully used to model attitude change in a social context. Next steps require data, and higher dimensional models. Here, we discuss an exploratory study that demonstrates an order effect when three question sets about *Climate Beliefs*, *Political Affiliation* and *Attitudes Towards Science* are presented in different orders within a larger study of $n = 533$ subjects. A quantum-like model seems possible, and we propose a new experiment which could be used to test between three possible models for this scenario.

Keywords: Attitude models · Quantum decision theory · Order effect

1 Modelling Attitude Change in a Social Context

How do the attitudes of a population vary according to its social makeup? Understanding the manner in which the social context of an individual will influence their attitudes is a difficult problem, but highly important. Privately held attitudes play a critical role in people's personal choices about their health, education, social groups, and housing, as well as the importance they attribute to national issues such as the environment, immigration and state security [1].

However, the way in which people express their attitudes is highly contextual. How will a given person think about 'global warming' vs 'climate change'? What if their daughter has just had her house flooded? Or if they are about to make a very large tax payment that includes a carbon component? People's attitudes are not static immutable objects, but change in response to persuasion [2], and attempts to maintain cognitive consistency [3]. We often express different attitudes in accordance with the social context we find ourselves in [4], and it is frequently the case that an explicitly expressed attitude is quite different from an internally held one [5]. As a further complication, many factors beyond the social setting itself are involved, from worldviews and cognitive styles [6–8], through to more traditionally studied factors such as education and demographics.

© Springer International Publishing Switzerland 2015
H. Atmanspacher et al. (Eds.): QI 2014, LNCS 8951, pp. 119–131, 2015.
DOI: 10.1007/978-3-319-15931-7_10

This complexity makes attitude change and opinion formation very difficult to model. While dual process models exist (such as the Elaboration Likelyhood Model (ELM) [9]; and the Heuristic-Systematic Model (HSM) [10]), this paper demonstrates a *framing effect* [11] which such models struggle to explain.

In the following section we will briefly introduce a model of attitude change that has been developed by two of us (Kitto & Boschetti) which uses a quantum-like approach. This model shows promise of unifying a number of cognitive variables into one consistent model of attitude change. Testing this model will require datasets which combine a number of variables which are not traditionally collected together, and for this reason, Sect. 2 will introduce some preliminary results from an extensive survey recently collected in the Australian context. We will show that there is evidence to believe that a weak order effect is at work when subjects are asked about their attitudes to science, politics and climate change. This leads us to propose an experimental scenario which could test between a collection of classical, quantum and quantum-like models.

1.1   A Quantum-Like Model of Attitude Change

A recent set of papers by the authors [12–14] have proposed a quantum-like model of attitude change, which allows for a natural explanation of framing effects. More details can be found in those papers, but in brief, this model makes use of the following key concepts.

The *cognitive state* $|A\rangle$ of an agent A is represented as a vector in a Hilbert space. This state is an objective feature of the model (i.e. it is a representation of how the agent currently thinks) but it cannot be objectively recovered (i.e. it can only be measured within a social context, or *framing* of an issue).

The *framing* of a social issue is represented by the choice of orthonormal basis states (e.g. $\{|0\rangle_p, |1\rangle_p\}$) which mathematically represent the cognitive state in that context. Within the particular frame (represented by p) used to denote an issue under consideration by the agent A, the state $|1\rangle_p$ denotes a case where the agent is in complete agreement with that interpretation of the issue, and $|0\rangle_p$ the case where they completely disagree. The current model utilises two types of frame; a *local* frame which represents the way an agent understands the issue under consideration, and *global* frames, which represent the combined attitudes of a particular social group (currently generated using a k-means style clustering algorithm [14]).

The *personality* of individual agents is modelled using two parameters which specify the psychological need that an agent A feels for *cognitive consistency*, $0 < w_i(A) < 1$, (i.e. making decisions that are highly correlated, or consistent, with their current cognitive state) and *social cohesion*, $0 < w_s(A) < 1$, (i.e. a bias towards making decisions that are similar to those of the social group to which A currently belongs, allowing A to 'fit in' with their current social context). These weights can range over a population of agents, providing a rough social parameterisation, and should match data about the society under consideration in the model. Thus, a society that values social conformity is likely to have more agents with a high $w_s(A)$ value, and one which values individualism would consist of more agents with a high $w_i(A)$, but other scenarios can be imagined. The model then considers the orientation of each agent's local frame to result from an attempt to navigate these two different drives, which may prove to compete with one another in the mind of the agent. Far more details about these parameters are provided in [13], but it is important to realise that they are not fixed. Introducing more frames will require more parameters (in order to model the time dynamics as they are introduced in (2)), and which ones to use must be a modelling decision. Is the model aiming to describe group cohesion vs individualism? In this case the above two parameters would be a logical choice. However, in a model that was aiming to describe attitudes to work then it might be more appropriate to use personality variables derivative from the "big-5" [15], or even something else.

Cognitive dissonance [3] suggests that agents who make decisions that are very different from their current cognitive states will experience a feeling of discomfort which may cause them to alter their cognitive state. We make use of *Binary entropy*, $H(P) \equiv -P\log_2 P - (1-P)\log_2(1-P)$, as a measure of this discomfort, where P is the probability of an agent making a decision given their current cognitive state and the context in which they are currently making that decision. Agents have a propensity (dependent upon their personality parameters) to align their cognitive states towards their current framing of a problem. Thus, agents are driven to update their cognitive state to align more closely with their decisions if they have a high consistency, and to update their individual framing of a problem to a closer alignment with the global frame to which they currently identify if they have a high need for social cohesion. Defining Θ as the angle between the agent's current state $|A\rangle$, and the $|1\rangle$ axis in their current global context, and θ as performing a similar function in their local frame, allows for the specification of an entropy measure for each agent [14]

$$H(|A\rangle, \theta, \Theta) = w_i(A)H_b(P(\theta)) + w_s(A)H_b(P(\Theta)). \tag{1}$$

Depending upon the social dynamics to be described the system is then updated in time, with agents making decisions, and then updating their cognitive states and individual framings of an issue to reflect the decisions made, their social context, and their personality variables [14].

If the decision was in the local frame, then only the cognitive state of the agent is updated (within the local frame). Thus, an agent who has made a decision within a certain framing of a problem will shift their state towards the decision ('yes' or 'no', represented by $|1\rangle_p$ and $|0\rangle_p$ respectively) that they made in the context (denoted by p). The size of this shift is defined as dependent upon two factors: (1) the personality profile of the agent (given in this case as w_i, as it represents the desire of an agent to align their cognitive state with their local frame); (2) the angle θ. Writing θ_0 for the angle between the agent's state and the $|0_p\rangle$ axis, and θ_1 for the angle between their state and the $|1_p\rangle$ axis, the new angle between the agent's state and the frame will become:

$$\text{if } A \text{ decides } \begin{cases} \text{to act: } \theta_1(|A\rangle_{t+1}, w(A)) = \theta_1(|A_t\rangle) \times w(A) \\ \text{not to act: } \theta_0(|A\rangle_{t+1}, w(A)) = \theta_0(|A_t\rangle) \times w(A) \end{cases} \tag{2}$$

where $w(A)$ depends upon the comfort of A with holding an attitude that is dissonant from their decision. Thus, for this update process $w(A) = w_i(A)$. Agents who make a decision that agrees with the attitude expressed in that frame will thus experience a rotation of their cognitive state by a certain distance dependent upon their personality towards the $|1_p\rangle$ axis (recall that θ is the distance between the $|1_p\rangle$ axis and the current state of the agent $|A\rangle$), and agents who disagree with that attitude will experience a rotation of their cognitive state in the opposite direction.

If the decision was made in the global frame, then both the cognitive state of the agent and their local frame are updated (with reference to their global frame). Thus, in addition to the update of the cognitive state that is represented in Eq. (2), the local frame of the agent will shift towards the global axis that represents the decision made by the agent. The amount by which the local frame shifts is given by an equivalent version of Eq. (2), thus the new angle between the local frame and the global frame is given by (2), but with $w(A) = w_s(A)$.

Over time, we expect the agents to self-organise towards a scenario where they are highly aligned within groups who all hold similar ideologies (or global frames). This process can be measured by the total entropy of the system, given by a summation of each agent's individual entropy

$$H = \sum_{i=1}^{N} H(|i\rangle, \theta_i, \Theta_i). \tag{3}$$

1.2 Alternative Quantum Inspired Models

We note that a few other models exist which could be used to model the same complex social scenarios. One example is a dynamic update semantics which uses non-commutative logics to describe changes in epistemic states in a society of agents [16–19]. These models take a formal approach to quantum logic, and so can be classified as pure classical and/or quantum models. Similarly, standard Quantum Decision Theory [20] can also be adapted to the modelling of attitude change. In Sect. 3 we will consider the QQ-model due to Wang & Busemeyer [21] which like all of these models precisely matches standard quantum time evolution. This model provides a very strong test which must be satisfied by any quantum inspired model which matches the standard quantum axioms. This will lead us to the possibility of testing between classical, quantum, and the weaker quantum-like model presented above.

2   Attitudes to Climate Change, Science and Politics

Understanding how such a model will work in a realistic setting requires an extensive data set. We must be able to connect personality data with a Hilbert space representation of attitudes, and to then find a way in which to connect this space to measurement outcomes. In particular, the way in which order of presentation might change expressed attitudes must be studied, as this would start to provide an indication as to what the topology of attitude space might be. For example, should we expect the cognitive state of an individual to lie in one large n-dimensional Hilbert space? Or should attitudes lie in a set of incompatible subspaces and so exhibit order effects? Perhaps the spaces are more than incompatible, and cannot be framed in the same space at all? (As for example the momentum of an electron and its spin are modelled in two different Hilbert spaces.)

Many possible scenarios could be examined, but some have been attracting more interest than others of late, and so already have extensive datasets available. For example, the complex nexus of climate belief and worldviews has attracted considerable interest in recent years [6, 7, 22], and provides an interesting link between many variables that could prove useful to testing and extending this model. Of particular interest to the current model, a set of results have been obtained demonstrating a strong link between attitudes to climate change and the expressed worldview of a subject [7]. According to this *cultural cognition thesis*, personality types that can be classified as egalitarian and communitarian tend to worry about environmental risks such as climate change, while individualists tend to reject such claims of environmental risk (worrying instead about too much governmental control). Due to the current imperative to understand the attitudes of populations to climate change a large amount of data is being generated, and so many opportunities exist to create new models of attitude change in this setting. Here, we will discuss one recent survey which explored the attitudes held by the Australian public towards Climate Change, Science, and Politics. This section will introduce one particular result from that study, as it seems to hold promise for exhibiting quantum-like effects. Later sections will make explicit predictions about what a secondary follow up study would find.

2.1 An Australian 2013 Election Survey

The survey used was adapted from one that was originally developed to study attitudes towards environmental issues in the general public with the intention of helping scientists to better design communication and engagement processes [6]. That paper reports upon the full set of scales probing cognitive styles, political ideologies, worldviews and environmental attitudes etc. that were explored in the survey. The surveys were run at three different times: (a) in 2011, (b) in 2013, a few weeks before the Australian General Election and (c) in 2013, a few weeks after the Australian General Election. The description and analysis of the 2011 survey can be found in [6], where each cognitive construct is described. A full analysis of the 2013 surveys is currently under way. In order to explore the ways in which framing a question might affect the resultant attitudes, the 2013 surveys were administered in 4 different orders of presentation.

Climate Beliefs: This question asked respondents "What best describes your thoughts about climate change?" with possible choices: "I don't think that climate change is happening", "I have no idea whether climate change is happening or not", "I think that climate change is happening, but it's a natural fluctuation in Earth's temperatures", "I think it is happening and I think that humans are largely causing it". This question is taken from [22], where a record of responses over the last 4 years is discussed. Two other questions were also added to this section the survey in an attempt to gain further insight into the responses obtained: (1) "How important is the issue of climate change to you?" and (2) "How certain are you of your own position on climate change?" with responses ranging through {Very Unimportant, Moderately Important, Important, Important, Very Important} and {Extremely Uncertain, Uncertain, Moderately Certain, Certain, Extremely Certain} respectively.

Political Affiliation: "On the following scale, please indicate how you identify your political views" with choices: {Very liberal, Moderately liberal, Neither liberal nor conservative, Moderately conservative, Very conservative}.

Attitudes Towards Science: This is a construct of 5 questions with {Strongly disagree, Disagree, Neutral, Agree, Strongly agree} as available choices. The 5 questions in the construct were: (1) I strongly believe in science. (2) I believe science can provide solutions to environmental problems. (3) I do not believe science can provide solutions to social problems. (4) Science has caused more problems than it has resolved. (5) I am reluctant to use technology (including computers and models) to address complex natural and social problems.

While six different orders of presentation are possible for three sets of questions, it was decided that concentrating on just four orders provided the best compromise between increasing the size of the subject pools for each order, and exploring a variety of different possibilities:

Order A: {Climate Beliefs, Attitudes Towards Science, Political Affiliation},
Order B: {Attitudes Towards Science, Climate Beliefs, Political Affiliation},
Order C: {Political Affiliation, Attitudes Towards Science, Climate Beliefs},
Order D: {Attitudes Towards Science, Political Affiliation, Climate Beliefs}.

Participants were recruited nationally within Australia using an on-line research only internet panel, administered by ORU, an online fieldwork company with QSOAP 'Gold Standard' and the new Global ISO 26362 standard accreditation. The online panel consisted of a group of community members who have explicitly agreed to take part in web-based surveys from time to time. In return they were offered a small non-cash incentives for completing the task, such as points towards shopping credits. The selection process utilised by ORU guarantees a sample that is strongly representative of the Australian population.

2.2 An Order Dependency for Climate Change Belief

All data analysis was performed using the R statistical environment [23]. The total number of respondents was 533, with $A_n = 148$ (27.7%), $B_n = 131$ (24.6%), $C_n = 132$ (24.8%), $D_n = 122$ (22.9%), as the breakdown into the various order categories. ORU split the demographics of the pools evenly across the four different orderings as far as was possible. Table 1 also compares the responses to the

Climate Beliefs question with the fourth CSIRO national survey [22], and shows that the sampled respondents are generally representative of the larger Australian population, although with a slight bias away from the "I don't think that climate change is happening" response and towards "I have no idea whether climate change is happening or not".

Table 1. The contingency table for the question: *What best describes your thoughts about climate change?* showing order of presentation in columns, response obtained across rows, and Pearson residuals listed underneath in parentheses. The last two columns compare responses to the Climate Beliefs question in the current study with the fourth CSIRO national survey of Australian attitudes to Climate Change [22].

Climate change is:	A	B	C	D	Total	Study	CSIRO
Not happening	8	10	2	0	20	3.8 %	7.6 %
	(1.04)	(2.29)	(−1.33)	(−2.14)			
I don't know	15	12	10	13	50	9.4 %	6.3 %
	(0.30)	(−0.08)	(−0.68)	(0.46)			
Happening but natural	60	53	47	43	203	38.1 %	38.8 %
	(0.48)	(0.44)	(−0.46)	(−0.51)			
Happening & human caused	65	56	73	66	260	48.8 %	47.3 %
	(−0.85)	(−0.99)	(1.07)	(0.84)			
Total	148	131	132	122	533	(n = 533)	(n = 5219)

Questions exhibiting order dependencies were found using chi-square tests of independence (*Climate Beliefs, Political Affiliation,* and *Attitudes to Science*). Each separate test of independence involved the four orders and the relevant response category variables. Three significant chi-square results were obtained: two in the *Climate Beliefs* scale: "What best describes your thoughts about climate change?" ($\chi^2(9, N = 533) = 17.89$, p = 0.036, Cramers's V = .105) and "How important is the issue of climate change to you?" ($\chi^2(12, N = 533) = 22.23$, p = 0.035, Cramer's V = .118); as well as one question in the *Attitudes towards science* scale: "I do not believe science can provide solutions to social problems" ($\chi^2(12, N = 533) = 21.07$, p = 0.049, Cramer's V = .115).

Fully understanding these significant rejections of independence is difficult, as many factors are involved. However, considering the dominant residuals reveals a very interesting pattern. Firstly, we note that a strong contribution to the significant χ^2 values comes from the people who express the view that climate change is not happening. Indeed, the top row of Table 1 is responsible for 70.8 % of the obtained value, with a further 19.9 % arising from those who believe that climate change is happening and human caused. A disproportionate amount of the variance depends upon a comparatively small subset of the population (n = 20, or 3.8 %), and three of the order categories for this response had expected values just under 5 ($A_e = 5.55, B_e = 4.92, C_e = 4.95, D_e = 4.58$, note that this table still satisfies the standard assumption that 80 % or more of the expected counts should be larger than 5). This means that larger pool of denialists is required before we can feel confident in declaring that we have indeed found an order dependence for this question, however, paying careful attention to these two response categories reveals an interesting pattern of behaviour that is somewhat masked by the dominant effect of the top row. While orders A-B show a decrease from the expected value of climate 'believers', C-D show a slight increase in the same subset. A similar but reversed pattern occurs for those who do not believe that climate change is occurring. Reconsidering the question ordering reveals a significant difference between these two categories; in C-D the *Climate Beliefs* questions were asked last. Furthermore, turning our attention to the third row of Table 1 (which lists the responses of those who think that climate change is happening, but just a natural fluctuation of the Earth's temperatures), we see a set of residuals that exhibit the same $\{+, +, -, -\}$ signature, although of a much smaller magnitude. This suggests that a merger of both denialist positions (i.e. rows 1 and 3) could lead to a test for independence that was less dependent upon the extreme denialist position. This aggregation leads to a $\chi^2(6, N = 533) = 8.11$ which is not significant at the 5 % level (p = 0.230), however, the same $\{+, +, -, -\}$ signature persists across the residuals. The other two significant results did not yield this intriguing signature.

It appears that framing a question about whether a subject believes in climate change within a political *and* scientific context is having a weak impact upon the response obtained. This framing results in a shift of subject responses towards belief, with climate change 'denialists' less likely to deny, and 'believers' more likely to believe that anthropogenic climate change is happening. Interestingly, framing climate belief questions in just a scientific context appears to have the opposite impact (as exhibited by order group B).

We propose an interaction between the *Political Affiliation* and *Attitudes Towards Science* is required, which would, when the two sets of questions are combined, result in a slight bias towards belief in anthropogenic climate change. A higher dimensional version of the model discussed in Sect. 1.1 can describe this effect, but alternative approaches are possible.

One such alternative model is based upon Quantum Decision Theory (QDT) [20] and a recent refinement called the QQ model [21]. Both models predict that incompatibility between questions results when answering one question reframes the perspective from which a subject will view the next one. Thus, both models would predict that the space in which people make decisions about climate change expands in orders C-D, which moves them towards framing the question in a different way (and so sometimes giving a different response). The model proposed by Wang & Busemeyer [21] creates a very strong condition that must be satisfied by quantum models. However, as a pure quantum model, it is highly restrictive, and would rule out the time update proposed in Eq. (2) above. Unfortunately, this model also requires that questions be asked consecutively, with no intervening questions or information provided, which makes the application of this test to surveys such as that discussed in Sect. 2 difficult. In what follows we will briefly introduce the QQ model, before attempting to adapt the current survey to a form where it might be applied in a three way scenario that could eventually test between classical, pure quantum, and quantum-like models of attitude change.

3   An Quantum Approach: The QQ Model

Denoting the projector representing the probability of responding yes to question Q_A as $\mathbf{P}_{Ay}$ (similarly that of responding no as $\mathbf{P}_{An}$) allows for an examination of how different sets of questions affect a cognitive state in some larger attitude space (let us assume this is a Hilbert space). According to the QQ Model proposed by Wang & Busemeyer [21], a necessary condition for producing order effects in a full quantum model is that a set of questions (for now call them Q_A and Q_B) be non-commuting: $\mathbf{P}_{Ay}\mathbf{P}_{Bn} \neq \mathbf{P}_{Bn}\mathbf{P}_{Ay}$. This reflects the manner in which asking question Q_A creates a *comparative context* for further questions (in this case question Q_B). The first question (in this case Q_A) is denoted as a *non-comparative context*. This allows for the definition of the comparative context in which a question (say Q_B) was asked:

$$TP_{Q_B} - P(By) = 2 \cdot P(AyBy) - 2\theta_{AB}\sqrt{P(By)} \cdot \sqrt{P(Ay)}, \qquad (4)$$

where $P(\dots)$ is the probability of the given response (yes or no) to the question denoted (Q_A or Q_B), $TP_B = P(AyBy) + P(AnBy)$ is the probability of answering yes to question Q_B in the comparative context of question Q_A, and θ_{AB} is the *similarity* between the two questions as represented by their projections:

$$\theta_{AB} = \frac{P(AyBy) - TP_{Q_B} + P(By)}{2\sqrt{P(By)} \cdot \sqrt{P(Ay)}}. \qquad (5)$$

4   A Three-Way Scenario

The data from Table 1 suggests that a dual comparative context of *Attitudes to science* and *Political affiliation* shifts subjects towards a higher rate of belief in climate change, across both denialist and belief positions.

Wang & Busemeyer rightly claim that the QQ model makes strong predictions for a three question scenario [21]. For example, the similarity parameters for three consecutive questions A, B and C should satisfy a triangle equality:

$$\theta_{AB} + \theta_{BC} = \theta_{AC}. \qquad (6)$$

This is a very interesting requirement, and it allows for a strong test to see if a system is exhibiting the fully quantum behaviour predicted by the QQ model.

We propose that a strong test of whether the QQ model applies to attitude change (in particular attitudes to climate change) could be constructed by taking three questions from the above survey and asking them consecutively. We propose that three questions from the above survey have a high likelihood of revealing a significant order effect in the protocol required by the QQ model:

A: What best describes your thoughts about climate change?
B: Please indicate how you identify your political views.
C: I do not believe science can provide solutions to social problems.

If asking *A*, *B*, and *C* in the six possible orders reveals a significant order effect then applying the QQ model would enable a determination of whether this was due to quantum behaviour. Indeed, if the similarity measure between each of these questions satisfies (6) then this would be a very strong proof that the system was exhibiting the quantum behaviour expected by the QQ model, severely restricting the form of time evolution exhibited by this system.

However, it is important to realise that the quantum-like behaviour exhibited by the QQ model is of a purely quantum form, and that there is no *a priori* reason why this system might not violate classical probability (hence reveal quantum-like behaviour), but fail to satisfy the QQ model. Indeed, the time evolution model proposed in [14] (and briefly introduced in Sect. 1.1) is not of a standard quantum form, although it is unitary in nature [12]. We would not expect a system that exhibits this behaviour to satisfy the QQ model.

This allows for a compelling test to be performed that would allow for a determination of what type of mathematical model this system of attitudes actually satisfy. Thus, the experiment proposed above would provide a straightforward way of determining whether the system of interrelating attitudes exemplified by climate change belief, attitudes towards science, and political affiliation is quantum, quantum-like or classical in nature.

4.1 Limitations of the QQ Model

While the QQ model provides a very powerful battery of tests that can be used to determine whether a system is exhibiting quantum behaviour, it does face some limitations. Firstly, and perhaps most pertinent to the present study, it is not particularly relevant to general survey scenarios. These usually consist of scales with multiple questions, and multiple responses, and so a direct application of the QQ model is generally not possible for such real world scenarios. Secondly, satisfaction of the QQ model requires that the system under consideration exhibit what we might term exact quantum behaviour. This is a very strong requirement, and many quantum-like models have been proposed in the QI community that do not have such a pure quantum form. The attitude model discussed above is just one such example, but Khrennikov also proposes models unlikely to satisfy this requirement (see e.g. [24]). A further battery of tests needs to be created, and perhaps most usefully, we envisage a hierarchy of tests that could be applied to a system exhibiting contextual behaviour, with an associated classification of the system as quantum, quantum-like and classical. Finally, we note that even a fully quantum system might not satisfy the QQ model if the associated subspaces cannot be represented in one space (as is the case with momentum and spin in a standard quantum system). We anticipate that this is highly likely to occur in many complex contextual systems, and so it is important that the model only be applied in the correct circumstances.

5 Conclusions

Even small effects such as the one discussed in this paper could prove highly significant in the modern world (e.g. in a very close election that has a focus upon the issue of climate change). Politicians already know that governments rise or fall on their ability to sell highly emotive issues such as climate change within the 'right' context. Indeed, Australian elections since the mid-1970's have always been won by a margin[1] of less than 10 %, which means that an effect of the size reported here (slightly over 10 %) would prove significant for any election fought on the issue of climate change. We note that the last two Australian federal elections have indeed featured climate change policy as a key dividing issue between the two major parties, and this issue is likely to become more controversial as the effects of climate change become more severe. However, few techniques exist for analysing the way in which public issues are framed in public debates. This means that the signature discovered in the residuals analysis performed in Sect. 2.2 offers a intriguing statistical approach that merits further investigation in its own right.

It is essential that quantum inspired models become more applicable to real modelling problems. Many of the tests and models so far proposed have considered simple datasets with a small number of incompatible measurements, or toy models in low dimensional spaces. However, the rise of big data opens up many opportunities, and with a new battery of complex models and tests that can be applied to real world datasets and problems we would find many more opportunities to progress.

This paper has provided an initial discussion of a real world dataset that exhibits an interesting order effect. This exploratory data was collected in the hope that it could be used to prime a quantum-like model of attitude change in a social context, and indeed it provides a baseline step towards this goal. Attempting to understand the order effect obtained by performing a standard χ^2 analysis has left us with a proposal for a strong experimental test, which could determine if the time evolution that was exhibited by this system should be considered quantum (as is exemplified by the QQ model), quantum like, or classical in nature. Future work will be devoted to performing this experiment and analysing its results.

Acknowledgements. We thank Peter Bruza for his many contributions to early discussions about this work, and the possible use of the QQ model.

References

1. Petty, R.E., Wegener, D.T.: Attitude change: multiple roles for persuasion variables. In: Gilbert, D., Fiske, S., Lindzey, G. (eds.) The Handbook of Social Psychology, pp. 323–390. McGraw-Hill, New York (1998)

---

[1] See http://en.wikipedia.org/wiki/List_of_Australian_federal_elections for the actual margins.

2. Seiter, R.H., Gass, J.S.: Persuasion, Social Influence, and Compliance Gaining, 4th edn. Allyn & Bacon, Boston (2010)
3. Cooper, J.: Cognitive Dissonance: 50 Years of a Classic Theory. Sage, Thousand Oaks (2007)
4. Bond, R., Smith, P.B.: Culture and conformity. Psychol. Bull. **119**, 111–137 (1996)
5. Greenwald, A.G., Banaji, M.R.: Implicit social cognition: attitudes, self-esteem, and stereotypes. Psychol. Rev. **102**, 4–27 (1995)
6. Boschetti, F., Richert, C., Walker, I., Price, J., Dutra, L.: Assessing attitudes and cognitive styles of stakeholders in environmental projects involving computer modelling. Ecol. Model. **247**, 98–111 (2012)
7. Kahan, D.M., Braman, D., Slovic, P., Gastil, J., Cohen, G.L.: The second national risk and culture study: making sense of - and making progress in - the American culture war of fact. Technical report, Yale Law School (2007). Public Law Working Paper No. 154. SSRN: http://ssrn.com/abstract=1017189 or http://dx.doi.org/10.2139/ssrn.1017189
8. Lewandowsky, S., Gignac, G.E., Oberauer, K.: The role of conspiracist ideation and worldviews in predicting rejection of science. PLOS ONE **8**, e75637 (2013)
9. Petty, R.E., Cacioppo, J.T.: Communication and Persuasion: Central and Peripheral Routes to Attitude Change. Springer, New York (1986)
10. Chaiken, S.M.: The heuristic model of persuasion. In: Zanna, P., Olson, J.M., Herman, C.P. (eds.) Social Influence: The Ontario Symposium, vol. 5, pp. 3–39. Erlbaum, Hillsdale (1987)
11. Tversky, A., Kahneman, D.: The framing of decisions and the psychology of choice. Science **211**(4481), 453–458 (1981)
12. Kitto, K., Boschetti, F., Bruza, P.: The quantum inspired modelling of changing attitudes and self-organising societies. In: Busemeyer, J.R., Dubois, F., Lambert-Mogiliansky, A., Melucci, M. (eds.) QI 2012. LNCS, vol. 7620, pp. 1–12. Springer, Heidelberg (2012)
13. Kitto, K., Boschetti, F.: The effects of personality in a social context. In: Knauff, M., Pauen, M., Sebanz, N., Wachsmuth, I. (eds.) Proceedings of the 35th Annual Conference of the Cognitive Science Society, pp. 2740–2745. Cognitive Science Society, Austin (2013)
14. Kitto, K., Boschetti, F.: Attitudes, ideologies and self-organisation: information load minimisation in multi-agent decision making. Adv. Complex Syst. **16**(2 & 3), 1350029 (2013)
15. Costa, P.T., McCrae, R.R.: Normal personality assessment in clinical practice: the neo personality inventory. Psychol. Assess. **4**(1), 5–13 (1992)
16. Gärdenfors, P.: Knowledge in Flux: Modeling the Dynamics of Epistemic States. MIT Press, Cambridge (1988)
17. Baltag, A., Smets, S.: Correlated knowledge: an epistemic-logic view on quantum entanglement. Int. J. Theor. Phys. **49**(12), 3005–3021 (2010)
18. Blutner, R.: Questions and answers in an orthoalgebraic approach. J. Logic Lang. Inform. **21**(3), 237–277 (2012)
19. Graben, P.B.: Order effects in dynamic semantics. Top. Cogn. Sci. **6**(1), 67–73 (2014)
20. Busemeyer, J., Bruza, P.: Quantum Models of Cognition and Decision. Cambridge University Press, Cambridge (2012)
21. Wang, Z., Busemeyer, J.R.: A quantum question order model supported by empirical tests of an a priori and precise prediction. Top. Cogn. Sci. **5**, 689–710 (2013)

22. Leviston, Z., Price, J., Malkin, S., McCrea, R.: Fourth annual survey of Australian attitudes to climate change: interim report. Technical report, CSIRO, Perth, Australia (2014)
23. R Development Core Team: R: A Language and Environment for Statistical Computing. R Foundation for Statistical Computing, Vienna, Austria (2008)
24. Khrennikov, A.Y.: Ubiquitous Quantum Structure. Springer, Heidelberg (2010)

Towards a Quantum Probability Theory
of Similarity Judgments

James M. Yearsley$^{(\boxtimes)}$, Emmanuel M. Pothos, James A. Hampton,
and Albert Barque Duran

Department of Psychology, City University London,
London EC1V 0HB, UK
james.yearsley.1@city.ac.uk

Abstract. We review recent progress in understanding similarity judgments in cognition by means of quantum probability theory (QP) models. We begin by outlining some features of similarity judgments that
have proven difficult to model by traditional approaches. We then briefly
present a model of similarity judgments based on QP, and show how it
can solve many of the problems faced by traditional approaches. Finally
we look at some areas where the quantum model is currently less satis-
factory, and discuss some open questions and areas for further work.

1 Introduction

1.1 Background

The study of similarity judgments is central to many branches of psychology (e.g.
Goldstone 1994; Pothos 2005), and this is one reason why the various attempts
to formalize similarity judgments have received much attention and debate (see
e.g. Goodman 1972). Another reason is that similarity is often assumed to correspond to some kind of measure of the 'distance' between concepts in psychological space. Any proposed similarity measure based on this concept must obey
various restrictions arising from the fact that (dis-)similarity functions as a metric on psychological space. For this reason models of similarity lend themselves
particularly well to empirical refutation, and this feature alone may explain some
of the popularity of this subject.

The classic demonstration of the failure of similarity judgments to respect the
restrictions one would expect of a metric is due to Tversky (1977). Two of the
empirical features of similarity judgments that Tversky reported are particularly
striking: The first is a lack of symmetry in certain similarity judgments, whilst
the second, dubbed the diagnosticity effect, is a particular type of contextuality.
We outline both effects below.

1.2 Asymmetry

A similarity judgment is often a directional comparison of one stimulus with
another; for example, how similar is A to B? Directionality can arise from the

© Springer International Publishing Switzerland 2015
H. Atmanspacher et al. (Eds.): QI 2014, LNCS 8951, pp. 132–145, 2015.
DOI: 10.1007/978-3-319-15931-7_11

syntax of the similarity comparison, when it is linguistically framed, but it is often a simple consequence of the fact that the relevant stimuli cannot be simultaneously presented. In the latter case, the temporal ordering of the stimuli imposes directionality structure in the similarity comparison. Whenever there is directionality in a similarity comparison, there is a potential for asymmetry.

Tversky (1977) asked participants to indicate their preference for one of two statements, e.g., '(North) Korea is similar to (Red) China' vs. 'China is similar to Korea'. Most participants preferred the former to the latter statement (this demonstration involved several other pairs of counties and was generalized to other kinds of stimuli). An important insight into why such asymmetries arise relates to an understanding of the similarity process as an interpretative one. Tversky's (1977) participants would know far less about Korea than China. Therefore, asserting that Korea is similar to China is like a process of attempting to understand the more limited representation of Korea in terms of the more extensive representation for China. China is like a cognitive reference point (cf. Rosch 1975) and the statement 'Korea is similar to China' can be considered as more informative or providing more potential for new inferences regarding Korea, on the basis of the more extensive knowledge about China (cf. Bowdle and Medin 2001). An important objective in providing a formal model of similarity asymmetries is exactly to understand how ideas like cognitive reference points or information flow may be modelled.

Most researchers accept Tversky's (1977) claim that the asymmetry in similarity judgments in the Korea, China example arises because of differences in the extent of knowledge between the two stimuli. But, asymmetries in similarity judgments can also arise in other ways. For example, Polk et al. (2002) identified asymmetries based on just differences in the frequency of occurrence of one of the compared stimuli (the highest similarity was observed when comparing the low frequency stimulus with the higher frequency one). Also, Rosch (1975) discussed asymmetries arising when comparing a less prototypical stimulus with a more prototypical one (similarity in this direction higher, than in the reverse direction). It is possible that some such asymmetries can be explained in the same way as asymmetries arising from differences in the amount of knowledge, since we may have more knowledge (in the form of a greater number of associations) for more prototypical stimuli. However, there may be other asymmetries which arise from purely perceptual properties and, in such cases, an approach based on extent of knowledge is inadequate.

It should hardly need mentioned that asymmetries are extremely difficult to reconcile with the idea of similarity-as-distance. Indeed symmetry is one of the basic assumptions of any metric function. It is however possible to modify the similarity measure to explicitly include terms that break the symmetry of similarity judgments, but these modifications have to be included by hand and are thus rather unsatisfactory. What would be preferable is some mechanism that can produce asymmetries in some circumstances in in a more natural way. We will see below that the QP approach provides such a mechanism.

1.3 Diagnosticity

Another of Tversky's (1977) seminal proposals is that of the diagnosticity effect. In a typical trial, participants were asked to identify the country most similar to Austria, from a set of alternatives including Hungary, Poland, and Sweden. Participants typically selected Sweden. However, when the alternatives were Hungary, Sweden, Norway, participants typically selected Hungary. Thus, the same similarity relation (e.g., the similarity between Sweden and Austria vs. Hungary and Austria) appears to depend on which other stimuli are immediately relevant, showing that the process of establishing a similarity judgment may depend on the presence of other stimuli, not directly involved in the judgment.

Analogous context effects also appear in decision making. Consider a choice between two options. According to the so-called similarity effect, introducing an option which is equally attractive to one of the existing ones leads to an increase in the probability of the dissimilar option (e.g., Trueblood et al., in press). The diagnosticity effect has been harder to replicate, even though Tversky (1977) did report alternative demonstrations, based on variations of the stimuli. His explanation was that the diagnosticity effect arises from the grouping of some of the options. For example, when Hungary and Poland are both included, their high similarity makes participants spontaneously code them with their obvious common feature (Eastern Europe), which, in turn, increases the similarity of the other two options, through the absence of this common feature (Austria and Sweden would become similar because they are neither in Eastern Europe, rather they are in Western Europe).

As with the case of asymmetries, the diagnosticity effect is difficult to square with the notion of similarity as a distance measure on psychological space. Note however that unlike asymmetries, the diagnosticity effect has proven hard to replicate. This may indicate either that the effect is fragile, or perhaps even that it is not a genuine effect but rather an artefact of the particular set up used by Tversky. We will return to this issue below.

1.4 Discussion

We have discussed two specific empirical challenges to the idea the similarity judgments can be thought of as measuring distance in some psychological space. Of course, there is nothing particularly surprising about this. It is highly improbable that information about concepts is stored and processed in the brain in a way that can be faithfully mapped onto a Euclidean 'concept space.' Thus by the same token it should hardly be surprising if similarity judgments between some concepts resist embedding in such a concept space. Nevertheless such models have proven surprisingly popular, perhaps in part because they provide a lucid account of the cognitive process that leads to a particular similarity judgment. That is, although the work of Tversky (1977) casts doubt on the adequacy of the concept of similarity-as-distance to provide an empirical description of similarity judgments, at least some of the reason for the popularity of the idea is due to the fact it provides a very compelling description of the process of these judgments.

One of the challenges for any alternative theory of similarity judgments is to provide a similarly compelling account of how these judgments arise from simple computations in some appropriate psychological space. We will see that the QP approach, although possessing some attractive features, still has room for improvement.

2   The Quantum Model of Similarity Judgments

In this section we will present an alternative model for similarity judgments based on Quantum Probability theory (QP). The use of QP for modelling these types of judgments follows on from a number of recent attempts to describe various phenomena in psychology, and the social sciences more generally, using non-classical models of probability. In brief, there is some consensus that certain types of probabilistic reasoning, in situations where there is not just uncertainty but also a form of incompatibility between the available options (see e.g. Busemeyer et al. 2011), may be better modelled using QP than by classical probabilities theories such as Bayseian models. For examples and a more detailed justification of the use of QP in this context see e.g. Aerts and Gabora (2005), Atmanspacher et al. (2006), Busemeyer and Bruza (2011), Khrennikov (2010).

Our discussion of the QP model follows closely the account given in Pothos et al. (2013). We will begin with a concise account of the main features of the quantum similarity model. We will then consider some of the details of the model in more depth.

2.1   Outline of the Model

The basic ingredient in our quantum model is a complex vector space H (strictly a Hilbert space), representing the space of possible thoughts, which may be partitioned into (vector) subspaces, H_i, each of which represents a particular concept. The subspace corresponding to concept A may be associated with a projection operator P_A. The set of subspaces relevant to a particular set of similarity judgments need not be disjoint or complete, so that a particular thought may be associated with more than one concept. Although a realistic psychological space may have very high dimensionality, the important features can often be captured by a model with a much smaller effective concept space.

The knowledge state is given by a density operator, ρ on H. It corresponds, broadly speaking, to whatever a person is thinking at a particular time. For example, the knowledge state could be determined by the experimental instructions, or alternatively it could represent the expected degree of knowledge of naïve participants. Note that in in some cases it may be more appropriate to model the knowledge state as a pure state $|\psi\rangle$, but this is not the most general possibility and is unlikely to be appropriate for describing an inhomogeneous group of participants.

Finally the similarity between two concepts A and B is computed as

$$\mathrm{Sim}(A, B) = \mathrm{Tr}(P_B P_A \rho P_A), \tag{1}$$

which, if the knowledge state is pure, reduces to

$$\text{Sim}(A, B) = |P_B P_A |\psi\rangle|^2. \qquad (2)$$

2.2 Comments

Initial State. We will discuss how this model can reproduce asymmetries in similarity judgments below, but for now note that this effect does not follow by itself from the non-commutation of the operators P_A, P_B etc. Suppose we were to choose as an initial knowledge state the maximally mixed state corresponding to an equal prior probability for any thought, $\rho \sim 1_H$. Whether this a reasonable choice depends of course on the model, but it is easily seen that such a state leads to symmetric judgments of similarity whatever P_A and P_B. We see therefore that the specification of the initial knowledge state is an important part of this model and must be done in a reasonably principled way.

Subspaces. Subspaces of the knowledge space represent different concepts, like China. A subspace could be a ray spanned by a single vector, or a plane spanned by a pair of vectors, or a three dimensional space spanned by three vectors, etc. Suppose that the China subspace is spanned by two orthonormal vectors, $|v_1\rangle$ and $|v_2\rangle$ (that is, the China subspace is two-dimensional; we will shortly consider how meaning may be ascribed to $|v_1\rangle, |v_2\rangle$). That is, $|v_1\rangle$ and $|v_2\rangle$ are basis vectors for the China subspace. Then, the concept of China is basically all the vectors of the form $a|v_1\rangle + b|v_2\rangle$, where $|a|^2 + |b|^2 = 1$ (as is required for a state vector in quantum theory). Note that this statement is different from, though obviously related to, the statement that a category corresponds to a region of psychological space (Ashby and Perrin 1998; Nosofsky 1984). So, to represent China with a subspace is to assume that the concept China is the collection of all thoughts, $a|v_1\rangle + b|v_2\rangle$, which are consistent with this concept. For example, our knowledge of China would include information about culture, food, language etc. The representation of China as a subspace implies that all these properties have to be contained in the China subspace. Therefore, the greater the range of thoughts we can have about a concept (e.g., properties or statements), the greater the dimensionality of the subspace. If we represent China as a two dimensional subspace and Korea as a one dimensional subspace, this means that we can have a greater range of thoughts for China, than for Korea, which is equivalent to assuming that we have greater knowledge for China than for Korea.

Note that a thought of the form $|\psi\rangle = a|v_1\rangle + b|v_2\rangle$ is neither about $|v_1\rangle$ nor $|v_2\rangle$, but rather reflects the potentiality that the person will end up definitely thinking about $|v_1\rangle$ or $|v_2\rangle$[1]. For example, if $|a| > |b|$, then this means that the person has a greater potential to think of $|v_1\rangle$ than $|v_2\rangle$. In QP theory, states like $a|v_1\rangle + b|v_2\rangle$ are called superposition states and the fact that we cannot

---

[1] It is often asserted that a superposition state such as $|\psi\rangle$ represents thinking about $|v_1\rangle$ *and* $|v_2\rangle$ at the same time. This is incorrect. The correct interpretation of such a state is that it represents thinking about neither $|v_1\rangle$ *nor* $|v_2\rangle$ (Griffiths 2002).

ascribe definite meaning to such states is the result of a famous theorem (the Kochen-Specker theorem).

Since the China concept is represented by a subspace spanned by vectors $|v_1\rangle$ and $|v_2\rangle$, the mathematical expression for China is a projector denoted as $P_{China} = |v_1\rangle\langle v_1| + |v_2\rangle\langle v_2|$ (although this decomposition is not unique.) Thus, following from the example above, if we think about the Chinese language, then $|\psi\rangle = |Chinese\rangle$, and $P_{China}|Chinese\rangle = |Chinese\rangle$, showing that this is a thought included in the China concept (but, the China concept would include many other thoughts). More generally the range of thoughts $|\psi\rangle$ such that $P_{China}|\psi\rangle = |\psi\rangle$ is the range of thoughts consistent with the concept of China or, equivalently, the thoughts which are part of the concept of China.

Finally we consider the meaning of vectors $|v_1\rangle$ and $|v_2\rangle$, in the claim that they span the China subspace. We could consider each such vector as a separate, distinct property of China. However, in general, different subsets of properties of a particular concept are likely to correlate with each other. For example, the properties relating to Chinese food are likely to correlate with properties relating to the general health of the average Chinese person. We so interpret $|v_1\rangle$ and $|v_2\rangle$ linearly independent combinations of all the thoughts that make up the concept of China. How to determine the set of appropriate vectors, properties, or dimensions is an issue common to all geometric approaches to similarity. Recent work, especially by Storms and collaborators (e.g., De Deyne et al. 2008), shows that this challenge can be overcome, for example, through the collection of similarity information across several concepts or feature elicitation. Then, the relatedness of the properties will determine the overall dimensionality of the concept.

Similarity. Given a particular subspace and an appropriate knowledge state vector, we can examine the degree to which the state vector is consistent with the subspace. In quantum theory, this operation is achieved by a projector. A projector can be represented by a matrix, which takes a vector and projects it (lays it down) onto a particular subspace. For example, if P_{China} is the projector onto the China subspace, then the projection $P_{China}|\psi\rangle$ represents the match between the current knowledge state and China, in other words, it computes the part of the vector $|\psi\rangle$ which is restricted or contained in the China subspace.

It is now easy to measure the consistency between a subspace and a state vector, from the projected vector. The length of the projection squared can be shown to be the probability that the state vector is consistent with the corresponding subspace. For example, the probability that a thought $|\psi\rangle$ is consistent with the China concept equals $|P_{China}|\psi\rangle|^2 = \langle\psi|P_{China}|\psi\rangle$. If the state vector is orthogonal to a subspace, then the probability is 0. In the more general language of density matricies this can be written as,

$$p(China) = \langle P_{China}\rangle_\rho = \text{Tr}(P_{China}\rho) \tag{3}$$

Thus the probability that the initial knowledge state is consistent with the concept China is given by the expectation value of P_{China}, computed in the initial knowledge state. We propose that the similarity between two concepts is determined by the sequential projection from the subspace corresponding to the first concept to the one for the second concept. Roughly, this corresponds to the idea that the similarity comparison is a process of thinking about the first of the compared concepts, followed by the second. Similarity in the quantum model is about how easy it is to think about one concept, from the perspective of another. The similarity between, e.g., Korea and China may therefore be written as,

$$\text{Sim}(\text{Korea}, \text{China}) = \text{Tr}(P_{\text{China}} P_{\text{Korea}} \rho P_{\text{Korea}}), \tag{4}$$

or

$$\text{Sim}(\text{Korea}, \text{China}) = |P_{\text{China}} P_{\text{Korea}} |\psi\rangle|^2, \tag{5}$$

in the special case that the initial knowledge state is pure.

2.3 Asymmetry

Suppose we are interested in how similar Korea is to China. When there is no particular directionality implied in the judgment we can either average the result from both directionalities or determine the directionality in another way (Busemeyer et al. 2011). However, similarity judgments are often formulated in a directional way (Tversky 1977). When this is the case, we suggest that the directionality of the similarity judgment determines the directionality of the sequential projection, i.e., the syntax of the similarity judgment matches the syntax of the quantum computation. For example, the similarity of Korea to China would involve a process of thinking about Korea (subject, mentioned first) and then China (object, mentioned second), which corresponds to

$$\text{Sim}(\text{Korea}, \text{China}) = |P_{\text{China}} P_{\text{Korea}} |\psi\rangle|^2 \tag{6}$$

Let us consider the justification for this formula in more detail. Suppose the initial state is $|\psi\rangle$. From this initial state, the probability to think about Korea is $|P_{\text{Korea}} |\psi\rangle|^2$. If the person thinks that the current state matches the Korea subspace, then the new state is revised to become the normalized projection of the previous state onto the Korean subspace, so that $|\psi_{\text{Korea}}\rangle = P_{\text{Korea}} |\psi\rangle / |P_{\text{Korea}} |\psi\rangle|$. Finally, the probability that this conditional state is consistent with China equals $|P_{\text{China}} |\psi_{\text{Korea}}\rangle|^2$. Thus, $|P_{\text{China}} |\psi_{\text{Korea}}\rangle|^2 |P_{\text{Korea}} |\psi\rangle|^2$ exactly computes the sequence of probabilities for whether $|\psi\rangle$ is consistent with the Korea subspace and whether the (normalized) projection of $|\psi\rangle$ onto Korea is consistent with the China subspace. The product rule then follows from,

$$|P_{\text{China}} |\psi_{\text{Korea}}\rangle|^2 |P_{\text{Korea}} |\psi\rangle|^2 = |P_{\text{China}} (P_{\text{Korea}} |\psi\rangle) / (|P_{\text{Korea}} |\psi\rangle|)|^2 |P_{\text{Korea}} |\psi\rangle|^2$$
$$= |P_{\text{China}} P_{\text{Korea}} |\psi\rangle|^2 \tag{7}$$

(Busemeyer et al. 2011).

As we noted above in order to generate asymmetries in similarity judgments we need some principle for fixing the initial state. Usually we will (partly) fix the initial knowledge state by demanding that it is unbiased, that is, that there is equal prior probability that the initial state is consistent with either, say, Korea or China. Such an assumption is analogous to that of a uniform prior in a Bayesian model. Then, it is straightforward to show that $\text{Sim}(\text{Korea}, \text{China}) \sim |P_{\text{China}}|\psi_{\text{Korea}}\rangle|^2$, whereby the vector $|\psi_{\text{Korea}}\rangle$ is a normalized vector contained in the Korea subspace. Therefore, the quantity $|P_{\text{China}}|\psi_{\text{Korea}}\rangle|^2$ depends on only two factors, the geometric relation between the China and the Korea subspaces and the relative dimensionality of the subspaces.

Although there is not space here for a full discussion, we note briefly that it is possible to argue against Eq.(6) as a viable measure of the similarity between A and B in the following way. Equation(6) is basically the joint probability to think about A and then B. A more natural notion of the 'distance' between A and B would rather be the conditional probability to think about B given we are initially thinking about A. In this case it follows that we should divide Eq.(6) by the probability of thinking about Korea, given the initial state. However this gives a result that is symmetric with respect to A and B when these are represented by rays.

The counterargument to this is that these similarities are not best thought of as 'objective' distances (even in a psychological space), but rather as subjective or perceived ones. This is already apparent in the fact that the representation of the stimuli depends on the extent of knowledge of these stimuli (high vs low subspace dimensionality in the case of China-Korea), and it is reasonable that the perceived similarity should also depend on the extent to which a subject may be thinking about a stimuli prior to the comparison. That A is similar to B is much less likely to occur to a subject not initially thinking about A. This line of argument is similar to that discussed in Aerts et al. (2011), where asymmetric judgments arise from the existence of a 'point of view' vector. Unfortunately space does not allow us to discuss the relationship between these approaches. Likewise, the connections between the emergence of similarity in the QP model and other models which directly include asymmetric similarity metrics (e.g. Jones et al. (2011) and Michelbacher (2011)) must await discussion elsewhere. Both of these issues will be taken up in Yearsley et al. (in preparation).

2.4   Diagnosticity

A modification of the basic similarity calculation to take into account context is motivated by Tversky's (1977) diagnosticity effect, one of the most compelling demonstrations in the similarity literature. In his experiment, participants had to identify the country most similar to a particular target, from a set of alternatives, and the empirical results showed that pairwise comparisons were influenced by the available alternatives. Such an influence can be accommodated within the quantum similarity model.

Previously, we have assumed that the initial state is unbiased between the stimuli, since we have no reason to assume participants are more likely to be thinking about any particular stimulus. However sometimes what a person is thinking just prior to a comparison cannot be assumed to be irrelevant to the comparison. Suppose that the similarity of A and B is computed in a way that has to take into account the influence of some contextual information, C, which is represented by a particular subspace. This information C could correspond to the alternatives in Tversky's (1977) diagnosticity task. The similarity between A and B should then be computed as,

$$\text{Sim}(A, B) = |P_B P_A |\psi'\rangle|^2 = |P_B|\psi'_A\rangle|^2 |P_A|\psi'\rangle|^2, \tag{8}$$

where $|\psi'\rangle = |\psi_C\rangle = P_C|\psi\rangle/|P_C|\psi\rangle|$ is no longer a state vector neutral between A and B, but rather one which reflects the influence of information C. If we minimally assume that the nature of this contextual influence is to think of C, prior to comparing A and B, then

$$\text{Sim}(A, B) = |P_B P_A |\psi'\rangle|^2 = |P_B P_A (P_C|\psi\rangle)/(|P_C|\psi\rangle|)|^2$$
$$= |P_B P_A P_C|\psi\rangle|^2/|P_C|\psi\rangle|^2. \tag{9}$$

In other words, if the similarity comparison between A and B involves first thinking about A and then about B, then the same similarity comparison, in the context of some other information, C should involve an additional first step of first thinking about C. Additional contextual elements correspond to further prior projections, though note that eventually this process must break down (there must be a limit to how many proximal items can impact on a decision).

As before, the link with probability justifies the choice of $|P_B P_A P_C|\psi\rangle|^2$, since

$$|P_B P_A P_C|\psi\rangle|^2 = |P_B P_A|\psi_C\rangle|^2 |P_C|\psi\rangle|^2 = |P_B|\psi_{AC}\rangle|^2 |P_A|\psi_C\rangle|^2 |P_C|\psi\rangle|^2, \tag{10}$$

where $|\psi_C\rangle = (P_C|\psi\rangle)/(|P_C|\psi\rangle|)$ and $|\psi_{AC}\rangle = (P_A|\psi_C\rangle)/(|P_A|\psi_C\rangle|)$. Therefore, the similarity comparison between A and B is now computed in relation to a vector which is no longer neutral, but contained within the C subspace. Depending on the relation between subspace C and subspaces A and B, contextual information can have a profound impact on a similarity judgment. Also, the term $|P_C|\psi\rangle|^2$ affects the overall magnitude of the similarity comparison, but we assume that a computation like $|P_B P_A P_C|\psi\rangle|^2$ can lead to a sense of similarity in relation to other, matched computations. Such an assumption follows from discussions on the flexibility of similarity response scales, e.g., depending on the range of available stimuli (Parducci 1965).

Compared to the case of asymmetries, the account of the diagnosticity effect in the QP model is more heuristic. One needs to accept a very particular model of the influence of the context items on the similarity judgment, and it is hard to see how this could be convincingly motivated (we take up this challenge in Yearsley et al. (in preparation)). A more reasonable place to include such effects would be in the choice of initial knowledge state. Nevertheless the main empirical findings are reproduced well in this model, and the approach also gives some qualitative predictions about when the effect is likely to be present or absent, based on the geometric relationships between the stimuli in psychological space. Any attempt to go beyond this model will therefore have to meet a stern challenge of both matching or bettering the predictions of this model while also being more convincingly motivated.

3   Open Questions and Areas for Further Work

Below we give a (incomplete) list of problems with the current quantum model and open questions for further research. Some of these are issues which have been raised already, but it is useful to collect them in one place.

3.1   How Do We Fix the Initial State?

One obvious problem with the quantum model as presented is that it relies on a particular choice of initial state in order to reproduce the asymmetry/diagnosticity effects, but it gives little by way of explanation for this choice. Even in set ups where one can partially fix the initial state by demanding it be unbiased, as outlined above, this typically leaves many degrees of freedom unfixed. Furthermore even this partial fixing is somewhat unsatisfactory since it has a very classical feel to it, one is essentially fixing prior probabilities rather than prior amplitudes.

What is needed is firstly a reliable way to determine the knowledge state of a group of participants, and secondly a reliable way to manipulate this knowledge state, i.e. to be able to prime participants to have reasonably arbitrary knowledge states. We noted above that a more convincing way to model the diagnosticity effect would be by direct manipulation of the initial knowledge state to reflect the set of available choices, and this will be one test of any theory that fixes the initial state.

3.2   Can We Model Asymmetries Due to Frequency/Prototypicality?

An important gap in the current quantum model concerns how to deal with asymmetries arising from differences in the frequency of presentation of stimuli, or from their differing prototypicality. This failure is particularly striking when we note that there appears to be an obvious way to include such effects. Presumably what distinguishes a prototypical stimulus from a non-prototypical one, or a stimulus presented many times from one presented only infrequently is the increased potentiality for a participant to think about this stimulus. In other words, suppose $|A\rangle$ corresponds to a more prototypical/frequently presented stimulus and $|B\rangle$ to a less prototypical/frequently presented one. Then one obvious way to encode this difference is to set the initial knowledge state to be $|\psi\rangle = N(a|A\rangle + b|B\rangle)$, with N some suitable normalization factor and $|a| > |b|$. Unfortunately it is easy to show that whilst this approach does lead to asymmetries in predicted similarity judgments, it predicts the opposite effect from that empirically observed, i.e. this model predicts $\text{Sim}(A, B) > \text{Sim}(B, A)$.

We would therefore like an account of how differences in frequency/prototypicality can lead to asymmetries in the quantum model, or at the very least a good explanation of why a simple manipulation of the initial state, as suggested above, is not the right way to proceed.

3.3   Is There Genuine Contextuality in Similarity Judgments?

One of the reasons why the treatment of the diagnosticity effect is currently unsatisfactory in this model is that quantum theory naturally includes a certain amount of contextuality, but this is not what is responsible for diagnosticity in the QP model. As it stands this represents a lost opportunity, since a context effect in similarity judgments that followed from the contextuality of QP would be a very powerful, admittedly a posteriori, prediction. It would be interesting to see if a new explanation for the diagnosticity effect can be devised which makes better use of the properties of QP, or alternatively if the genuine contextuality of QP leads to additional predictions. Of course, it may also turn out that the current approach to context in the diagnosticity model (with its sensitivity to grouping) is the optimal way to proceed.

3.4   Are There Novel Quantum Predictions?

Following on from the previous point, it is important to understand whether the QP model makes any novel predictions about similarity judgments in particular cases. These could either take the form of new qualitative effects, or of quantitatively accurate predictions for similarity judgments between some simple artificial stimuli.

3.5   Can the Quantum Similarity Model Be Extended?

As well as extracting new predictions from the current QP model, it is interesting to ask whether the model may be extended in some way to cope with new types of judgment. Many of the possible extensions are not tied particularly to similarity judgments, but may be incorporated into QP models of many different types of judgments. There is not space here to discuss all the possible extensions of the QP model, but we will instead focus on a single possibility, the role of memory effects in the QP model.

A model of memory could be included in the QP scheme in at least three ways; firstly one might consider a process of forgetting whereby information about the stimuli is gradually lost. This may have the effect of reducing the effective dimension of the knowledge subspace spanned by each stimuli, and so could potentially change the size or even direction of any asymmetry effects. A second possibility is to include memory recall as a constructive process in these models, so that comparing a present stimulus with a past one may depend on whether one is asked to recall the presence or absence of certain features of the stimuli. A final radical possibility is that holding a stimulus in ones short term memory may allow thoughts about that stimulus to interact with other thoughts and memories, potentially resolving ambiguities and collapsing any superpositions of distinct possibilities. Thus it may be that quantum effects are less likely to occur the longer participants have to process the stimuli.

These are just some of the many options for extensions to the QP model. We believe these present exciting possibilities for future research directions.

3.6   Can We Frame Quantum Similarity as a Process Theory?

Perhaps the most serious concern with the quantum model is that it is not currently clear how to extract from the mathematics of the theory a picture of what similarity judgments are really about. Partly this is an inherent difficulty with quantum theory as a model for anything. Indeed, the history of attempts to decipher what quantum theory as applied to physics is really about is long, tortuous and largely unproductive. However there are some difficulties with this model that go beyond the usual problems with the interpretation of QP.

At first glance it seems like an interpretation of similarity judgments in QP in terms of the thought process involved should be obvious, indeed we explicitly motivated the order of the projection operations above by regarding the similarity judgment Sim(A,B) as a process of thinking about A followed by thinking about B. However in actual fact things are slightly more complicated than this. The first complication is that it is not the order of the projection operators that is important so much as their positions relative to the knowledge state ρ. In the above we jumped the gun somewhat by calling this the initial knowledge state, but really its role is confined to ensuring judgments are not biased. There is nothing in principle to stop us computing similarity by starting from a completely mixed state, thinking about A followed by B and then demanding that our final knowledge state be unbiased in the sense above. This leads an identical expression for Sim(A,B) but with the opposite ordering of the projection operators. One could also imagine demanding including both an initial and a final knowledge state.

Another difficulty with interpreting the current model is the problem, already mentioned, of establishing the correct initial states and subspaces for particular similarity judgments. However it is possible to argue that this problem is no more severe than that encountered by other approaches to representing stimuli in psychological space.

A final difficulty with QP as a process theory of similarity judgments concerns what happens when we make sequential judgments, of the kind involved in the forced choice tasks of Tvesrky (1977). The difficulty here is that, according to QP, after judging the similarity between A and B, our knowledge state is no longer ρ, but rather

$$\rho' = (P_B P_A \rho P_A P_B)/\text{Tr}(P_B P_A \rho P_A P_B) \tag{11}$$

That is, performing the similarity judgment between A and B collapses the initial state ρ into the new state ρ'. Such a collapse is not currently included in the quantum model.

Thus we can see that although attractive in many ways, the 'narrative' given by the QP theory relating to what happens during a similarity judgment is far from complete. This presents us with a problem but also with an opportunity. It is possible that by focusing on making the QP model a better description of the process of making similarity judgments, we may simultaneously clear up some of the technical problems, such as how to account for other types of asymmetry.

4   Conclusions

So what are we to conclude about the current status of the QP approach to similarity judgments? In this contribution we have been particularly harsh on the approach, and we haven't shirked from pointing out some of the flaws. However it is worth remembering that this approach does deal very well with asymmetries due to differences in the level of knowledge, providing a good qualitative account of the observed similarity judgments as well as the outline of an account of the process by which these judgments are made. In the case of diagnosticity although the details of the model are less well motivated it does provide a good fit to the current data. It is also worth pointing out that the alternatives to the QP model largely involve putting in asymmetry factors by hand. Still, the QP model could not be said to be convincing in its current form. Technical problems aside, the challenge is to convert some of the obvious parallels between similarity judgments and QP (order effects, contextuality etc.), into both a broad range of accurate empirical predictions/explanations and a convincing narrative of the cognitive processes behind similarity judgments. However it would be wrong to be overly pessimistic. The QP approach to similarity judgments is more than just an alternative to a particular classical theory of similarity-as-distance. Instead it is better seen as just one possible application of an entirely new way of thinking about cognition that may also be applied to constructive judgments, belief updating, moral dynamics and many other areas of research in cognition. The QP approach to similarity may be still in its infancy, but one should be prepared to accept such teething troubles when the reward is the possibility of a revolution in our understanding of cognition.

Acknowledgments. E.M.P. and J.M.Y. were supported by Leverhulme Trust grant no. RPG-2013-00. Further, E.M.P. was supported by Air Force Office of Scientific Research (AFOSR), Air Force Material Command, USAF, grants no. FA 8655-13-1-3044. The US Government is authorized to reproduce and distribute reprints for Governmental purpose notwithstanding any copyright notation thereon.

References

Aerts, D., Gabora, L.: A theory of concepts and their combinations II: a Hilbert space representation. Kybernetes **34**, 192–221 (2005)

Aerts, S., Kitto, K., Sitbon, L.: Similarity metrics within a point of view. In: Song, D., Melucci, M., Frommholz, I., Zhang, P., Wang, L., Arafat, S. (eds.) QI 2011. LNCS, vol. 7052, pp. 13–24. Springer, Heidelberg (2011)

Ashby, G.F., Perrin, N.A.: Towards a unified theory of similarity and recognition. Psychol. Rev. **95**, 124–150 (1988)

Atmanspacher, H., Romer, H., Wallach, H.: Weak quantum theory: formal framework and selected applications. Weak quantum theory: complementarity and entanglement in physics and beyond. Found. Phys. **32**, 379–406 (2006)

Bowdle, B.F., Medin, D.L.: Reference-point reasoning and comparison asymmetries. In: Moore, J.D., Stenning, K. (eds.) Proceedings of the 23rd Annual Conference of the Cognitive Science Society, pp. 116–121. Psychology Press, New York (2001)

Busemeyer, J.R., Bruza, P.: Quantum Models of Cognition and Decision Making. Cambridge University Press, Cambridge (2011)

Busemeyer, J.R., Pothos, E.M., Franco, R., Trueblood, J.: A quantum theoretical explanation for probability judgment errors. Psychol. Rev. **118**, 193–218 (2011)

De Deyne, S., Verheyen, S., Ameel, E., Vanpaemel, W., Dry, M.J., Voorspoels, W., Storms, G.: Exemplar by feature applicability matrices and other Dutch normative data for semantic concepts. Behav. Res. Meth. **40**, 1030–1048 (2008)

Goldstone, R.L.: The role of similarity in categorization: providing a groundwork. Cognition **52**, 125–157 (1994)

Goodman, N.: Seven strictures on similarity. In: Goodman, N. (ed.) Problems and Projects, pp. 437–447. Bobbs-Merrill, Indianapolis (1972)

Griffiths, R.B.: Consistent Quantum Theory. Cambridge University Press, Cambridge (2002)

Jones, M.N., Gruenenfelder, T.M., Recchia, G.: In defense of spatial models of lexical semantics. In: Carlson, L., Hlscher, C., Shipley, T. (eds.) Proceedings of the 33rd Annual Conference of the Cognitive Science Society, pp. 3444–3449. Cognitive Science Society, Austin (2011)

Khrennikov, A.Y.: Ubiquitous Quantum Structure: From Psychology to Finance. Springer, Berlin (2010)

Michelbacher, L., Evert, S., Schtze, H.: Asymmetry in corpus-derived and human word associations. Corpus Linguist. Linguist. Theor. **7**(2), 245–276 (2011)

Nosofsky, R.M.: Choice, similarity, and the context theory of classification. J. Exp. Psychol. Learn. Mem. Cogn. **10**, 104–114 (1984)

Parducci, A.: Category judgment: a range-frequency model. Psychol. Rev. **72**, 407–418 (1965)

Polk, T.A., Behensky, C., Gonzalez, R., Smith, E.E.: Rating the similarity of simple perceptual stimuli: asymmetries induced by manipulating exposure frequency. Cognition **82**, B75–B88 (2002)

Pothos, E.M.: The rules versus similarity distinction. Behav. Brain Sci. **28**, 1–49 (2005)

Pothos, E.M., Busemeyer, J.R., Trueblood, J.S.: A quantum geometric model of similarity. Psychol. Rev. **120**, 679–696 (2013)

Rosch, E.: Cognitive reference points. Cogn. Psychol. **7**, 532–547 (1975)

Trueblood, J.S., Brown, S.D., Heathcote, A., Busemeyer, J.R.: Not just for consumers: context effects are fundamental to decision-making. Psychol. Sci. **24**(6), 901–908 (2013)

Tversky, A.: Features of similarity. Psychol. Rev. **84**, 327–352 (1977)

Yearsley, J.M., Pothos, E.M., Hampton, J.A., Barque Duran, A.: Context effects in similarity judgments (in preparation)

Positive Operator-Valued Measures in Quantum Decision Theory

Vyacheslav I. Yukalov[1,2]($\boxtimes$) and Didier Sornette[1,3]

[1] Department of Management, Technology and Economics, ETH Zürich,
Swiss Federal Institute of Technology, 8092 Zürich, Switzerland
syukalov@ethz.ch
[2] Bogolubov Laboratory of Theoretical Physics,
Joint Institute for Nuclear Research, Dubna 141980, Russia
yukalov@theor.jinr.ru
[3] Swiss Finance Institute, C/o University of Geneva,
40 Blvd. Du Pont D'Arve, 1211 Geneva 4, Switzerland
dsornette@ethz.ch

Abstract. We show that the correct mathematical foundation of quantum decision theory, dealing with uncertain events, requires the use of positive operator-valued measure that is a generalization of the projection-valued measure. The latter is appropriate for operationally testable events, while the former is necessary for characterizing operationally uncertain events. In decision making, one has to distinguish composite non-entangled events from composite entangled events. The mathematical definition of entangled prospects is based on the theory of Hilbert-Schmidt spaces and is analogous to the definition of entangled statistical operators in quantum information theory. We demonstrate that the necessary condition for the appearance of an interference term in the quantum probability is the occurrence of entangled prospects and the existence of an entangled strategic state of a decision maker. The origin of uncertainties in standard lotteries is explained.

Keywords: Decision theory · Quantum information processing · Decisions under uncertainty · Quantum probability · Positive operator-valued measure · Entangled prospects

1 Introduction

Techniques of quantum theory are nowadays widely employed not only for physics problems but also in such fields as quantum information processing and quantum computing [1–5]. Another example is the theory of quantum games [6]. A scheme of artificial quantum intelligence was suggested [7,8]. Applications of quantum techniques to cognitive sciences are also quickly growing.

Actually, the idea that human decision making could be characterized by quantum techniques was advanced long ago by Bohr [9,10]. Since then, a number

© Springer International Publishing Switzerland 2015
H. Atmanspacher et al. (Eds.): QI 2014, LNCS 8951, pp. 146–161, 2015.
DOI: 10.1007/978-3-319-15931-7_12

of publications have discussed the possibility of using quantum techniques in cognitive sciences, as is summarized in the recent books [11–13].

Von Neumann [14] mentioned that the theory of quantum measurements can be interpreted as decision theory. There is, however, an important difference between the standard situation in quantum measurements and the often occurring case in realistic decision making. Usual measurements in physics problems are operationally testable, resulting in well defined numerical values of the measured observables. In decision making, however, it is common to deal with composite events requiring to take decisions in uncertain situations. While the final decision should also be operationally testable, intermediate steps often involve uncertainty that is not operationally testable. The correct description of such uncertain composite prospects requires the use of more elaborate mathematics than the projection-valued measure commonly employed for standard physics problems.

In our previous papers [15–19], we have developed Quantum Decision Theory (QDT) whose mathematical basis rests on the theory of quantum measurements and quantum information theory. The strategic state of a decision maker was represented by a wave function. As is well known, a wave function characterizes an isolated quantum system. However, in real life, no decision maker can be absolutely isolated from the society where he/she lives. That is, the characterization of a strategic decision-maker state by a wave function is oversimplified. Simple methods of quantum mechanics are not sufficient for a realistic description of a decision maker that is a member of a society. Being an open system, a decision maker has to be described by a statistical operator, similarly to any non-isolated system in quantum theory, which requires the use of the ramified techniques of quantum statistical theory [20–22].

One could think that, for describing simple psychological laboratory experiments, there is no need of invoking statistical operators and it would be sufficient to just use pure states characterized by wave functions, since most lab-based tests on cognition deal with subjects that are typically isolated and the experiments have limited durations. However, in quantum theory, as is well known, the necessity of using density matrices is dictated by the existence of interactions not merely at the present moment of time, but also at any previous times, which is always relevant for any alive being. In addition, a system is termed open if interactions have been present not only with similar systems, but with any surrounding. Thus, humans are always subject to interactions with many other people as well as with various information sources, such as TV, radio, telephone, internet, newspapers, and so on. All these numerous interactions always influence decision makers making them, without doubt, open systems. In order to reduce a decision maker to a pure quantum-mechanical system for a pure laboratory experiment, it would be necessary to make a surgical operation deleting all memory and information from the brains of these poor decision makers. The usual lab tests, fortunately, do not require this, so that decision makers have to be always treated as open systems described by statistical operators.

It is worth stressing that a theory based on statistical operators includes, as a particular case, the pure-state description. So that all results obtained in the general consideration can be straightforwardly reduced to the latter case by taking the statistical operator in the pure form $|\psi \rangle\langle \psi|$.

The goal of the present report is threefold. First, we present the extension of QDT to the most general case when the decision-maker strategic state is characterized by a statistical operator. Second, we demonstrate that the correct mathematical description of uncertain composite events has to be described by a positive operator-valued measure generalizing the projection-valued measure used in quantum mechanics. Third, we show that decision making under uncertainty is a rather common phenomenon that happens in the delusively simple problem of choosing between lotteries and illustrate this by an explicit example.

The important feature of our approach is that we employ the rigorous mathematical techniques developed in the theory of quantum measurements and quantum information theory. In order that the reader with background in psychology would not confuse mathematical notions used in our paper, we give the necessary definitions, trying at the same time to keep the exposition concise. Details can be found in the books [1,2,4,5,23–26] and review articles [3,27].

2 Operationally Testable Events

The operationally testable events in QDT can be characterized by analogy with operationally testable measurements in quantum theory. Quantum events, obeying the Birkhoff-von Neumann quantum logic [28], form a non-commutative non-distributive ring $\mathcal{R}$. The nonempty collection of all subsets of the event ring $\mathcal{R}$, including $\mathcal{R}$, which is closed with respect to countable unions and complements, is the event sigma algebra Σ. The algebra of quantum events is the pair $\{\Sigma, \mathcal{R}\}$ of the sigma algebra Σ over the event ring $\mathcal{R}$. An elementary event A_n is represented by a basic state $|n\rangle$ generating the event operator defined as a projector

$$\hat{P}_n \equiv |n\rangle\langle n|. \tag{1}$$

The space of mind of a decision maker is a Hilbert space $\mathcal{H}$ that is a closed linear envelope of the basis $\{|n\rangle\}$ spanning all admissible basic states. The strategic state of a social decision maker is a statistical operator $\hat{\rho}$ that is a trace-class positive operator normalized to one. The algebra of observables in QDT is the family $\{\hat{P}_n\}$ of the event operators whose expected values define the event probabilities

$$p(A_n) \equiv \mathrm{Tr}\hat{\rho}\hat{P}_n \equiv \langle \hat{P}_n \rangle, \tag{2}$$

with the trace over $\mathcal{H}$. From this definition, it follows:

$$\sum_n p(A_n) = 1, \qquad 0 \le p(A_n) \le 1,$$

hence the family $\{p(A_n)\}$ forms a probability measure. By the Gleason theorem [29], this measure is unique for a Hilbert space of dimensionality larger than two. In the theory of quantum measurements, the projectors $\hat{P}_n$ play the role of observables, so that, for an event A_n, one has the correspondence

$$A_n \rightarrow \hat{P}_n \equiv |n\rangle\langle n|. \tag{3}$$

For a union of mutually orthogonal events, there is the correspondence

$$\bigcup_n A_n \rightarrow \sum_n \hat{P}_n, \tag{4}$$

which results in the additivity of the probabilities:

$$p\left(\bigcup_n A_n\right) = \sum_n p(A_n). \tag{5}$$

The procedure described above is called the standard measurement.

Let us emphasize that all formulas of this and following sections are valid for an arbitrary statistical operator, which includes the pure form $\hat{\rho} = |\psi\rangle\langle\psi|$ as a trivial particular case.

3   Operationally Uncertain Events

It may happen that one cannot tell whether a particular event has occurred, but it is only known that some of the events A_n could be realized. This is what is called an uncertain or inconclusive event.

Assume that the observed event A is a set $\{A_n\}$ of possible events. Although the events A_m and A_n are orthogonal for $m \neq n$, in the case of the uncertain event A, they form not a standard union but an *uncertain union* that we shall denote as

$$A \equiv \{A_n\} \equiv \biguplus_n A_n \tag{6}$$

in order to distinguish it from the standard union $\bigcup_n A_n$. The uncertain event A is characterized by the wave function

$$|A\rangle = \sum_n a_n |n\rangle, \tag{7}$$

where $|a_n|^2$ play the role of weights for the events A_n. Now, instead of the correspondence (4) for the standard union, we have the correspondence

$$\biguplus_n A_n \rightarrow \hat{P}_A \equiv |A\rangle\langle A|. \tag{8}$$

Note that $\hat{P}_A$ is not a projector.

The probability of the uncertain event A reads as

$$p(A) = p\left(\biguplus_n A_n\right) = \sum_n |a_n|^2 p(A_n) + q(A), \tag{9}$$

where the second term

$$q(A) \equiv \sum_{m \neq n} a_m^* a_n \langle m | \hat{\rho} | n \rangle \tag{10}$$

is caused by the interference of the uncertain subevents A_n that are called *modes*. The probability $p(A)$ of the uncertain event A, represented by the uncertain union (6), does not equal the sum of the event probabilities $p(A_n)$. In that sense, the uncertain union (6) is not additive with respect to partial events A_n, contrary to the probability of the standard union (5).

4   Composite Non-entangled Prospects

Composite events are termed prospects. These can be sorted in two classes, entangled and non-entangled [30]. This classification is based on the theory of Hilbert-Schimdt spaces [31,32], as is explained below.

It is well known that quantum-mechanical wave functions, pertaining to a Hilbert space, can be either entangled, or non-separable, and non-entangled, or separable. Similarly, by constructing the appropriate Hilbert-Schmidt space, it is possible to introduce the notions of entangled, or non-separable operators, and of non-entangled, or separable operators. We need this classification for a bipartite system, that is, consisting of two parts, although the definition can be straightforwardly generalized for a multi-partite case.

Let us consider a bipartite quantum system, with one subsystem corresponding to a Hilbert space $\mathcal{H}_A$ and the other, to a Hilbert space $\mathcal{H}_B$. The subsystem, defined in $\mathcal{H}_A$, is characterized be a set of operators, acting on $\mathcal{H}_A$. For what follows, we keep in mind the operators of observables represented by the projectors of operationally testable events. The set of operators on $\mathcal{H}_A$ forms an algebra of observables $\mathcal{A}$. Respectively, the subsystem in $\mathcal{H}_B$ is characterized by an algebra $\mathcal{B}$ acting on $\mathcal{H}_B$. For any two operators $\hat{A}_1$ and $\hat{A}_2$ in the algebra $\mathcal{A}$, it is possible to introduce a scalar product

$$(\hat{A}_1, \hat{A}_2) \equiv \mathrm{Tr}_A \hat{A}_1^+ \hat{A}_2,$$

where the trace is over the space $\mathcal{H}_A$, inducing the Hilbert-Schimdt norm

$$||\hat{A}|| \equiv \sqrt{(\hat{A}, \hat{A})}.$$

Then the operator algebra $\mathcal{A}$, complemented by the above scalar product, becomes a Hilbert-Schmidt space. The same can be done for the algebra $\mathcal{B}$ becoming a Hilbert-Schmidt space with the scalar product defined in the same way.

The system, composed of two parts, is a composite system defined in the tensor-product Hilbert space $\mathcal{H}_A \otimes \mathcal{H}_B$. The operator algebra $\mathcal{A} \otimes \mathcal{B}$ acts on this tensor-product space. For any two operators $\hat{C}_1$ and $\hat{C}_2$ of the latter algebra, one defines the scalar product

$$(\hat{C}_1, \hat{C}_2) \equiv \mathrm{Tr}_{AB} \hat{C}_1^+ \hat{C}_2,$$

with the trace over the space $\mathcal{H}_A \otimes \mathcal{H}_B$. Thus, the algebra $\mathcal{A} \otimes \mathcal{B}$, complemented by this scalar product, becomes a composite Hilbert-Schmidt space. In this way, the operators of a Hilbert-Schmidt space can be treated similarly to the vectors of a Hilbert space.

One tells that the operator $\hat{C}$, acting on the composite Hilbert-Schmidt space, is separable, or not-entangled, if and only if it can be represented as

$$\hat{C} = \sum_\gamma \hat{C}_{\gamma A} \otimes \hat{C}_{\gamma B},$$

where $\hat{C}_{\gamma A}$ and $\hat{C}_{\gamma B}$ are the operators from the related algebras of observables, acting on $\mathcal{H}_A$ and $\mathcal{H}_B$, respectively. Such separable operators have been widely used in scattering theory [33]. On the contrary, if the operator cannot be reduced to the separable form, it is termed non-separable, or entangled.

The classification of the operators onto separable and entangled is intensively employed in quantum information theory [1–5], where one considers statistical operators. In quantum decision theory [15–19], this classification is applied to prospect operators. A prospect operator that cannot be represented in the separable form is called entangled or non-separable, while when it can be reduced to that form, it is termed non-entangled, or separable. Similarly, the prospects, represented by the corresponding prospect operators, can be distinguished onto entangled and non-entangled. Exactly this classification will be used below.

Suppose we consider two elementary events A_n, represented by a vector $|n\rangle$ from a Hilbert space $\mathcal{H}_A$, and B_α, represented by a vector $|\alpha\rangle$ from a Hilbert space $\mathcal{H}_B$. The composite event, formed by these two elementary events, is treated as a tensor product $A_n \otimes B_\alpha$. In this notation, the event A_n is assumed to happen after the event B_α. The composite event $A_n \otimes B_\alpha$ is represented by the vector

$$|n\alpha\rangle = |n\rangle \otimes |\alpha\rangle \tag{11}$$

from the tensor-product Hilbert space

$$\mathcal{H}_{AB} \equiv \mathcal{H}_A \otimes \mathcal{H}_B. \tag{12}$$

The composite event of observing A_n and B_α induces the correspondence

$$A_n \otimes B_\alpha \;\rightarrow\; \hat{P}_n \otimes \hat{P}_\alpha, \tag{13}$$

where

$$\hat{P}_\alpha \equiv |\alpha\rangle\langle\alpha|$$

is a projector in $\mathcal{H}_B$.

The strategic state is now a statistical operator $\hat{\rho}$ on the tensor-product space (12). The joint probability of the composite event (13) becomes

$$p(A_n \otimes B_\alpha) = \mathrm{Tr}\hat{\rho}\hat{P}_n \otimes \hat{P}_\alpha \equiv \langle \hat{P}_n \otimes \hat{P}_\alpha \rangle, \tag{14}$$

with the trace over the space (12). The composite event (13) is the simplest composite event, which enjoys the factor form, being composed of two elementary events, and being called *non-entangled*.

More complicated structures arise when at least one of the events is a union. It is important to emphasize the difference between the standard union and the uncertain union introduced in (6).

When the composite event is a product of an elementary event A_n and a standard union of mutually orthogonal events B_α, we can employ the known property of composite events:

$$A_n \bigotimes \bigcup_\alpha B_\alpha = \bigcup_\alpha A_n \bigotimes B_\alpha.$$

In the right-hand side here, we have the union of mutually orthogonal composite events, since B_α are assumed to be mutually orthogonal. Therefore

$$p\left(A_n \bigotimes \bigcup_\alpha B_\alpha\right) = \sum_\alpha p(A_n \bigotimes B_\alpha). \tag{15}$$

That is, the probability of a composite event, with one of the factors being the standard union of mutually orthogonal events, is additive. Such events are also termed non-entangled.

It is important to stress that the used terminology is in agreement with the notions of separable and non-entangled operators, as is formulated at the beginning of this section. Really, in the present case, the bipartite system is described by the tensor product of the algebras of observables $\mathcal{A} \equiv \{\hat{P}_n\}$ and $\mathcal{B} \equiv \{\hat{P}_\alpha\}$. The event $A_n \bigotimes \bigcup_\alpha B_\alpha$ induces the event operator that has the form

$$\hat{P}\left(A_n \bigotimes \bigcup_\alpha B_\alpha\right) = \sum_\alpha \hat{P}_n \bigotimes \hat{P}_\alpha,$$

corresponding to the definition of a separable, or non-entangled operator.

5 Composite Entangled Prospects

The situation is essentially different when dealing with an uncertain union. In that case, composite events are represented by prospect operators that cannot be represented in the separable form.

Let us have such an uncertain union

$$B \equiv \{B_\alpha\} \equiv \biguplus_\alpha B_\alpha \tag{16}$$

corresponding to a vector

$$|B\rangle = \sum_\alpha b_\alpha |\alpha\rangle. \tag{17}$$

The composite event, or prospect

$$\pi_n = A_n \bigotimes B = A_n \bigotimes \biguplus_{\alpha} B_\alpha, \tag{18}$$

corresponds to the prospect state

$$|\pi_n\rangle = |n\rangle \bigotimes |B\rangle = \sum_{\alpha} b_\alpha |n\alpha\rangle. \tag{19}$$

The composite event (18) induces the correspondence

$$\pi_n \; \rightarrow \; \hat{P}(\pi_n) \equiv |\pi_n\rangle\langle\pi_n| \tag{20}$$

defining the prospect operator $\hat{P}(\pi_n)$.

At this point, it is necessary to make an important comment clarifying the notion of entanglement. The latter is correctly defined when it is explicitly stated what object is considered and with respect to which parts it is entangled or not. Recall that, in quantum mechanics, one considers the entanglement of a wave function of a composite system with respect to the wave functions of its parts, which are not arbitrary functions. Wave functions can be defined as eigenfunctions of Hamiltonians. In the case of statistical operators, one considers their entanglement or separability with respect to statistical operators of subsystems, but not with respect to arbitrary operators [1–5]. In the general case of operators from a Hilbert-Schmidt space, one considers their entanglement with respect to the operators from the corresponding Hilbert-Schmidt subspaces, but not with respect to arbitrary operators not pertaining to the prescribed subspaces.

The prospect state (19) could be qualified as not entangled with respect to arbitrary functions from the Hilbert spaces $\mathcal{H}_A$ and $\mathcal{H}_B$. However, the function $|B\rangle$ does not correspond to an operationally testable event, while exactly the latter are of our interest. Hence the formal separability of (19) in the Hilbert space is of no importance. What is important is the separability or entanglement of operationally testable events.

In our case, the operationally testable events correspond to the related projectors forming the algebras of observables $\mathcal{A} \equiv \{\hat{P}_n\}$ and $\mathcal{B} \equiv \{\hat{P}_\alpha\}$. Complementing them by the appropriate scalar products, we get the corresponding Hilbert-Schmidt spaces. A prospect π_n is characterized by the prospect operator (20). According to the general theory, a prospect operator is separable if and only if it can be reduced to the linear combination of the tensor products of operators from the Hilbert-Schmidt subspaces. However, the prospect operator (20) reads as

$$\hat{P}(\pi_n) = \sum_{\alpha} |b_\alpha|^2 \hat{P}_n \bigotimes \hat{P}_\alpha \; + \; \sum_{\alpha \neq \beta} b_\alpha b_\beta^* \hat{P}_n \bigotimes |\alpha\rangle\langle\beta|.$$

The first term in the right-hand side does correspond to the definition of separability, while the second term does not, since $|\alpha\rangle\langle\beta|$, with $\alpha \neq \beta$, does not pertain to the algebra of observables $\mathcal{B} \equiv \{\hat{P}_\alpha\}$. Hence, the prospect operator (20) is not separable, that is, it is entangled. Respectively, prospect (18), corresponding to this prospect operator can also be termed entangled, since it cannot be represented as a union of mutually orthogonal events. The entangling properties of operators can be quantified by the measure of entanglement production [34–36]. The amount of entanglement produced in the process of decision making can be calculated as shown in Ref. [37].

The prospect states (19) are not necessarily orthogonal and do not need to be normalized to one. Because of this, the prospect operators, generally, are not projectors. However, the resolution of unity is required:

$$\sum_n \hat{P}(\pi_n) = \hat{1}_{AB}, \tag{21}$$

where $\hat{1}_{AB}$ is the unity operator in the space (12). The family $\{\hat{P}(\pi_n)\}$ composes a *positive operator-valued measure*.

The prospect probability

$$p(\pi_n) \equiv \mathrm{Tr}\hat{\rho}\hat{P}(\pi_n) \equiv \langle \hat{P}(\pi_n) \rangle, \tag{22}$$

with the trace over space (12), becomes the sum of two terms:

$$p(\pi_n) = f(\pi_n) + q(\pi_n). \tag{23}$$

The first term

$$f(\pi_n) \equiv \sum_\alpha |b_\alpha|^2 p(A_n \bigotimes B_\alpha) \tag{24}$$

contains the diagonal elements with respect to α, while the second term

$$q(\pi_n) \equiv \sum_{\alpha \neq \beta} b_\alpha^* b_\beta \langle n\alpha | \hat{\rho} | n\beta \rangle \tag{25}$$

is formed by the nondiagonal elements. By construction and due to the resolution of unity (21), the prospect probability (22) satisfies the properties

$$\sum_n p(\pi_n) = 1, \qquad 0 \leq p(\pi_n) \leq 1, \tag{26}$$

which makes the family $\{p(\pi_n)\}$ a probability measure.

Expression (25) is caused by the quantum nature of the considered events producing interference of the modes composing the uncertain union (16). Because of this, the term (25) can be called the *quantum factor, interference factor*, or *coherence factor*. The quantum term (25) may be nonzero only when prospect (18) is *entangled* in the sense of the nonseparability of the prospect operator in the Hilbert-Schmidt space.

Classical probability has to be a marginal case of quantum probability. To this end, we have to remember the quantum-classical correspondence principle advanced by Bohr [38]. This principle tells us that classical theory is to be the limiting case of quantum theory, when quantum effects vanish. In the present case, this implies that when the quantum interference factor tends to zero, the quantum probability has to tend to a classical probability. Such a process is also called *decoherence*. According to the principle of the quantum-classical correspondence, we have

$$p(\pi_n) \ \rightarrow \ f(\pi_n), \qquad q(\pi_n) \ \rightarrow \ 0, \tag{27}$$

which means that the decoherence process leads to the classical probability $f(\pi_n)$. Being a probability, this classical factor needs to be normalized, so as to satisfy the conditions

$$\sum_n f(\pi_n) = 1, \qquad 0 \leq f(\pi_n) \leq 1. \tag{28}$$

As a consequence of the above equations, the interference factor enjoys the properties

$$\sum_n q(\pi_n) = 0, \qquad -1 \leq q(\pi_n) \leq 1. \tag{29}$$

The first of these equations is called the *alternation condition*.

One should not confuse the effect of decoherence, based on the quantum-classical correspondence principle, when quantum measurements are reduced to classical, with the Kochen-Specker theorem [39] stating the impossibility of simultaneous embedding of all commuting sub-algebras of the algebra of quantum observables in one commutative algebra, assumed to represent the classical structure of the hidden-variables theory, if the Hilbert space dimension is at least three. This theorem places certain constraints on the permissible types of hidden-variable theories, which try to explain the apparent randomness of quantum mechanics as a deterministic model featuring hidden states. The theorem excludes hidden-variable theories that require elements of physical reality to be non-contextual, i.e., independent of the measurement arrangement. The exclusion of such hidden variables is exactly due to the existence of quantum entanglement.

Our consideration has nothing to do with hidden variables. We do not intend to replace quantum theory by a classical theory with hidden variables. Vice versa, the whole of our approach is completely based on the standard techniques of quantum theory and all results are in full agreement with the known properties of quantum theory. Being always in the frame of quantum theory, we consider a very well known effect called *decoherence* that manifests the transition from quantum to classical behavior. This effect is intimately connected with the quantum-classical correspondence principle, formulated by Bohr and widely used in quantum theory. According to this principle, the results of quantum theory reduce to those of classical theory, when quantum effects, such as entanglement and interference, are washed out. The effect of decoherence is well understood and described in the frame of quantum theory [40–42].

As is mentioned above, the quantum term arises only when the considered prospect is entangled in the sense of the nonseparability of the prospect operator in the Hilbert-Schmidt space. The other necessary condition for the existence of the quantum term is the entanglement in the strategic state $\hat{\rho}$. To illustrate that a disentangled strategic state does not produce interference, let us take the system state in the disentangled product form

$$\hat{\rho} = \hat{\rho}_A \bigotimes \hat{\rho}_B.$$

Then, the quantum interference term becomes

$$q(\pi_n) = \sum_{\alpha \neq \beta} b_\alpha^* b_\beta \langle n|\hat{\rho}_A|n\rangle \langle \alpha|\hat{\rho}_B|\beta\rangle.$$

Taking into account the normalization condition

$$\text{Tr}_A \hat{\rho}_A = \sum_n \langle n|\hat{\rho}_A|n\rangle = 1,$$

we get

$$\sum_n q(\pi_n) = \sum_{\alpha \neq \beta} b_\alpha^* b_\beta \langle \alpha|\hat{\rho}_B|\beta\rangle = 0.$$

As a result, we find

$$q(\pi_n) = \langle n|\hat{\rho}_A|n\rangle \sum_n q(\pi_n) = 0.$$

So, the disentangled strategic state does not allow for the appearance of a nontrivial quantum interference term.

The quantum term (25) is a random quantity satisfying a very important property called the *quarter law* [16–19]. For a prospect lattice, $\mathcal{L} \equiv \{\pi_n : n = 1, 2, \ldots N_L\}$ the absolute value of the aggregate quantum factor can be estimated as

$$|\bar{q}| \equiv \frac{1}{N_L} \sum_{j=1}^{N_L} |q(\pi_j)| = \frac{1}{4}. \tag{30}$$

The value $1/4$ for the aggregate attraction factor can be shown [43] to arise for a large class of distributions characterizing the attraction factors of different decision makers.

Expression (24), corresponding to classical probability, is defined as an objective term, whose value is prescribed by the prospect utility, justifying to call this term the *utility factor*. The quantum term (25) describes the attractiveness of the prospect to a decision maker, so that it is named the *attraction factor* [15–19]. A prospect π_1 is more useful than π_2, if and only if $f(\pi_1) > f(\pi_2)$. A prospect π_1 is more attractive than π_2, when and only when $q(\pi_1) > q(\pi_2)$. And a prospect π_1 is preferable to π_2, if and only if $p(\pi_1) > p(\pi_2)$. Hence, a prospect can be more useful but less attractive, as a result being less preferable.

6   Uncertainty in Standard Lotteries

It can be shown [30], that the necessary condition for the quantum term to be nonzero requires that the considered prospect be entangled and the strategic state $\hat{\rho}$ also be entangled. This implies that the decision is made under uncertainty [44].

A typical situation in decision making is when one chooses between several lotteries. One may ask what kind of uncertainty is ascribed to such a choice between the lotteries.

Suppose we consider a family $\{L_n\}$ of lotteries enumerated with the index $n = 1, 2, \ldots, N_L$. Each lottery is the set

$$L_n = \{x_i,\ p_n(x_i):\ i = 1, 2, \ldots\} \tag{31}$$

of payoffs x_i and payoff probabilities $p_n(x_i)$. A decision maker has to choose one of these lotteries.

The choice between the lotteries is a random procedure involving uncertainty. First of all, when choosing a lottery, one does not know exactly what would be a payoff whose occurrence is characterized by the related probability. Moreover, in each choice, there always exists uncertainty caused by two reasons. One reason is the decision-maker doubt about the objectivity of the setup suggesting the choice. The other origin of uncertainty is caused by subjective hesitations of the decision maker with respect to his/her correct understanding of the problem and his/her knowledge of what would be the best criterion for making a particular choice. Let us denote by B_1 the decision-maker confidence in the empirical setup as well as in his/her ability of making a correct decision. Then B_2 corresponds to the disbelief of the decision maker in the suggested setup and/or in his/her understanding of the appropriate criteria for the choice. The combination of belief and disbelief is the set

$$B = \{B_1, B_2\} = \biguplus_\alpha B_\alpha \qquad (\alpha = 1, 2).$$

In this way, even choosing between simple lotteries L_n, one actually confronts the composite prospects

$$\pi_n = L_n \bigotimes B, \tag{32}$$

where the event of selecting a lottery L_n is denoted by the same letter, which should not lead to confusion. The choice is made under uncertainty incorporated into the set $B = \{B_1, B_2\}$ of belief and disbelief.

The prospect probability is given by (23). The utility factor, characterizing the objective part of the probability, in the case of the choice between the lotteries can be defined [16,19] as

$$f(\pi_n) = \frac{U(\pi_n)}{\sum_n U(\pi_n)}, \tag{33}$$

ordering the prospects according to their expected utilities

$$U(\pi_n) = \sum_i u(x_i) p_n(x_i), \tag{34}$$

where $u(x_i)$ is a utility function. The attraction factors can be evaluated as is explained in the previous section.

For example, dealing with the prospect lattice $\mathcal{L} = \{\pi_1, \pi_2\}$, in which the prospect π_i is more attractive than π_j, the prospect probabilities are estimated by the expressions

$$p(\pi_i) = f(\pi_i) + 0.25,$$
$$p(\pi_j) = f(\pi_j) - 0.25. \tag{35}$$

To illustrate how the procedure described above works, let us consider the lotteries discussed by Kahneman and Tversky [45]. Consider, for instance, the lotteries

$$L_1 = \{6, 0.45 \mid 0, 0.55\}, \qquad L_2 = \{3, 0.9 \mid 0, 0.1\}.$$

Calculating their expected utilities, we assume, for simplicity, linear utility functions $u(x) = cx$. The corresponding utility factors of both the lotteries are equal,

$$f(\pi_1) = 0.5, \qquad f(\pi_2) = 0.5.$$

The second prospect is more attractive, being more certain. Then, employing rule (35), we have

$$p(\pi_1) = 0.25, \qquad p(\pi_2) = 0.75.$$

The experimental results of Kahneman and Tversky [45] are

$$p_{exp}(\pi_1) = 0.14, \qquad p_{exp}(\pi_2) = 0.86,$$

where $p_{exp}(\pi_i)$ is the ratio of the number of the decision makers, choosing the lottery L_i, to the total number of participants. Within the statistical errors of ± 0.1 of these experiments, our theoretical prediction agrees with the empirical results.

Another example by Kahneman and Tversky [45] is the choice between the lotteries

$$L_1 = \{6, 0.001 \mid 0, 0.999\}, \qquad L_2 = \{3, 0.002 \mid 0, 0.998\},$$

which enjoy the same utility factors

$$f(\pi_1) = 0.5, \qquad f(\pi_2) = 0.5,$$

as in the previous example. The uncertainties of the two lotteries are close to each other. However, the gain in the first prospect is essentially larger, which makes it more attractive, hence, the second prospect less attractive. As a result, the prospect preference reverses, as compared to the previous case, with the prospect probabilities

$$p(\pi_1) = 0.75, \qquad p(\pi_2) = 0.25.$$

The experimental data of Kahneman and Tversky [45] are

$$p_{exp}(\pi_1) = 0.73, \qquad p_{exp}(\pi_2) = 0.27.$$

Thus our theoretical prediction practically coincides with the empirical data.

We also have analyzed a number of other experimental examples, obtaining good agreement of our theoretical predictions with empirical results. However, we shall not overload the present report by the description of all these experiments, which will be the topic of a separate paper.

7   Conclusion

Decision making very often meets the necessity of deciding under uncertainty. Applying quantum techniques to decision making, one has to use the appropriate mathematical tools. We have shown that the correct mathematical foundation of quantum decision theory, dealing with uncertain events, requires the use of positive operator-valued measure that is a generalization of the projection-valued measure. The latter is used for operationally testable events, but cannot be applied to uncertain events typical of decision making under uncertainty. Such operationally uncertain events require the use of the operator-valued measure. In decision making, one has to distinguish composite non-entangled events from composite entangled events. The accurate mathematical formulation of entangled events is based on the notion of entangled or nonseparable prospect operators in a Hilbert-Schmidt space. This should not be confused with the entanglement of functions in a Hilbert space. The operationally testable events are called modes. Therefore the entanglement of such events can be termed *mode entanglement.*

According to the principle of quantum-classical correspondence, classical probabilities can be treated as a limiting case of quantum probabilities, when the effect of decoherence is present. We consider the occurrence of classical probabilities exactly in this sense, which is completely in the frame of quantum theory. We stress that the Kochen-Specker theorem, proving the impossibility of non-contextual hidden variables has no relation to our approach.

Quantum probability can be essentially different from the form of classical probability only for entangled events, defined through the mode entanglement in a Hilbert-Schmidt space. The necessary condition for the appearance of a quantum interference term in the quantum probability is the occurrence of entangled prospects and the existence of an entangled strategic state of a decision maker. The origin of uncertainties in standard lotteries is explained. Our approach makes it possible to provide theoretical predictions that are in good numerical agreement with the results of empirical observations.

Our approach is principally different from those of other authors [11] in several basic points. First, we develop a general theory based on rigorous mathematics of quantum measurement theory and quantum information theory, which can be applied to any decision-making processes. Different from [11] and others, we do not construct special schemes for studying some particular problems. Second, we give a mathematically correct definition of quantum joint probabilities as the probabilities of composite events realized in different measurement channels and represented in tensor-product Hilbert spaces. In contrast, other authors usually consider a single Hilbert space and deal with the Lüders probabilities of consecutive events, which are, actually, transition probabilities, but cannot be treated as conditional probabilities [30]. Third, we emphasize the necessity of entangled events for the appearance of quantum effects, such as the arising interference. Fourth, we define the entanglement of operationally testable events as mode entanglement described by the nonseparable prospect operators in a Hilbert-Schmidt space. Fifth, our theory allows for quantitative predictions of decision making, without any fitting parameters, including quantitative explanations of classical decision-making paradoxes. This makes our approach unique, since there is no other approach that could be compared with empirical results without invoking fitting parameters.

References

1. Williams, C.P., Clearwater, S.H.: Explorations in Quantum Computing. Springer, New York (1998)
2. Nielsen, M.A., Chuang, I.L.: Quantum Computation and Quantum Information. Cambridge University, Cambridge (2000)
3. Keyl, M.: Fundamentals of quantum information theory. Phys. Rep. **369**, 431–548 (2002)
4. Vedral, V.: Introduction to Quantum Information Science. Oxford Press, Oxford (2007)
5. Barnett, S.M.: Quantum Information. Oxford Press, Oxford (2009)
6. Eisert, J., Wilkens, M.: Quantum games. J. Mod. Opt. **47**, 2543–2556 (2000)
7. Yukalov, V.I., Sornette, D.: Scheme of thinking quantum systems. Laser Phys. Lett. **6**, 833–839 (2009)
8. Yukalov, V.I., Yukalova, E.P., Sornette, D.: Mode interference in quantum joint probabilities for multimode bose-condensed systems. Laser Phys. Lett. **10**, 115502 (2013)
9. Bohr, N.: Light and life. Nature **131**, 457–459 (1933)
10. Bohr, N.: Atomic Physics and Human Knowledge. Wiley, New York (1958)
11. Busemeyer, J.R., Bruza, P.: Quantum Models of Cognition and Decision. Cambridge University, Cambridge (2012)
12. Bagarello, F.: Quantum Dynamics for Classical Systems. Wiley, Hoboken (2013)
13. Haven, E., Khrennikov, A.: Quantum Social Science. Cambridge University, Cambridge (2013)
14. von Neuman, J.: Mathematical Foundations of Quantum Mechanics. Princeton University, Princeton (1955)
15. Yukalov, V.I., Sornette, D.: Quantum decision theory as quantum theory of measurements. Phys. Lett. A **372**, 6867–6871 (2008)
16. Yukalov, V.I., Sornette, D.: Processing information in quantum decision theory. Entropy **11**, 1073–1120 (2009)
17. Yukalov, V.I., Sornette, D.: Physics of risk and uncertainty in quantum decision making. Eur. Phys. J. B **71**, 533–548 (2009)
18. Yukalov, V.I., Sornette, D.: Mathematical structure of quantum decision theory. Adv. Complex Syst. **13**, 659–698 (2010)
19. Yukalov, V.I., Sornette, D.: Decision theory with prospect interference and entanglement. Theory Decis. **70**, 283–328 (2011)
20. Bogolubov, N.N.: Lectures on Quantum Statistics, vol. 1. Gordon and Breach, New York (1967)

21. Bogolubov, N.N.: Lectures on Quantum Statistics, vol. 2. Gordon and Breach, New York (1970)
22. Yukalov, V.I.: Theory of cold atoms: basics of quantum statistics. Laser Phys. **23**, 062001 (2013)
23. Wheeler, J.A., Zurek, W.H.: Quantum Theory and Measurement. Princeton University Press, Princeton (1983)
24. Kraus, K.: States, Effects, and Operations. Springer, Berlin (1983)
25. Holevo, A.S.: Statistical Structure of Quantum Theory. Springer, Berlin (2001)
26. Holevo, A.S.: Probabilistic and Statistical Aspects of Quantum Theory. Springer, Berlin, Berlin (2011)
27. Holevo, A.S., Giovannetti, V.: Quantum channels and their entropic characteristics. Rep. Prog. Phys. **75**, 046001 (2012)
28. Birkhoff, G., von Neumann, J.: The logic of quantum mechanics. Ann. Math. **37**, 823–843 (1936)
29. Gleason, A.M.: Measures on the closed subspaces of a Hilbert space. J. Math. Mech. **6**, 885–893 (1957)
30. Yukalov, V.I., Sornette, D.: Quantum probabilities of composite events in quantum measurements with multimode states. Laser Phys. **23**, 105502 (2013)
31. Reed, M., Simon, B.: Methods of Modern Mathematical Physics, vol. 1. Academic Press, New York (1980)
32. Gohberg, I.: Semi-separable operators along chains of projections and systems. Math. Anal. Appl. **125**, 124–140 (1987)
33. Gillespie, J.: Separable operators in scattering theory. Phys. Rev. **160**, 1432–1440 (1967)
34. Yukalov, V.I.: Entanglement measure for composite systems. Phys. Rev. Lett. **90**, 167905 (2003)
35. Yukalov, V.I.: Evolutional entanglement in nonequilibrium processes. Mod. Phys. Lett. B **17**, 95–103 (2003)
36. Yukalov, V.I.: Quantifying entanglement production of quantum operations. Phys. Rev. A **68**, 022109 (2003)
37. Yukalov, V.I., Sornette, D.: Entanglement production in quantum decision making. Phys. At. Nucl. **73**, 559–562 (2010)
38. Bohr, N.: Collected Works. The Correspondence Principle, vol. 3. North-Holland, Amsterdam (1976)
39. Kochen, S., Specker, E.P.: The problem of hidden variables in quantum mechanics. J. Math. Mech. **17**, 59–87 (1967)
40. Zurek, W.H.: Decoherence, einselection, and the quantum origin of the classical. Rev. Mod. Phys. **75**, 715–776 (2003)
41. Schlosshauer, M.A.: Decoherence and the Quantum-to-Classical Transition. Springer, Berlin (2007)
42. Joos, E., Zeh, H.D., Kiefer, C., Giulini, D.J., Kupsh, J., Stamatesku, I.O.: Decoherence and the Appearance of a Classical World in Quantum Theory. Springer, Berlin (2010)
43. Yukalov, V.I., Sornette, D.: Quantum probabilities and entanglement for multimode quantum systems. J. Phys. Conf. Ser. **497**, 012034 (2014)
44. Yukalov, V.I., Sornette, D.: Conditions for quantum interference in cognitive sciences. Top. Cogn. Sci. **6**, 79–90 (2014)
45. Kahneman, D., Tversky, A.: Prospect theory: an analysis of decision under risk. Econometrica **47**, 263–292 (1979)

Games, Politics, and Social Aspects

Aesthetics as Incentive: Privacy in a Presence Culture

Christian Flender[✉]

Faculty of Economics and Behavioral Sciences,
University of Freiburg, Freiburg, Germany
christian.flender@wvf.uni-freiburg.de

Abstract. With information technology penetrating every aspect of human life privacy is "literally" present in industrialized societies. Nonetheless, even in academic circles privacy remains a contested concept and its meaning is far from consensual among consumers, customers, citizens, patients, and institutions. This essay departs from a fusion of presence and linguistic expression and argues that the many failed attempts to draw a clear boundary around the concept of privacy (secrecy, information control, access restrictions, etc.) are missing out on language being a medium that overcomes the separation between humans and things (physical and informational). In a presence culture where language is a mediator, quantum concepts like indeterminacy, context, and inseparability are not simply metaphorical. Rather, they reconcile humans with the world of things in which privacy turns from an abstract concept to a tangible presence.

Keywords: Privacy · Presence · Quantum concepts · Aesthetics

1 Introduction

"What is it like to live in the information age?" is a question that besets many scholars of our time concerned with impacts of information technology upon individuals, institutions, and society at large [1, 2]. Mobile devices, smart homes, and the many Internet services, just to name a few instances of information technology, alter entrenched norms of communication and association and constantly change human behaviors, attitudes, economic relations, and social configurations. With personal data fueling the many applications of highly connected endpoints, privacy, a concept that dates back to pre-industrialized times, gained new attention. Ever since its inception, privacy has posed the question of concealment and exposure: where does the private end and where does the public begin?

Privacy has been defined from a multitude of perspectives. Often it appears as a concept and basis for law, economic policy, and security appliances. Some authors have argued that privacy is a right to be let alone [3]. In order for individuals to make free decisions and develop personality a restricted space to do

© Springer International Publishing Switzerland 2015
H. Atmanspacher et al. (Eds.): QI 2014, LNCS 8951, pp. 165–176, 2015.
DOI: 10.1007/978-3-319-15931-7_13

so is requirement. Like one's home with walls, doors, and access restrictions, consumers, customers, citizens, patients, and institutions shall have the right to draw a separation line between a private realm of data usage and a public space where they don't mind being exposed to others. Informational self-determination is a cornerstone of data protection legislation in many countries, and, in democratic societies, it accounts for the need of individuals and institutions to draw this separation line [4].

However, with the ease and comfort to make things public by means of information technology exercising privacy rights has become increasingly difficult. Once personal data has reached unwanted recipients, information control is hard if not impossible. Data is easily reproduced and disseminated beyond control and accountability [5]. Enormous benefits come along with eased information exchange and ways to express in digital public. Transaction costs are reduced, association with like-minded others is easier than ever before, and showing who one is on the Web contributes to self-development and fulfillment of social needs and desires [6]. Nonetheless, maintaining a protected space separated from public remains a key challenge in the twenty-first century. Economic policy, law, and privacy technology aim at addressing this challenge and balancing the many conflicting interests, e.g. new business models based on "Big Data" vs. personal rights. All their attempts depart from a consensual notion of privacy, i.e. an understanding of what exactly needs to be protected. But even in academic circles privacy remains a contested concept. Its meaning is far from consensual among consumers, customers, citizens, patients, and institutions.

In this essay it is argued that difficulties in getting a grip on privacy are due to a still predominating meaning culture [7] that struggles with expressing privacy in linguistic terms. In such a culture the meaning of concepts like privacy stands for or represents something, e.g. a right. In opposition to a meaning culture, a presence culture takes linguistic expressions as a medium that overcomes the separation between privacy stakeholders (consumers, citizens, etc.) and physical and informational things (shopping preferences, political views, rights, etc.). Presence is a mode of privacy that is achieved by ways of accessing things as they are available and show up in the world, i.e. within language and not from a bird's eye view. Privacy presents itself to each individual as a mode of concealment and exposure beyond privacy preferences being explicable in a representational fashion. Quantum concepts like indeterminacy, context, and inseparability reconcile individuals with their (self-) expressions and so they are not metaphorical or representational in the sense of standing for something, i.e. physical effects. Rather, they provide the very means to render privacy towards tangible presence. A heightened privacy-awareness opens the arena for an aesthetic dimension that so far has remained untouched. Even more important, it may trigger forthcoming generations to engage with the topic beyond a mere take-or-leave-it approach[1].

In the next section privacy is discussed from the perspective of Cartesian dualism where individuals refer to themselves as subjects as opposed to the

---

[1] Thinking of privacy as an obsolescent model would constitute such an attitude.

world of things. In such a meaning culture an ontic-ontological divide is presupposed and here it is elaborated with reference to privacy. In Sect. 3, presence is introduced as a way of achieving access to what is available within language. Quantum concepts like indeterminacy, context, and inseparability ground presence as a mode of being-in-the-world by pushing the quest for meaning of concepts to its boundary. Section 4 proposes to think about privacy as grounded in a presence culture. In a presence culture the ontic-ontological divide of Cartesian dualism is disarmed. Here, as a mode of concealment and exposure, privacy is a tangible presence of aesthetic value. Conclusions are drawn in the last section.

2   Privacy in a Meaning Culture

In an article on presence historian and literature critic Gumbrecht notes [8]:

"In a meaning culture the dominant form of human self-reference will always correspond to the basic outline of what Western culture calls 'subject' and 'subjectivity', that is, it will refer to a bodiless observer who, from a position of eccentricity vis-à-vis the world of things, will attribute meaning to these things."

What Gumbrecht describes is what many privacy scholars do when defining their subject matter. At the center of quite a few definitions of privacy is the subject or thinking individual, i.e. the *res cogitans* as French philosopher René Descartes (1596–1650) named it [9]. The thinking person is separated from the external world of material things, i.e. the *res extensae*. Metaphysically, the subject, its ability to reflect and make use of language is over, beneath, or beyond the material substance of physical reality. Accordingly, privacy as defined in the Cartesian tradition uses linguistic expressions to attribute meaning to things and thinking subjects, e.g. in terms of abstract rights.

As one of the most cited definitions the right to be let alone accounts for individuals making free decisions while inhabiting an autonomous space for self-development and recreation [3]. In Germany, informational self-determination is a derived basic right and attributes to each individual in society the legal ability to decide what personal data is disclosed, when, how, to what extent, and to whom [4]. The subject or individual is at the center of such meaning attributions.

In an economic context, privacy is often reduced to personal data, i.e. attributes of or about an individual [10]. Such attributes stand for or represent customers or citizens in the flesh and turn into a tradable asset like a customer profile or digital dossier[2] Here, again, the meaning of privacy is an attribution in a narrative or descriptive fashion.

Sociologically, privacy is expressed as a dynamic boundary regulation process oscillating between concealment and exposure [12]. How this process materializes remains an open question. What are concrete situations in which concealment

---

[2] This is not to say that individuals in the flesh can be identified. Anonymization aims at preventing identification. However, it is a myth that privacy only matters to person-identifying information [11].

and exposure apply? How to define such situations without abstracting to much from individual idiosyncrasies or falling into relativism?

Ontically, privacy is a right, a tradable asset, or a boundary regulation process. Ontologically, however, in a meaning culture and the Cartesian tradition, there remains the unbridgeable gap or chasm between the subject or *res cogitans*, its preferences, attitudes, and behaviors, and the material or bodily substrate to which it refers, i.e. the subject in the flesh or the *res extensae*. What privacy is does not reduce to what it emerges from.

Positivists may claim that privacy simply is a right, a tradable asset, or a boundary regulation process. No interpretation is required. Positivism is the epistemological correlate of realism in ontology. Here, things exist out there independent of our sensory and cognitive faculties. It would be naïve to deny ontic experience. Ontically, there is no need for interpretation or meaning attribution. Things are the way they show up as available or present. Privacy is a derived human right. Where is interpretation required? Here it is: privacy is a tradable asset or a boundary regulation process. Thus, epistemically, the meaning of privacy varies from one discourse (law) to another (economics or sociology). Positivism forces interpretation and meaning attribution as long as the ontic-ontological divide is not addressed. Ontologically, one won't be able to say what privacy is as long as one merely talks about privacy in the realm of epistemology.

In physics, presumably the most rigorous of all natural sciences, interpretation and meaning attribution, for a long time, were out of the question. When in 1900 Max Planck (1858–1947) discovered the quantum this situation changed. It seemed that the microscopic realm of compact particles lacked reality while macroscopic objects like chairs or books, i.e., tangible things, didn't. Physics entered a meaning culture where interpretation was unavoidable. Up to this day, many interpretations about physical reality stand side by side, e.g. the Copenhagen interpretation or the many-worlds theory. In a meaning culture, like for the concept of privacy, there is no consensus about the *res extensae* let alone the *res cogitans*.

In the following section, attempts to attribute meaning to concepts like privacy will be pushed to their boundary. An interdisciplinary approach that allows doing so is quantum interaction (QI). QI provides an open-minded and intellectually-inspiring platform to investigate quantum concepts and effects in a broad context spanning across the natural and social sciences, engineering, and the humanities and arts.

3   Presence or Why Quantum Concepts are not Metaphorical

When today's users of computing devices like smart phones or tablet computers access the Internet they are confronted with a particular design of their device at hand. In the process of developing such devices linguistic expression and meaning attribution is at play. Back in the early 1980s, when commercial operating systems with their graphical user interfaces emerged, they offered a space on the screen that resembled a work desk with utilities like folders, bins, and an area where work items and files could be placed in such a way that suits the person at work. Metaphors like the desktop have accompanied engineering and science ever since the industrial revolution. Think of the image of a moving person or good travelling from a point of departure to a destination. How many artifacts did the metaphor of moving subjects and objects inspire to ease transportation and free persons or goods from their limited capacity to move in space? Cars, bikes, trains, trucks, and many other transportation mechanisms have been subject to metaphorical meaning attributions, at least in the process of development.

A metaphor is a linguistic expression (a text, formula, or, more generally, a signifier) that stands for or represents a thing in context (the signified), e.g., a wooden work desk, and that is applied to another context, e.g. an interface of a computing device. Interpreting online privacy as a human right takes the imagination of an autonomous, self-determined individual and applies it to the context of Internet services. Likewise, the structure and behavior of physical particles expressed in algebraic terms is subject to application in economics or computer science [10,13–16]. In this sense concepts acquire meaning by shifting conventional use from one discourse to another. The act of meaning attribution involves an adjustment of perspective. It literally opens a novel view on the phenomenon at hand and opens a space for innovation and creativity.

Quantum concepts are special. They raise the question of how the very act of meaning attribution works. What fascinates scholars within and apart from physics and what raises this question is the quantum enigma, i.e. the apparent "mystery" where subjectivity enters the arena of descriptions or attributions of meaning to materiality [17]. Paradigmatic to this mystery is the double-slit experiment.

In the double-slit experiment particles like photons or electrons run through two slits. On a screen behind the slits appears an interference pattern, i.e. a pattern of dark and white bands indicating particles to behave like waves. A wave is a series of crests and troughs and when two or more waves arrive at the same time and space, they either add up or cancel each other out. The result is an interference pattern. If an experimenter wants to know the slit a particle actually run through at a particular point in time, the interference pattern disappears. On the screen only one dark band appears. This indicates that matter and energy behave like discrete particles. The measurement or observation at one of the slits makes photons or electrons to behave like discrete particles and thus they do not behave like waves spread out and extended in space. Both measurement contexts are incompatible. It is not possible to reduce wave-like matter and energy to particle-like matter and energy and vice versa (wave-particle duality). In the wave scenario the slit a particle runs through is not determined. Particles seem to run through both slits simultaneously. After an act of measurement a particle runs through either one or the other slit. The slit through which a particle passes is determined with the measurement performed upon it. Beforehand, like in the wave case, it is indeterminate (measurement problem).

What is the meaning of materiality according to this paradox? Does the *res extensae* refer to a wave, a particle, or both? What's the role of language and formal expression within such meaning attributions?

At first sight it appears that the quantum enigma or measurement problem is confined to a meaning culture. Observations made in experiments are expressed in numbers and formal terms. Numerical and algebraic concepts stand for or represent the signified physical phenomena. The mathematical tools developed to describe quantum effects were generalized by quite a few authors [18,19]. This made them apt for metaphorical use, e.g. use in computer science or economics. As an illustrative example take State-Context-Property (SCoP) systems which have been successfully applied to model concepts themselves [20–22]. In a paper on quantum effects in conversations it was shown that concepts within language use can have a topological structure transcending subject-object dualities [14]. A subject-object duality presupposes an ontic-ontological divide or Cartesian dualism and is paradigmatic for meaning attributions. For instance, a scientist attributes meaning to her object of investigation; let's say the meaning of matter and energy is there being either a wave, a particle, or both!? In such a meaning case materiality and linguistic expression seem at odds. In a presence culture, however, understanding the meaning of things (objects or subjects, physical or informational) are always already at work. As the philosopher Noë put it though in a slightly different way by referring to perception and concepts, the meaning of things and their presence arrive at the party together [23]. Things are present, even when there is no direct sensory affection involved. Think of your neighbor next door, who is present as absent. He is there, you can go next door and visit him without him being in sight, i.e. without perceiving him visually or hearing noises coming from next door. Thus, beyond perception, abstract concepts like privacy can be present in absence without attributing significance like in a meaning culture where linguistic expressions refer to or represent things. Accordingly, quantum effects in a presence culture are not representational, and, therefore, they are not metaphorical either. In summary, meaning and presence can go well together. Their distinction is not binary.

4   Privacy in a Presence Culture

In 1959 a short book titled "Gelassenheit" was published in Germany[3] [25]. In this book Martin Heidegger (1889–1976) gives a Memorial Address to the composer Conradin Kreutzer (1780–1849) at the hundredth anniversary of his death. The Memorial Address, amongst other topics, talks about technical devices in the atomic age. At the time the Address was given technology promised to solve the scarcity of natural resources and the supply of abundant energy. Always skeptical about calculative rationality and technological enthusiasm, the author meditates about a forgotten style of thinking that is rooted or grounded in a presence culture. Despite his skepticism towards the Cartesian tradition characterized by a relation of man to the world that is a technical one and was

---

[3] An English translation appeared in 1966 [24].

developed in the seventeenth century first and only in Europe [24], he wasn't as naïve as rejecting a meaning culture outright. For him a fusion or amalgamation of meaning attribution and presence was not contradictory. On page 54 he states [24]:

"But will not saying both 'yes' and 'no' this way to technical devices make our relation to technology ambivalent and insecure? On the contrary! Our relation to technology will become wonderfully simple and relaxed. We let technical devices enter our daily life, and at the same time leave them outside, that is, let them alone, as things which are nothing absolute but remain dependent upon something higher. I would add this comportment toward technology which expresses 'yes' and at the same time 'no' by an old word, releasement[4] toward things".

At the time the Memorial Address was given privacy was not yet a major concern. Concern was more a fear of groundlessness typical of a meaning culture or post-metaphysical age where there is an infinite number of representations or interpretations of any given phenomenon as well as domination of the ontic over, beneath, or beyond the ontological. Discourse of thinking appeared in light of an uprising atomic age. Today, half a century later, with information technology at the forefront in many realms of global society, personal information and "Big Data" are said to be the oil, or, to put in quantum terms, the uranium of the twenty-first century. It is striking to see quantum interaction as a fusion of the atomic and the information age with the exit from nuclear and fossil-fuel energy only being a symptom of this fusion. More fundamental than the energy revolution may be an epistemological shift towards releasement, i.e. a mode of concealment and exposure that takes personal data not to represent subjects as opposed to things.

The following paragraph draws from the second part of discourse on thinking. In a conversation on a pathway, a scholar, a scientist, and a teacher develop such an epistemological shift, and, while doing so, they achieve a reconciliation of meaning and presence. Releasement towards personal data and openness towards their meanings is the cornerstone of privacy in a presence culture.

The conversation starts with thinking in a meaning culture understood as representing as a kind of willing. To think is to will and will is to think. In contrast, in a presence culture thinking is non-willing or waiting upon instead of waiting for. It involves a negation directed at willing, a negation that renounces willing. Non-willing or waiting upon is the preparation for releasement. In a quantum world there is indeterminacy. The state of a quantum system is not determined before measurement is performed upon it (cf. double-slit experiment in Sect. 3). That what is not yet known ontologically is the negative that renounces willing[5] Weaning from will is context-dependent. It stands in contrast to a context or mode where we attribute or represent meaning. According to a scholar in the conversation on a pathway [24]:

---

[4] Releasement is not to confuse with composure, calmness, or unconcern which all may come with a connotation of passivity and indecisiveness.

[5] In contrast, what is not yet known epistemologically is due to lack of information or knowledge.

"This representing, for instance, places before us what is typical of a tree, of a pitcher, of a bowl, of a stone, of plants, and of animals as that view into which we look when one thing confronts us in the appearance of a tree, another in the appearance of a pitcher, this in the appearance of stones, many in the appearance of plants, and many in the appearance of animals."

Likewise, placing privacy before us in terms of a right, a tradable asset, or a boundary regulation process is an act of the will, which is a meaning attribution. However, such a confrontation is always open in the sense of surrounded by a horizon. In a meaning culture this surrounding region as it stands in itself is missed out. An interpretation or act of meaning attribution singles out things and describes them ontically from a bird's eye view within a region. In a presence culture privacy as encircled by a horizon of meaning comes to meet us either as a right, an asset, or a process. It comes to meet us as its region that itself is at once an expanse and an abiding. Privacy is present as absent, it is near at a distance and distant in its nearness. The presence of privacy that goes hand in hand with its meaning is that-which-regions as an abiding expanse, an openness that returns to and rests in itself and thus no longer confronts us or stands against a subject. The fusion of meaning and presence is quite well illustrated in the conversation on a pathway [24]:

"Scientist: I must confess that I can't quite represent in my mind all that you say about a region, expanse and abiding, and about return and resting."

"Scholar: Probably it can't be represented at all, in so far as in representing everything has become an object that stands opposite us within a horizon."

"Scientist: Then we can't really describe what we have named?"

"Teacher: No. Any description would reify it."

"Scholar: Nevertheless it lets itself be named, and being named it can be thought about"

"Teacher: only if thinking is no longer representing."

This returning to and resting in itself of that-which-regions can in fact be named and thought about by means of quantum terms. In a paper on quantum effects in language it was argued that in a conversation like the one on a pathway, concepts acquire a topological structure that transcends any opposition between subjects and objects [14]. That-which-regions is topological and inseparably connected to itself. It can be named without attributing meaning. In a conversation interactive pathways emerge from speech enacted from a person's *Dasein* in such a way that conversational pathways entangle and cannot be reduced to the acts from which they emerged. In a region meaning and presence arrive together. Here time is not chronological. Time returns to and rests in that-which-regions. The suspension of the will involved in the fusion of meaning and presence is not passivity. Neither is it activity understood as an action that transforms a pre-state to a post-state. Remember indeterminacy for which there are no pre-determined states. Thus the chronotope of privacy as a mode of concealment and exposure is releasement, a way of thinking beyond activity and passivity, open to meaning or understanding while not reducing it to a right, and asset, or a boundary regulation process.

At this point, some readers might legitimately ask what we gain from a reconciliation of meaning and presence for all practical purposes. An answer is ready-to-hand. Our globalized society and economy rests and relies upon trust. As recent media coverage illustrates, ideological thinking is still omnipresent with mass surveillance and censorship only being a few symptoms. Sticking to privacy and the dominant role information technology plays in daily life, releasement as a mode of bridging the ontic-ontological divide may enable forthcoming generations to engage with the topic beyond a mere take-it-or-leave it approach. Often users of Internet services claim that they don't have anything to hide and thus don't fear inappropriate data usage. Some privacy advocates develop a mild form of paranoia and experience chilling effects, i.e. they observe prevention from associating freely with others in fear of being tracked and traced. Both extremes are legitimate and not unusual for post-metaphysical societies. An exit strategy that follows neither one of the extremes nor does it embrace groundlessness as quite a few meditative practices do is art. Art broaches post-metaphysical thinking and opens spaces for aesthetic experience. Science is art. Enabling scientists to question their own presuppositions, i.e., their place in a meaning culture, distinguishes science like art from other cultural practices where meaning attribution and metaphysical thinking is unavoidable and even desired.

5   Conclusion

This essay embraced a non-binary distinction between presence and meaning in regards to privacy. As basic human rights are concerned, privacy has become a crucial concept in the information age. Since the emergence of a way of thinking that was coined second-order observation, i.e., a way of observing one's self and the things in the world in the very act of observation, meaning attribution has been the dominant intellectual mode of inquiry [7]. According to this way of thinking about privacy an infinite number of representations or interpretations of concealment and exposure are possible. Privacy as a right, as a tradable asset, or as a boundary regulation process are only three of the many meanings people refer to when actually withdrawing from public or exposing themselves. Surveys and polls witness that digital citizens are concerned about privacy and the secondary use of their personal data [10,26]. It is no wonder that most consumers, customers, citizens, patients, and institutions do have an opinion about privacy and an idea about its meaning. However, it's likewise not surprising that consensus is difficult to achieve given the many conflicting interests among, for instance, citizens (e.g. freedom of speech) and governments (e.g. security).

In a meaning culture, grounding privacy in the material world, at first sight, seems paradoxical with regard to the many abstract definitions. In the first place, a right, a tradable asset, and a boundary regulation process do not refer to a particular individual in the flesh. Taking quantum concepts into account dissolves this paradox. Quantum theory raises the question of what materiality actually is and how it refers to linguistic expressions. Indeterminacy as that what is not yet known ontologically grounds meaning in a presence culture. Meaning is always relative to a spatial vantage point, not only in perception. For instance, one's right to informational self-determination is present in absence even when not actually exercised. Its context is law. Likewise, actually exercising informational self-determination depends on a context grounded in our daily encounters with information technology. Thinking of language as a mediation between subjects and things (physical and informational) inseparably connects subjects and things as that-which-regions, a topological structure typical for a presence culture. A conversation like the one between a scholar, a scientist, and a teacher illustrates that meaning can be grounded in a presence culture where time is not chronological but spatial. The act of will suspension is not a falling into passivity. Neither is it an active attempt to make use of metaphors, i.e. to apply the meaning of privacy from one context (e.g. law) to another (e.g. computer science). Rather, in a presence culture, waiting upon and non-willing are conditions of possibility for a heightened privacy-awareness, i.e. an awareness of the many paradoxical meanings of the concept. That-which-regions transcends subject-object dualities and Cartesian dualism and opens the possibility for aesthetic experience.

How can art as science and science as art help us to trigger forthcoming generations to engage with the topic beyond a mere take-it-or-leave-it approach? As basic human rights are concerned the relevance of privacy in the current age is doubtless. The means to achieve privacy-awareness may indeed draw from quantum interaction (QI). At the heart of QI and privacy is the subject and its relation to the public in terms of objects (physical and informational) being accessible or given to others and even everyone else. Objects are open within a region that surrounds meanings. Conceiving privacy in such a way requires being-in or waiting upon into the openness of what is given beyond relativistic and metaphysical interpretations.

Thinking privacy as a regional, spatial, or topological concept is not to deny realism. In pre-twentieth century ontology realism is about being of objects or things (Seiendes). No interpretation is required. As laid out in the section on the double-slit experiment, for positivists in pre-twentieth century ontology there is no need for interpretation. That is fair enough. But is there consensus about results of the experiment? If not, can interpreting the results be avoided? From a positivist viewpoint in twenty-first century ontology isn't the result simply the way it is (presence) although interpretation (meaning) is not denied or impossible? In twenty-first century ontology realism is also about being of objects or things (Sein), however, not as opposed to the subject. Privacy in a presence culture is neither abstract nor simply theoretical as opposed to practical or empirical. Privacy as that-which-regions eludes any of the isms. It can be named without representing or interpreting it in terms of something else. Its literal appearance and written form (Seiendes) - in this essay and the many other sources and disciplines - will never exhaust its being (Sein). A non-binary distinction between presence and meaning is an oxymoron. However, it is even more than a linguistic style once it has been grasped that paradoxes and contradictions constitute the interpretation pole within oscillations between meaning and presence.

For all practical purposes QI develops tools to conduct science as traditionally conceived. For the purpose of reconciling subjects and things in the information age it may help us to embody and cope with a chronotope that is aptly described as a broadening present. Information technology tracks and traces our journeys. Here forgetting is fundamentally different to the way, and more difficult than, we, as humans, are capable of. At the same time the future is increasingly difficult to forecast (e.g. global financial crisis, Fukushima, etc.).

"Between the 'new' inaccessible future and the new past that we no longer (want to) have behind ourselves, we have begun to feel that the present is becoming broader and that the rhythm of time is slowing down" [7].

References

1. Nissenbaum, H.: Privacy in Context: Technology, Policy, and the Integrity of Social Life. Stanford University Press, Palo Alto (2010)
2. Solove, D.: Understanding Privacy. Harvard University Press, Cambridge (2008)
3. Warren, S., Brandeis, L.: The right to privacy. Harvard Law Rev. **4**, 193–220 (1890)
4. Westin, A.: Privacy and Freedom. Atheneum, New York (1967)
5. Weitzner, D., Abelson, H., Berners-Lee, T., Feigenbaum, J., Hendler, J., Sussman, G.: Information accountability. Commun. ACM **51**, 82–87 (2008)
6. Buchmann, J.: Internet Privacy - Eine Multidisziplinäre Bestandsaufnahme/ A Multidisciplinary Analysis. Springer, Heidelberg (2012)
7. Gumbrecht, H.U.: Production of Presence: What Meaning Cannot Convey. Stanford University Press, Stanford (2004)
8. Gumbrecht, H.U.: Presence achieved in language (with special attention given to the presence of the past). Hist. Theor. **45**, 317–327 (2006)
9. Descartes, R.: Descartes: Meditations on First Philosophy: With Selections from the Objections and Replies. Cambridge University Press, Cambridge (1996)
10. Flender, C., Müller, G.: Type indeterminacy in privacy decisions: the privacy paradox revisited. In: Busemeyer, J.R., Dubois, F., Lambert-Mogiliansky, A., Melucci, M. (eds.) QI 2012. LNCS, vol. 7620, pp. 148–159. Springer, Heidelberg (2012)
11. Müller, G.: Die Mythen von Transparenz und Sicherheit im Internet. Ansprache zur Verleihung der Ehrendoktorwürde der TU Darmstadt (2011)
12. Altman, I.: The Environment and Social Behavior: Privacy, Personal Space, Territory, and Crowding. Brooks/Cole Publishing Company, Monterey (1975)
13. Lambert-Mogiliansky, A., Zamir, S., Zwirn, H.: Type indeterminacy: a model of the KT (Kahneman-Tversky)-man. J. Math. Psychol. **53**, 349–361 (2009)
14. Flender, C., Kitto, K., Bruza, P.: Beyond ontology in information systems. In: Bruza, P., Sofge, D., Lawless, W., van Rijsbergen, K., Klusch, M. (eds.) QI 2009. LNCS, vol. 5494, pp. 276–288. Springer, Heidelberg (2009)
15. Busemeyer, J., Lambert-Mogiliansky, A.: An exploration of type indeterminacy in strategic decision-making. In: Bruza, P., Sofge, D., Lawless, W., van Rijsbergen, K., Klusch, M. (eds.) QI 2009. LNCS, vol. 5494, pp. 113–127. Springer, Heidelberg (2009)
16. Bruza, P., Kitto, K., Nelson, D., McEvoy, K.: Entangling words and meaning. In: Proceedings of the 2nd International Symposium on Quantum Interaction (QI 2008). University of Oxford (2008)

17. Rosenblum, B., Kuttner, F.: Quantum Enigma: Physics Encounters Consciousness. Oxford University Press, Oxford (2011)
18. Aerts, D.: Foundations of quantum physics: a general realistic and operational approach. Int. J. Theor. Phys. **38**, 289–358 (1999)
19. Busemeyer, J., Wang, Z., Townsend, J.: Quantum dynamics of human decision-making. J. Math. Psychol. **50**, 220–241 (2006)
20. Gabora, L., Aerts, D.: Contextualizing concepts using a mathematical generalization of the quantum formalism. J. Exp. Theor. Artif. Intell. **14**(4), 327–358 (2002)
21. Aerts, D., Gabora, L.: A state-context-property model of concepts and their combinations I: the structure of the sets of contexts and properties. Kybernetes **34**(1&2), 167–191 (2005)
22. Aerts, D., Gabora, L.: A state-context-property model of concepts and their combinations II: a hilbert space representation. Kybernetes **34**(1&2), 192–221 (2005)
23. Noë, A.: Varieties of Presence. Harvard University Press, Cambridge (2012)
24. Heidegger, M.: Discourse on Thinking. Harper and Row, New York (1966)
25. Heidegger, M.: Gelassenheit, 15. Auflage. Klett-Cotta (2012)
26. Acquisti, A., Grossklags, J.: Privacy and rationality in individual decision making. IEEE Secur. Priv. **3**, 26–33 (2005)

A Quantum Formalization for Communication Coordination Problems

Jürgen Hahn(✉) and Paul Weiser

Department of Geodesy and Geoinformation, Vienna University of Technology,
Gusshausstrasse 27-29, 1040 Vienna, Austria
{hahn,weiser}@geoinfo.tuwien.ac.at

Abstract. Humans have developed several strategies to ensure that communication is successful. For example, humans take another person's perspective into account when they design the content of a message. Furthermore, communicated messages exhibit frequent level of detail changes due to the interactive nature of conversations. In this paper, we look at an instance of spatial knowledge transfer that occurs if one person requests route instructions from a knowledgeable source. More specifically, using a quantum cognition approach, we model the process of perspective taking in such a scenario. Our work contributes to the ongoing research effort to make information systems capable of mimicking human-style communication.

Keywords: Communication coordination problems · Referring expressions · Quantum cognition · Order effect · Hilbert space model

1 Introduction

1.1 Statement of the Problem

The ability to communicate is a critical feature for the exchange of knowledge across individuals. A special case of (spatial) knowledge transfer is the exchange of route directions between two human agents, i.e., a knowledgeable source and a target lacking the necessary knowledge to perform a way-finding task between two or more points in geographic space [34].

Most (if not all) communication settings are highly interactive and require all speakers to contribute to the conversation if it is to be successful [10]. For example, when humans communicate routes they are capable of taking another person's perspective [14] to take that person's (assumed) spatial knowledge into account. This means that the level of detail at which information is presented is a function of its recipient, i.e., a tourist will likely receive different information than somebody from town. Additionally, the interactive nature of human communication allows the speaker to adjust the level of detail over the course of the conversation, if the recipient signals that this is necessary [34], for example if an initial assumption made by the speaker is not met.

© Springer International Publishing Switzerland 2015
H. Atmanspacher et al. (Eds.): QI 2014, LNCS 8951, pp. 177–188, 2015.
DOI: 10.1007/978-3-319-15931-7_14

In contrast, today's routing services can neither adapt to a person's individual information needs, nor do they allow for much interaction with the system (cf. [28,31,34]). One reason for this mismatch is the lack of formal models that can help to design next-generation information systems capable of mimicking human-style communication.

In this work, we present a formalism that accounts for perspective taking in human communication settings. In a conversation between humans, referring expressions (words or word phrases) are used to uniquely identify instances of objects. For example, the word "dog" in the utterance "Look at the dog!" is used to identify a particular instance of a dog, out of an environment with mostly non dogs and does not refer to the category of a dog. However, the successful usage of referring expressions depends on whether the other person's perspective is taken into account. In other words, person A increases the likelihood that expression e is understood by person B, if A considers whether B will understand it. This paper argues that perspective taking in communication exhibits an order effect (See Sect. 2.2) and can be modeled by applying principles from quantum cognition. Order effects occur if the sequence of two or more actions or utterances result in different outcomes.

1.2   Motivating Example and Analysis

Consider the following excerpt of a dialogue between a tourist who is visiting Vienna (T = Target) and requesting route instructions from a Viennese (S = Source).

1. T: Excuse me, sir! Can you tell me how I get to [...]
2. S: [...] , and then you pass *Stephansdom* to your left, [...]
3. T: um, wait, *Stephansdom*?
4. S: ... Where are you from?
5. T: Paris.
6. S: *Hmm, ok Stephansdom*, that's a *cathedral* similar to *Notre Dame...*
7. T: ... Ok
8. S: So, once you have passed the *cathedral* to your left, you ...

This small example illustrates the use of referring expressions (RE) in every day language. REs are linguistic selectors that uniquely identify an instance of a category. As such they map a word (or a word phrase) onto a real-world object with the intention that it is recognized and identified in a conversation. Note that referring expressions are indicated by the subscript RE while we use the subscript LM if we talk about the landmark as a real-world object. In line 2, S makes use of the proper noun $Stephansdom_{RE=LM}$ as part of the requested route instruction. Note that objects (e.g., landmarks) in the example conversation are generally not visible to either person (See Clark and Wilkes-Gibbs [11] for a discussion of experiments using REs for visible objects).

Because T cannot visually identify the object S refers to as $Stephansdom_{RE}$, T needs to judge the likelihood that mapping the RE onto the real-world object

Stephansdom$_{LM}$ is successful once she follows the route. As can be seen in line 3, however, T does not believe that she can map the term *Stephansdom$_{RE}$* and asks for clarification. We can now assume that for T *Stephansdom$_{RE}$* is a meaningless and arbitrary combination of symbols [19], while for S the term is grounded in a rich set of experiential knowledge (cf. [6]). As a consequence T's only choice (if she wants to maximize conversation success) is to ask for clarification on this term. We can speculate that, in case S had considered T's non-familiarity with *Stephansdom$_{LM}$* (i.e., taken her perspective) he would not have used the RE in the first place. This means that the order at which the perspective is taken into account (before or after the initial generation of the instruction) affects the resulting RE.

When confronted with T's request for clarification, S realizes that the use of *Stephansdom$_{RE=LM}$* is inadequate for conversation success. Then, with the goal to add contextual information, S asks T where she is from. Setting up such background knowledge lets S find a comparative instance (i.e., *Notre Dame$_{LM}$*) and switch to the term *cathedral$_{RE}$* instead (same object but more general concept). S assumes that this change in level of detail (cf. [35]) results in a more successful instruction. Note that other strategies, e.g., selecting an entirely different landmark for the same instruction, are equally valid but not considered here.

Our example helped to reveal several effects that occur frequently in communication settings. Both the correct use of referring expressions and the ability to provide corresponding adjustments of level of detail are essential to maximize conversation success. Information that is perfectly acceptable for S can be meaningless to T. The construction of messages exhibits an order effect through perspective taking. That is, depending on whether S takes T's perspective before the generation of a message or after T signaled trouble understanding, the resulting RE and its success during conversation can differ.

1.3   Organization of the Paper

The remainder of the paper is structured as follows. First, we briefly review literature concerned with "grounding meaning through communication" and order effects. In Sect. 3 we introduce the properties of a Hilbert Space and discuss the calculation of unitary transformations necessary to model the order effect. With this background, we formalize perspective taking (and the resulting order effect) using the example of exchanging route instructions (See Sect. 4). The paper concludes with a discussion of the presented results and possible future work.

2   Related Work

2.1   The Grounding Model of Communication

Humans have developed a particularly rich set of capabilities to communicate ideas, thoughts, and feelings. Communication often makes use of speech acts, i.e., utterances that can change the state of the world (cf. [5,29]). For example, declarations can have legal and social consequences ("I pronounce you man and wife") while requests can get people to do physical things ("Could you pass me the salt please?"). Others allow the transfer of knowledge across individuals, e.g., assertions of belief ("I'm telling you, the capital of Australia is Canberra not Sydney!"). The success of speech acts, however, depends on whether the utterance receives an uptake from its recipient [8]. Conversely, if a request is not considered by its addressee it has no effect.

In general, communication is an interactive endeavor, i.e., it occurs as a joint activity [8,11] between two or more individuals and requires turn-taking actions by all participants in order to be successful. In this work, we only consider verbal communication between two individuals, but the same concepts hold true for non-verbal communication and several contributors to conversation. Clark [8] defined a framework that proposes that if communication is to be successful any information-bearing utterance must be: (1) attended to, (2) identified, (3) understood, and (4) considered by both listener and speaker. Attendance means that an utterance is heard. Identification means that the message needs to be decoded on a syntactic level ("Did she say Soup or Soap?"). Understanding means that a message needs to be decoded on a semantic level ("did she mean (river) bank or (money) bank"). Finally, consideration means that a message receives an uptake by the participant ("She said pass me the salt", so I give it to her or refuse to do so).

If any of the four stages fails, both participants can engage in a sequence of repair steps to make sure that the utterance is mutually understood. This process is called "grounding through communication" [9]. That is, any utterance needs to be part of common ground [30] (joint knowledge) of all individuals participating in a conversation. For example, consider the following sample of a request for route information:

1. T: Can you tell me the way to the Goethehaus?
2. S: Güterhaus?
3. T: Goethehaus!
4. S: ok sure...

In this example, S was not able to identify the destination (line 2) for which T requested a description (line 1). S initiates a repair sequence by uttering what she understood to be the destination (line 2). This is in turn rejected by T by uttering the correct destination again (line 3). S then accepts the task (line 4) and continues with the next relevant turn, i.e., the actual route instruction. In this example, utterances in lines 1 through 4 were necessary to ground the meaning of Goethehaus from the perspective of both individuals. Goethehaus as the destination for the route and the fact that T wants to be guided there has become part of common ground for both individuals.

2.2   Order Effect

Perreault [23] defined order effect as "the relative position of an item in an inventory of questions or stimuli" that "may uniquely influence the way in which a respondent reacts to the item". Order effects are well known in quantum physics where quantum models were developed and are used to predict outcomes. Atmanspacher et al. [4] classified types of order effects and presented a relation to the field of psychology. The analogies of a non-commutativity model (quantum model) and mental operations especially in the field of linguistics are discussed by Beim Graben [16].

For example, Anderson [3] showed that if subjects are asked to judge whether they find a person likable depending on a list of descriptive adjectives the outcome is a function of the order at which the adjectives were listed. A first attempt to model order effects was provided by Hogarth et al. [20], but Busemeyer et al. [7,32] showed that a quantum model approach can produce more accurate results. Wang et al. [33] also argued for a quantum approach to model order effects stating that "... drawing a conclusion from one judgment or decision changes the context and disturbs the cognitive system, which affects the next judgment or decision, producing order effects, ... ".

In our example conversation mentioned in Sect. 1, an order effect occurs because the referring expression used to describe the landmark $Stephansdom_{LM}$ depends on whether S takes T's perspective or not. Initially, S does not take T's perspective and produces $Stephansdom_{RE}$ to refer to the landmark necessary for the description. After T signaled the rejection of the expression, S takes T's perspective (by introducing contextual information, i.e., T is from Paris) and produces the alternative referring expression *cathedral*. We can speculate that if S had taken T's perspective in the first place, $Stephansdom_{RE}$ might not have been produced at all, because we can assume that S knows the expression requires specific knowledge and is not a universally suitable.

2.3 Category to Instance Adjustment

Generally, the process of changing from an instance to a category can be seen as a process of learning in which a limited number of instances are generalized to categories ([15], page 123). Prototype theory [26] demonstrated that some instances are more typical than others for describing a category. For example, in Europe and the U.S., a sparrow is more typical than a penguin for the category bird [26]. Quantum formalizations for prototype theory were demonstrated by Aerts et al. [1,2] and applied to the field geographic information systems (GIS) by Hahn et al. [17,18]. Further investigations in particular for similarity judgments are made by the Quantum Interaction community [24,36].

In our example conversation (See Sect. 1), S changes from the instance *Stephansdom* to the category *cathedral* after he realized that *Stephansdom* is inappropriate. Therefore, the instance to category switch is a function of the order effect that occurs as a result of S taking (or not taking) T's perspective.

3   Properties of Quantum Models and Hilbert Spaces

Quantum models use a particular vector space known as Hilbert space. Hilbert spaces are capable to model order effects like the one discussed in Sect. 1. In this section we only provide a brief introduction to the concept of a Hilbert Space. For an extensive introduction we refer to Hughes introduction [21].

A Hilbert space $\mathcal{H}$ is a vector space with real or complex scalar values α called amplitudes or coordinates. Within this space an inner product between two vectors $|x\rangle, |y\rangle \in \mathcal{H}$ is defined. The Dirac notation [12] of the inner product and the corresponding formula is shown in Eq. 1. The (*)-operator (on top of vector x_i) changes both the column vector to a row vector and the sign from the imaginary part (if present) of the scalar value.

$$\langle x|y\rangle = \sum_i x_i^* \cdot y_i \tag{1}$$

The inner product of a vector $|x\rangle$ can be used to calculated the square of the length $\langle x|x\rangle = \sum_i x_i^* \cdot x_i$ which represents a probability value. A Hilbert space is spanned by base vectors and as a result of the orthonormal property of base vectors the inner product of two base vectors $|x\rangle, |y\rangle$ equals zero $\langle x|y\rangle = 0$ and their length equals one $\langle x|x\rangle = 1$.

To represent a state $|v\rangle$ of a (cognitive) system a linear combination of the base vectors including coordinates/amplitudes [13] is used. The state vector $|v\rangle$ represented with base vectors $|x_1\rangle, \ldots, |x_n\rangle$ and amplitudes $\alpha_1, \ldots, \alpha_n$ for an n-dimensional Hilbert space is shown in Eq. 2.

$$|v\rangle = \alpha_1|x_1\rangle + \alpha_2|x_2\rangle + \ldots + \alpha_n|x_n\rangle \tag{2}$$

A change in the system (e.g., the transformation of one state vector $|x\rangle$ into another state vector $|y\rangle$)can be achieved by operators. One class of operators are projectors, projecting a state vector onto the dimension identified by the basis vector (or space). For example, the projection operator P_1 projects the state $|v\rangle$ onto the basis vector $|x_1\rangle$, which the following equation shows: $\alpha_1|x_1\rangle = P_1|v\rangle$.

Transformations of a set X of orthogonal vectors to another set Y of orthogonal vectors are done by unitary transformations [25]. Unitary transformations are represented by matrices. The elements of the matrix represent transition amplitudes between two state vectors. Two examples of unitary matrices are shown in Eqs. 9 and 10. Unitary transformations U preserve inner products between vectors $|x\rangle, |y\rangle$ (See Eq. 3).

$$\langle x|U^\dagger U|y\rangle = \langle x|I|y\rangle = \langle x|y\rangle \tag{3}$$

The characteristic feature for unitary transformations is that the multiplication of the conjugate transposed form $U^\dagger$ with the base form U results in the identity matrix I as shown in Eq. 4.

$$U^\dagger U = I \tag{4}$$

3.1   Unitary Transformation Matrices

Unitary transformations describe the transition amplitudes from one state (base) $|x\rangle$ to another state (base) $|y\rangle$. With the unitary transformation the correlation between the states is represented. How unitary transformation matrices act on the states $|x\rangle$ and $|y\rangle$ is shown in Eq. 5.

$$|x\rangle = \boldsymbol{U}\,|y\rangle \tag{5}$$

The dimension of the unitary transformation matrix depends on the dimension of the Hilbert space. For a two dimensional Hilbert space the unitary transformation matrix can be represented ([21], page 18) by Eq. 6.

$$\boldsymbol{U} = \boldsymbol{R_\theta} = \begin{pmatrix} cos\theta & -sin\theta \\ sin\theta & cos\theta \end{pmatrix} \tag{6}$$

This unitary transformation depends on the angle θ. If the amplitudes for the state vectors $|x\rangle$ and $|y\rangle$ are known, the angle θ can be calculated.

If the dimension of a Hilbert space increases, the calculation of the unitary matrix can not be done in an algebraic way. For this cases Busemeyer et al. ([7], page 327) invented a fitting algorithm. In the field of quantum information Nielsen et al. ([22], page 194) presented an approximation algorithm to build unitary matrices.

4 A Formal Model for Perspective Taking

This section introduces the formalization for the order effect as a result of perspective taking during a conversation. We use the example of exchanging route instructions between two human agents as introduced in Sect. 1.

We assume the Hilbert space (Sect. 3) represents reality from which humans make experiences and gain knowledge. Every person perceives reality from another perspective, thus their knowledge about the world differs from person to person (e.g., color-blindness in people [27]). We can model this property by assuming that every person uses another base of this Hilbert space. From now on, we call this base the perspective or background knowledge of a particular person.

During a communication process the perspectives of its participants meet and if the conversation is to be successful, a common ground (an interpretation of a term shared by everyone) has to be found. The more background knowledge people share the less likely it is that misunderstandings will happen (see for example [10]). Less shared background knowledge increases the likelihood that misunderstandings will occur. This issue can be addressed with a Hilbert space model. We model perspectives as basis in a Hilbert space and use the inner product to transform from one base into the other. The transformation from one perspective to another is done by a unitary transformation described in Sect. 3.

For our formalization we limit the background knowledge to two instances mentioned in the example route instruction. With this it is possible to represent the two bases as shown in Fig. 1. The amount of experience (background knowledge) is represented by the vector amplitudes α_1 and α_2 for S and β_1 and β_2 for T. This results in a two dimensional Hilbert space.

We assume that S has a lot of experience with *Stephansdom*, thus uses it as a landmark for his description. Therefore, we assume the probability of α_1^2 is almost one. A restriction of the model is that the probabilities for both instances have to sum up to one. The consequence is that the probability for *Notre Dame* equals $\alpha_2^2 = 1 - \alpha_1^2$. T's experiences are represented by amplitudes β_1, β_2.

Formalizing the background knowledge of S and T, the amplitudes are combined with base vectors $\alpha_i|S_i\rangle$ and $\beta_i|T_i\rangle$, respectively. The linear combination of the two base vectors represents the mental state of S or T. The mental state $|v_S\rangle$ of S is represented in Eq. 7. The mental state $|v_T\rangle$ of T is represented with base vectors $|T_i\rangle$ in Eq. 8.

$$|v_S\rangle = \alpha_1|S_{Stephansdom}\rangle + \alpha_2|S_{NotreDame}\rangle \qquad (7)$$

$$|v_T\rangle = \beta_1|T_{Stephansdom}\rangle + \beta_2|T_{NotreDame}\rangle \qquad (8)$$

As basis vectors $|S_{Stephansdom}\rangle, |S_{NotreDame}\rangle$ the unit vectors, e.g., $\langle S_{Stephansdom}| = \begin{pmatrix} 1 & 0 \end{pmatrix}$, are selected. This fixes the base vectors for S according to the mental state $|v_S\rangle$. The mental state $|v_S\rangle$ is the starting vector for building the common ground. S has somehow included the background knowledge of T into the description. This inclusion is modeled as a unitary transformation operator (technically a unitary matrix) given in Eq. 9. The conjugate transposed of the matrix (Eq. 9) shown in Eq. 10 models the other direction (T -> S). Each element of the unitary matrices includes base vectors for both bases: $|S_{Stephansdom}\rangle, |S_{NotreDame}\rangle, |T_{Stephansdom}\rangle, |T_{NotreDame}\rangle$. With this fact, the amplitudes of T (in T's base) can be reflected in amplitudes of S's base and vice versa.

$$U_{ST} = \begin{pmatrix} \langle S_{Stephansdom}|T_{Stephansdom}\rangle & \langle S_{NotreDame}|T_{Stephansdom}\rangle \\ \langle S_{Stephansdom}|T_{NotreDame}\rangle & \langle S_{NotreDame}|T_{NotreDame}\rangle \end{pmatrix} \qquad (9)$$

$$U_{ST}^\dagger = U_{TS} = \begin{pmatrix} \langle T_{Stephansdom}|S_{Stephansdom}\rangle & \langle T_{NotreDame}|S_{Stephansdom}\rangle \\ \langle T_{Stephansdom}|S_{NotreDame}\rangle & \langle T_{NotreDame}|S_{NotreDame}\rangle \end{pmatrix} \qquad (10)$$

Both unitary matrices (Eqs. 9 and 10) can be calculated by a fitting algorithm mentioned in Sect. 3.1. The result of the fitting algorithm produces the unitary matrices U_{ST} and U_{TS}. Because we only discuss the two dimensional case the matrix is a rotation matrix shown in Eq. 6. As a result, the rotation angle θ can be calculated and interpreted as a similarity measure of the two bases (background knowledge) of S and T. The larger the angle the bigger the difference between S and T's background knowledge.

The mental state vectors $|v_S\rangle$ and $|v_T\rangle$ can be used to formalize the route description and the order effect. In line 2 of our example conversation, S decides to mention *Stephansdom* as the referring expression for the landmark *Stephansdom*. We formalize this decision process by using a Feynman path [13]. The path from the base state $|v_S\rangle$ considers first the perspective of S, and then takes the perspective of T into account (See Eqs. 11 and 12).

$$\gamma_1 = |v_S\rangle \rightarrow |S_{Stephansdom}\rangle \rightarrow |T_{Stephansdom}\rangle \qquad (11)$$

$$\gamma_1 = \langle T_{Stephansdom}|S_{Stephansdom}\rangle\langle S_{Stephansdom}|v_S\rangle \qquad (12)$$

$$\gamma_2 = \langle T_{NotreDame}|S_{NotreDame}\rangle\langle S_{NotreDame}|v_S\rangle \qquad (13)$$

The path is calculated with inner products e.g.: $\langle T_{Stephansdom} | S_{Stephansdom} \rangle$. This inner product also represents a kind of similarity measure, i.e.: of the basis vectors $|S_{Stephansdom}\rangle$ and $|T_{Stephansdom}\rangle$. Feynman paths for all instances of the Hilbert space can be calculated and result into amplitudes. In our example, amplitude γ_1 stands for *Stephansdom* whereas γ_2 for *Notre Dame*. The amplitudes are converted back into probabilities with Eq. 14. The probability of *Stephansdom* is at top, that is the reason why S mentions it. A graphical representation of this path and the Hilbert Space model is included in Fig. 1a.

$$prob(\text{Stephansdom}) = \| \langle T_{Stephansdom} | S_{Stephansdom} \rangle \langle S_{Stephansdom} | v_S \rangle \|^2 \quad (14)$$

The answer from T to S mentioning Stephansdom is "um, ...", which gives S the signal that Stephansdom is not known. As a reulst S takes the perspective of T into account. In order to do so S has to estimate the background knowledge/ perspective of T. The only information S can use to estimate is that Stephansdom is not present in T's background knowledge. As a result the estimated background knowledge S has for T hardly equals the real background knowledge of T. On behalf of this S evaluates the word Stephansdom including the perspective of T. Therefore, S first considers T's perspective and then his own perspective. This order effect changes the path shown in Eq. 15. The amplitudes δ_1 and δ_2 are converted back into probabilities which results in a lower probability for *Stephansdom*. A graphical representation of the this order is included in Fig. 1b.

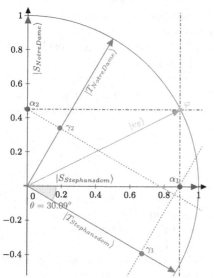

(a) Starting from the mental state of S (indicated by φ) first the perspective of S is taken into account (α_1, α_2 indicated by the dash-dotted lines) followed by the perspective of T (γ_1, γ_2 dotted lines).

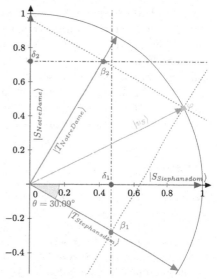

(b) Starting from the mental state of S (indicated by φ) first the perspective of T is taken into account (β_1, β_2 indicated by the dotted lines) followed by the perspective of S (δ_1, δ_2 dash-dotted lines).

Fig. 1. A Hilbert space showing the results of the order effect if the bases/perspectives of S and T are different. The difference can be seen in the different outcomes for amplitudes $\gamma_1, \gamma_2, \delta_1, \delta_2$. The angle θ can be interpreted as a similarity measure for the two bases.

$$\delta_1 = |v_S\rangle \rightarrow |T_{Stephansdom}\rangle \rightarrow |S_{Stephansdom}\rangle \tag{15}$$

$$\delta_1 = \langle S_{Stephansdom}|T_{Stephansdom}\rangle\langle T_{Stephansdom}|v_S\rangle \tag{16}$$

The difference between this path and the first path (Eq. 11) is the factor $\langle T_{Stephansdom}|v_S\rangle$. The factor represents which base is taken in consideration first. The second factor ($\langle S_{Stephansdom}|T_{Stephansdom}\rangle$) seems different but is in fact equal due to the unitary property of unitary matrices: $\langle S_{Stephansdom}|T_{Stephansdom}\rangle = \langle T_{Stephansdom}|S_{Stephansdom}\rangle$.

5   Conclusion and Future Research

This paper presented a quantum model formalization for an order effect that can occur due to perspective taking in human communication coordination problems. We discussed the example of an exchange of route instructions between a knowledgeable source (S) and a person requesting route information (T). In such a scenario, an order effect occurs if the source of information (S) evaluates the perspective of (T) first, as opposed to evaluate his perspective first and then taking T's perspective into account. The two forms of evaluation (1st T then 2nd S vs. 1st S then 2nd T) can lead to different outcomes if the likelihood of the best referring expression is judged. Our model made use of a 2D-Hilbert space and using unitary transformation to model the perspectives. Additional research has to be carried out to calculate unitary transformations for higher dimensional Hilbert spaces to model richer domains (more instances).

A logical next step would also be to address more sophisticated level of detail switches that occur frequently in communication settings. Our approach would also benefit from an evaluation with real-world data.

The motivation of this paper was the fact that today's information systems fall short in offering a natural way of interaction. We believe that our work makes an important step towards the construction of such formal models that can help to improve current information systems.

References

1. Aerts, D., Gabora, L.: A theory of concepts and their combinations i: the structure of the sets of contexts and properties. Kybernetes **34**(1/2), 167–191 (2005)
2. Aerts, D., Gabora, L.: A theory of concepts and their combinations ii: a hilbert space representation. Kybernetes **34**(1/2), 192–221 (2005)
3. Anderson, N.H.: Primacy effects in personality impression formation using a generalized order effect paradigm. J. Pers. Soc. Psychol. **2**(1), 1 (1965)
4. Atmanspacher, H., Römer, H.: Order effects in sequential measurements of noncommuting psychological observables. J. Math. Psychol. **56**(4), 274–280 (2012)
5. Austin, J.L.: How to do Things with Words - The William James Lectures delivered. Harvard University, Cambridge (1955)
6. Barsalou, L.W.: Perceptual symbol systems. Behav. Brain Sci. **22**(04), 577–660 (1999)

7. Busemeyer, J.R., Bruza, P.D.: Quantum Models of Cognition and Decision. Cambridge University Press, Cambridge (2012)
8. Clark, H.H.: Using Language. Cambridge University Press, Cambridge (1996)
9. Clark, H.H., Brennan, S.E.: Grounding in communication. In: Resnick, L.B., Levine, J.M., Teasley, S.D. (eds.) Perspectives on Socially Shared Cognition, pp. 127–149. American Psychological Association (1991)
10. Clark, H.H., Schaefer, E.F.: Collaborating on contributions to conversations. Lang. Cogn. Process. **2**(1), 19–41 (1987)
11. Clark, H.H., Wilkes-Gibbs, D.: Referring as a collaborative process. Cognition **22**, 1–39 (1986)
12. Dirac, P.A.M.: The Principles of Quantum Mechanics, vol. 27. Oxford University Press, Oxford (1981)
13. Feynman, R.P.: The Character of Physical Law, vol. 66. MIT press, Cambridge (1967)
14. Fussell, S.R., Krauss, R.M.: Understanding friends and strangers: the effects of audience design on message comprehension. Eur. J. Soc. Psychol. **19**(6), 509–525 (1989)
15. Gärdenfors, P.: Conceptual Spaces: The Geometry of Thought. MIT press, Cambridge (2004)
16. Graben, P.B.: Order effects in dynamic semantics. Top. Cogn. Sci. **6**(1), 67–73 (2014)
17. Hahn, J., Frank, A.U.: Context determines the features which need to show on a map, produced on demand. In: 1st International Workshop on Context for Business Process Management (CBPM 2013), Eight International and Interdisciplinary Conference on Modeling and Using Context (CONTEXT 2013) Annecy, Haute-Savoie, France (2013)
18. Hahn, J., Frank, A.U.: Select the appropriate map depending on context in a hilbert space model (SCOP). In: Atmanspacher, H., Haven, E., Kitto, K., Raine, D. (eds.) QI 2013. LNCS, vol. 8369, pp. 122–133. Springer, Heidelberg (2014)
19. Harnad, S.: The symbol grounding problem. CoRR, cs.AI/9906002 (1999)
20. Hogarth, R.M., Einhorn, H.J.: Order effects in belief updating: the belief-adjustment model. Cogn. Psychol. **24**(1), 1–55 (1992)
21. Hughes, R.I.G.: The Structure and Interpretation of Quantum Mechanics. Harvard University Press, Cambridge (1992)
22. Nielsen, M.A., Chuang, I.L.: Quantum Computation and Quantum Information. Cambridge University Press, Cambridge (2010)
23. Perreault Jr., W.D.: Controlling order-effect bias. Public Opin. Q. **39**(4), 544–551 (1975)
24. Pothos, E.M., Busemeyer, J.R., Trueblood, J.S.: A quantum geometric model of similarity. Psychol. Rev. **120**(3), 679 (2013)
25. Reichenbach, H.: Philosophic Foundations of Quantum Mechanics. Courier Dover Publications, New York (1944)
26. Rosch, E., Mervis, C.B.: Family resemblances: studies in the internal structure of categories. Cogn. Psychol. **7**(4), 573–605 (1975)
27. Sacks, O.: The Island of the Colour-Blind. Pan Macmillan, Sydney (1997)
28. Schmidt, M., Weiser, P.: Web mapping services: development and trends. In: Peterson, M.P. (ed.) Online Maps with APIs and WebServices, pp. 13–21. Springer, Heidelberg (2012)
29. Searle, J.R.: Speech Acts: An Essay in the Philosophy of Language. Cambridge University Press, Cambridge (1969)

30. Stalnaker, R.: Common ground. Linguist. Philos. **25**, 701–721 (2002)
31. Tenbrink, T., Winter, S.: Variable granularity in route directions. Spat. Cogn. Comput. **9**(1), 64–93 (2009)
32. Wang, Z., Busemeyer, J.R.: A quantum question order model supported by empirical tests of an a priori and precise prediction. Top. Cogn. Sci. **5**(4), 689–710 (2013)
33. Wang, Z., Solloway, T., Busemeyer, J.: New empirical tests of a quantum model for question order effects. In: 35th Annual Cognitive Science Conference (2013)
34. Weiser, P., Frank, A.U.: Cognitive transactions – a communication model. In: Tenbrink, T., Stell, J., Galton, A., Wood, Z. (eds.) COSIT 2013. LNCS, vol. 8116, pp. 129–148. Springer, Heidelberg (2013)
35. Weiser, P., Frank, A.U., Abdalla, A.: Process composition and process reasoning over multiple levels of detail. In: GI Science 2012 Extended Abstract (2012)
36. Yearsley, J.M., Photos, E.M., Hampton, J.A.: Towards a quantum probability theory of similarity judgements. In: 8th International Confreence on Quantum Interaction, Filzbach (2014)

Financial Payoff Functions and Potentials

Emmanuel Haven[(✉)]

University of Leicester, Leicester LE1 7RH, UK
eh76@le.ac.uk

Abstract. This paper attempts to argue that when considering a financial payoff function as a potential, one can begin to model how 'private' information is. Private information is probably best understood by juxtaposing it against the concept of 'public' information, i.e. information which is widely available via various freely accessible media platforms. The very simple model presented here allows us to make a case to compare public with private information. In economics and academic finance, a comparison of both such notions of information can prove to be a useful exercise especially in models where a more formal approach to information is needed. The argument made in this paper is based on using Fisher information and its relationship with a probability density function which itself is related to a wave function. The comparison between the level of available public information (proxied by total energy) and the payoff function (proxied by the potential function) is an important driver in determining the decay of the wave function.

1 Introduction

In common parlance, so called 'public information' can be defined as 'widely known information', i.e. non-privileged information. The concept of 'private information' may hint towards information which is held by a few. See also Haven [12] for uses of private information in economics. In a financial setting the comparison of those two types of information is often important as it pertains to basic concepts such as financial 'efficiency' and the existence of arbitrage profits[1]. As an example it is often said in any beginner's course in finance that so called 'strong-form efficiency' exists if asset prices will reflect private as well as public information. The goal of this paper is to provide for some initial ideas which may aid us to define better the notion of private information.

This paper is structured as follows. In the next section we briefly define what a financial payoff function is. In the section following we argue how private information may relate to the wave function. In Sect. 4, we aim to address why we would need a probability amplitude as a proxy for private information. In Sect. 5 we discuss the topic of tunneling which lies at the heart of the private information argument. A conclusion follows.

---

[1] Arbitrage profits are realized when the risk incurred to realize such profits is nil.

© Springer International Publishing Switzerland 2015
H. Atmanspacher et al. (Eds.): QI 2014, LNCS 8951, pp. 189–195, 2015.
DOI: 10.1007/978-3-319-15931-7_15

2   Financial Payoff Function and the Potential Function

In the realm of applications of physics principles to areas outside of physics, we can safely claim that two distinct movements are currently in operation on the research front. The 'econophysics' movement (Mantegna and Stanley [20]; Bouchaud [5,6] are some great examples) has been very active especially in applications to finance and economics. The other distinct movement is focused on using quantum mechanical principles to a variety of areas such as information retrieval (Cohen, Schvaneveldt, Widdows [8]); decision making (Busemeyer and Bruza [7]; Dzhafarov and Kujala [9]; Atmanspacher and Filk [3]; Aerts, Gabora and Sozzo [1]; Khrennikov [17,18]); biology (Asano, Basieva, Khrennikov et al. [2]); economics/finance (Khrennikov [18]; Hawkins and Frieden [14]; Haven and Khrennikov [10,11]; Baaquie [4]).

In some of the literature on using quantum mechanics in finance and economics, ideas have come forward on what to do with the all important 'potential function' which takes such a central place in all of physics. Two papers which discuss this within the quantum physics/finance area are by Li and Zhang [19]; Zhang and Li [22]. The recent presentation by Hawkins and Frieden [13] also discusses this.

A two dimensional financial payoff function can be defined as a mapping of an interval of prices onto a level of profit. The pattern of profit really determines the type of payoff function. As an example the finite square well potential could easily be interpreted as a payoff function which combines a so called 'box spread'[2] with a restriction where a certain price interval can not make any profit. Certain potentials in physics are not possible from a financial payoff point of view: the infinite square well is an example. No payoff in finance can have an infinite payoff. Furthermore, a financial payoff function when translated into real potential language would require time independent potentials. Payoff functions are only valid for a given period of time, as specified in the contracts of the underlying financial ingredients which make up that potential.

3   Private Information and the Wave Function

In this paper we make the assumption that the payoff function when set down contractually, is public information. As mentioned above, the payoff function is valid for a set period of time. What profits are realized depends on the behavior of the actual market. Before trading, any trader will know explicitly the precise functional form of the payoff function (since it is contractually set), but the trader

---

[2] To avoid any un-necessary financial vocabulary, a box spread combines a 'bull' spread and a 'bear' spread. The spreads themselves combine financial option contracts. The bull spread requires the buying of an option at a certain (strike) price; and the selling of another option at a higher (strike) price. The bear spread buys the option at the higher strike, but sells the option at the lower strike price. A strike price can be seen as a contractually determined price. When the time comes, to 'exercise the option', the market price can be higher or lower than that price.

only has 'some idea' (but surely not an exact idea) what the *likelihood* maybe of the position of the realized price in the set interval of the payoff function.

4   Why Quantum Mechanics?

The *quantum mechanical* source we require in the proposed model of this paper can be justified by four possible reasons:

1. we formalize private information with a wave function which serves as input to a probability density function.
2. this probability density function indicates a likelihood of a price occurring in the interval of prices of the payoff function.
3. the use of the Lagrangian function, using Fisher information, leads to show-breaking that the wave function follows a Schrödinger-like equation.
4. the likelihood of the price occurring will depend on: (a) whether tunnelling can occur; (b) the width of the payoff function and (c) the height of the payoff function.

The attentive reader will very quickly spot that reasons '1.' and '2.' above are insufficient to justify a quantum mechanical wave. Making the assertion that a quantum mechanical source of the wave function, as employed in this paper, is reasonable does beg for justification! If there exists some quantum state which relates to the financial event (determined by the set payoff function), does that state: (i) refer to information? or (ii) does it refer to some physical state? Is the quantum probability which ensues from the use of this wave function, subjective or objective? In effect, reason '3' is probably the strongest argument why it may be reasonable to make the analogy with using quantum mechanical wave functions as carriers of information.

Let us develop this argument now. We must start with the concept of Fisher information. This type of information measures basically the slope of a probability density function over the fluctuations x around an observed value x_0. As an example, if x symbolizes the noise around a value x_0, then Fisher information $I \equiv \int \frac{1}{P} \left(\frac{dP}{dx} \right) dx$, where $P(.)$ is the probability density function on noise x. Fisher information is well known in economics, but it exists under a different name: the so called Cramer-Rao bounds which measure the inverse of I. In Hawkins and Frieden [13,14] we can understand quite well how the wave function, as a probability amplitude, can 'live' within this macroscopic context. We now follow tightly Hawkins and Frieden [13]. The highlight of their beautiful argument consists in showing that it is reasonable to connect the probability amplitude, as the primal object in quantum mechanics, to the probability density function as used in the Fisher information measure. What are the components of this beautiful argument? The authors use Lagrangian optimization, a technique which is also well known in micro-economics. One needs to minimize: $\int \frac{1}{P} \left(\frac{dP}{dx} \right) dx + \sum_{n=1}^{N} \lambda_n \left[\int f_n(x)P(x)dx - \langle f_n(x) \rangle_{obs} \right]$. The first part of this equation is the objective function and the constraint (which is multiplied thus with the Lagrangian multipliers λ_n) indicates the divergence between the expected value of $f_n(x)$ obtained by using P and the average value obtained from the observations. This constraint can be found back in the ground-breaking work by Jaynes [15,16]. This optimization problem leads Hawkins and Frieden [13] to show that if P is set up via the probability amplitude: $P = \psi^2$: a Schrödinger-like differential equation is obtained: $\frac{d^2 \psi(x)}{dx^2} = \frac{1}{4} \left[\lambda_0 + \sum_{n=1}^{N} \lambda_n f_n(x) \right] \psi(x)$. We note that Reginatto [21] has shown that Fisher information is proportional to the quantum potential in the Bohmian mechanics set up.

This argument, we believe, shows how the wave function is related to the Fisher information measure and therefore it is palatable to use a wave function which has the probability amplitude characteristic in a macroscopic environment. Moreover, we can make the argument that this wave function does formalizes private information, since the narrowing of fluctuations around the true value x *can* indeed mean that there exists an increase in private information. The stress is on the word 'can' since of course such narrowing of fluctuations may also occur due to public announcements (say via some well known financial media channel). This addresses reason '1' to some extent. Reason '2' gives meaning to the probability density function within our context. The probability density function does not now measure fluctuations around a true value, but rather it indicates a likelihood of a price occurring in the interval of prices of the payoff function. Reason '4' is addressed in the next section.

5   Tunnelling

In Haven and Khrennikov [11] the way in which the 'finance form' of the real potential is formulated, allows for the argument that if this potential is non-zero it must be, there exists a source of arbitrage. In this paper we *generalize* the finance form of the potential by allowing it to be a payoff function. As mentioned above, the payoff function is contractually set. This means two essential things: (i) the functional form of this function is explicitly determined and (ii) the time period during which this payoff function can operate is set. As we explained above, the payoff function is public information. This paper's goal is to propose the early beginnings of a simple model which can give us an idea of how dense information is. We propose three key ingredients:

- First, we define with the word 'system', the set up of (i) the payoff function (publicly known) and (ii) the time dependent value of the asset price which moves relative to the set price contained in the contract. The time dependency is entirely determined, contractually, by the time interval for which the payoff function is valid.
- Second, we assume the total energy E of this 'system' symbolizes all the available public information relative to the timing of the payoff function.
- Third, we assume the level of total energy E relative to the functional form of the payoff function informs us about the possible decay of private information.

From a very basic physics point of view, if $E > V$ (when V indicates the potential function), then any incoming wave function (information) which approaches the payoff function (potential), will alter speed of movement, but the functional form of the wave function will not be affected. Hence, the ensuing probability density function is not altered. The situation is different when $E < V$, where tunnelling occurs and the functional form of the wave function, and especially its decay will depend very much on the width and height of the payoff function (potential function). This very basic mechanical model, can allow us to begin to model how financial efficiency in a particular market (here a market with payoff functions) behaves over a given period of time (as set by the time for which the payoff function is valid).

Consider the simple 'box spread' payoff function which stretches over the full positive valued X axis. The incoming wave function (information) decays tremendously rapidly and the information content of private information is very small, if we use the I measure which we defined above. In that sense do we want to claim that the wave function and private information are connected. We can think about the other extreme, the decay of a wave function when it hits, say a 'Dirac-δ' styled potential function. The type of decay will be such that the ensuing density function will exhibit a very steep gradient and thus a large level of private information.

This level of decay is in some sense already measured in very basic quantum mechanical terms. In Haven and Khrennikov [11] we make mention of the parameter $\kappa = \sqrt{\frac{2m}{\hbar^2}(V - E)^3}$ which is a decay parameter and it figures also in the transmission coefficient for waves to penetrate through barriers.

If $E < V$, as mentioned already above, we are in a situation where private information decays. This starting argument of $E < V$, also implies that $V = 0$ is impossible, since then $E < 0$. Thus, the payoff function can not be zero. In effect, there exists no financial rationale to define a zero payoff function.

6 Conclusion

We have attempted in this paper to provide for some rudimentary ideas on how we could begin to model the idea of private information. The private information as considered in this paper is set within a very peculiar financial context: i.e. the setting of payoff functions. The impctus for using the quantum-like wave function idea provides really from the work by Hawkins and Frieden [13,14]. A key argument in our paper is that there is good reason to believe that the level of private information needs to be high there where payoff functions obviously exhibit very large positive profits on very small domains of the interval of prices. This is why we mentioned the box spread and the Dirac-δ hypothetical payoff function. But this paper has not at all refined this potential measure in much depth. It is clear that a nascent formalism needs to be established to expand further on those ideas. One of the referees of this paper remarked that it may well be helpful to expand somewhat on whether a more advanced model could identify discrepancies between the acknowledged and actual influence of private

---

[3] m being mass and $\hbar$ being the Planck constant.

information. We have not mentioned this in this paper, but Fisher information has a very close connection with the error level between the estimate of a true value of a variable and the true value. This relationship can quite easily be applied to even the rudimentary framework we have considered in this paper. As an example in the case of a box spread, as described above, zero error would occur. Slight deviations from such a payoff functions would introduce errors. We hope we can expand on this in a future paper.

References

1. Aerts, D., Gabora, L., Sozzo, S.: Concepts and their dynamics: a quantum-theoretic modelling of human thought. Top. Cogn. Sci. **5**, 737–772 (2013)
2. Asano, M., Basieva, I., Khrennikov, A., Ohya, M., Tanaka, Yu., Yamato, I.: Quantum-like model of diauxie in escherichia coli: operational description of precultivation effect. J. Theor. Biol. **314**, 130–137 (2012)
3. Atmanspacher, H., Filk, T.: A proposed test of temporal nonlocality in bistable perception. J. Math. Psychol. **54**(3), 314–321 (2010)
4. Baaquie, B.: Interest rates in quantum finance: the Wilson expansion and Hamiltonian. Phys. Rev. E **80**, 046119 (2009)
5. Bouchaud, J.P.: An introduction to statistical finance. Physica A **313**, 238–251 (2002)
6. Bouchaud, J.P., Potters, M.: Theory of Financial Risks. Cambridge University Press, Cambridge (2000)
7. Busemeyer, J., Bruza, P.: Quantum Models of Cognition and Decision. Cambridge University Press, Cambridge (2012)
8. Cohen, T., Schvaneveldt, R., Widdows, D.: Reflective random indexing and indirect inference: a scalable method for discovery of implicit connections. J. Biomed. Inform. **43**(2), 240–256 (2010)
9. Dzhafarov, E.N., Kujala, J.V.: Selectivity in probabilistic causality: where psychology runs into quantum physics. J. Math. Psychol. **56**, 54–63 (2012a)
10. Haven, E., Khrennikov, A.: Quantum Social Science. Cambridge University Press, Cambridge (2013)
11. Haven, E., Khrennikov, A.: Quantum-like tunnelling and levels of arbitrage. Int. J. Theor. Phys. **52**(11), 4083–4099 (2013)
12. Haven, E.: Private information and the 'Information Function': a survey of possible uses. Theor. Decis. **64**(2–3), 193–228 (2007)
13. Hawkins, R.J., Frieden, B. R.: Fisher Information and Quantization in Financial Economics. ESRC (The Economic and Social Research of the United Kingdom) Seminar Series: Financial Modelling Post 2008: Where Next? (University of Leicester), January 2014
14. Hawkins, R.J., Frieden, B.R.: Asymmetric information and quantization in financial economics. Int. J. Math, Math. Sci. (2012). doi:10.1155/2012/470293
15. Jaynes, E.T.: Information theory and statistical mechanics. Phys. Rev. **106**, 620–630 (1957)
16. Jaynes, E.T.: Information theory and statistical mechanics II. Phys. Rev. **108**, 171–191 (1957)
17. Khrennikov, A.Y.: Classical and quantum mechanics on information spaces with applications to cognitive, psychological, social and anomalous phenomena. Found. Phys. **29**, 1065–1098 (1999)

18. Khrennikov, A.Y.: Ubiquitous Quantum Structure: from Psychology to Finance. Springer, Heidelberg (2010)
19. Li, Y., Zhang, J.E.: Option pricing with Weyl-Titchmarsh theory. Quant. Financ. 4(4), 457–464 (2004)
20. Mantegna, R., Stanley, H.E.: An Introduction to Econophysics: Correlations and Complexity in Finance. Cambridge University Press, Cambridge (1999)
21. Reginatto, M.: Derivation of the equations of nonrelativistic quantum mechanics using the principle of minimum fisher information. Phys. Rev. A **58**(3), 1775–1778 (1998)
22. Zhang, J.E., Li, Y.: New analytical option pricing models with Weyl-Titchmarsh theory. Quant. Financ. **12**(7), 1003–1010 (2010). doi:10.1080/14697688.2010.503659

Quantum Like Modelling
of the Nonseparability of Voters' Preferences
in the U.S. Political System

Polina Khrennikova[(⊠)]

School of Management, University of Leicester,
University Road, Leicester LE1 7RH, UK
pkl98@leicester.ac.uk

Abstract. Divided Government is nowadays a common feature of the U.S. political system. The voters can cast partisan ballots for two political powers the executive (Presidential elections) and the legislative (the Congress elections). Some recent studies have shown that many voters tend to shape their preferences for the political parties by choosing different parties in these two election stages. This type of behavior referred to by [36] as "ticket splitting" shows irrationality of behavior (such as preference reversal) from the perspective of traditional decision making theories (Von Neumann and Morgenstern [40], Savage [34]. It has been shown by i.e. [42] and also [25] that these types of preferences are "non-separable" and can be well accommodated in a quantum framework.

In this paper we use data from [36] to show first of all probabilistic violation of classical (Kolmogorovian) framework as a result of inconsistent Bayesian updating procedure among voters. We proceed with the depiction of the two observables (the President and Congress election contexts) with the aid of the quantum probability formula that incorporates the 'contextuality' of the decision making process through the interference term. Some of decision eigenvectors reconstructed from the statistical data induce the interference term of large magnitude exceeding one (a so called hyperbolic interference). We perform with help of our transition probabilities a state reconstruction of the voters' state vectors to test for the applicability of the generalized Born rule. This state can be mathematically represented in the generalized Hilbert space based on hyper-complex numbers.

Keywords: US Election system · Divided Government · Non-separability of preferences · Kolmogorov's probability theory · Contextuality · Interference · Generalized Born rule

1 Introduction

The application of the quantum models to phenomena outside the remit of quantum physics is not longer perceived as something exotic despite the novelty of this inter-disciplinary field (see [19] and [33] for a general account on the establishment of this field and its prospects both in relation to decision making and economics & finance). The quantum like models that actively pursue the mathematical framework and concepts of quantum physics to other social phenomena can serve as an accurate explanatory,

© Springer International Publishing Switzerland 2015
H. Atmanspacher et al. (Eds.): QI 2014, LNCS 8951, pp. 196–209, 2015.
DOI: 10.1007/978-3-319-15931-7_16

descriptive and also predictive instrument. The philosophy of the application at this stage bears a phenomenological character, without making a claim that the social and cognitive systems are exhibiting quantum features (i.e., that that human brain is a huge quantum system where neurons act like quantum particles or pointing to other possible sources of physical "quantumness" in the brain such as microtubules).

The domain of applications includes primarily decision making problems in economics and cognitive science [3–6, 10, 16, 23, 28, 29, 32]. Many of these findings focus on the violation of classical probabilistic scheme by Kolmogorov [26] and the axioms of Boolean logic of capturing the events and their relations in the context of decision-making. The most well-known effects that violate the classical representation of observables as random variables in the joint probability space are the conjunction and disjunction errors. Another context related effect is a so-called order effect that has been also successfully modeled in quantum framework e.g., [7, 24, 37].

Other application to the field of economics and expected utility are by [27, 35]. Many contributions were also achieved in the domain of financial instrument modelling and game theory [13, 17, 18] see also [1] for works in logic and concept combination. These and many other findings are successfully recapped in the books by [3, 20, 22].

A new domain of the application of quantum models is the political science, with first discussions on the possibility to model voters preferences in a quantum framework by [42] and a dynamical representation of the evolution of voters' preferences, including the impact of the so called election campaign "bath" by [25]. The work by [42] fostered for the motivation of the interdisciplinary application of quantum framework stating that:

> "Among all of the academic specialties customarily identified as social sciences, political science is perhaps the greatest "debtor" discipline, in the sense that so many of the theories and methods and models put to the task of understanding politics are borrowed from scholars working in other fields." [42], p. 83.

In this regard it seemed to be natural to search for inspiration in the domain of quantum physical models and their generalizations. In this paper we will go beyond the traditional quantum formalism in modelling our statistical data and consider a generalized quantum model obtained via extension of complex numbers to the hyper-complex algebra.

2   U.S. Political System and the Nonseparability Phenomenon

The US political system has a governance scheme based on divided partisan control formed by the so called executive power attributed to the President of the U.S. and the legislative power formed by the Congress of the U.S.[1]. Moreover, the political arena was historically dominated by two parties, the Democrats and the Republicans, where the U.S. is commonly regarded as a country with an established two party political system. Historically, the voters used to hold stable preferences by supporting the same political party in both the White House and (at least one) Houses of Congress elections. In this regard a large body of orthodox studies on voting preferences perceived such power accumulation as a matter of fact and argued that the divided government should

---

[1] Senate and the House of Representatives.

be perceived rather as a negative occurrence that inhibits the normal functioning of political system (see e.g., [2, 9, 30]). Similarly, [42] advocate that voters who strive to maximize their returns in terms of the political power would naturally choose the same party in both types of elections. This type of preference would be consistent with the postulates of modern "rational" decision theories [34, 40] implying completeness and invariance of the choices.

During the last 40 years the situations with power distribution began to change, in particular after the Watergate scandal related to the presidency of Richard Nixon.[2] The U.S. voters started to search to separate the political power at least based on the results of the election campaigns that did lead to the domination of Congress and White House by different political parties, a so called "gridlock". First attention to this phenomenon was paid by a well known political scientist, Morris Fiorina [14, 15], who explained this behavior of voters not as a random occurrence, but as a purposive (but not necessarily conscious) motivation to balance the political power as to sustain a less extreme political course (in either direction).

A recent study by [36] showed that voters are highly influenced by the information context related to the outcome of the elections. In particular, the voters strongly relate the outcomes of the Presidential elections to their subsequent decisions and often change their preferences in favor of another party in the Congress election. This phenomenon is called by [36] "nonseparability" of preferences, which implies that a particular informational context affects voter' belief state in a mode that is incompatible with their previous attitudes. In fact, more than a half of the respondents in the study by [36] exhibited such preference reversal, where the new informational context strongly changed the point of view of the participants. This effect was especially manifest for a large group of voters who initially didn't have any firm preferences for any party, where the additional information did elicit their preferences. In line with the psychological studies in decision theory by [21] we can witness based on this opinion pooling study that the all- inclusive context implying a stability of preferences doesn't exist in political environment. In the next section we will appeal to QL (quantum like models) to represent decision formation in such type of context dependent behavior.

2.1   Nonseparability in Quantum Framework

The first endeavor to incorporate the phenomenon of nonseparability through a static representation of the choice outcomes in a one-dimensional Euclidian space was in works by [15] and [36]. However, as pointed out by [42] the simplicity of this model entailed some limitations, such as a lack of dynamical representation of the decision maker's state evolution as well as no account has been made for the additional (contextual) factors impacting the preference emergence, i.e. the upcoming information and the mental characteristics of the voter.

For this reason a Hilbert space representation of the observables - the measurement context and its impact on the superposition of the initial mental state of the voters was proposed. The ultimate state decoherence into the particular eigenvectors is context

---

[2] For statistical data see e.g., http://www.loc.gov/rr/program/bib/elections/statistics.html.

depended, where a dynamical simulation that also accounted for the impact of the environmental context (the election campaign "bath") was proposed by [25].

This paper supports the above findings by showing a violation of the probabilistic updating of voters beliefs that yields in the violation of the classical probabilistic scheme, and in particular the Law of Total Probability by Kolmogorov [26]. Instead we appeal to quantum probability formula by von Neumann [41]. We prove that we can apply Born rule by reconstructing the superposition state for our observables from the obtained eigenvalues and the eigenvectors' squared probability amplitudes. Furthermore, we obtain such a large scale interference for one of our eigenvectors that constrains a (traditional) complex number Hilbert space representation of the observables, instead we propose for a hyperbolic Hilbert space state representation.

3   Non Separability Phenomenon and Violation of Classical Probabilistic Framework: Empirical Evidence

For the purpose of measuring how the phenomenon of "nonseparability" is reflected in the classical probabilistic scheme, we extracted the frequencies form the study [36] that interviewed 983 respondents[3] before the 1996 U.S. elections (with Bob Dole and Bill Clinton as presidential candidates). The interview had a within group design and was performed in three stages, that we will call "informational contexts" to test for the occurrence of nonseparability that we can interpret as preference reversal.

Firstly, a general question (Q1) was asked: *"Which party is the best choice for managing the U.S. Congress?"* (p. 748) This question was aiming to establish a baseline of the preferences, which subsequently would be compared to the conditional responses. This question was embedded in a context of similar questions about partisan preferences, which assumingly was related to the elimination of information storage among participants.

Secondly, the same respondents were contacted again and given following information context:

Q2 *"If Bob Dole were to be elected president, which would you prefer: a Republican Congress to help him pass his agenda or a Democratic Congress to serve as a check on his agenda?"*

Subsequently, the information in the question was reverted (Q3): *"If Bill Clinton were to be elected president, which would you prefer: a Republican Congress to help him pass his agenda or a Democratic Congress to serve as a check on his agenda?"*

We denote our baseline context question (Q1) answers as $C = \lambda$ {R, D, N}, corresponding to: "Democratic Congress", "Republican Congress" and "Don't know". We decided to include the participants who were uncertain as well (the "don't" know), since the amount of these participants is quite substantial in this study. Also, during the actual election campaign to "win" the voices of this group of voters (among them

---

[3] For the baseline question concerning the general preferences for Democratic/Republican Congress the sample consisted of 937 respondents.

e.g., Centrists, Liberal Republicans and Conservative Democrats) as well as of the inactive voters is of particular importance for the success of the main parties.

Next, in our mathematical formulation, the context for Dole (Q2) and Clinton (Q3) presidential election outcomes is denoted by $P = \mu \{R,D\}$. Questions (Q2) and (Q3) are conditional questions, which after informing about the outcomes R or D are again containing the same question as the (Q1) in order to elucidate once again the preferences for the parties in the Congress.

We summarize the frequencies obtained in the interviews in a table below. In the first row we summarize the frequencies of the answers of the unconditional question (Q1). The second and third row contains the answer frequencies of the conditional questions (Q2, Q3):[4]

Table 1. The summary of the outcome frequencies for each voting context

	C = D	C = R	C = N
Q1: Baseline (C)	0.323	0.406	0.271
Q2: Dole (P = R)	0.544	0.398	0.058
Q3: Clinton (P = D)	0.317	0.629	0.054

3.1 Law of Total Probability: Test for "Classicality" of Obtained Frequencies

According to [12] the Law of Total Probability and the notion of conditional probabilities were applied as the core inputs in the modern decision theory (in economics and other fields) throughout the 20th Century. The Law of Total Probability that is derived with the aid of Bayesian conditional probabilities [26] denotes the total probability of an outcome given its fulfillment through different distinct events. This formula obeys the principle of additivity and enables to express the occurrence of an outcome in our case p(C = λ) through conditional probabilities $p(C = \lambda|P = D)$, $p(C = \lambda|P = R)$ and the marginal probabilities given by $p(P = D)$ and $p(P = R)$. The $(P = D) \cap (P = R) = \emptyset$.[5]

In our study we deal with subjective formation of voters preferences, where the marginal probabilities encoded in the information contexts are objective probabilities, since we have the same amount of participants (N = 983) in our Dole/Clinton contexts we treat this probability as being equal i.e., $p(P = D) = p(P = R) = 0.5$. By inserting frequencies from Table 1 into the Law of Total Probability (the most common way is to approximate frequencies through probabilities in experimental studies) we calculate the baseline probabilities for events (C = R, C = D and C = R) and see if they correspond with the obtained results via their conditional realizations:

---

[4] The frequencies for conditional probabilities are taken from Table 1, p. 748 and the compound probabilities are taken from Table 2, p. 749. We should note that the baseline context, had N = 937 and Dole/Clinton contexts, N = 983.

[5] It should be denoted that the probabilities applied for statistical decision making (on the right hand of the formula of Total Probability) could be as well objective probabilities, calculated on the basis of the previous statistical experience as well as subjective probabilities, based on one's personal experience. Both of them are interpretations of the Bayesian probabilities.

$$p(C = \lambda) = p(P = D)p(C = \lambda|P = D) + p(P = R)(C = \lambda|P = R) \tag{1}$$

$$p(C = D) = 0.323 \neq p(P = D)p(C = D|P = D) + p(P = R)(C = D|P = R)$$
$$= 0.5 * 0.317 + 0.5 * 0.544 = 0.43 \tag{2}$$

$$p(C = R) = 0.406 \neq p(P = D)p(C = R|P = D) + p(P = R)(C = R|P = R)$$
$$= 0.5 * 0.629 + 0.5 * 0.398 = 0.514 \tag{3}$$

$$p(C = N) = 0.271 \neq p(P = D)p(C = N|P = D) + p(P = R)(C = N|P = R)$$
$$= 0.5 * 0.054 + 0.5 * 0.058 = 0.056 \tag{4}$$

Based on the result of Eqs. 2–4 we obtained a violation of the additivity rule of the conditional probabilities that constitute the baseline probability. This violation is due to the preference reversal that occurs in the different informational contexts, which change the mental (belief) state of the participants, especially for the 'don't know' outcome. This probabilistic judgment error is well known through the works by [8, 39] and others, where the obtained findings show that the disjunction of two conditional events is lower or higher as the compound outcome. The disjunction error and its mental origins are in detail discussed in [38]. An account for this fallacy with the aid of quantum physical framework has been proposed by numerous academics in the quantum community (see some references in the "Introduction" part.).

The main difference of our study is that the decision makers are uncertain between three different choices (whereas the classical studies on disjunction effect and violation of the "Sure Thing Principle" focus on two possible choices for simplicity of the analysis). Despite the more complex setting of this decision making task we observe a well recognized violation of the Sure Thing Principle.[6] Of course this decision making problem requires a more extended analysis of the frequencies for those voters, who have chosen C = R|{R, D} respective C = D|{R, D}, out of the C = N baseline sample. For now, if we would just oppose 2 choices; to cast the vote for any party (C = {R, D}) or abstain from expressing their preferences (C = N), we can observe that the frequency of voters who ultimately elucidate their preferences in Q2 and Q3 contexts equals to: 0.27 − 0.056 = 0.214 = 21.4 %.

We can conclude that the voters are not acting strategically i.e. they cannot decide whether to vote (they don't make the Bayesian conditional updating procedure) until the very moment when they certainly get the information about the events in question.[7]

---

[6] The Sure Thing Principle by Lenard Savage [34] simply put states: If a person is uncertain about her decision in a particular decision making context, but she knows that she will make decision A given that an event B occurs, but she also decided that he will make the decision A when B- obtains then the person should make the decision A even before knowing if B or B- obtained. As such it doesn't matter for her, whether she has obtained any information about events' B- and B-likeliness.

[7] From the point of view of quantum physics the voters in each setting are acting "coherently" as a result of the joint preparation procedure (in a more complex election campaign picture, we would have other sources of disturbance besides the interview, such as media campaign, newspapers, Internet etc.) In this study the authors articulate that they aim to perform three different question measurements on the *same* belief state of the voters, with no disturbance ("noise") in-between.

As such, we suggest that our observational contexts exhibit non-classicality from the point of view of traditional probability theory and a different state space representation would be necessary to accommodate our observables and their impact on the decision makers' belief state. We proceed with incorporating or probability outcomes in a generalized Law of Total Probability - the Quantum Probability formula that captures the interference of the complex probability amplitudes of the different decision outcomes -manifest in the superposition state of the voters. The representation of observables with help of quantum probability formula is of particular relevance to the field of political science since there are always present the so-called "swing voters" which find themselves in a kind of vacillation between various voting preferences.

4 Generalized Quantum Representation of Voters' Belief[8] State

Quantum probability formula is an extension of the classical Law of Total Probability with a special interference term; that can exhibit positive, negative or zero interference of the corresponding wave function. Moreover, the particular observational context can yield the traditional (cos) interference as well as a more exotic hyperbolic (cosh) interference for which a hyper-complex Hilbert space would be needed.[9] The Ψ – vectors are in a similar way constructed in the linear space over complex or hyperbolic numbers, where application of hyperbolic numbers enables to obtain interference amplitudes of larger magnitude. For more detailed elaboration see Appendix 6.

By using the quantum probability formula we calculate the interference angles (phases between beliefs) encoded in the additional interference term, which can yield either constructive interference or destructive interference of different magnitude between the beliefs. For the $C = D$ belief outcome we obtain:

$$
\begin{aligned}
p(C = D) = {}& p(P = D)p(C = D|P = D) + p(P = R)(C = D|P = R) \\
& + 2\cos\theta\sqrt{(p(P = D)p(C = D|P = D)p(P = R)p(C = D|P = R))}
\end{aligned}
\tag{5}
$$

$$
p(C = D) = 0.5 * 0.317 + 0.5 * 0.544 + 2\cos\theta\sqrt{0.5 * 0.544}
\tag{6}
$$

$$
\begin{aligned}
\cos\theta &= -0.257; \\
\theta &= 1.83.
\end{aligned}
\tag{7}
$$

This observable outcome yields $\cos\theta$ with negative sign implying a destructive interference (the absolute value of interference term is less than 1, denoting a trigonometric interference). Therefore, it is possible to represent it as $\cos$ of some angle (phase) of the mental state wave function. The same result obtains for the $(C = R)$:

---

[8] In this work we use the notions of belief state and mental state interchangeably.

[9] Where the state vector is represented with hyperbolic numbers $(x + y\,j$, were $j^2 = +1)$, instead of complex numbers.

$$cos\,\theta = -0.216;\ \theta = 1.79. \tag{8}$$

The interference effect for the $(C = N)$ decision outcome differs essentially from the $(C = D)$, $(C = R)$ outcomes. Here the interference is constructive and the interference term is of a very high magnitude. We can interpret it as a consequence of a strong contextuality effect. Such interference term cannot be represented in a trigonometric form, but though hyperbolic scheme as:

$$(C = N):\ \cosh\,\theta = 3.84;\ \theta = 2.021 \tag{9}$$

We can summarize that two of our decision outcomes exhibit destructive interference of sufficiently low (although nonzero) magnitude, trigonometric interference. This effect can well explain the preference reversal where the upcoming information alters the voters' preferences in favor of the respective party in the Congress elections. Consequently, those participants who do not have any firm preferences in the baseline context exhibit a strongly constructive interference; hyperbolic interference for which a hyperbolic Hilbert space representation is needed (see Appendix 6 and [22, 31]).

What are the implications of the results obtained with the Quantum probability formula for the decision-making formation in our study context? By applying the quantum formalism we can describe the voters' initial mental state as being in a superposition of three possible choices; to vote for the "Democratic Congress", $(C = D)$ to vote for the "Republican Congress", $(C = R)$ or prefer not to reply $(C = N)$ in which case the voter either doesn't know for which party to vote, or prefers not to bother, alternatively has a negative attitude to both of the parties.[10] As a result of the obtained information in the Q2 and Q3, corresponding to another measurement context, the belief state of the voters changes, interfering with the C = D and C = R probability amplitudes. As we have mentioned above, the voters that have a Ψ vector in eigenstate corresponding to $(C = N)$ that are avoiding making up their choice are mostly influenced by the information about the definite outcome of the presidential elections. The destructive interference makes the final probability of $(C = N)$ to evaporate, as the uncertainty is resolved. This is an important finding, since we are been able to show the exact degree of Q2 and Q3 impact on the different decision outcomes though the presence of the interference term.

In the next subsection we perform a state reconstruction for our for the belief state vector using the obtained probabilities for our decision outcomes $(C = D,\ C = R$ and $C = N)$.

4.1 Reconstruction of the Belief State by a Generalized Born Rule

The inverse Born Rule, which is the essential tool to reconstruct the superposition state of the system from the experimental data, enables us to obtain the initial mental state,

---

[10] We suggest that the meaning of the answer "don't know" in opinion pooling studies should be further studied, since many psychological studies, experiments, surveys in some sense "force" the respondents to make a particular choice, whereas abstaining from making a proposed choice can also be considered as a firm preference.

Ψ of the ("average") voter using the matrix of transition probabilities. The transition probabilities are in psychological context simply the conditional preferences that are firm preferences obtained after some measurement, which is the particular information contained in the question. We proceed with the assumption that the Ψ function collapse occurs as a result of measurement and yields some eigenvector amplitudes in its eigenvalues λ. The squared amplitudes provide us with the transition probabilities that we extract from (Table 1) and arrange in a transition probability matrix (Eq. 10).

This matrix is always stochastic, for fixed conditioning, the sum of conditional probabilities in each column has to be equal to one:

$$\begin{pmatrix} p(C=D|P=D) & p(C=D|P=R) \\ p(C=R|P=D) & p(C=R|P=R) \\ p(C=N|P=D) & p(C=N|P=R) \end{pmatrix}; \begin{pmatrix} 0.317 & 0.544 \\ 0.629 & 0.398 \\ 0.0539 & 0.058 \end{pmatrix} \tag{10}$$

We start with the reconstruction of the state vector in coordinates for the eigenvalue $(C = D)$. Its' squared amplitude corresponds to $p(C = D)$:

$$p(C = D) = |\Psi_1|^2 \tag{11}$$

$$\Psi_1 = \sqrt{p(P=D)p(C=D|P=D)} + e^{i\theta}\sqrt{p(P=R)p(C=D|P=R)} \tag{12}$$

By Euler's formula we obtain:

$$e^{i\theta} = cos\theta + isin\theta = -0.257 + 0.967i \tag{13}$$

$$\Psi_1 = \sqrt{(0.5*0.317)} + (-0.257+0.967i)\sqrt{(0.5*0.544)}$$
$$= 0.265 + 0.5i = |0.265 + 0.5i| = \sqrt{0.265^2 + 0.5^2} \tag{14}$$

$$|\Psi_1|^2 = 0.32 \tag{15}$$

In a similar way we reconstruct the state vector in coordinates corresponding to $(C = R)$ answer to obtain its probability:

$$\Psi_2 = \sqrt{p(P=D)p(C=R|P=D)} + e^{i\theta}\sqrt{p(P=R)p(C=R|P=R)}$$
$$= \sqrt{(0.5*0.629)} + (-0.216+0.976i)\sqrt{(0.5*0.398)} = 0.465 + 0.43 \tag{16}$$
$$= |0.465 + 0.435i| = \sqrt{0.465^2 + 0.435^2}$$

$$|\Psi_2|^2 = 0.405 \tag{17}$$

We were able to reconstruct the mental state vector coordinates in respect to eigenvalue corresponding to $C = N$ outcome by taking use of generalized Born rule, using operations with hyperbolic numbers:

$$\Psi_3 = \sqrt{p(P=D)p(C=N|P=D)} + e^{j\theta}\sqrt{p(P=R)p(C=N|P=R)} = \alpha + e^{j\theta}\beta \tag{18}$$

By the hyperbolic analogue of the Euler formula we obtain[11]:

$$e^{j\theta} = cosh\theta + jsinh\theta \tag{19}$$

By inserting the right hand side term (Eq. 18) we can represent the third state vector[12]:

$$\Psi_3 = A + jB = \alpha + e^{j\theta}\beta = (\alpha + cosh\theta\beta) + jsinh\theta\beta \tag{20}$$

$$|\Psi_3| = A^2 - B^2 = (\alpha + cosh\theta\beta)^2 - \beta^2 sinh\theta^2$$
$$= \alpha^2 + 2\alpha\beta cosh\theta + \beta^2(cosh\theta^2 - sinh\theta^2) \tag{21}$$

By inserting our frequencies into (Eq. 18) we proceed with the calculations:

$$\Psi_3 = \sqrt{0.5*0.054} + e^{j\theta}\sqrt{0.5*0.58} = 0.164 + 0.17e^{j\theta} \tag{22}$$

We express $e^{j\theta}$ through the Euler formula (Eq. 19):

$$\Psi_3 = (0.164 + 0.17cosh\theta) + 0.17jsinh\theta = 0.81 + 0.17jsinh\theta \tag{23}$$

By inserting the results of (Eq. 23) into (Eq. 21) we obtain:

$$|\Psi_3| = A^2 - B^2 = (0.164 + 01.17cosh\theta)^2 - 0.029sinh\theta^2$$
$$= 0.027 + 2*0.164*0.17*3.84 + 0.029 = 0.27 \tag{24}$$

We were able to reconstruct the mental state vector $\Psi = (\Psi_1, \Psi_2, \Psi_3)$ belonging to the Hilbert space over the hyperbolic algebra. *What is the aim of performing this state reconstruction procedure for psychological measurements?* The Born rule is the basic postulate of quantum theory to predict, for a given state Ψ outcomes' probabilities given some observables (operators) acting upon systems in the state Ψ; which in psychology can for instance be questions, informational contexts, internal aspects such a s memory etc. The possibility to apply Born rule to our data could give a basis for further application of dynamical quantum models; by knowing the initial mental state of the voter and the informational context we could proceed with modelling

---

[11] We remark that the elements of the complex hyperbolic algebra have the form: $z = x_1 + ix_2 + jx_3$, where x_j are real numbers. We set $\bar{z} = x_1 - ix_2 - jx_3$ and $|z|^2 = z\bar{z}$. In a hyperbolic space it could be the case that $|z|^2 < 0$ so that negative probabilities could appear. It should not be regarded as a problem since the negative probabilities are not present as "probabilities" of the results of the mental state measurements. (However, they can appear in theoretical models as the results of intermediate calculations.) For a detailed treatment of negative probabilities see, e.g., [11].

[12] $sinh\theta$ can be expressed as a relation: $sinh\theta^2 = cosh\theta^2 - 1$.

the state evolution as to predict the probabilities of the observable outcomes in the mental state Ψ function.

For instance for our observable we can select the canonical basis $e_1 = (1,0,0)$, $e_2 = (0,1,0), e_3 = (0,0,1)$. Thus the (hyper-complex) Born rule takes the form:

$$p(D) = |\langle \Psi, e_1 \rangle|^2, \; p(R) = |\langle \Psi, e_2 \rangle|^2, \; p(N) = |\langle \Psi, e_3 \rangle|^2 \qquad (25)$$

The question about Congress elections (Q1) can be represented as the diagonal operator $\hat{C}$ in the basis e_1, e_2, e_3. Since the matrix of transition probabilities is not doubly stochastic,[13] the questions Q2 and Q3 that informing about the Presidential elections outcomes cannot be represented by a Hermitian operator (in the hyper-complex Hilbert space). One would need to appeal to the hyper-complex analog of positive operator-valued measures (POVMs), see, e.g., [24] to model such type of experimental data.

5 Concluding Remarks

By analyzing the results of the opinion pooling study by [36] we have mathematically shown, how the upcoming information concerning the outcomes of an election campaign changes the preferences of the voters. In particular, the voters do cast ballots for different parties in Congress and President elections under the influence of the informational context. Moreover, the voters with no firm preferences form their opinions conditioned on the obtained information. But even when doing so, the voters are not following a traditional Bayesian updating procedure.

We have shown non-classicality of voters' behavior due to the incompatibility of the observational contexts that cannot be embedded into single classical probability space model. Based on the obtained probabilities we were able to reconstruct the initial mental state vector (belief state) of the voters that adheres to the generalized Born rule. We propose for the representation of the observables that act upon the voters' cognitive states in hyper-complex three-dimensional Hilbert space. Thus our probabilistic representation is not only non-classical (i.e., non-Kolmogorovian), but it neither can be described by canonical quantum formalism. Its generalization is in use.

We hope that the findings of this paper can provide for new insight on the applicability of alternative probabilistic and conceptual frameworks to the decision making problems in political science, by firstly of all motivating for the more broad interdisciplinary usage of quantum like models.

Acknowledgements. I would like to thank my supervisor Prof. Emmanuel Haven and the participants of the Quantum Interaction 2014 Conference for valuable insights and discussions that contributed to the completion of this paper. I also would like to thank the organizers of the QI2014 Conference for providing a great opportunity to discuss ideas and present new findings in this interdisciplinary field.

---

[13] As is the case for many other data from related findings on disjunction effects, e.g., Prisoners Dilemma, Hawaii vacation experiment, Gambling experiment [38]. For construction of the transition probability matrixes see e.g., [22]).

Appendix

Remarks on the construction of linear space with hyperbolic numbers.

The construction of hyper- complex Hilbert space is a simple generalization of the complex Hilbert space where instead of using a number field of complex numbers C one operates with hyperbolic number algebra (denoted by G) which differ in the form of the hyper-complex unit, where $j^2 = 1$ instead of $i^2 = -1$ as it is for C.

We remark that the same rules for multiplication, addition and subtraction apply for G as for C. The important difference between G and C is that C is a number field for which we can apply division operation, while G is just an algebra for which the division operation is not well- defined. To construct a linear space over C in its most simple form we apply the notion of Cartesian product of n complex numbers:

$$H = C \times C \times \ldots \times C \tag{26}$$

its elements can be denotes as:

$$z = (z_1, \ldots z_n), z_i \in C \tag{27}$$

with the basis in these coordinated having the form:

$$e_1 = (1, 0..0), \ e_2 = (0, 1..0), \ \ldots, e_n = (0, 0..1) \tag{28}$$

an arbitrary vector in such a linear space can be uniquely represented as:

$$z = z_1 e_1 + \ldots z_n e_n \tag{29}$$

For the hyperbolic numbers G we simply repeat the above linear space construction by building a hyper- complex linear space with G coordinates.

We remark that the basis for the vector coordinates (Eq. 29) is defined uniformly both for C and for G. The preference for application of the hyperbolic numbers for the linear space construction matters only for the choice of the vector coordinates, which however plays a central role, since the coordinates determine the probability amplitudes.

At the same time we should emphasize that in this modelling task we operate with Hilbert space constructed over the C number field or its generalization the G algebra, which can have any dimensionality depending on the n. We are not considering regarding C or G as being (two dimensional) linear spaces over $\mathbb{R}$ per se. This approach could be however theoretically speaking applied to other space modelling tasks that require multidimensional extensions of the number field C. Those could be quaternions, octonions etc., that are all encompassed in the notion of hyper- complex numbers.

References

1. Aerts, D., Sozzo, S.: Quantum structure in cognition: Why and how concepts are entangled. In: Song, D., Melucci, M., Frommholz, I., Zhang, P., Wang, L., Arafat, S. (eds.) QI 2011. LNCS, vol. 7052, pp. 116–127. Springer, Heidelberg (2011)
2. Alvarez, R.M., Schousen, M.: Policy moderation or conflicting expectations? Testing the intentional model of split- ticket voting. Am. Politics Q. **21**, 410–438 (1993)
3. Bruza, P., Busemeyer, J.R., Gabora, L.: Introduction to the special issue on quantum cognition. J. Math. Psychol. **53**(5), 303–305 (2009)
4. Busemeyer, J.R., Matthew, M., Wang, Z.: Quantum game theory explanation of disjunction effect. In: Sun, R., Miyake, N. (eds.) Proceedings of 28th Annual Conference of the Cognitive Science Society, pp. 131–135. Erlbaum, Mahwah (2006-a)
5. Busemeyer, J.R., Wang, Z., Townsend, J.: Quantum dynamics of human decision-making. J. Math. Psychol. **50**(3), 220–241 (2006-b)
6. Busemeyer, J.R., Bruza, P.D.: Quantum Models of Cognition and Decision. Cambridge University Press, Cambridge (2012)
7. Conte, E., Todarello, O., Federici, A., Vitiello, F., Lopane, M., Khrennikov, A., Zbilut, J.P.: Some remarks on an experiment suggesting quantum like behavior of cognitive entities and formulation of an abstract quantum formalism to describe cognitive entity and its dynamics. Chaos, Solitons Fractals **31**, 1076–1088 (2007)
8. Croson, R.: The disjunction effect and reason based choice in games. Organ. Behav. Hum. Decision Process **80**(2), 118–133 (1999)
9. Cutler, L.N.: To form a government. Foreign Aff. **59**, 126–143 (1980)
10. De Barros, J.A., Suppes, P.: Quantum mechanics, interference and the brain. J. Math. Psychol. **53**, 306–313 (2009)
11. De Barros, J.A.: Decision Making for inconsistent expert judgements using negative probabilities arXiv:1307.4101 (2013)
12. De Finetti, B.: Theory of Probability, vol. 2. Wiley, New York (1974)
13. Eisert, J., Wilkens, M., Lewenstein, M.: Quantum games and quantum strategies. Phys. Rev. Lett. **83**, 3077–3080 (1999)
14. Fiorina, M.P.: Retrospective Voting in American National Elections. Yale University Press, New Haven (1981)
15. Fiorina, M.P.: Divided Government, 2nd edn. Allyn and Bacon, Boston (1996)
16. Franco, R.: The conjunction fallacy and interference effects. J. Math. Psychol. **53**, 415–422 (2009)
17. Haven, E.: Analytical solutions of the backward Kolmogorov PDE via and adiabatic approximation to the Schrodinger PDE. J. Math. Anal. Appl. **311**, 439–444 (2005)
18. Haven, E.: Pilot- wave theory and financial option pricing. Int. J. Theor. Phys. **44**(11), 1957–1962 (2006)
19. Haven, E.: Elementary quantum mechanical principles and social science: Is there a connection? Rom. J. Econ. Forecast. **1**, 41–57 (2008)
20. Haven, E., Khrennikov, A.: Quantum Social Science. Cambridge University Press, Cambridge (2013)
21. Kahneman, D.: Maps of bounded rationality. Psychol. Behav. Econ. **93**(5), 1449–1475 (2003)
22. Khrennikov, A.: Ubiquitous Quantum Structure. Springer, Heidelberg (2010)
23. Khrennikov, A., Haven, E.: Quantum mechanics and violations of the Sure-Thing principle: the use of probability interference and other concepts. J. Math. Psychol. **53**, 378–388 (2009)

24. Khrennikov, A., Basieva, I., Dzhafarov, E.N., Busemeyer, J.R.: Quantum models for Psychological Measurements: An unsolved Problem, arXiv:1403.3654[q-bio.NC] (2014)
25. Khrennikova, P., Haven, E., Khrennikov, A.: An application of the theory of open quantum systems to model the dynamics of party governance in the U.S. political system. Int. J. Theor. Phys. **53**(4), 1346–1360 (2014)
26. Kolmogorov, A.N.: Foundations of Probability. Chelsea Publishing Company, New York (1933, 1950)
27. La Mura, P.: Projective Expected Utility. Mimeo, Leipzig Graduate School of Management (2006)
28. Lambert-Mogilansky, A., Zamir, S., Zwirn, H.: Type indeterminacy- A model of the KT (Kahneman-Tversky) – man. J. Math. Psychol. **53**, 349–362 (2009)
29. Lambert-Mogiliansky, A., Busemeyer, J.R.: Emergence and instability of individual identity. In: Busemeyer, J.R., Dubois, F., Lambert-Mogiliansky, A., Melucci, M. (eds.) QI 2012. LNCS, vol. 7620, pp. 102–113. Springer, Heidelberg (2012)
30. McCubbins, M.D.: Party politics, divided government and budget deficits. In: Politics, P. (ed.) Samuel Kernell. Brookings Institution, Washington (1991)
31. Nyman, P.: On the consistency of the quantum- like representation algorithm for hyperbolic interference. Adv. Appl. Clifford Algebras **21**(4), 799–811 (2011)
32. Pothos, E.M., Busemeyer, J.R.: A quantum probability explanation for violations of 'rational' decision theory. Proc. Royal Soc. B **276**(1165), 2171–2178 (2009)
33. Pothos, E.M., Busemeyer, J.R.: Can quantum probability provide a new direction for cognitive modeling? Behav. Brain Sci. **36**(3), 255–274 (2013)
34. Savage, L.J.: The Foundations of statistics. Wiley, New York (1954)
35. Shubik, M.: Quantum economics, uncertainty and optimal grid size. Econ. Lett. **64**(3), 277–278 (1999)
36. Smith, C.E., Brown, R.D., Bruce, J.M., Overby, M.: Party balancing and voting for congress in the 1996 national elections. Am. J. Polit. Sci. **43**(3), 737–764 (1999)
37. Trueblood, J.S., Busemeyer, J.R.: A quantum probability account of order effects in inference. Cogn. Sci. **35**(8), 1518–1552 (2011)
38. Tversky, A., Kahneman, D.: Extensional versus intuitive reasoning: The conjunction fallacy in probability judgment. Psychol. Rev. **90**, 293–315 (1983)
39. Tversky, A., Shafir, E.: The disjunction effect in choice under uncertainty. Psychol. Sci. **3**(5), 305–309 (1992)
40. von Neumann, J., Morgenstern, O.: Theory of Games and Economic Behaviour. Princeton University Press, Princeton (1953)
41. von Neumann, J.: Mathematical Foundations of Quantum Mechanics. Princeton University Press, Princeton (1955)
42. Zorn C., Smith C.: Pseudo – Classical Nonseparability and Mass Politics in Two Party Systems, arXiv:1107.0964 (2011)
43. Election statistics: http//www.loc.gov/rr/program/bib/elections/statistics.html. Accessed 01 April 2014

Transparency in Public Life: A Quantum Cognition Perspective

Ariane Lambert-Mogiliansky[1] and François Dubois[2,3]([⊠])

[1] Paris School of Economics, 48 Bd Jourdan, 75014 Paris, France
alambert@pse.ens.fr
[2] Department of Mathematics, University Paris Sud, Orsay, France
[3] Structural Mechanics and Coupled Systems Laboratory,
CNAM Paris, Paris, France
francois.dubois@math.u-psud.fr

Abstract. In this paper we investigate the implications of assuming that citizens are cognitively constrained for transparency in public life. We model cognitive limitations as reflecting a quantum property of people's mental representations of the world. There exists a multiplicity of incompatible (Bohr) complementary mental representations of a situation. As a consequence the framing of information plays a crucial role. We show that additional information can be detrimental to a quantum cognitively constrained agent: he may become more confused. We suggest some implications for the design of a public agency's website.

Keywords: Learning · Quantum cognition · Transparency

AMS classification: 81Q99, 91C99

Introduction

Transparency is among the most debated issues in modern public life. The development of information technology has given rise to hopes for a modern truly democratic state based on transparency. As noted by Beth Noveck [18], real applications have fallen short for those hopes. In part we suggest that this may be due to a narrow understanding of the concept of transparency. This paper is a contribution to the exploration of the links between access to information and transparency. The starting point is the recognition that access to information is not equivalent to transparency. Instead transparency is intimately related to learning. In this paper we suggest that a quantum approach to information processing by human receptors may shed some fruitful light on the public debate as well as provide insights of value for practical applications.

The information system community, among others, was early aware that in addition to the physical constraints, the transmission of information *e.g.*, about a new information system, is conditioned by cognitive limitations. Appealing to cognitive scientists they formulate those limitations in terms of "mental models", "cognitive frames" or "scripts" that simultaneously enable and constrain

© Springer International Publishing Switzerland 2015
H. Atmanspacher et al. (Eds.): QI 2014, LNCS 8951, pp. 210–222, 2015.
DOI: 10.1007/978-3-319-15931-7_17

understanding. Gioia writes about "definitions of (organizational) reality that serve as vehicule for understanding and action" (Gioia [9], p. 50). "They include assumptions, knowledge and expectations expressed symbolically through language, visual images, metaphors and stories. Frames are flexible in content and structure having variable dimensions that skift in salience and content by context and over time" (Orlikowsky and Gash [19]).

In economics, we talk about "framing effects" when alternative descriptions of one and the same decision problem induce different decisions from agents. Kahneman and Tversky [13] address framing effects by making the crucial point that "the true objects of evaluation are neither objects in the real world nor verbal descriptions of those objects; they are mental representations". To capture this feature, framing effects have been modelled as the "process of constructing a representation", *i.e.*, as a measurement performed on the (quantum) state of the agent (Lambert-Mogiliansky, Zamir and Zwirn [16]). In Lambert-Mogiliansky and Busemeyer [14], we show how this approach is consistent with a number of central theories in psychology including *e.g.*, Self perception and provides a tractable approach to questions related to identity and self-control. In this paper, we introduce element of a theory of learning based on those premises and suggest that it provides a fruitful way to capture some of the above mentioned concerns expressed by practitioners.

We propose that the cognitive process involved in information processing includes two steps: i. receiving information framed according to some representation; ii processing information in terms of ones preferred representation. This learning process is not Bayesian as soon as we allow for Bohr complementarity of representations. The issue of learning by non-classically minded agents has been approached in Danilov and Lambert Mogiliansky [4,5] and more recently in Busemeyer and Bruza [1].

A central result in learning theory is that Bayesian updating (under weak conditions) converges to the truth. However critics have been raised on several aspects of Bayesianism (see *e.g.* Gilboa, Postlewaite and Schmeidler [11]. Departures from Bayesian updating may occur because they undervalue or overvalue priors (*e.g.*, Epstein Noor Sandroni [8]). Alternative approaches have been developed in connection with Maxmin Expected Utility (Gilboa and Schmeidler [10]) and Multiple priors (Hanany and Klibanoff [12]). Our approach implies a novel departure from Bayesian updating appealing to the recent success of the quantum formalism in psychology and in social sciences (for a survey of recent advances see Khrenikov [15] and Busemeyer and Bruza [1].

1 Learning by Non-classically Minded Agents

It is a common place that human beings are not capable of holding very complex picture in mind (cf "small worlds" in Savage 1954). They consider reality focusing on one perspective at a time and show difficulty switching perspective as amply documented. What the quantum approach entails is that this inability to seize reality in its full richness has far reaching consequences beyond incomplete knowledge. When the perspectives are incompatible in the agent's mind, his understanding of reality does not look like a puzzle that is assembled progressively, instead the evolution of the picture of reality is subjected to disturbances (discrete jumps) which entails specific properties of the learning process.

In the present context the parallel with QM can be described as follows: the system is the subjective picture about the world, it is a psychic object. To gain information on the mental picture of the world two things can be done. One may add some information about the outside world. And one may perform a measurement of the picture by means of introspection. New information about the world transforms the picture (in a way similar to a preparation procedure). Thereafter, the agent processes information *i.e.*, he "updates" his beliefs. This is modeled as a measurement that projects the new state (picture) onto one of the possible pictures defined by his preferred representation (see below). Figure 1 is a well-known ambiguous picture. The mind may perceive a rabbit or a duck. Both pictures are complete representations of the drawing: they confer a "meaning" to every detail. The brain oscillates between the two or settle for either one of them but cannot perceive both simultaneously. Both pictures are true but they are incompatible in the mind.

1.1   The Basic Model

Let the state (of understanding) of an agent be called a mental picture, we denote it $|\varphi\rangle \in \mathbb{H}$ where $\mathbb{H}$ is the Hilbert space of mental pictures of the (relevant) world. The present analysis addresses uncertainty exclusively linked to quantum indeterminacy reflecting cognitive constraints *i.e.*, we shall be working exclusively with pure states. A distinctive feature of non-classical systems is the existence of dispersed pure states referred to as "intrinsic uncertainty". It is closely related to two other features of non-classical systems: the existence of incompatible measurements and the impact of the measurements on the state.[1]

The Notion of Measurement. Before entering into the analysis let us remind of some basic notions and how they relate to our issue. Generally, a measurement is an interaction between a system and some measurement device, which yields some result, the outcome of the measurement that we can observe and record. Two measurements are compatible if they, roughly speaking, can be performed simultaneously or more precisely, if the performance of one measurement does not affect the result of the other.

In our context a measurement is an introspective operation that acts on the agent's mental picture. The agent's asks himself a question and an answer, the

---

[1] If a state is dispersion-free, *i.e.*, the outcome of every possible measurement is uniquely determined, there is no reason for the state to change. If all pure states are dispersion-free then measurements do not impact on pure states and therefore all measurements are compatible. On the contrary, if a state is dispersed then by necessity it will be modified by an appropriate measurement. On the other hand, the change in a pure state is the reason for incompatibility of measurements. The initial outcome of a first measurement is not repeated because the system has been modified by a second measurement (see Danilov and Lambert-Mogiliansky [4,5]).

Fig. 1. What do you see?

outcome of the mental process is brought to consciousness. We propose that the cognitive limitations documented by practitioners can be modelled as the result of incompatible mental operations that act on the mental picture.

A Preferred Frame. We shall assume that the agent seeks information *because he has some concern in mind e.g.*, he wants to make a decision. This assumption is consistent with psychological and neurobiological evidence that human cognitive processes (including perception) are structured by some form of intentionality.

Generally, a representation is an observable R with eigenvalues $\{r_1, ... r_n\}$ interpreted as the possible "eigenpictures" belonging the representation R^2. The agent's state, a mental picture can written as a superposition of the possible eigenpictures in any representations of the (relevant) world:

$$|\varphi\rangle = \sum_i \lambda_i |r_i\rangle, \quad \sum_j \lambda_i^2 = 1, \ \lambda_i \in \mathbb{R}.$$

A decision problem is defined as a correspondance from $D : \mathbb{H} \rightarrow A$ where $\mathbb{H}$ is the space of mental pictures of the world and A the set of actions. For each (mentally represented) state of the world, it defines which actions the agent wants to undertake.

Hypothesis 1
There exists a representation R^* such that D is a coarsening of R^*.[3]

Hypothesis 1 implies that if the agent receives (maximal) information framed in representation R^* he will know exactly what to do. We also say that R^* is fully congruent with D. Generally, D has a lower dimensionality than $\mathbb{H}$, *i.e.*, distinct eigenpictures can induce the same action.

---

[2] All the representations R, R^*, *etc.* that we consider in this contribution have eigenspaces of dimension exactly equal to one. All these eigenstates are maximal information states for the individual.

[3] A measurement M' is coarser than M if every eigenset of M is contained in some eigenset of M', see Danilov and Lambert-Mogiliansky [4,5] p. 334.

The Cognitive Process. In our context, it is in place to explicitly decompose the cognitive process of learning into two steps:

Step 1: Preparation
The first step of the mental process is gaining information expressed within some representation $R \neq R^*$ (or frame - we use the terms interchangeably). It corresponds to a fully deterministic evolution of the mental picture. It operates on the initial state(picture) so as to project it onto the one eigenpicture reflecting the information content provided (see below for a concrete example). In the terminology of QM it resembles a process of preparation[4]: $|\varphi\rangle \rightarrow |\varphi'\rangle = |r_i\rangle$, where $|r_i\rangle$ is an eigenpicture of the R representation.

Step 2: Measurement
After having received the information, the agent processes information i.e., updates his mental picture (r_i) with respect to his preferred representation R^*. This is a non-deterministic evolution which we model as a measurement. We first express $|\varphi'\rangle = |r_i\rangle$ in terms of the eigenpictures of the preferred representation, R^*, $|r_i\rangle = \sum_j \gamma_j |r_j^*\rangle$ applying R^* we obtain

$$R^*|\varphi'\rangle \rightarrow |r_j^*\rangle \text{ with probability } \gamma_j^2.$$

We see that after completing the cognitive process corresponding to interpreting the information in his own mental model, the agent's actual state of information is some $|r_j^*\rangle \neq |r_i\rangle$. The two states are not mutually exclusive (orthogonal) but they are incompatible in his mind which captures the cognitive limitation.

1.2   Analysis: The Value of New Information

We now develop a simple argument showing that information can increase the agent's relevant uncertainty. Uncertainty (intrinsic) is measured by the entropy *of dispersion*[5] in terms of the preferred representation: let $|\varphi\rangle = \sum_j \nu_j |r_j^*\rangle$, since γ_j^2 is the probability for obtaining eigenpicture $|r_j^*\rangle$ after the measurement R^*, the (intrinsic) uncertainty associated with φ is defined

$$H(\varphi) = -\sum_j \nu_j^2 \log \nu_j^2$$

For the purpose of the argument, we shall assume that the agent's mental state is initially an eigenpicture of his preferred representation $|\varphi\rangle = |r_2^*\rangle$. This state reflects information that is perfectly congruent with R^* but is not framed in R^{*6}. But the agent is not aware of r_2^* unless he updates "his beliefs" which corresponds to the (measurement) operation of R^*. If he did, he would obtain

---

[4] In the process of preparation a system is put into a specific state.

[5] We talk about the entropy of *dispersion* rather than of probability distribution, because we are dealing with a pure state. See discussion above.

[6] In the example "learning that the administration lacks standard of ethics" is equivalent to learning "it is worthwhile to complaint". The point is before the agent processed the information in his own frame (step 2), he is not aware of this.

$$R^*|\varphi\rangle = |r_2^*\rangle$$

He would then be fully determined with respect to the decision problem. There would not be any (relevant) uncertainty left with $\nu_2 = 1$ we have $H(\varphi) = 0$. But assume that instead he acquires new information relative to another but related aspects of the issue. We denote this representation P. This corresponds to steps 1 of the cognitive process above. The mental state $|\varphi\rangle$ is prepared into $|\varphi'\rangle$ equal to some $|p_i\rangle$. "Enriched" with this new information, the agent now updates his mental picture with respect to his preferred representation (step 2):

$$|\varphi'\rangle = |p_2\rangle = \sum_j \gamma_j |r_j^*\rangle \rightarrow \text{any}|r_j^*\rangle \text{ with probability } \gamma_j^2 \neq 1$$

We see that while he previously potentially "knew" r_2^* (but was unaware of it) he is now is a state of hesitation where he believes that there is only a probability of $\gamma_2^2 < 1$ that the "true" eigenpicture is r_2^*.[7] The acquisition of new information has triggered the loss of some information leaving the agent in a state of intrinsic uncertainty captured by a strictly positive entropy:

$$H(\varphi') = -\sum_j \gamma_j^2 \log \gamma_j^2 > 0.$$

Proposition 1. *Assume that the agent's mental state is one eigenpicture of his preferred representation, acquiring additional information in terms of a representation that is not compatible with the preferred one leads to confusion measured by increased dispersion entropy.*

This is the central result of this paper. When two representations are incompatible in the agent's mind. Additional information is not always beneficial to the agent. It is unambiguously detrimental when the starting point is an eigenpicture of the preferred representation as illustrated in the argument above: the new information induces a strict loss of information implying confusion with respect to the concerns of the agent. More generally *i.e.*, starting from an arbitrary eigenpicture (with non zero dispersion entropy) as in the example below, new information may either decrease or increase dispersion entropy.

We illustrate the result in Proposition 1 in Fig. 2 where the dimensionality of a representation is 2. The broad line corresponds to the preparation stage and the thin lines to the measurement.

Remark 1. In our case r_2^* is true because it reflects an information congruent with R^* and $|p_i\rangle$ is also true. The agent is not mistaken. He simply cannot hold in one single picture both informations. The introspective operation when processing information p_2 involves the whole (cognitively limited) mind and therefore upsets earlier held beliefs.

---

[7] After the introspective process, he will end up believing r_2^* with some probability less than 1.

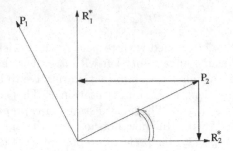

Fig. 2. Detrimental information

Classical Cognition. In order to better understand the result above let us consider the classical counter-part of the argument above. It is well-known that the quantum model includes the classical one as a special case when all measurements commute. It is important for the argument that follows to understand that we are not considering all possible classical models but the classical model corresponding to the quantum one where all the premises are the same except that all measurements commute. We below discuss other possible classical approaches.

We next consider a classical situation where all representations are compatible in the citizen's mind. He can synthesize all information without constraint. Formally, this is expressed as follows. For simplicity let both P and R^* be two dimensional as in the illustrative example of Fig. 2. When P and R^* are compatible, a picture (a state) can have values in both representations simultaneously. This means that a state or picture can be represented as a vector in the four dimensional tensor product space $P \times R^*$ spanned by the eigenvectors $\{|p_1 r_1^*\rangle, |p_1 r_2^*\rangle, |p_2 r_1^*\rangle, |p_2 r_2^*\rangle\}$. Generally the picture (state of mind) ψ of the citizen is as before expressed as a superposition of the basis vectors: $|\psi\rangle = c_1|p_1 r_1^*\rangle + c_2|p_1 r_2^*\rangle + c_3|p_2 r_1^*\rangle + c_4|p_2 r_2^*\rangle$, $\sum_{i=1}^{4} c_i^2 = 1$. Since we are dealing with a classical agent this can be interpreted as a belief state b (a random variable) in boolean space $\Omega = \{\omega_1, ..., \omega_4\}$ with $\omega_1 = p_1 r_1^*$, $\omega_2 = p_1 r_2^*$, $\omega_3 = p_2 r_1^*$, $\omega_4 = p_2 r_2^*$:

$$b = \alpha_1 \omega_1 + \alpha_2 \omega_2 + \alpha_3 \omega_3 + \alpha_4 \omega_4 \tag{1}$$

with $\alpha_i = c_i^2$, $i = 1, ..., 4$ and reads as follows: the agent believes that with probability α_1 the true state is ω_1. Now in order to compare with the quantum case above assume that the agent initially has an information that is completely correlated with r_2^* so $prob\{r^* = r_1^*\} = 0$ implying $prob\{\omega = \omega_1\} = prob\{\omega = \omega_3\} = 0$. The priors b_0 writes

$$b_0 = \frac{\alpha_2}{\alpha_2 + \alpha_4} \omega_2 + \frac{\alpha_4}{\alpha_2 + \alpha_4} \omega_4. \tag{2}$$

The agent now receives information in a way similar to the subsection above. So he receives information along P, he learns p_2 implying $prob\{p = p_1\} = 0$ implying $prob\{\omega = \omega_2\} = 0$. the agent processes that information *i.e.*, updates his priors into posteriors

$$b_1 = \omega_4.$$

The agent is now fully informed of the state of the world. So compared with the priors (2) there is no loss of information as in the quantum updating case.

Proposition 2. *In the classical counter-part of the quantum model, additional information never increases the agent's uncertainty.*

Proposition 2 underlines the implications of quantum cognitive limitations. In the absence of such limitations, *i.e.*, when all representations are compatible in the mind of the agent, information is always beneficial and - in the classical counter part model - it reduces entropy. While if the citizen is cognitively limited, information can turn confusing.

Remark 2. It must be emphasized that the reasoning above relies on our assumption that we are dealing with a classical counter part where the agent learns that $r^* = r_2^*$ with probability 1 (corresponding to the pure state in the quantum model). If we relax slightly this assumption (*i.e.*, allowing for incomplete information), the result in proposition 1 could be approached with a classical model *of a different flavor*. Assume the agent has priors that puts nearly all the weight (but not all) on r_2^* so $\alpha^1 \neq 0$ and $\alpha^3 \neq 0$ as in b in (1). Next, he receives information p^2. If according to the agent's structural model, that information is highly correlated with r_1^* (which is not the case in the original model) he updates his beliefs and puts more weight on ω_1 and ω_3 than he initially had. He is now less certain about what to do than he was before he got the information. His new beliefs exhibit a distribution with higher entropy. However, he has not *lost information* as in the quantum case. Instead the interpretation is that *his priors were wrong* so new information brought him closer to the truth. So a legitimate question is: are we only talking about interpretation or do quantum cognitive limitations really have a more profound bearing on learning?

Oscillating for Ever. Bayesian learning operates within a Boolean algebra. The objective is to learn the parameters of the model of the system.[8] Provided the priors are not inconsistent with the true model, we know (Schwartz 1965) that starting from any such priors Bayesian updating converges to the true state.

With quantum learning, we are in a Hilbert space, that is there exists a variety of *resolutions* of the system *i.e.*, a variety of representations, of valid theories of the system. *Those descriptions are not alternative to each other but complementary (in the sense of Bohr).* As a consequence there exists no single true complete information state but a multiplicity of equally true maximal information states. Therefore, the state of knowledge of a quantum minded individual does not converge with new information but oscillates for ever. Consider again the example above. After the agent performed the introspective measurement R^*, if the agent is being asked about his understanding in P, he will perform a new measurement of the eigenpicture resulting from the first measurement

---

[8] Some consider also Bayesain updating with multiple priors (see *e.g.*, Hanany and Klibanov [12]). But there is no consensus as to how to proceed - in sharp contrast with Bayesian updating of single priors.

and p_2 will not be recovered with probability 1. Performing those measurements alternately, he will keep oscillating without converging *i.e.*, without being able to settle for a definite value in both P and R^* simultaneously.[9]

Of course this example is simplistic and the agent might simply remember p_2. But in more sophisticated context, we expect the modification of the mental picture to be effective. Moreover, our focus is on the consequences for decision-making of lost information which are far from self-evident.

2   Application: Transparency in Public Life

We next address the issue of providing access to public information and its relationship with transparency in terms of the theory developed above. Consider a situation where a citizen suspects that there has been some serious wrongdoing and he must decide whether or not to file a formal complaint against a public administration. Since that is costly to him he wants to collect information to evaluate his chance of winning.

The government makes available information *e.g.*, on a website. Information can be expressed and organized according various principles. For instance some information concerns the extent of responsibility and discretion at various step of decision-making. Another informs about the ethical rules various bureaus obey. Yet, another set of information takes the perspective of the personnel and informs about the conditions for recruitment and promotion. The assumption is that the different perspectives are incompatible in the citizen's mind. When he thinks in moral/ethical terms, he cannot simultaneously envision the implication of the allocation of responsibilities for the quality of decisions or the quality competence emerging from the recruitment/promotion system. Therefore we define three non-commuting operators which for simplicity are two-valued: R_1 {rule-bounded ($|R\rangle$), discretionary ($|D\rangle$)}; R_2 {High ethical standards ($|E\rangle$), No ethical standards ($|U\rangle$)}; R_3 {Competent ($|C\rangle$), Incompetent ($|I\rangle$)}. We assume one representation R_2 is fully congruent with D the decision problem *i.e.*, whether he should file a complaint of not.[10] The initial state can be expressed in any of the representation:

$$|\varphi\rangle = \lambda_{11}|R\rangle + \lambda_{12}|D\rangle = \lambda_{21}|E\rangle + \lambda_{22}|U\rangle = \lambda_{31}|C\rangle + \lambda_{32}|I\rangle.$$

In Fig. 3 we depict the case when the citizen learns the administration is competent (green plain arrow) and when he learns the process is discretionary (blue plain arrow).

Recall that R_2^* (in red) is fully congruent with the requirements of decision-making. When provided the information framed according to R_1 and learning

---

[9] The general result is a transposition into cognition of the basic feature of quantum mechanics namely that it is not possible for complementary properties to have a determinate value simultaneously.

[10] If the citizen pictures the administration as lacking ethical standard, that comforts his suspicion and he will definitely file a complaint. Conversely, if he is convinced the administration has high ethical standards, he will not file.

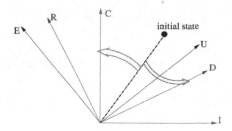

Fig. 3. Transparency in public life; incompatible mental frames of an administration

e.g., that the administration is competent. Instead of decreasing uncertainty with respect to decision-making, the new information actually increases uncertainty (dispersion entropy) thereby creating confusion in the agent's mind. The initial state (doted line) was pretty close to U, the new state C is almost equidistant to both E and U. In contrast learning that the decision processes are discretionary (projecting onto D) though not fully congruent, reduces decision uncertainty. As we see the extent of congruence is of paramount importance for cognitively constrained agents. In contrast with the classical model where at worst orthogonal information is useless, we know from proposition 1 that information can be detrimental; the citizens get confused (increased dispersion entropy).

Proposition 3. *The government can increase citizens' confusion by providing information along a representation that is little congruent with the citizens' concerns.*

This result implies that in our framework, truthful information can be used to manipulate the citizens away from their concerns in order to affect their decisions. The next section shows how full access to information can lead to confusion.

Sequential Information Acquisition: The Architecture of the Website.
In this subsection we explore some implications of the results above for the architecture of the administration's website. Consider now a representation as a complete set of commuting observable. So for instance in R_3, beside competence (in terms of formal education), the website provides a description of the principles for selection in recruitment, of the principles governing evaluation for promotion, a description of the rules and processes to be followed (from the point of view of their complexity/simplicity), etc. Similarly for the other representations *e.g.*, R_4 provides information about the standards for decisions, the appeal procedures etc.

Assume the website aims at providing full access to information. If the architect does not have in mind the quantum structure of the citizens' mind, the website will most probably be constructed so the progression in the tree mixes elements from different representations. Each new step entails a projection on a subspace of the representation to which the information belongs. But as we next show that has implication for the information previously "pictured", it is "lost" in the updating *i.e.*, in the necessity for the citizen to be coherent *i.e.*, fit information in one coherent to him picture.

To see this consider the following path. To facilitate the reading we let the eigenvalues of R_1 be labeled as a_i and R_2 as b_i the two representations are complementary in the mind of the citizen. Assume the citizen state is $|\psi\rangle = |b_1\rangle = \sum_{i=1}^{3} \lambda_i |a_{1i}\rangle$. This means that his knowledge is an eigenpicture of R_2, he has a determinate understanding of the administration in that representation. Now the website guides him further with information "*non* a_3". The picture of the citizen evolves from

$$|b_1\rangle = \sum_{i=1}^{3} \lambda_i |a_i\rangle \rightarrow |\psi'\rangle = \frac{\lambda_1}{\sqrt{\lambda_1^2 + \lambda_2^2}} |a_1\rangle + \frac{\lambda_2}{\sqrt{\lambda_1^2 + \lambda_2^2}} |a_2\rangle \neq |b_1\rangle$$

So the citizen is less indeterminate with respect to R_1 but he lost the determination he had in R_2. With $|a_i\rangle = \sum_{j=1}^{3} \gamma_{ij} |b_{1j}\rangle$ we can now write the citizen's state of information in R_2: $|\psi'\rangle = \frac{\lambda_1}{\sqrt{\lambda_1^2 + \lambda_2^2}} \sum_{j=1}^{3} \gamma_{1j} |b_j\rangle + \frac{\lambda_2}{\sqrt{\lambda_1^2 + \lambda_2^2}} \sum_{j=1}^{3} \gamma_{2j} |b_j\rangle$. After redistribution in terms of the b_j: $|\psi'\rangle = \left(\frac{\lambda_1}{\sqrt{\lambda_1^2 + \lambda_2^2}} \gamma_{11} + \frac{\lambda_2}{\sqrt{\lambda_1^2 + \lambda_2^2}} \gamma_{21} \right) |b_1\rangle + \left(\frac{\lambda_1}{\sqrt{\lambda_1^2 + \lambda_2^2}} \gamma_{12} + \frac{\lambda_2}{\sqrt{\lambda_1^2 + \lambda_2^2}} \gamma_{22} \right) |b_2\rangle + \left(\frac{\lambda_1}{\sqrt{\lambda_1^2 + \lambda_2^2}} \gamma_{13} + \frac{\lambda_2}{\sqrt{\lambda_1^2 + \lambda_2^2}} \gamma_{23} \right) |b_3\rangle$. So we see that in R_2 the citizen is represented by a relatively complex superposition of all 3 possible eigenpictures of R_2. If he walks out from the website now, he is definitely more confused than when he started: he has no clear picture of anything. Adding yet another information belonging to a third representation will make his updating toward R_2 even more difficult.

Any learning process about a sufficiently complex system proceeds by step which can be identified as the sequential acquisition of coarse information. For quantum cognitively constrained citizens this corresponds to a sequence of preparation followed by possibly incompatible measurements. The more complex the system the more likely the cognitive constraints are binding *i.e.*, the agent is not capable of synthesizing all information in one picture. Instead information is organized in a number of alternative perspectives of the system corresponding to alternative (incompatible) representations. We have the following claim

Claim. i. Sequential acquisition of information can be particularly confusing if it mixes inputs from different representations. ii. Full access to information about a complex system is generally not beneficial to cognitively constrained agents.

The first claim is illustrated in the example above. The second claim follows from recognizing that the more complex a system, the more likely information about it involves a number of incompatible representations. The claim demonstrates the distinction between access to information and transparency. One implication is that an ill-intentioned webarchitect while providing full access to information can manipulate citizens so they give up their ambition to file a complaint whatever the initial state of mind. In other words transparency can be defeated precisely by providing full access to information.

3   Concluding Remarks

This paper is a first exploration of learning by cognitively limited agents where the limitations are modeled appealing to quantum like characteristics of the mind. A main motivation is that the quantum approach has shown successful in explaining behavioral anomalies in decision-making while it also seems able to capture concerns expressed by practitioners dealing with information transmission and communication. In particular, the fact that i. people reason about reality within the frame of some a representation ("mental script") or as we call it, a mental picture, ii, the multiplicity of potential representations of reality generates specific problems for information transmission and learning. We model cognitive limitations in terms of the multiplicity of Bohr complementary mental representations of one and the same reality. We find that under intrinsic uncertainty, additional information may contribute to increasing the confusion of people. The analysis reveals a new significance of informational congruence which allows shedding some light on the issue of transparency in public life. In particular, we find that indeed access to information is not equivalent to transparency and that even truthful and full access to information can be exploited to manipulate cognitively constrained people. Future research will aim at extending the argument to a setting with uncertainty due to both incomplete information and intrinsic uncertainty. It will also establish the asymptotic properties of learning by quantum minded agents and perform a systematic comparison with non-Bayesian learning models.

References

1. Busemeyer, J.R., Bruza, P.: Quantum Models of Cognition and Decision. Cambridge University Press, Cambridge (2012)
2. Busemeyer, J.R., Wang, Z., Townsend, J.T.: Quantum dynamics of human decision-making. J. Math. Psychol. **50**, 220–241 (2006)
3. Busemeyer, J.R., Weg, E., Barkan, R., Li, X., Ma, Z.: Dynamic and consequential consistency of choices between paths of decision trees. J. Exp. Psychol. Gen. **129**, 530–545 (2000)
4. Danilov, V.I., Lambert-Mogiliansky, A.: Measurable systems and behavioral sciences. Math. Soc. Sci. **55**, 315–340 (2008)
5. Danilov V.I., Lambert-Mogiliansky, A.: Decision-making under non-classical uncertainty. In: Proceedings of the second interaction symposium (QI 2008), pp. 83–87 (2008)
6. Danilov, V.I., Lambert-Mogiliansky, A.: Expected utility under non-classical uncertainty. Theory Decis. **2010**(68), 25–47 (2010)
7. Dawes, S.: Stewardship and usefulness: policy principles for information-based transparency. Gov. Inf. Q. **27**(4), 377–383 (2010)
8. Epstein, L., Noor, J., Sandroni, A.: Non-Bayesian updating: a theoretical framework. Theor. Econ. **3**, 193–229 (2008)
9. Gioia, D.: Symbols, script and sense-making: creating meaning in the organizational experience. In: Sims, H., Gioia, D. Jr., Associates (eds.) Thinking Organization. Jossey Bass San-Fransisco, pp. 49–74 (1986)

10. Gilboa, I., Schmeidler, D.: Maxmin utility with non-unique priors. J. Math. Econ. **18**, 141–153 (1989)
11. Gilboa, I., Postlewaite, A., Schmeidler, D.: Rationality of beliefs or: why Savage's axioms are neither necessary nore sufficient for rationality. Synthese **187**, 11–31 (2012)
12. Hanany, E., Klibanov, P.: Updating preferences with multiple priors. Theor. Econ. **2**, 261–298 (2007)
13. Kahneman, D., Tversky, A. (eds.): Choices, values and frames. Cambridge University Press, New York (2000)
14. Lambert-Mogiliansky, A., Busemeyer, J.R.: Quantum indeterminacy in dynamic decision-making: self-control through identity management. Games **3**(2), 97–118 (2012)
15. Khrennikov, A.: Ubiquitous Quantum Structure - from Psychology to Finance. Springer, Berlin (2010)
16. Lambert-Mogiliansky, A., Zamir, S., Zwirn, H.: Type indeterminacy - a model of the KT(Khaneman Tversky)- man. J. Math. Psychol. **53**(5), 349–361 (2009)
17. La Mura, P.: Projective expected utility. J. Math. Psychol. **53**, 408–414 (2009)
18. Noveck, B.: Wiki Government: How Technology Can Make Government Better, Democracy Stronger, and Citizens More Powerful. Brookings Institution Press, Washington DC (2009)
19. Orlikowsky, W.J., Gash, D.C.: Technological frames: making sense of information technology in organizations. ACM Trans. Inf. Syst. (TOIS) **12**(2), 174–207 (1994)
20. Savage, L.: The Foundation of Statistics. Dover publication inc, New York (1954)

Games with Type Indeterminate Players
A Hilbert Space Approach to Uncertainty and Strategic Manipulation of Preferences

Ariane Lambert-Mogiliansky[1] and Ismael Martínez-Martínez[2]([✉])

[1] Paris School of Economics, 48 Boulevard Jourdan, 75014 Paris, France
alambert@pse.ens.fr
[2] Düsseldorf Institute for Competition Economics (DICE), Heinrich Heine Universität Düsseldorf, Universitätsstraße 1, 40225 Düsseldorf, Germany
ismael@imartinez.eu

Abstract. We develop a basic framework encoding preference relations on the set of possible strategies in a quantum-like fashion. The Type Indeterminacy model introduces quantum-like uncertainty affecting preferences. The players are viewed as systems subject to measurements. The decision nodes are, possibly non-commuting, operators that measure preferences modulo strategic reasoning. We define a Hilbert space of types and focus on pure strategy TI games of maximal information. Preferences evolve in a non-deterministic manner with actions along the play: they are endogenous to the interaction. We propose the Type Indeterminate Nash Equilibrium as a solution concept relying on best-replies at the level of eigentypes.

Keywords: Type Indeterminacy · Superposition of preferences · Hilbert space of types · Type Indeterminate Nash Equilibrium

1 Introduction

The Type Indeterminacy model (TI) provides a benchmark for the study of decision-makers characterized by quantum-like uncertain preferences (Lambert-Mogiliansky *et al.* 2009). The 'constructive preference perspective' *à la* Kahneman and Tversky reminds of certain aspects of the Quantum formalism, in particular relative to the notion of superposition of states and of non-commutativity of measurements. The analogy between the non-commutativity of observables in Quantum Mechanics and the intrinsic uncertainty of preferences in Decision Theory comes from viewing the decision-situations as possibly non-commuting operators that measure the preferences of the decision-maker. The novel contribution of this approach is the proposal of encoding the preference relations on the set of possible strategies in a quantum-like fashion (*i.e.*, orthonormal basis and Hermitian operators), and not the game strategies as was done in previous studies.[1] This

---

[1] For monographic overviews of other achievements in quantum-like decision making, Busemeyer and Bruza (2012), Khrennikov (2010), and Haven and Khrennikov (2012).

© Springer International Publishing Switzerland 2015
H. Atmanspacher et al. (Eds.): QI 2014, LNCS 8951, pp. 223–239, 2015.
DOI: 10.1007/978-3-319-15931-7_18

allows for capturing important features in behavioral economics as it defines a TI player as an agent who is *not simultaneously endowed with a preference order over all possible subsets of alternatives* (Lambert-Mogilianksy and Busemeyer 2012). When applied to Game Theory, the type of a TI agent emerges as a consequence of the choice of actions within the interactions with the other players, rather than being fully exogenous.[2] The Type Indeterminacy approach has already shown to be fruitful in providing explanation to a wide range of behavioral anomalies in simple decision-making (e.g., violations of transitivity and of the Principle of Indifference of Irrelevant Alternatives; Lambert-Mogiliansky *et al.* 2009). After the present proposal of extending the formalism to games with TI players, we conjecture that the further development of equilibrium concepts for TI games can provide important insights in a wide range of behavioral patterns in interactive situations.

This work seeks to define the most basic elements of a theory of games with Type Indeterminate players, so we keep the notation as close as possible to the standard one in Game Theory and we consider only basic knowledge of vector spaces to be required for the reading. The paper is structured as follows. In Sect. 2, we first establish how a finite number N of mutually exclusive preference relations of a player (called eigentypes) can be modeled as an orthogonal basis of a N-dimensional vector space: The Hilbert Space of Types. We introduce two postulates: *(i)* the superposition of preferences is a valid type, and *(ii)* the choice of actions affects preferences.[3] We discuss the probabilistic interpretation of this framework and how the intrinsic uncertainty in the preferences relates to a model of non-commuting decision-situations.[4]

Section 3 introduces the basic elements for the study of TI games, the interactions between TI players. The preferences of a TI player are represented as a unit length vector giving her type as a linear combination of the elements of an orthonormal basis. When the player faces several non-commuting decision-situations, the Hilbert Space of Types admits several orthonormal basis of eigentypes related to each other by means of basis transformation matrices. These are basic operations in any linear space. In this contribution, we focus only on TI games with maximal information, so that the whole structure of eigentypes and their relations is known. We discuss how the timing of a TI game defines a partially ordered set of decision-situations which may imply a sequence of projections of

---

[2] This is an idealized model for agents whose type may change in the decision-making process, formalizing the idea that *in these situations – of violation of procedural invariance – observed preferences are not simply read off from some master list; they are actually constructed in the elicitation process*, as argued by Kahneman and Tversky (2000, p. 504).

[3] They are inspired by the Principle of Superposition and the Postulate of Measurement and Observables in Quantum Mechanics, respectively.

[4] Under some simplifying conditions, a TI model can yield the same predictions as a 'classical' Bayesian framework.

the preferences as a consequence of the path defined by the choice of actions. This 'evolution' of preferences is endogenous to the interaction between TI players and is, in general, non-deterministic. We also discuss a definition for the Type Indeterminate Nash Equilibrium (henceforth TINE). The TINE is proposed as a solution concept for TI games whose main feature is that the choices of actions are best-responses at the level of the eigentypes, while the overall utility for the player is computed at the level of the type. Generally, the type is a linear superposition of several eigentypes, and the composition of this combination is affected by the choice of actions in a non-deterministic evolution. This idea of *cashing-on-the-go* is introduced in the Assumptions 1 and 2. A TINE specifies the equilibrium strategy of each player as the collection of the best-replies of all possible eigentypes of each player, as well as the expected resulting profile of preferences of the players as a consequence of their plays along the game. A TINE implies an expected utility level for all the players.

We analyze an example in Sect. 4. We consider a simple game with two players illustrating how to operate with the computational machinery in a Hilbert Space of Types, and it emphasizes the notion of actions as projectors, and the strategic value of manipulating other players' intrinsically indeterminate preferences. We conclude in Sect. 5 with some final remarks.

2   Types as Superpositions in a Hilbert Space

In this paper an agent is characterized by her type. The type captures maximal information about the agent's preferences over the actions in interactive decision-situations. The TI approach defines an agent as a measurable system. Such a system is characterized by its state: an element in a Hilbert space endowed with a set of operators (measurements).[5]

Definition 1. *Let O be the set of possible outcomes of an interaction between players. Then, a preference relation of the player i over the set of outcomes O is a binary relation denoted by $\succsim_i (O \times O)$.*[6]

Definition 2. *Let $R_i(O) = \{\succsim_i^{(n)}\}_{n=1}^N$ be a set of N different preference relations over a set of outcomes. We associate them in a bijection with a set*

---

[5] For a more general discussion in terms of ortholattices, see Danilov and Lambert-Mogiliansky (2008). We restrict ourselves to separable and finite-dimensional Hilbert spaces defined over the field of real numbers.

[6] Given two elements $o_j, o_k \in O$, $o_j \sim o_k$ denotes the indifference between both of them defined as $o_j \succsim_i o_k$ and $o_k \succsim_i o_j$, and $o_j \succ_i o_k$ denotes the strict preference for o_j defined as $o_j \succsim_i o_k$ and not $o_k \succsim_i o_j$. A utility function u_i representing $\succsim_i$ is a real-valued function defined over O and satisfying $u_i(o_1) \geq u_i(o_2) \Leftrightarrow o_1 \succsim_i o_2 \; \forall o_1, o_2 \in O$.

$\Theta_i = \{\theta_i^{(n)}\}_{n=1}^N$ of orthonormal vectors in a Hilbert space. Then, Θ_i is an ortho-normal basis of a Hilbert space of dimension N.[7]

From the bijection $R_i(O) \leftrightarrow \Theta_i$, we equivalently refer to the preference relations of a player and to the corresponding vectors of the orthonormal basis. We denote both of them by Θ_i from now on to lighten the notation.

Definition 3. *Let Θ_i be the set of orthonormal vectors in a bijection with the set of preference relations of player i. Then, we denote by T_i the N-dimensional Hilbert space of the types of player i, $T_i \equiv Span(\Theta_i)$, spanned by the orthonormal basis of preference relations of player i.*

Definition 4. *Let a player i be described in terms of a Hilbert space of types T_i. Then, the type of the player is fully characterized by a state-vector $t_i \in T_i$ such that $\|t_i\| = 1$.*

The state of a system is expressed in terms of vectors of the Hilbert space with unit length as a requirement to be a probability framework.[8]

Postulate 1. *Let T_i be the Hilbert space of types spanned by the possible prefer-ences of the player, $\{\theta_i^{(n)}\}_{n=1}^N$. Then, every type of the form $t_i = \sum_{n=1}^N c_n \theta_i^{(n)}$, with $c_n \in \mathbb{R}$, and $\sum_{n=1}^N c_n^2 = 1$, is also a unit length vector belonging to the same Hilbert space, $t_i \in T_i$. Hence, any linear combination of preferences (eigentypes) of a player is itself a proper type of the player.*

This Postulate 1 represents a major departure from the standard models in Deci-sion and Game Theory, where the linear combinations of types are understood as tools for computing expected values when the other players lack information about the proper type of a player. In a TI game, any superposition is a proper type itself, meaning that the type of an agent is in general characterized by several mutually exclusive preference relations.[9] For the rest of this paper we use the term *type* of a player to denote *a superposition of mutually exclusive*

---

[7] As a simplifying remark, a preference relation defined over a set of M alternatives is, generally, composed of a list of the order of $C_{M,2}$ elements, the combinatorial number counting how many different pairs we can form with the collection of M elements. Imagine a decision-maker i who can conceive only two monotonic ways of ranking the elements: either in a 'positive' way $M \succsim_i^{(+)} \ldots \succsim_i^{(+)} 1$ or in a 'negative' way $1 \succsim_i^{(-)} \ldots \succsim_i^{(-)} M$. Then, the number of eigentypes required to describe our thought-agent is just $N = 2$, because there are only two possible preference relations even though each of these relations contains many pairwise comparisons between the elements in the outcome set. Please note that due to the interactive nature of the game-theoretical settings, we will usually find more complex representations.

[8] All the elements of the form λt_i (with $\lambda \neq 0$) represent the same state of the system as t_i, with $\|t_i\| = 1$.

[9] At this initial stage of our research, we restrict the model to pure types. We do not consider mixed types (represented by density matrices) that are expression of incomplete information. We deal exclusively with situations of *maximal information*, where all the uncertainty is intrinsic.

preference relations, which are referred to as the *eigenpreferences* or the *eigen-types* associated to each decision-making node.

The players' choices of actions reflect the type of the players. Nevertheless, when observing the choice of an action, we do not directly learn about the preferences: we observe the type *modulo strategic reasoning*. Note that this is standard in game theory but it acquires a new meaning in our context. The notion of intrinsic uncertainty entails that the players' type must be defined together with the decision-nodes to which they are confronted along the game.[10]

For any decision-situation d, player i has a set of possible actions $A_i(d)$ among which she can choose. Taking actions reveals information about the underlying preferences which are present in the type of the player. It is therefore natural to understand the actions as related to the outcomes of some sort of measurements of the type. Let the set $\Theta_i(d)$ contain those preference relations (eigentypes) that can be actualized for the player i in the state of preferences (type) t_i when facing a decision-situation d. Then, the choice of a particular action $a_i(d)$ implies the transition of the player i's type from the initial state t_i to an outcoming state t'_i, resulting from the measurement process. We model this transition as a projection onto the subspace of types spanned by the eigentypes supporting the chosen action,[11] as a consequence of strategic reasoning. Formally,

Definition 5. *Let $a_i(d) \in A_i(d)$ be a particular action that can be chosen by the player i at a decision-situation d, and let us assume that $a_i(d)$ is the preferred action for a certain number $M \leq N$ of eigentypes $\{t_1, \ldots, t_M\} \in \Theta_i(d)$. Then, the matrix $P_{a_i(d)} = \sum_{t_1, \ldots, t_M} t_m t_m^T$ is the projector associated to the action $a_i(d)$.[12]*

Postulate 2. *For the player i facing a given decision-situation d, the chosen action $a_i(d) \in A_i(d)$ is the outcome of a measurement of her preferences. The type of player i after making her decision in decision-situation d is $t'_i = P_{a_i(d)} t_i / \|P_{a_i(d)} t_i\|$, where t_i is the type before making the decision.*

If one action is preferred only by one particular eigentype, the outcoming preferences of the player only contain the information of the eigentype that was actualized with the selected action. Usually, an action may be preferred by *several* of the eigentypes belonging to the initial superposition. The outcoming preferences of the player are then a superposition of all those eigentypes. If one and the same action is preferred by all the eigentypes, the projector is the identity

---

[10] We below return in more detail to the distinction between the observed choice and the underlying preferences.

[11] This follows in the spirit of Lüders' postulate, a generalization of the so-called von Neumann's Postulate for Pure States, which applies only for nondegenerate spectrums of observables. We consider our manuscript presents a self-contained exposition of the use of the Hilbert spaces for describing the space of types in Game Theory. For the reader deeply interested in the interpretation of the *measurement postulate* in Quantum Mechanics, we suggest Chap. 8 of *The Logic of Quantum Mechanics* by E.G. Beltrametti and G. Cassinelli (1981), as well as A. Khrennikov (2009), Int. J. of Quant. Inf., 7, 1303-1311.

[12] The row-vector t_m^T is the transposition of $t_m \in \mathcal{T}_i$, and $P_{a_i(d)}$ is a $N \times N$ matrix.

matrix and the outcoming preferences of the player i after taking such action, t_i', are identical to the incoming preferences, t_i. The projections corresponding to the possible actions are orthogonal, and the Hilbert space of types T_i can be decomposed as the direct sum of the subspaces associated to each of the actions (this relates to spectral decomposition). We note that in the case we were interested in a single move corresponding to a single measurement, the Postulate 2 would imply Bayesian updating.

Let the state of the preferences of the player i be given by the type t_i as a superposition of the eigentypes in $\Theta_i(d)$, according to Postulate 1. Hence, strategic reasoning performed at the level of the eigentypes determines which action each eigentype chooses if given a chance to act. The actual observed action chosen by the player i depends on the probability of actualization of each eigentype, defined by her incoming type t_i expressed in terms of the eigenvectors corresponding to the actions available in decision-situation d.

Definition 6. *Let t_i be the preferences vector-state of the player i when facing a decision-situation d expressed as in the Postulate 1, $t_i = \sum_{n=1}^{N} c_n \theta_i^{(n)}$, with $c_n \in \mathbb{R}$, and $\sum_{n=1}^{N} c_n^2 = 1$, and let each of the possible actions $a_i(d) \in A_i(d)$ be associated to an orthogonal projector $P_{a_i(d)}$ reflecting the strategic reasoning. Then, a particular action $a_i(d)$ will be selected by the player i in the decision-situation d with a probability given by $p\big(a_i(d)\big|t_i\big) = \|P_{a_i(d)}t_i\| = \sum_{m=1}^{M} c_m^2 \leq 1$, with $\{c_m\}_{m=1}^{M}$ being the linear coefficients of those eigentypes $\{\theta_i^{(m)}\}_{m=1}^{M} \subseteq \Theta_i(d)$ for which the action $a_i(d)$ is the preferred one.*

Intrinsic Uncertainty and Types: The Hilbert space of types provides a suitable framework for describing agents with intrinsic uncertainty involved in the strategic interactions. We have to emphasize that by *intrinsic uncertainty* we mean a kind of uncertainty different from the uncertainty due to incomplete information and different from the strategic uncertainty which arises when considering mixed strategies (we deal only with pure strategies in this paper). The realization of a particular action $a_i(d)$ when the player i is making a decision in the decision-situation d will, in general, alter the preferences of the agent with respect to another decision-situation d', as a consequence of projecting the preferences t_i of the player onto the subspace of types supporting $a_i(d)$.

Let $\Theta_i(d)$ and $\Theta_i(d')$ be two sets of eigentypes representing the preference relations for the player i facing two different decision-situations d and d', respectively. Let us assume for clarity of the exposition that both sets contain the same number N of elements.[13] In the particular case that $a_i(d)$ is supported by only one eigentype θ_i, one may think that this measurement process clears *all* the uncertainty about the preferences of the agent, but this is not true when the decision-situations are incompatible or, equivalently, they represent non-commuting measurements of the agent's type (in plain words, if order effects may arise). The vectors $\theta_i' \in \Theta_i(d')$ then form an alternative orthonormal basis

---

[13] We shall deal with the problem of coarse measurement in the future.

spanning $\mathcal{T}_i$. The two sets of vectors $\Theta_i(d)$ and $\Theta_i(d')$ are related by a basis transformation matrix, $B_i^{(d',d)} : \mathcal{T}_i \to \mathcal{T}_i$, such that every vector represented in terms of coordinates with respect to one basis is uniquely determined in terms of the other one. When the chosen action $a_i(d)$ is supported by only one eigentype, let us say $\theta_i^{(m)}(d)$, preferences of player i are fully determined with respect to decision-situation d. But player i's preferences when facing the next decision-situation d' are given by $t'_i = B_i^{(d',d)}\theta_i^{(m)}$. Thus, the vector t'_i is, in general, a superposition of several eigentypes in $\Theta_i(d')$. When the decision-situations d and d' commute, the dimensionality of the type space is given by the tensor product of the type space corresponding to each decision-situation. If this is the case, the corresponding preferences are characterized by some independence and the analysis can be fully classical.[14]

3   Games with TI Players

A TI game is an interacting situation where the agents are modeled as Type Indeterminate players. A TI player i is a decision-maker facing a set of decision-situations D_i, for which the player i's preferences are actualized when the decision is made, interpreted as the outcome of a measurement process, following Postulate 2. The following elements define a TI player: the set D_i of decision-situations in which player i has to take an action; the collection $\Theta_i = \{\Theta_i(d)\}_{d \in D_i}$ of the sets $\Theta_i(d)$ of eigentypes giving the orthonormal basis of eigenpreferences of the player i in each decision-situation $d \in D_i$, as in Definition 2; and the initial type of the player i, $t_i^0 \in \mathcal{T}_i$, given as an element of the Hilbert space of types spanned by the basis of the decision-situations corresponding to player i, Θ_i, as in Definition 3.

A TI game is of maximal information if every decision-situation of the game is identified and common knowledge; every orthonormal basis $\Theta_i(d) \in \Theta_i$ associated to each decision-situation $d \in D_i$ is common knowledge, as well as the relation among them, $B_i^{(d';d)}$, for every pair $d, d' \in D_i$; and the initial type t_i^0 of every player is known and common knowledge. A TI game is defined as $\Gamma \equiv \langle I, \mathcal{D}, \mathcal{T}, \langle t_i^0, A_i, \{u_i(\cdot)\}_{d \in D_i}\rangle_{i \in I}\rangle$, where I is the set of TI players taking part in the game, labeled by $i \in I$; $\mathcal{D} = \mathcal{D}(D, \leq)$ is the partially ordered set of the decision-situations in the game. This ordering comes from the time structure of the game, which equips the set $D = \cup_{i \in I} D_i$ with an ordering relation $\leq$ of temporal nature, and where D_i is the set of decision-situations in which the player i has to participate; $\mathcal{T} \equiv \bigotimes_{i \in I} \mathcal{T}_i$ is the Hilbert space of types describing the type for all the agents in the game, with the set $\Theta = \{\Theta_i\}_{i \in I}$ of all the orthonormal basis associated to each player's eigenpreferences; t_i^0 gives the initial type of each player i; $A_i = \{A_i(d)\}_{d \in D_i}$ is the collection of sets specifying the available actions for each player i, at each of her decision-situations; and $u_i(\cdot) : \Theta_i(d) \times A_i(d) \times A_{-i}(d) \to \mathbb{R}$ is the payoff function for each player i.[15]

---

[14] Note that commuting decision situations do not preclude statistical correlations.

[15] Just for notation, $A_{-i}(d)$ represents the actions available for all the players other than i that are involved in the decision-situation d. Then, $u_i[\theta_i(d), a_i(d), a_{-i}(d)]$

The already defined partially ordered set $\mathcal{D}$ is obtained when considering the collection of decision-situations of the game together with the ordering imposed by the timing of the game. After understanding the actions as projections in the space of preferences (see Postulate 2), we find a richer structure that can be defined over $\mathcal{D}$. Given the specification of payoffs $\{u_i(\cdot)\}_{d \in D_i}$, we have interpreted the actions as the projections defined by the underlying structure of preferences of the agents (see Definition 5), modulo strategic reasoning. Then, we can associate each decision-situation node $d \in D$ to a projector acting over the type of the players who make their decision at the node d.

It follows directly that the partially ordered set of decision-situations $\mathcal{D}$, together with the specification of the preferred action for each of the available eigentypes, defines a partially ordered set of projectors. In order not to overload the notation, we assume from now on that $\mathcal{D}$ can refer also to the partially ordered set of projectors actualized along the path of the game. Therefore, for every TI game Γ defined we build the set Σ of all possible paths of measurement along the game, from the root to each of the possible end nodes of the game. For a given path $\sigma_l \in \Sigma$, of length L, we have a chain of projectors of length up to L associated to the path along the game $\sigma_l \mapsto (P_{a_i(d_1)}, P_{a_i(d_2)}, \ldots, P_{a_i(d_L)})$, with the index $d_1 < d_2 < \ldots < d_L$ giving the order in which the L decision-situations are reached when the chain describes the play of the game.

Projections and Endogenous Evolution of Preferences: In standard game theory the preferences of a given agent are expressed in terms of a *utility function* defined only over the different end nodes of the game. The purpose of this section is to clarify certain aspects characterizing the theory of TI games which departs from both the standard and the non-deterministic approaches to the definition of the utility which clearly rely on the temporal invariance of the players' preferences. A main feature of the TI games is that the preferences are *endogenous*, they are a part of the outcome of the game as a result of the choices that are made. We can say that the preferences of the agents are initially the motivation for but finally the consequence of the choices along the path of decisions. The chain of projections defined in the play of the game determines the *evolution* of the players' preferences. Within this framework, the possibility for a *strategic manipulation* of the other players' preferences arises as a new field of interaction among the agents, as we will see in the example below.

The idea of preferences that evolve along with the taken action is not completely new. It was initially discussed from the point of view of consistent planning and welfare economics. See, *e.g.*, the discussions by Schoeffler (1952) and Harsanyi (1953). Peleg and Yaari (1973) defined the notion of *equilibrium consumption plan* for the optimal behavior of agents immersed in multi-stage decision processes with certain preferences that evolve deterministically. This original approach referred to as 'agent-form games' consists in defining a sequence of decision-makers, one for each decision-stage. A thorough discussion on cred-

---

gives the utility associated to eigenpreferences $\theta_i(d)$ when facing an interaction (a_i, a_{-i}) in the decision-situation d.

ible equilibria in agent-form games is given by Ferreira, Gilboa and Maschler (1995). This seminal discussion suggests considering *situations where a player is a group of individuals. [...] Such a player is to some extent a decision-making unit, but it does not have a utility function of its own* (Ferreira *et al.* 1995).

At first glance, one might think that a TI game could be properly described also as an *agent-form* game as in Ferreira *et al.* (1995). As we shall attempt to show, a proper TI game has a richer structure because it allows for the strategic manipulation of preferences. Moreover, because preferences are represented in a Hilbert space of types, superposition of *a priori* incompatible aspects (eigentypes) of the personality of the agent are by definition valid types and they may interfere when computing the overall utility level of the agent who is facing the different decision-situations. In a Hilbert space of types, the superposition of eigentypes is itself a proper type of the agent (Postulate 1). If the action taken by a player is the best-reply of several eigentypes, the resulting superposition must be the basis for computing the utility level of the agent. Since taking actions generally alters the type of the agent, we propose that in order to compute the utility value of an action one should not wait until the last node of the game. This means that we consider that the agent acts as if he was cashing in utility along with the game. He may actually experience utility after taking the action. But we can also think that he 'savours' (experiences before the actual outcome). There are several reasons for this. Most importantly, since the strategic reasoning is performed by the eigentypes (who know their preferences as in a standard game) they have to compute the utility associated with the different actions in order to identify the best-reply. If they reasoned from the end node, their own preferences would play no role and the computation would be extremely complex as they would have to calculate at each step the expected type of the agent arising from the possible actions to determine the end node (expected) type. Moreover, such an approach would not allow for the central novel features brought about by Type Indeterminacy.

To understand better, let us consider a path $\sigma_l \in \Sigma$ along a TI game Γ, containing two particular decision-situations d and d' such that player i has to take an action for d some steps before she takes an action for d', following the timing of the game represented by the ordering $\leq$. According to Postulate 2, the state-vector t_i giving the player i's preferences is affected by the course of actions such that $t_i^{(\text{before } d)} \neq t_i^{(\text{after } d)} \neq t_i^{(\text{before } d')} \neq t_i^{(\text{after } d')}$ holds.[16] We thus propose to consider the idea of *cashing-on-the-go*, so that the payoffs, rewards or punishments are received when the preferences are actualized through the actions which are taken. Therefore, for each possible play of the game given as a path $\sigma_l \in \Sigma$, we can define the total utility of the path as the collection of all the contributions of the payoffs received when solving each decision-situation with respect to the preferences governing the affinities of the player in each step.

---

[16] The particular exception $t_i^{(\text{after } d)} = t_i^{(\text{before } d')}$ is found if d strictly precedes d' in the path, or if all of the intermediate decision-situations between d and d' are trivially associated to the identity projector.

In plain words, we model the reader of this paper enjoying the reading at present time, as well as enjoying past readings in the past (now you only enjoy the memory of them) and future readings in the future, instead of all enjoyment being at the end of the game of her or his life when final preferences of the agent, in general, do not coincide with the preferences motivating each particular choice along the path of life. Experience conditions and modifies preferences, and the TI framework mirrors and formalizes this effect.

Solution Concept: The optimal play in a TI game arises from the strategic reasoning at the level of the eigentypes. This implies the strategies are defined such that one action is selected by each eigentype of every player.[17] We propose the notion of Type Indeterminate Nash Equilibrium (TINE) as a solution concept for the TI games. A TINE builds on the notion of the players' mutual best-replies as the standard Nash equilibrium does. The major distinction now is that the best-replies are computed at the level of the eigentypes of each player.[18] The actual play of a player is, in addition, determined by the probability for the different eigentypes to actualize according to the Definition 6.

Following Postulate 2, the actions taken in the decision-situations along the play of the game define a path of projection. This path of projections determines the state of the outcoming preferences of the players after the interactions. Resulting preferences of a TI player are endogenous to the game, they arise in the process of interaction. The outcome of a TI game includes the payoffs of the players, and the outcoming profile of preferences. We proceed in this section as follows. First, we define a TINE as the profile of the (pure strategy) best-reply of all the eigentypes of all players, a complete algorithm for the players' action in the game. See the Definitions 7 to 9. Second, we compute the overall utility of the paths in the Definitions 10 and 11. We propose the *cashing-on-the-go* for solving TI games in the Assumption 2.[19] Third, we compute the profile of outcoming types of the players which, in general, are different from the initial types. The play alters the preferences in accordance with Postulate 2 (Projection), and we formalize it in the Definition 12.

In game theory, the definition of a *strategy* implies an algorithm specifying what actions are chosen by a player i in every possible situation in the game. An action has to be assigned to every node, irregardless of whether some previous action forbids some nodes to be reached: the strategy specifies a fully fledged and contingent instruction for the complete play. When considering TI players, a strategy s_i in a TI game has to explicitly specify the action that is selected by every possible eigentype that a player i can incarnate in each decision-situation.

---

[17] Note that for this first work we consider only pure strategies.

[18] The situations that can be analyzed with the notion of Nash Equilibrium are contained in the TI framework as an oversimplified case where only one eigentype exists for each player and therefore, the type and the eigentype trivially coincide.

[19] *Cashing-on-the-go* has been introduced to deal with the fact that the initial preferences of TI players are, in general, altered along the path of the game as already discussed.

Definition 7. *Let a TI player i face a number K of decision-situations with a set $\Theta_i(d_k)$ of eigentypes associated for each decision-situation $d_k \in D_i$. A strategy of a TI player s_i is a complete algorithm for her play in the TI game, and it contains one action $a_i\big(\theta_i^{(n)}(d_k)\big)$ for each and every of the N eigentypes $\theta_i^{(n)} \in \Theta_i(d_k)$ associated to each of the K decision-situations $d_k \in D_i$ in which the player i takes part in the game. Therefore, s_i is a collection of $N \times K$ elements,*

$$s_i = \Big(a_i\big(\theta_i^{(1)}(d_1)\big),\ a_i\big(\theta_i^{(2)}(d_1)\big),\ \ldots,\ a_i\big(\theta_i^{(N)}(d_1)\big);\ \ldots$$
$$\underbrace{a_i\big(\theta_i^{(1)}(d_k)\big),\ a_i\big(\theta_i^{(2)}(d_k)\big),\ \ldots,\ a_i\big(\theta_i^{(N)}(d_k)\big);\ \ldots}_{\text{One action for each of the } N \text{ eigentypes in each } d_k}$$
$$a_i\big(\theta_i^{(1)}(d_K)\big),\ a_i\big(\theta_i^{(2)}(d_K)\big),\ \ldots,\ a_i\big(\theta_i^{(N)}(d_K)\big)\Big).$$

Assumption 1. *The optimal strategy of a TI player arises from the optimality of the actions at the level of the eigentypes: every eigentype of every player best-responds to the expected play of the other players computed from the best-replies of the eigentypes that enter their current type, weighted by the coefficients of superposition in every decision-situation (node) of the game.*

Definition 8. *Let $A_i(d)$ be the set of available actions for the player i facing decision-situation $d \in D_i$, and let $A_{-i}(d)$ be the set of available actions for all the other players $I\backslash\{i\}$ taking part in the interaction. For every given action profile of the other players $a_{-i}(d)$, we can define the preferred action (best-reply) of each one of the eigentypes $\theta_i^{(n)} \in \Theta_i(d)$ of the player i in the decision-situation d. We denote this by $a_i^*\big[\theta_i^{(n)}, a_{-i}\big]$ such that $a_i^*\big(\theta_i^{(n)}, a_{-i}\big) \in \arg\max_{a_i(d)\in A_i(d)} u_i\big[\theta_i^{(n)};\, a_i(d), a_{-i}(d)\big]$.*

Definition 9. *A particular profile of strategies $(s_i^*; s_{-i}^*)$ constitutes a Type Indeterminate Nash Equilibrium of a TI game when they are the collection of all the eigentypes of every player best-responding to every eigentype of the other players, in the sense of Definition 8, so that $u_i\big[\theta_i^{(n)};\, a_i^*(d), a_{-i}^*(d)\big] \geq u_i\big[\theta_i^{(n)};\, a_i(d), a_{-i}^*(d)\big]$ $\forall\, a_i(d) \in A_i(d)$, holds for every eigentype $\theta_i^{(n)} \in \Theta_i(d)$ of every player $i \in I$, at every decision-situation $d \in D_i$.*

We can denote by $\sigma^* = \sigma(s_i^*; s_{-i}^*)$ the equilibrium path of the game obtained from the combination of these strategies, optimized at the level of the eigenpreferences. The outcome of the TINE includes: (i) the overall utility level of every TI player, and (ii) the final state of preferences of every TI player (see Definitions 11 and 12 below). According to the Postulate 2, when the preferred action $a_i^*(d)$ is taken a the player i, her outcoming preferences t_i' are the result of projecting the incoming type t_i onto the M-dimensional subspace ($M \leq N$) of the preference relations (eigentypes) supporting that particular action as their preferred one in the strategic interaction. And according to the Postulate 1, this superposition of eigenpreferences is now also a proper type of the player given by $t_i' = \sum_{m=1}^M c_m' \theta_i^{(m)}$, with $c_m' \in \mathbb{R}$, and $\sum_{m=1}^M c_m'^2 = 1$.

Definition 10. *Let the player i face a decision-situation d with the preferences given by a type $t_i \in \mathcal{T}_i$, and let $a^*_{-i}(d)$ be the actions chosen by the other players. Then, the utility cashed by the player i when taking the action $a^*_i(d)$ as in Definition 8 is the weighted utility of the M eigenpreferences where the weights are given by the coefficients in the superposition:* $u_i[t'_i; a^*_i(d), a^*_{-i}(d)] = \sum_{m=1}^M c'^2_m u_i[\theta^{(m)}_i; a^*_i(d), a^*_{-i}(d)].$[20]

Assumption 2. *We compute the overall utility of the players involved in a TI game as the addition of the local utilities cashed by the type of each of the players in the decision-situations along the path of play.*

Definition 11. *Let $\sigma_l \in \Sigma$ be a path $\sigma_l = \{d_1, \ldots, d_L\}$, induced by the strategy profile $(s^*_i; s^*_{-i})$. Then, the total utility for the player i in the play following path σ_l is given by $u_i[\sigma_l] = \sum_{d_l \in \sigma_l} u_i[a^*_i(d_l), a^*_{-i}(d_l)]$, with the utility of the preferred actions given in the Definition 10.*[21]

Definition 12. *Given a path of play σ_l, and the state-vector of initial preferences of a TI player i denoted by $t^0_i \in \mathcal{T}_i$, the outcoming preferences of the TI player i are computed by the consecutive application of the projections as a consequence of the actions taken along the path of play $t^{(\text{end})}_i = \prod_{d_l \in \sigma_l} P_{a^*_i(d_l)} t^0_i$ for every player $i \in I$.*

After the discussion presented up to this point of the paper, the Definition 12 translates into computations by means of the Definition 5 and the Postulate 2.[22] This determines a process of all the players *updating their knowledge* about the state of preferences of themselves and the other players in the game. The projections reflect the evolution of the types resulting from the choice of actions (modeled as the measurement of preferences) originated by the eigentypes' strategic reasoning, so the rule for updating knowledge is a constituent part of the solution of the game.

4   Example

The following example is motivated by the one presented in Lambert-Mogiliansky (2010). *The story:* Alice (player A) is a Tenured Professor at University who starts working with her new student Bob (player B). Bob is finishing his Master studies and later on he can choose to work with Alice for a PhD. For the long-term, Alice wants Bob to agree to cooperate with her in a very specific idea of

---

[20] Note that the utility defined above is linear in the probabilistic content of the outcoming preferences (compare c'^2_m to Definition 6).

[21] When some paths become 'branches' including moves of chance, the utility shall be considered in expected terms.

[22] The notation $\prod_{d_l \in \sigma_l} P_{a^*_i(d_l)} t^0_i$ for the subsequent application of projectors has to be understood in the sense of the composition of operators, $P_{a^*_i(d_L)} \cdots P_{a^*_i(d_2)} P_{a^*_i(d_1)} t_i{}^{i^0}$.

research. Bob is indeterminate with respect to his willingness to engage in this specific topic which appeals to open-mindness. Bob is also indeterminate with respect to his taste for personal challenges.[23] Timing of the game as follows.

(First) Alice is currently Bob's Master thesis advisor and she has two different ideas to propose him for his Master thesis: either a standard problem (S) or an intricate one (I). *(Second)* once Alice offers a specific topic, Bob can work on his Master thesis either on a routine basis (R) or adopting a more creative approach (C). Bob's preferences regarding his Master thesis are given by two different contributions θ_1 and θ_2.[24] The first one reflects Bob's necessity to get his Master studies finished so a personal challenge for his final dissertation is not very desirable. The second one reflects the joy for a motivated student when solving a challenge. *(Third)* After Bob finishes his Master thesis, Alice invites him (Inv) for a PhD collaborating in her specific project. *(Fourth)* Bob can accept (A) or reject (R) such offer. Bob's preferences in this stage are given by two choice-making eigentypes: τ_1 if he is open-minded and willing to work with Alice, or τ_2 if he will not trust her very specific idea and will refuse her as PhD advisor.

Elements of the TI game: $I = \{$Alice, Bob$\}$, labeled as A and B, respectively. $D_A = \{1; 4\text{--}7\}$, and $D_B = \{2\text{--}3; 8\text{--}11\}$ are the decision-situations for A and B, respectively. The space of types is such that player A has a unique and trivial type, while $\mathcal{T}_B = \mathrm{Span}(\{\theta_1, \theta_2\}) = \mathrm{Span}(\{\tau_1, \tau_2\})$. The decomposition for the player A is trivial in the sense that there is no indeterminacy relevant to the game for this player. The player B presents two sets of eigentypes, associated to the measurements of the θ-preferences in nodes 2–3 and of the τ-preferences in nodes 8–11, with

$$\begin{pmatrix} \theta_1 \\ \theta_2 \end{pmatrix} = \begin{pmatrix} \sqrt{0.4} & \sqrt{0.6} \\ \sqrt{0.6} & -\sqrt{0.4} \end{pmatrix} \begin{pmatrix} \tau_1 \\ \tau_2 \end{pmatrix} \tag{1}$$

giving the correlations between the orthonormal basis. The initial state for the player A is fully determined, and for the player B we have $t_B^0 = (\sqrt{0.6}, \sqrt{0.4})_\theta$, as given parameters. From (1), t_B^0 is given in coordinates of the τ-basis of eigen-preferences by $t_B^0 = (\sqrt{0.96}, \sqrt{0.04})_\tau$. Specification of the payoffs: (i) The payoffs that both players will receive from their collaboration in the Master thesis are given in the following two matrices:

θ_1	S	I		θ_2	S	I	
R	(0; 0)	(−10; 20)	and	R	(0; 0)	(5; 20)	,
C	(−5; 0)	(−15; 70)		C	(−5; 0)	(10; 70)	

$$\tag{2}$$

representing $(u_B^{\theta_1}, u_A)$ and $(u_B^{\theta_2}, u_A)$, respectively. Alice's payoff structure represents the fact that she would prefer at this point of her collaboration with the student to give him a difficult problem. On the other hand, Bob's payoff

---

[23] We assume the open-mindness and the taste for personal challenge are not the same psychological features but they are somehow related.

[24] We shall understand this two different aspects of Bob's personality as two orthogonal eigentypes of θ-preferences. See Definition 2.

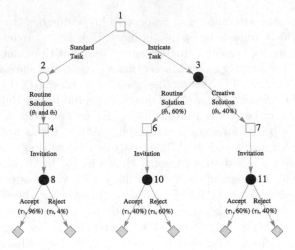

Fig. 1. Reduced game tree showing only actions that will be taken according to strategic reasoning. The probabilities for each type being realized are written in the links.

structure reflects that for the eigentype θ_1, receiving a standard offer is always more pleasant, as well as working in a routine basis is always more profitable, regardless of the task being the standard or the intricate one. For the eigentype θ_2, a personal challenge is more enjoyable and then receiving an intricate task is more pleasant than receiving a standard problem; as well as dealing with the intricate task in the creative way is the most preferred action, but if the received task is the standard one, delivering a routine solution is fine. (*ii*) For doing the PhD, Bob will get a fixed amount of utility u due to the degree he earns and the scholarship he receives, regardless of who is his supervisor (the τ_i eigentypes as choice-making types have already been explained above). For Alice, who really wants to see her new idea developed, if Bob agrees (A) to work with her, she will receive $u_A(A, Inv) = 200$ or $u_A(R, Inv) = 0$ if he rejects and goes with another advisor. Attending to the payoffs given in the matrices (2), the θ_1-type contribution to Bob's personality makes him prefer a routine (R) solution to a standard task (S) proposed by Alice as well as if it were the case that she offers the intricate one (I), while the θ_2-type contribution wills to give a routine (R) solution to a standard task (S), but a creative one to an intricate problem (I).

From the setup of the TI game, Bob's initial type is the pure state $t_B^0 = (\sqrt{0.6}, \sqrt{0.4})_\theta$, which according to the Postulate 1 reflects that Bob's personality is composed of the characteristics of θ_1 and θ_2, with weights of 60 % and 40 %, respectively.

Two possible paths: σ_1: At node 2, after Alice offered a standard task (S), Bob will always give a routine solution (R). Because of Alice's standard proposal, there is no contradiction between the willingness of the two contributions to Bob's personality, so Bob's reaction does not clear the indeterminacy in his preferences in the sense of realizing a particular θ_i. σ_2: At node 3, after Alice offered an intricate task (I), the two contributions to Bob's personality disagree on the desired action to take. At this point, the action he takes will project his preferences onto θ_1 if he goes for a routine solution (R), or onto θ_2 if he goes for a creative solution (C). See the Postulate 2.

For both paths, the utilities have to be computed in expected terms since there are some non-deterministic lotteries. In the case of σ_1, there is only one move of chance: the final measurement on τ. In σ_2 there are two moves of chance: the initial measurement on θ, and final the measurement on τ. It is worth to note that in this second case, the composition of the incoming pure state for the final measurement differs depending on what was the outcome of the initial measurement. Taking these observations into account, the game tree of the game can be reduced to the one shown in Fig. 1. See the different composition of the pure states for the final measurement (recall that Alice is interested on getting Bob to accept the research project).

Utilities and TINE: Utility levels $u_A[\sigma_1] = 0.96 \cdot 200 = 192$, and $u_B[\sigma_1] = u$ are trivial. For the second path, $u_A[\sigma_2] = p_3(\theta_1)\{u_A(R, I) + p_{10}(\tau_1)u_A(A, Inv) + p_{10}(\tau_2)u_A(R, Inv)\} + p_3(\theta_2)\{u_A(C, I) + p_{11}(\tau_1)u_A(A, Inv) + p_{11}(\tau_2)u_A(R, Inv)\}$ gives $u_A[\sigma_2] = 0.6(20 + 0.4 \cdot 200 + 0.6 \cdot 0) + 0.4(70 + 0.6 \cdot 200 + 0.4 \cdot 0) = 136$, and $u_B[\sigma_2] = p_3(\theta_1)\{u_B(\theta_1, R, I) + p_{10}(\tau_1)u_B(\tau_1, A, Inv) + p_{10}(\tau_2)u_B(\tau_2, R, Inv)\} + p_3(\theta_2)\{u_B(\theta_2, C, I) + p_{11}(\tau_1)u_B(\tau_1, A, Inv) + p_{11}(\tau_2)u_B(\tau_1, R, Inv)\}$ gives $u_B[\sigma_2] = 0.6(-10 + 0.4 \cdot u + 0.6 \cdot u) + 0.4(10 + 0.6 \cdot u + 0.4 \cdot u) = u - 2$. Then, the Type Indeterminate Nash Equilibrium of this game is such that Bob's preferred actions are Routine Solution (R) both for θ_1 and θ_2 eigentypes, when confronting a Standard Task. Thus, when Alice proposes the Standard Task (S), Bob's preferences are projected only in the last stage of the game, with the non-deterministic measurement of the choice-making types τ_1 and τ_2 with high probability of Bob accepting the PhD project, the ultimate purpose of Alice. This example can be considered as a simplified model of self-control in the sense that in this interaction, Alice restrains herself from overwhelming Bob with a difficult task when he is under the pressure of finishing his Master thesis, so that his willingness to engage in the PhD project remains intact.

5   Discussion

Bob's final decision, i.e., whether to accept or to reject the PhD proposal is a measurement with respect to the τ-eigentypes of preferences. As it is reflected in the Fig. 1, the composition of his final preferences is affected by the presence (or absence) of a previous projection onto any of the θ_i's. The interesting feature is that this measurement will determine Bob's final preferences in the game, but it is Alice who has the power to manipulate the composition of his preferences by means of her initial choice. The sequence of measurements, if some of these are non-commuting, forces an evolution of the preferences that can be selected by the players directly with their choice of strategies, a distinctive contribution of the Type Indeterminacy model: an open door towards a theory of games with full interaction between the agents. Kvam *et al.* (2014) provide empirical evidence supporting the TI model.[25]

One of the first extensions which can be considered in this research program is the introduction of time-dependent preferences. When selecting the most preferred action, each eigentype is responsible not only of what happens in the present interacting situation, but also of how such outcome conditions the future composition of the type of the player as a consequence of the measurement process. In the example that we have illustrated, we considered both situations (the Master Thesis and the future collaboration) to be equally weighted as a simplifying assumption for the ease of exposition. Nevertheless, the introduction of the appropriate terms to represent constant discount rates, hyperbolic discounting as well as different kinds of myopia (the ability of each eigentype to forecast, for example, only a few number of steps ahead) can be easily contained in the formulation, enriching the effects that can be described.[26] The study of the dynamics of the Type Indeterminate interactions can contribute to the conceptual discussion suggested by Daniel Kahneman: *"Is the intuitively attractive judgment or course of action in conflict with a rule that the agent would endorse?"* (Kahneman 2003).

Despite some conceptual differences, the TI approach shares one of the nicest characteristics of the Projective Expected Utility model introduced by La Mura (2009). The Definition 10 can also be written as a bilinear form, and therefore we can introduce very naturally some interferences (penalties or rewards) due to the agents experiencing the superposition of some (confronting or reinforcing) contributions by some of the mutually exclusive eigentypes. Since the eigentypes are orthonormal by definition, this makes very easy to think about contradictory contributions in the personality and preferences of the players.

The eigentypes represent the associative or intuitive level of the reasoning process, while the notion of the type as a linear superposition of these eigenpreferences subject to the measurement process implies the existence of a rule-governed level of reasoning contained in the functional form adopted for the definition of the utility along the path. The TI approach departs from the standard assumption of reference-independence, because the final states are no longer the only carriers of utility. It retains the tractability of expected utility theory however, and respects the paradigm of utility maximization at all levels of reasoning. In this way the TI model challenges the claim by Kahneman and Thaler (2006) that when considering some *virtuous choices that people make may involve a lack of empathy for the future self who will have to live with the choice [...] it is unlikely that these conflicting choices are both utility maximizing.* The concept of Type Indeterminate Nash Equilibrium builds on the best-replies of the

---

[25] The extension from pure states to the formulation in terms of density matrices has been excluded from this paper to avoid computational complexity, in order to keep the discussion as fundamental and formal as possible according to our best.

[26] See, *e.g.*, Lambert-Mogiliansky and Busemeyer (2012) on self-control within the framework of one TI decision-maker with temporal discounting. A classical discussion of several models of time-dependent preferences can be found in Loewenstein (2008).

(potential) eigentypes of the players in a way similar to an agent-form game, and at the same time, the TINE reflects optimization at the level of the player through the maximization of the overall expected utility along the path of the game.

References

Busemeyer, J.R., Bruza, P.: Quantum Models of Cognition and Decision. Cambridge University Press, Cambridge (2012)

Danilov, V.I., Lambert-Mogiliansky, A.: Math. Soc. Sci. **55**, 315–340 (2008)

Ferreira, J.L., Gilboa, I., Maschler, M.: Games Econ. Beh. **10**, 284–317 (1995)

Haven, E., Khrennikov, A.: Quantum Social Science. Cambridge University Press, Cambridge (2012)

Harsanyi, J.C.: Rev. Econ. Stud. **21**, 204–213 (1953)

Kahneman, D.: Am. Econ. Rev. **93**(5), 1449–1475 (2003)

Kahneman, D., Tversky, A.: Choice, Values and Frames. Cambridge University Press, Cambridge (2000)

Kahneman, D., Thaler, R.H.: J. Econ. Perspect. **20**(1), 221–234 (2006)

Khrennikov, A.: Ubiquitous Quantum Structure: From Psychology to Finance. Springer, Heidelberg (2010)

Kvam, P.D., Busemeyer, J.R., Lambert-Mogiliansky, A.: An empirical test of type-indeterminacy in the Prisoner's Dilemma. In: Atmanspacher, H., Haven, E., Kitto, K., Raine, D. (eds.) QI 2013. LNCS, vol. 8369, pp. 213–224. Springer, Heidelberg (2014)

La Mura, P.: J. Math. Psycol. **53**, 408–414 (2009)

Lambert-Mogiliansky, A.: Paris School of Economics Working Paper, 2010-20 (2010)

Lambert-Mogiliansky, A., Busemeyer, J.R.: Games **3**, 97–118 (2012)

Lambert-Mogiliansky, A., Zamir, S., Zwirn, H.: J. Math. Psycol. **53**, 349–361 (2009)

Loewenstein, G.: Exotic Preferences, Behavioral Economics and Human Motivation. Oxford University Press, Oxford (2008)

Peleg, B., Zaari, M.E.: Rev. Econ. Stud. **40**(3), 391–401 (1973)

Schoeffler, S.: Am. Econ. Rev. **42**(5), 880–887 (1952)

Non-Locality and Entanglement

Temporal Non-Locality: Fact or Fiction?

Günter Mahler[✉]

Institute for Theoretical Physics I,
University of Stuttgart,
70550 Stuttgart, Germany
mahler@itp1.uni-stuttgart.de
http://www.itp1.uni-stuttgart.de/institut/arbeitsgruppen/mahler

Abstract. The status of quantum non-locality, last not least its temproal versions, depend on the interpretational platform one is willing to adopt. The so-called consistent history approach claims to be "Copenhagen style done right"; this interpretation challenges the standard notion of quantum non-locality. As a kind of illustration I discuss some recent theoretical and experimental results in the context of temporal Bell inequalities. I believe the physics behind is typically much less clear than taken for granted.

Keywords: Non-locality · Consistent quantum theory · Frames · Temporal Bell inequalities · Quantum histories · Weak measurements

1 Introduction

Quantum weirdness cannot be removed, only tamed. For that purpose various strategies have been proposed: Amend the theory by means of hidden variables [1], by the postulate of position as a preferred observable combined with the wave-function as a so-called "pilot-wave" [2], or the introduction of *ad hoc* rules for "spontaneous collapse" [3]. Alternatively keep the basic theory untouched, but change the concept of probability [4], modify the rules of ordinary (classical) logic [5], or impose restrictions on the accessible event space [6].

It is fair to say that neither of these proposals have found general acceptance in the physics community [7], a fact that one should bear in mind when attempting to transfer quantum inspired modelling beyond its original realm. Nevertheless, the use of a specific interpretation can hardly be avoided. For the analysis of quantum processes in time the consistent history scheme [6,8,9] promises to be most appropriate and illuminating.

1.1 Non-Locality

The fundamental equation of motion, the Schrödinger equation, is said to be local (in time and space) in the sense that it contains only low order derivatives. (Such derivatives can be interpreted to test but a tiny environment around a given point

© Springer International Publishing Switzerland 2015
H. Atmanspacher et al. (Eds.): QI 2014, LNCS 8951, pp. 243–254, 2015.
DOI: 10.1007/978-3-319-15931-7_19

in space-time.) Solutions thus depend on boundary- and initial- conditions only, there are no memory effects.

But this limitation does not exclude other forms of non-locality: Spatial non-locality could be associated with the superposition of differently localized states (a rather common situation); double-slit experiments are explicitly based on the superposition of two spatially separate peaks at positions x_1 and x_2. Such a scheme can be extended also to the time-domain: The role of the slits is then taken over by two windows in time, t_1 and t_2. For an experimental realization of the latter, based on matter waves, see [10]. However, both these kinds of non-locality are not necessarily restricted to the quantum domain: Classical waves suffice; the required precison might present a serious obstacle, though.

Eventually, a loss of temporal sequentiality [11] may indicate the breakdown of "histories"; and last not least, physical interactions between events are routinely termed non-local, if they are too far apart in space and too close together in time to be induced by any signals even at the speed of light. Such "spooky actions at a distance" are the subject of the standard Bell inequalities [12]. These and their temporal versions [13] challenge the classical idea of realism.

2   Consistent Quantum Theory (CQT)

CQT suggests to introduce probabilities and stochastic processes as part of the foundations, not just as an *ad hoc* addition [8]. Any probability theory has to be based on a sample space of mutually exclusive events E. Subsets of E form a so-called Boolean algebra ("event algebra"). A classical indicator function is introduced to tell us whether or not an event has a certain property F. A quantum event is associated with a quantum property F_j given by the eigenvalue of some observable $\hat{F}$ (or the eigenvalues of a set of commuting observables). The corresponding eigenfunctions $|F_j>$ specify the projectors,

$$\hat{P}_j = |F_j><F_j| \qquad \hat{P}_j\hat{P}_k = \delta_{jk}\hat{P}_j, \tag{1}$$

by which the observable can be re-written as

$$\hat{F} = \sum_j F_j\hat{P}_j. \tag{2}$$

One notes that the projectors also serve as the quantum analogue of the indicator function: They allow to "test" the corresponding quantum state $|\Psi>$, a vector in Hilbert-space. The quantum event algebra corresponding to the sample space

$$\hat{I} = \sum_j \hat{P}_j \quad \text{(decomposition of identity)} \tag{3}$$

consists of all projectors of the form

$$\hat{R} = \sum_j \pi_j\hat{P}_j \quad \pi_j = 0,\ 1. \tag{4}$$

The concrete values π_j are at our disposal, they specify $\hat{R}$.

2.1   Frameworks

Each such Boolean event algebra constitutes a "language"; this language (or description) is based on mutually compatible properties, i.e., commuting operators $\hat{F}^{(\mu)}$. For any given Hilbert-space (i.e., a given system) there are infinitely many such frameworks, each related with some other set of observables $\hat{F}^{(\nu)}$ which, however, does not commute with the previous set, $\hat{F}^{(\mu)}$, $\nu \neq \mu$. These alternative descriptions are incompatible: statements referring to a combination of such incompatible frames are neither true nor false, they are "meaningless",

$$F_j^{(\mu)} \cap F_k^{(\nu)} \text{ meaningless, if } \hat{F}^{(\mu)} \hat{F}^{(\nu)} \neq \hat{F}^{(\nu)} \hat{F}^{(\mu)}. \tag{5}$$

This means that logic (i.e., the possibility to assign truth values) is contextual. "Unicity does not hold", there is no classical realism, no unique exhaustive description [6]. Instead there are mutliple layers of reality. These ideas are consistent with Bohr's complementary, but much more general, cf. also [14].

Fundamental rule of CQT: At any instant make sure to use only one single framework. The violation of this rule may easily lead to paradoxes; in the following we will encounter attempts to combine different frames, cf. Sects. 5 and 6.

The framework to be used does not follow from CQT ("freedom of choice"). In that sense this scheme is incomplete. The selection of a framework has to be founded on some kind of symmetry-breaking: possible sources can be virtual, e.g., the questions being asked by the experimenter [8], or to follow from a material "selection mechanism" imposed by a macroscopic (quasi-classical) environment [9], which may even be explicitly time-dependent ("delayed choice", cf. [8]).

In quantum mechanics the probability distributions follow from the Born rule,

$$p(F_j) = \mathrm{Tr}\{\Psi \hat{P}_j\}, \tag{6}$$

$$p(G_k) = \sum_k p(F_j)| < F_j|G_k > |^2. \tag{7}$$

$|\Psi >$ is the respective quantum state of the system, $|F_j >, |G_k >$ are eigenstates of the (in general) non-commuting operators $\hat{F}, \hat{G}$. This assignment of probabilities is non-contextual; in fact, this frame-independence can be shown to imply the Born rule [9].

2.2   Quantum Histories

A quantum history is a sequence of quantum events E with properties $\hat{F}^{(\mu)}$ at successive discrete time instances $t_\mu, \mu = 1, 2, \ldots f$. Any such f-step history Y^β is a member of a so-called history-Hilbert-space (tensor space[1]),

---

[1] Tensor product spaces are thus introduced not only for composite systems at a given time, but also for a single system at various discrete times. For the former the symbol $\otimes$ is used, for the latter the symbol $\odot$.

$$\hat{Y}^\beta = \hat{F}^{(1)} \odot \hat{F}^{(2)} \odot \cdots \hat{F}^{(f)}, \tag{8}$$

$$\hat{I} = \sum_\alpha \hat{Y}^\alpha \quad \text{(decomposition of identity)}, \tag{9}$$

$$\hat{Z} = \sum_\alpha \pi_\alpha \hat{Y}^\alpha \quad \pi_\alpha = 0, 1. \tag{10}$$

The unitary dynamics is specified by the evolution operator $\hat{U}(t_f, t_i) = \hat{U}(t_i, t_f)^\dagger$. For convenience we switch to the Heisenberg-picture, i.e. the wave-function is time independent and given by $|\Psi(0) >$, while the evolution is carried by the operators, $\hat{F}(t_2) = \hat{U}(t_2, t_1)\hat{F}(t_1)\hat{U}(t_1, t_2)$. Introducing for the history Y^β the so-called chain operator

$$\hat{K}(\hat{Y}^\beta) = \hat{F}^{(f)}\hat{U}(t_f, t_{f-1})\hat{F}^{(f-1)}\hat{U}(t_{f-1}, t_{f-2})\cdots\hat{U}(t_2, t_1)\hat{F}^{(1)}, \tag{11}$$

one defines the consistency of histories α, β (each with respect to the same sequence of times) by the requirement

$$< \Psi(0)|\hat{K}(\hat{Y}^\alpha)\hat{K}(\hat{Y}^\beta)\Psi(0) > = 0 \quad \text{for } \alpha \neq \beta \tag{12}$$

Consistency is always relative to the underlying dynamics.

3   Weak Measurements

Measurements are active processes, in which system and environment interact in a specific way. "Strong measurements" are able to resolve the eigenvalue spectrum of the measured observable $\hat{F}$. The associated back-action on the system is routinely described by projectors $\hat{P}$ inducing a "collapse" of the original wave-function $|\Psi >$ onto the respective eigenstate of $\hat{F}$; this collapse may alternatively be interpreted to imply an updated probability conditioned by the reading of the correlated measurement apparatus (gain of information) [8].

A weak value F^w of an operator $\hat{F}$ refers to an initial state $|i >$ and a final state $|f >$ (Schrödinger picture), i.e., to a scenario involving pre- and post-selection:

$$|\Psi >= \begin{cases} |i > \text{ for } t = t_1, \\ |f > \text{ for } t = t_2. \end{cases} \tag{13}$$

Requiring $< i|f > \neq 0$, the weak value is defined as [15]

$$F^w \equiv \frac{< f|\hat{F}|i >}{< f|i >} \tag{14}$$

and is, in general, complex. If $|i >$ and $|f >$ are almost orthogonal, anomalously large weak values F^w result. These values can no longer be understood in any classical way as properties related to the eigenvalues of $\hat{F}$. Instead, a simple operational meaning of F^w can be found by considering the operator $\hat{F}$ as a weak perturbation on the initial state,

$$|i' >= \exp{(-i\epsilon\hat{F})}|i > . \tag{15}$$

With the strength parameter ϵ going to zero, one finds for the ratio of transition probabilities with/without perturbation [15]

$$\lim_{\epsilon \to 0} \left(\frac{p_\epsilon}{p} \right) \equiv \frac{|<f|i'>|^2}{|<f|i>|^2} \approx 1 + 2\epsilon \, \Im(F^w). \tag{16}$$

$\Im(x)$ denotes the imaginary part of x. Contrary to a strong measurement this "weak measurement" is unable to resolve the eigenvalue spectrum of $\hat{F}$ and thus does not update the original wavefunction: There is no "collapse".

Concrete applications of the weak value often involve continuous measurements, cf. Sect. 7.1.

4 Realism

According to [9] a theory may be called "realistic", if a system S "is formulated entirely in terms of entities and concepts referring to S itself". An operationalist formulation would have to be based on a "cut", i.e., includes entities external to S; such entities are observers/agents and measurement apparatus'. Classically inspired realism demands that all quantum observables $\hat{F}^{(\mu)}$ have pre-existing values. As these values do not follow from the quantum state $|\Psi>$ alone, we assume that they are implicitly specified by a set of so-called "hidden variables". While the actual values of these variables are unknown by definition, their assumed presence means that quantum mechanics would have to be incomplete.

4.1 Pair-Correlations and Sum Rules

Let us start from the following two assumptions:

i. "Classical realism": All observables exist, independent of measurement.
ii. "Non-invasive measurability (NIM)": It is possible to determine any one observable with arbitrary small perturbations on the other observables.

For convenience we restrict ourselves to observables $\hat{F}^{(\mu)}, \mu = 1, 2, \ldots f$, which can only take the values $F^{(\mu)} \pm 1$. As a consequence also the values for the pair-correlations ($\mu \neq \nu$) are simply given by

$$C_{\mu\nu} = C_{\nu\mu} = F^{(\mu)} F^{(\nu)} = \pm 1, \tag{17}$$

For given (finite!) f there are exactly f cyclic pairs $\{C_{12}, C_{23}, \ldots C_{(f-1,f)}, C_{f1}\}$. Under the assumption of realism these correlations have all definite values, forming a data set of the type $D = \{\pm 1, \pm 1, \pm 1, \cdots \pm 1\}$. There are $d = 2^f$ possible data sets. One easily convinces oneself that specific sums of such correlations can be selected, which take up only two different values – for any data set. If we consider, e.g., $f = 3$ and the cyclic pairs (12), (23), (31), we find for each of the $d = 8$ possible data sets

$$S_\pm(3) \equiv \pm[C_{12} + C_{23}] + C_{31} = +1 \pm 2 \tag{18}$$

Similarly, for $f = 4$ and the cyclic set (12), (23), (34), (41) there are $d = 16$ data sets. For each of them

$$S(4) \equiv C_{12} + C_{23} + C_{34} - C_{41} = \pm 2, \tag{19}$$
$$S_{\pm}(4) \equiv |C_{12} - C_{41}| \pm [C_{23} + C_{34}] = \pm 2, \tag{20}$$
$$S_{||}(4) \equiv |C_{12} - C_{41}| + |C_{23} + C_{34}| - 1 = \pm 1. \tag{21}$$

4.2   Inequalities

The actual data set D, while taken to be controlled by the hidden variables, is not known. We may represent our ignorance by a distribution function for the hidden variables and thus for the choice of data sets. Irrespective of the type of distribution the ensemble averages for the above sums are thus bounded by inequalities. The first two read:

$$\overline{|S_{\pm}(3) - 1|} \leq 2, \tag{22}$$
$$\overline{|S(4)|} \leq 2. \tag{23}$$

5   The Standard Bell Inequalities

5.1   Quantum Implementation

We consider a two-spin system (A, B) with the following $f = 4$ local observables:

$$\hat{F}^{(1)} = \hat{\sigma}_{\theta_1}(A), \quad \hat{F}^{(2)} = \hat{\sigma}_{\theta_2}(B),$$
$$\hat{F}^{(3)} = \hat{\sigma}_{\theta_3}(A), \quad \hat{F}^{(4)} = \hat{\sigma}_{\theta_4}(B). \tag{24}$$

These local operators $\hat{\sigma}_{\theta_\mu}$ denote the spin polarization of spin A(B) in the direction specified by the angle θ_μ, $\mu = 1, 2, 3, 4$. They commute pairwise for different spins (i.e., odd/even indices). Based on "classical" realism the pair correlations should be $C_{\mu\nu} = C(\theta_\mu, \theta_\nu) = \pm 1$. Restricting ourselves to the 4 cyclic correlations as of Eq. (19), the bounds for the ensemble average Eq. (23) becomes the Bell inequality [12]

$$\overline{|S(4)|} = |\overline{C(\theta_1, \theta_2)} + \overline{C(\theta_3, \theta_2)} + \overline{C(\theta_3, \theta_4)} - \overline{C(\theta_1, \theta_4)}| \leq 2. \tag{25}$$

In quantum mechanics the ensemble averages are identified as expectation values. Assuming the system to be prepared in a maximal entangled state, the so-called EPR-state $|\Psi_{EPR}>$, the pair correlations between spin A and spin B read, e.g.,

$$\overline{C(\theta_1, \theta_2)} \equiv <\Psi_{EPR}|\hat{\sigma}_{\theta_1}(A) \otimes \hat{\sigma}_{\theta_2}(B)|\Psi_{EPR}> =$$
$$- \cos(\theta_2 - \theta_1) = \overline{C(\theta_2 - \theta_1)}. \tag{26}$$

Note that the correlation only depends on the difference between local measurement angles. Analogue results are obtained for the other 3 possible frames, (θ_1, θ_4), (θ_3, θ_2), (θ_3, θ_4).

5.2   Violation of Inequalities

Combining all these 4 frames and choosing $\theta_1 = 0$, $\theta_2 = \Delta\Phi$, $\theta_3 = 2\Delta\Phi$, $\theta_4 = 3\Delta\Phi$, one finds

$$\overline{|S(4)|} = |3\cos\Delta\Phi - \cos(3\Delta\Phi)|. \tag{27}$$

For $\Delta\Phi = \pi/4$ the right-hand side is $2\sqrt{2} > 2$, which would violate the Bell inequality Eq. (25). The violation is confirmed experimentally (cf. [16]).

However, the various properties $\hat{F}^{(\mu)}$ entering the inequalities are (in part) incompatible: Neither can they all jointly be measured, nor is there a consistent description in the sense of CQT (see Sect. 2.1). So, if such a combination is considered acceptable, "spooky actions at a distance" (a form of spatial non-locality) seem to be unavoidable [17,18]. The story about possible loopholes in the experimental tests of the Bell inequalities is vividly told in [19].

5.3   Classical Statistical Simulation

Feynman believed that a probabilistic simulation had to be equivalent to a (local) hidden variable theory, and thus there should be no chance for such a simulation [20]. However, by applying a specific positive phase-space distribution $P(\alpha)$ Drummond et al. [21] were able to do just this for optical Bell violations. The trick is that the underlying phase space variables α are continuous and complex rather than the integer or half-integer eigenvalues considered in a standard probabilistic description. Nevertheless their statistical moments exactly reproduce the quantum correlations. Such simulations can even be surprisingly efficient. There are limitations, though: The effective variables corresponding to the spin-projections go outside their quantum bounds ±1. This is reminescent of weak measurements, cf. Sect. 3.

A purely classical statistical model in terms of such variables α may thus account for violations of Bell inequalites. One should be aware of this possibility for statistical models outside physics (where descriptions often suffer from ambiguities in the proper choice of fundamental variables to begin with).

6   Temporal Bell Inequalities

6.1   Quantum Implementation

Let us consider the unitary time-evolution of a single spin-system, specified by the Hamiltonian

$$\hat{H} = \frac{\hbar\omega}{2}\hat{\sigma}_x. \tag{28}$$

ω is a parameter, which will turn out to control the unitary dynamics. In the following we restrict ourselves to the single time-dependent operator (Heisenberg-picture)

$$\hat{F}^{(j)} \equiv \hat{\sigma}_z(t_j) \quad j = 1,\ldots f. \tag{29}$$

f is the number of discrete time points specifying a certain history. In general, this operator does not commute for different times. One easily convinces oneself that the (symmetrized) two-time correlation function is given by the expectation value

$$\overline{C(t_i, t_j)} \equiv \frac{1}{2} < \Psi(0)|(\hat{\sigma}_z(t_i)\hat{\sigma}_z(t_j) + \hat{\sigma}_z(t_j)\hat{\sigma}_z(t_i))|\Psi(0) > =$$
$$\cos(\omega(t_j - t_i)) = \overline{C(t_j - t_i)}. \tag{30}$$

Remarkably it has the same form as the pair correlation function Eq. (26); the correlation is translational invariant and only depends on the time-difference. Temporal Bell inequalities can be understood to refer to such f-step histories.

For the $f = 3$-case with $t_1 = 0, t_2 = \Delta t, t_3 = 2\Delta t$ one expects, according to Eq. (18) and [22],

$$\overline{S_\pm(3)} = \pm(\overline{C(0, \Delta t)} + \overline{C(\Delta t, 2\Delta t)} + \overline{C(0, 2\Delta t)} \geq -1. \tag{31}$$

It is convenient (also for experimental tests, see below) to re-write the inequality $\overline{S_-(3)} \geq -1$ in terms of so-called conditioned probabilites $p(x|y)$, which are defined as the probability to find x under the condition y. In the following x is the eigenstate ± 1 at time t_f, y the eigenstate ± 1 at some earlier time t_i. Given $|1(t_1) >$ as the initial state one shows that [22],

$$p(+1(t_3)| + 1(t_1)) - p(+1(t_2)| + 1(t_1)) \cdot p(+1(t_3)| + 1(t_2)) \geq 0, \tag{32}$$
$$p(+1(2\Delta t)| + 1(0)) - [p(+1(\Delta t)| + 1(0))]^2 \geq 0. \tag{33}$$

The last line follows assuming translational invariance (just like for the correlation functions) and identifying the three time points as before.

6.2   Violation of Inequalities

Taking into account Eq. (30) one concludes that

$$\overline{S_\pm(3)} = \pm 2\cos(\omega\Delta t) + \cos(2\omega\Delta t) \geq -1, \tag{34}$$

which can be violated by a proper choice of Δt. The extension to a $f = 4$-times history with the same three time points as before, supplemented by $t_4 = 3\Delta t$, is straight forward. The corresponding sum rule reads, in analogy to Eq. (27),

$$\overline{|S(4)|} = |3\cos\omega\Delta t - \cos(3\omega\Delta t|. \tag{35}$$

This equation gives $2\sqrt{2}$ for $\Delta t = \pi/(4\omega)$ and thus would violate the constraint of Eq. (23).

However, the original multi-step histories violate "temporal locality". Indeed, for $f > 2$ there are intermediate measurement events, for which non-invasive measurability (NIM) and thus translational invariance does not hold. As a consequence, the two-time correlation function for the total duration of the history,

$t_f - t_1$, factorizes into the respective two-time correlations between adjacent time points (loss of memory). This means for $f = 3(4)$

$$\overline{C(2\Delta t)} \rightarrow \left(\overline{C(\Delta t)}\right)^2, \tag{36}$$

$$\overline{C(3\Delta t)} \rightarrow \left(\overline{C(\Delta t)}\right)^3, \tag{37}$$

respectively, and the temporal Bell inequalities are necessarily fulfilled.

In order to violate these inequalities one has to circumvent the invasiveness. This can most easily be done by splitting the whole history into separate 2-step histories, and by that breaking the temporal cycle. For such sub-histories translational invariance always holds, they only depend on a single parameter, the respective waiting time $t_{j+1} - t_j$. However, the overlapping sub-histories (t_1, t_2) and (t_1, t_f) – referring to different times – do not form a consistent family of histories in the sense of CQT. The possible violation of the temporal Bell inequalities is thus reminescent of the violation of the standard Bell inequalities by combining incompatible frames.

As an example consider the decomposition of the 3-step history $\{0, \Delta t, 2\Delta t\}$ into one history with waiting time Δt and one with waiting time $2\Delta t$. In a "two-shot experiment" both the 2-time correlations become measurable, and with these data the temporal Bell inequality can, indeed, formally be violated for a proper choice of Δt. Based on a single spin in a Diamond defect center the authors of [23] have performed such an experiment showing a violation of Eq. (33).

7 Alternative Approaches

7.1 Temporal Bell for Weak Measurements

Let us consider a continuous signal $I^w(t)$ weakly depending on the variable $\hat{F}(t)$ of a single spin such that ΔI reflects the difference of signal between the momentary eigenvalues $F(t) = \pm 1$:

$$I^w(t) = I_0 + \frac{\Delta I \cdot F(t)}{2} + \xi(t). \tag{38}$$

I_0 is the background signal, $\xi(t)$ a noise term, cf. [24]. Again, with $t_2 - t_1 = \Delta t, t_3 - t_1 = 2\Delta t$ we obtain from a single trace $I^w(t)$ the two correlations $C^w(\Delta t)$ and $C^w(2\Delta t)$, each corresponding to pre-and post-selected time-signals. Averaging is performed here over the reference-time t_1. In the limit of weak coupling the resulting correlations should fulfill the weak form of the corresponding temporal Bell inequality Eq. (31),

$$S_-^w(3) = -2C^w(\Delta t) + C^w(2\Delta t) \geq -\frac{\Delta I}{2}. \tag{39}$$

Like for its original version $\overline{S_-(3)} \geq -1$ violations require separate 2-time histories – which, indeed, underly the experimental scheme [24]. The inequality is violated down to $-3/4\Delta I$ on the right-hand side.

7.2   Quantum Entanglement in Time

For the temporal Bell inequality the observer measures a single spin having a choice between different observation times. Also in the following example [25] a single spin is considered, but the observer chooses two different measurement directions specified by the unit-vectors $a(t_j), b(t_j)$ at two pre-set times t_j, $j = 1, 2$. Selecting the 4 operators,

$$\hat{F}^{(1)} = \hat{\sigma}_b(t_2), \quad \hat{F}^{(2)} = \hat{\sigma}_a(t_1),$$
$$\hat{F}^{(3)} = \hat{\sigma}_b(t_1), \quad \hat{F}^{(4)} = \hat{\sigma}_a(t_2), \tag{40}$$

the Bell-like inequality based on the sum rule Eq. (19) reads

$$\overline{|S(4)|} = |\overline{C(at_1, bt_2)} + \overline{C(at_1, bt_1)} + \overline{C(at_2, bt_1)} - \overline{C(at_2, bt_2)}| \leq 2. \tag{41}$$

In this case the correlation functions are independent of the initial state $|\Psi >$ and given by the scalar product

$$\overline{C(at_i, bt_j)} = a(t_i) \cdot b(t_j). \tag{42}$$

For 2-times non-invasiveness is guaranteed. But in order to violate the Bell-inequalities one has to choose at each time t_j incompatible frames $\{a(t_j), b(t_j)\}$. Indeed, the choice for maximum violation is:

$$a(t_1) = \frac{1}{\sqrt{2}}(b(t_1) + b(t_2)), \tag{43}$$

$$a(t_2) = \frac{1}{\sqrt{2}}(b(t_1) - b(t_2)). \tag{44}$$

An experimental realization has been presented in [26].

8   Summary and Remarks

The notion of nonlocality potentially defines a broad field of different physical phenomena. Here we have restricted ourselves to quantum limitations on the co-existence of discrete observables over space or time.

In consistent quantum theory (CQT) the essence of non-classical features is traced back to the invalidity of "unicity", i.e. the lack of any exhaustive, complete description. Instead we encounter a multiplicity of (mutually incompatible) frames based on one and the same Hilbert-space; there is no frame which is in principle superior to the other. The appropriate selection ("symmetry breaking") depends on the concrete embedding, e.g., the design of the experimental scenario.

The (theoretical or experimental) violation of the standard as well as the temporal Bell inequalities is interpreted to result from the combination of incompatible frames or inconsistent histories, respectively (in conflict with the "fundamental rule of CQT"). Quantum nonlocality becomes unmasked as a – possibly convenient – fiction.

In any case, such non-classical features are typically restricted to what one might call "laboratory physics". This is the realm of detailed control, achievable, e.g., in nano-physics (small Hilbert-spaces). Quantum weirdness usually does not survive on the macroscopic level. Indeed, the physical world around us overwhelmingly appears classical, due to the notorious phenomenon of decoherence [27].

Nevertheless, there are macroscopic quantum phenomena (like superconductivity). Less spectacular is the quantization of collective excitations related to many-body systems (cf., e.g., plasmons, magnons, phonons), or the effective spin-behavior exhibited by a restricted 2-level subspace within an atomic multi-level system, say. Identical classical models allow for identical (canonical) quantization procedures – irrespective of the underlying "meaning" of the observables.

In general, however, there is no clear recipe for quantizing an existing classical model, let alone for jumping directly to an "effective Hilbert-space" description. It is therefore still controversial, whether surprisingly stable "quantum-like features" could, indeed, persist in the macro-domain even outside physics. Recent proposals (ordered with increasing distance from physics) include the biological space [28], the medical space (see, e.g., [29]), and the opinion space [30].

Acknowledgments. I thank Hermann Haken, Stuttgart, for valuable discussions.

References

1. Bell, J.S.: On the problem of hidden variables. Rev. mod. Phys. **38**, 447 (1966)
2. Goldstein, S.: Bohmian mechanics and the quantum revolution. Synthese **107**, 145 (1997). arxiv:quant-ph/9512027 (1995)
3. Ghirardi, G.C., Rimini, A., Weber, T.: Unified dynamics for microscopic and macroscopic systems. Phys. Rev. D **34**, 470 (1986)
4. Asano, M., Basieva, I., Khrennikov, A., Ohya, M., Yamato, I.: Non-Kolmogorovian approach to the context-dependent systems breaking the classical probability law. Found. Phys. **43**, 895 (2013)
5. Birkhoff, G., von Neumann, J.: The logic of quantum mechanics. Ann. Math. **37**, 823 (1926)
6. Hohenberg, P.C.: Colloquium: an introduction to consistent quantum theory. Rev. mod. Phys. **82**, 2835 (2010)
7. Schlosshauer, M., Kofler, J., Zeilinger, A.: A snapshot of foundational attitudes toward quantum mechanics. Stud. Hist. Phil. Mod. Phys. **44**, 222 (2013)
8. Griffiths, R.B.: Consistent Quantum Theory. Cambridge University Press, Cambridge (2002)
9. Friedberg, R., Hohenberg, P.C.: Compatible quantum theory. Rep. Progr. Phys. (2014). http://physics.nyu.edu/~pch2/CQT-resub.pdf (submitted)
10. Lindner, F., et al.: Attosecond double-slit experiment. Phys. Rev. Lett. **95**, 040401 (2005)
11. Filk, Th: Temporal non-locality. Found. Phys. **43**, 533 (2013)
12. Clauser, J.F., Horne, M.A.: Experimental consequences of objective local theories. Phys. Rev. D **10**, 526 (1974)
13. Leggett, A.J., Garg, A.: Quantum mechanics versus macroscopic realism: is the flux there when nobody looks? Phys. Rev. Lett. **54**, 857 (1985)

14. Primas, H.: Basic elements and problems of probability theory. J. Sci. Explor. **13**, 573 (1999)
15. Dressel, J., Malik, M., Miatto, F.M., Jordan, A.N., Boyed, R.W.: Colloqium: understanding quantum weak values: basics and applications. Rev. mod. Phys. **86**, 307 (2014)
16. Aspect, A., Grangier, P., Roger, G.: Experimental realization of Einstein-Podolski-Rosen-Bohm Gedanken experiment. Phys. Rev. Lett. **49**, 91 (1982)
17. Salart, D., Baas, A., Branciard, C., Gisin, N., Zbinden, H.: Testing the speed of 'spooky action at a distance'. Nature **454**, 861 (2008)
18. Yin, J., et al.: Lower bound on the speed of non-local correlations without locality and measurement choice loopholes. Phys. Rev. Lett. **110**, 260407 (2013)
19. Gill, R. D.: Time, finite statistics, and Bell's fifth position. arXiv:quant-ph/0301059 (2003)
20. Feynman, R.P.: Simulating physics with computers. Int. J. Theor. Phys. **21**, 467 (1982)
21. Drummond, P.D., Opanchuk, B., Rosales-Zárate, L., Reid, M.D.: Simulating bell violations without quantum computers. Phys. Scr. **T160**, 014009 (2014)
22. Huelga, S.F., Marshall, T.W., Santos, E.: Temporal bell-type inequalities for two-level Rydberg atoms coupled to a high-Q resonator. Phys. Rev. A **54**, 1798 (1996)
23. Waldherr, G., Neumann, P., Huelga, S.F., Jelezko, F., Wrachtrup, J.: Violation of temporal bell inequality for single spins in a diamond defect center. Phys. Rev. Lett. **107**, 090401 (2011)
24. Rusko, R., Korotkov, A.N., Mizel, A.: Signatures of quantum behavior in single-qubit weak measurements. Phys. Rev. Lett. **96**, 200404 (2006)
25. Brukner, C., Taylor, S., Cheung, S., Vedral, V.: Quantum entanglement in time. arxiv:quant-ph/0402127 (2004)
26. Fedrizzi, A., Almeida, M.P., Broome, M.A., White, A.G., Barbieri, M.: Hardy's paradox and violation of a state-independent bell inequality in time. Phys. Rev. Lett. **106**, 200402 (2011)
27. Zurek, W.H.: Decoherence, einselection, and the quantum origin of the classical. Rev.mod. Phys. **75**, 715 (2003)
28. Briegel, H.J., Popescu, S.: Entanglement and intra-molecular cooling in biological systems? A quantum thermodynamic perspective. arxiv:0806.4552 (2009)
29. Milgrom, L.R.: Conspicious by its absence: the memory of water, macro-entanglement, and the possibility of homeopathy. Homeopathy **96**, 209 (2007). Comment by Leick, P.: Homeopathy **97**, 51 (2008)
30. Lambert-Mogiliansky, A., Dubois, F.: Transparency in public life: a quantum cognition perspective. In: Atmanspacher, H., et al. (eds.) QI 2014. LNCS, vol. 8951, pp. 210–222. Springer, Heidelberg (2015)

Intentional Quantum Dynamics: Entangling Choices and Goals

Robert Shaw$^{(\boxtimes)}$ and Jeffey Kinsella-Shaw

Center for the Ecological Study of Perception and Action,
University of Connecticut, Storrs, USA
roberteshaw@aol.com, jmkshaw@gmail.com

Abstract. An unresolved problem in psychology is prospective control, i.e., the question of how information about what is intended to be done can influence what is being done [22]. Over the past quarter century we have addressed this issue by working toward an intentional dynamics approach based on the Feynman path integral. From initial to final condition, i.e., from goal-selection to goal-satisfaction, the kernel of the integral's transform, $K(t_1, t_0)$, somehow propagates a path that solves a two-point boundary problem just as any constrained particle must. Here we treat choices at choice-points (including the initial, current, and final states) encountered along goal-paths as superpositions. Intention, or goal selection, is hypothesized to be just another word for entanglement whose path stability can be measured using quantum correlation. Also, we hypothesize that objects' multiple uses (affordances) encountered along the way can be treated as superpositions that "collapse" as the goal-paths are successfully propagated. Under this approach, we hypothesize that intentional activities are made possible by the system's entanglement dynamics – the progressive making and breaking of entanglements in order to stay on a goal-path.

1 Introductory Remark

The question that motivated this conference and the formation of the Mind-Matter Society is whether and to what extent there is an interaction between psychology and quantum mechanics – either theoretically or empirically. The current paper suggests one way in which to characterize such an interaction. It is not unusual for quantum physicists to claim there to be an intrinsic connection between their field and psychology. Here is one such instance offered by Schwartz, Stapp, and Beauregard [12]: "Quantum theory is built upon the practical concept of intentional actions by agents. Each such action is a preparation that is expected or intended to produce an experiential response or feedback. For example, a scientist might act to place a Geiger counter near a radioactive

This material is based upon work supported by the National Science Foundation under INSPIRE Track 1 grant BCS-1344725. Any opinions, findings, and conclusions or recommendations expressed in this material are those of the authors and do not necessarily reflect the views of the National Science Foundation.

© Springer International Publishing Switzerland 2015
H. Atmanspacher et al. (Eds.): QI 2014, LNCS 8951, pp. 255–270, 2015.
DOI: 10.1007/978-3-319-15931-7_20

source and expect to see the counter either 'fire' during a certain time-interval or not 'fire' during that interval. The experienced response, 'Yes' or 'No', to the question, 'Does the counter fire during the specified interval?', specifies one bit of information. Quantum theory is thus an information-based theory built upon the preparative actions of information seeking agent" (p. 9).

Psychology has been developing as a science but without a clear idea of what kind of science it might become. As quantum theory developed it soon became clear that it differed from classical mechanics in very important ways. Rather than being local and deterministic, it proved to be nonlocal and nondeterministic, instead of *either_or* but *not both* logic, because of superposition it has an *either_or* and *both* logic. Similarly, ecological psychology is dramatically different from classical psychology (i.e., behaviorism and cognitivism) in an analogous way. Next, an important way is discussed.

2   Ecological Laws as Analogous to Quantum Laws

Classical mechanical laws apply to predict events: Given the appropriate initial conditions (i.e., the mass and layout of three balls A, B, and C so that if $event_1$ occurs (e.g., ball A strikes ball B), then $event_2$ (i.e., ball B strikes ball C) necessarily (lawfully) follows. Traditionally, psychological laws have been assumed to take the same causal form: Given the appropriate initial conditions, normal organisms (with proper learning history, attending to stimulus, and so forth), then if $event_1$ occurs (a stimulus event), then $event_2$ (a response event) typically (lawfully) follows. Here, as Skinner [19] suggests, the stimulus, although not truly a force, acts like a force and the 'control law' (next state function), although not truly a law, acts like a law to move the organism into its next state from which it emits the observed behavior. If the state transition is associative, then this form of law fits a *stimulus-response behaviorism*; however, if the state transition involves a representation, or symbol, then this form of law fits *cognitive psychology* (Fodor & Pylyshyn [5]).

This classical law form, however, fits neither quantum phenomena nor ecological psychology phenomena (e.g., intentional dynamics); rather, they both take a different law form. It is generally agreed that quantum mechanical laws do not predict events with absolute certainty, as deterministic classical laws are supposed to do; rather they predict only the probability that subsequent observations (measurements) will follow from previous observations (measurements) if a certain relationship holds between a state function and characteristic properties of the situation (Wigner [23]). As indicated, ecological psychology requires laws that operate similarly.

Consider a rule for the perceptual control of action (Gibson [6]), say, as formulated from the perspective of a prey engaged in a prey-predator competition. *If you (the prey) intend to escape the predator, whose image is expanding in your optic array, then intend to move so as to make the predator's image contract!* Here, analogous to the quantum law formulation, the law relates a previous observation (information) to a subsequent observation. The quantum mechanical interpretation of intentional dynamics has a similar form.

The Table below compares the different laws discussed. Both forms of the classical law (I and II) relate event to event, while the quantum-type law form (III and IV) relate information to information through a function that is the complex conjugate of the characteristic property of that information. In the quantum case, a state function does so, while in the intentional dynamics case, a path function (an effectivity) does so.

	KIND OF LAW	FORMULATION
I.	Classical mechanics	$event_1 \rightarrow law \rightarrow event_2$
II.	Classical psychology	$stimulus \rightarrow law \rightarrow response$
III.	Quantum mechanics	$observation_1 \rightarrow law \rightarrow observation_2$
IV.	Ecological psychology	$perception_1 \rightarrow law \rightarrow perception_2$

3 Background

Two decades ago, we wrote a paper for a Neurodynamics conference entitled "Modeling systems with intentional dynamics: A lesson from quantum mechanic" [13] There we discussed the putative relevance and significance of Feynman's path integral, FPI (or, 'sums over histories') approach to quantum theory for developing a psychology of goal-directed behavior. A little later, we showed how the FPI might also be relevant to neuroscience by using it to model fundamental cerebellar activities [8,15]. Fifteen years later Ittai Flascher completed an experimental dissertation in our laboratory whose data was modeled quite well by a Markov chain Monte Carlo rendition of a Feynman path integral [4]. And, more recently, we showed how intentional dynamics might be treated under a thermodynamics framework [16]. Today we are continuing that program by providing some reasons to believe goal-directed systems are best understood when treated as quantum systems rather than classical systems. An inventory of the most relevant quantum theory concepts to be adopted includes superposition, interference, entanglement, and quantum correlation.

4 Introduction

Historically, attempts to provide traditional scientific accounts of systems that appear end-directed were stymied by the general ban on teleological reasoning. Such explanations have been deemed unworthy for two reasons: First, they violate mechanistic principles by invoking *time-backward* causation that puts effects before causes and, second, because they depend on, to use Einstein's words, "spooky action-at-a-distance" that violates the consensus view that distal influences cannot produce proximal effects without acting through mediating causal chains. Indeed, the concept of field was originated to be the mechanism for filling this empty gap.

In modern physics these objections no longer hold – and were even ill-founded in classical physics since notable examples of both backward causation and action-at-a-distance existed but were ignored. Hamilton's principle of least action and Maxwell's vector potential are two such cases. We briefly review the history of these shibboleths and the reasons they were over-turned to help set up our thesis that many systems (e.g., least action paths, black holes) do, in fact, exhibit *prototypic intentional dynamics* – the term we use to identify goal-directed systems and to refer to principled aspects of their common dynamics. But note carefully, a prototype is not yet the final form but is a basis from which a final form might eventually follow.

To emphasize how ubiquitous goal-directedness is in nature, we begin with a rather odd case.

5   The Intentional Black Hole

Let's allow ourselves to entertain a wild hypothesis. What if intentionality were rooted in the fabric of space-time as a ubiquitous physical phenomenon, then shouldn't it show up in some ways that are independent of living systems. Perhaps, there is 'prototyping' in nature whose expression in living systems is but a derivative outcome of something far more basic. Consider the following curious case of the "intentional" black hole as evidence that intentional connections might be as fundamental in nature as causal connections. (For clarification. see note at end of Sect. 11.)

Most of us have a nodding acquaintance with those denizens of deep space known as "black holes". However let us remind ourselves of some of their key properties. A black hole is a celestial object, probably a massive old star that has collapsed under its own gravitational attraction so that particles trapped inside its boundary, or event horizon, cannot escape with a velocity less than that equal to the speed of light. There is also a boundary outside the black hole such that objects that cross it are captured and dragged into the black hole.

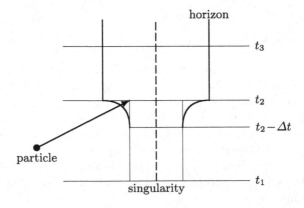

Fig. 1. Particle colliding with a black hole.

Figure 1 shows the make-up of a black hole to include a singularity, a point in space of essentially zero dimensions surrounded by a horizon. The temporal trace of the singularity is depicted as a dark vertical line with time running upward (note the order of time tags). The event boundary is depicted as the cross-section of two cylindrical sleeves of different radii, $(t_1 - t_2)$ and $(t_2 - t_3)$. A nonlinear jump in the size of the radius of the cylindrical boundary takes place whenever a particle is swallowed by the black hole at time t_2. Although the radial increment must be a discrete jump to accommodate the particle mass instantaneously added to the black hole, the field properties surrounding the black hole require that the transition from the smaller to the larger radius be smooth and continuous. Hence, there is a conflict here between quantum theory and general relativity: On the one hand, causality requires that the radial change be a retarded potential and not take place until *after* the particle is swallowed (i.e., the effect must follow the cause), whereas, on the other hand, the field property requires an advanced potential so that the smooth transition indicated by the arcs connecting $(t_2 - \Delta t) - t_2$ must take place *before* the arrival of the particle (Thorne [21], pp. 417–418).

In other words, if the horizon is to undergo the smooth continuous change field theory demands, then it must begin expanding before the particle arrives – a clear case of an anticipatory response where the effect precedes the cause! Note especially, that the degree of the expansion must be specific to (i.e., informed by) the mass of the particle and its time of impact. Does the black hole then somehow "know" the intention of the particle? If it were sentient, we would ask three questions: (a) In what form is the information about the impending collision of the particle made available to the black hole? (b) How is that prospective information detected by it? And (c) how is the anticipatory response of the horizon's radius controlled by the prospective information?

This may all sound quite farfetched, but the alternative explanation is no less so. For if there is no prospective information, then it must instead be a case of action-at-a-distance without any way to specify the black hole's control parameters. If so, then how does the distal particle cause the black hole to begin its early responding? To avoid action-at-a-distance and to preserve both the causality condition and the continuity principle that underwrites relativistic field theory, we have no choice but to postulate an information field that is co-extensive with the gravitational field. (It is important to note that this assumption of an information field is a hidden variable theory and inconsistent with Bell's famous theorem, namely, that no physical theory of local hidden variables can ever reproduce all of the predictions of quantum mechanics.)

There is no known energetic field to support the prospective information needed to specify the hole's advanced response to the particle's impending collision; nor is there any known mechanism present in the hole for detecting and using such information to effect that anticipatory response. Hence the mystery.

This black hole example is dramatic but not a standard one. Here is a standard example. It is possible to polarize two particles in a single quantum state such that when one particle is observed to be spin-up, the other one will always be observed to be spin-down, and vice versa. This result holds despite the fact that it is impossible to predict which set of measurements will be observed. As a result, measurements performed on one system seem to *instantaneously* influence the other system entangled with it – regardless of how far apart they are.

Now let the second particle be a black hole, then we seem to have an analogous case of "spooky action-at-a-distance" that is somehow brought about by the two objects being entangled. Hence the mystery of the anticipatory black hole seems just another instance of the mystery of entanglement in general.

6   Moved by Applied Forces or by Choosing Best Next Step

Nineteenth century mechanics formulated particle motion paths in two ways: in differential equations that expressed Newton's laws of motion and gravitational attraction and in Lagrange's integral equations that expressed Hamilton's principle of stationary (i.e., "least") action. Newton's laws explained motion by means of forces applied to the particle, step-by-step (i.e., dx/dt-by-dx/dt), from an agency located in the environment (and assumed in the initial conditions). In contrast to Newton, Lagrange explained a particle's motion by integrating the difference between its kinetic and potential energy (a quantity called the Lagrangian density). Hamilton's principle of stationary action asserts that particles prefer those paths that are at equilibrium along the path of average Lagrangian density. This is the so-called "least", or better, *stationary action path*, as compared to all other paths along which action (the time integral of energy) never changes (hence, the term stationary action path).

Lagrange's action integral method always yields a path that satisfies a condition known as the Euler-Lagrange equation and that coincides with Newton's solution. The two methods are formally equivalent, in the sense that they always give the same particle trajectory as their solution, and, as we shall see, they both entail the involvement of intentionality in their dynamical explanations. Let us see what this means.

If a particle is pushed by Newtonian forces applied to it from the outside, agency is externalized such that the particle has no choice but to move as made to. By contrast, if a particle must find which path out of all possible paths is the least action path, then it seems to require a particle to make choices. Thus it seems that it has intentions. For this reason, Poincaré [11] called Hamilton's principle "an offence to reason" because it apparently anthropomorphizes particles by requiring that they choose so as to satisfy a criterion (i.e., exhibit an intention). Furthermore no mechanistic explanation has ever been given for how a particle is able to do this intentional task.

Physicists have typically expressed their chagrin at the apparent need for a particle to consider its choices, especially when only the Newtonian path is considered real – the Lagrangian defined paths being mere possibilities, mathematical fictions, and thus not to be numbered among the physical entities populating the universe. For not being actually allowed by the laws of nature, how could they have any real status even if particles could choose. Such choosing would be nonphysical since it allows them to violate conservation laws. Hence no particle can have such freedom! But still they seem to. Another mystery!

In spite of this apparent absurdity, a closer look at both Newton's and Lagrange's mechanical accounts shows them both to be riddled with intentions.

7   A Pox on both of Your Houses

Why then do physicists not simply stay with the Newtonian account to avoid such particle chicanery? One reason is that this account has its own problems. If the particle only goes where external forces make it go, how do the external forces themselves get directed? A regress to the most prior initial conditions seems unavoidable (like Aristotle's prime mover regress). Could initial conditions not be explained as the product of prior application of the laws? It seems not, for initial conditions are complementary to dynamical laws in the sense that not only can they not be explained by such laws, but are needed if the laws as stated in their general form (differential equations) are to be made specific to a given situation. Without the initial conditions, the laws have no power of prediction or explanatory relevance [10].

Even if we assume the particle were a free agent, how could it make such choices? It would need to be enveloped in some kind of information field that informs it about the best next step to take. But then it must possess an information detection system and some means to act in a self-controlled manner. But this requires particles to have complex interiors that house *inter alia* an on-board action potential and a control mechanism that allows it to be guided by that information along its intended goal-path. This is of course contrary to fact.

For particles with simple interiors, such as electrons and photons, are known to abide by Hamilton's principle and to follow stationary action paths (if not constrained to do otherwise). For this reason, Poincaré's objection to Hamilton's principle seems quite reasonable – even though the principle has never been abrogated in nature. Thus there must be another story that honors both Poincaré's reasonable objection and Hamilton's valid principle. There is. And it is called Feynman's "sum over histories" approach to quantum physics. We consider it next.

8   Deriving Hamilton's Principle from the Sum over Histories

Feynman's strategy was to treat the behaviors of particles as following probabilistic waves rather than simple trajectories [3]. All possible paths are allowed, even non-physical ones. Through constructive and destructive wave interference (or positive and negative phase correlation), the set of possible trajectories is "sculpted away" until just those paths remain which are as close to the least action path as Heisenberg's Uncertainty Principle would allow. Hence the path selected is not where the particle *actually* is but where it is *most likely* to be found. The outcome of this move to quantum field theory is that the particle is constrained to follow the path left standing after all other paths have been cancelled by phase interference. In this way, the least action path simply emerges from the pack, therefore, making it *unnecessary for the particle to select its own path*. A law of nature does the choosing.

Here, however, determinism (simple location and certainty) is traded off in favor of a tolerable degree of indeterminism (distributed location and uncertainty). As a result this approach succeeds in removing the "offense to the reason" that so bedeviled Poincaré and others. In other words, the particle need not choose its path because it is constrained to follow the preferred path automatically.

Although the experts agree that the process works and even allows the other quantum strategies to be derived from it, whether it is physical or just mathematical is still an open question. Even expert physicists were perplexed by Feynman's suggestion that phase interference somehow acted simultaneously across all possible paths to automatically find the particle's preferred path. An anecdote told by one expert reveals how incredible Feynman's claim seemed to most physicists at the time and to many even today [2].

> Thirty-one years ago [1949!], Dick Feynman told me about his "sum over histories" version of quantum mechanics. "The electron does anything it likes," he said. "It just goes in any direction at any speed, forward or backward in time, however it likes, and then you add up the amplitudes and it gives you the wave-function." I said to him, "You're crazy." But he wasn't. (p. 336)

It is now generally conceded that Feynman's method is so fundamental that all other forms of quantum theory can be derived from it. Also, it has been shown to be useful throughout a wide domain of physical phenomena.

A major difficulty is encountered however when we try to understand how Feynman's path integral does its job without violating the dictum that nothing (with non-zero resting mass) can travel faster than the speed of light. It would seem therefore, according to Feynman's own words, that the particle must check each path in its entirety before choosing the right one – quite an impossible task, unless it could do so instantaneously in disregard of the relativistic limits (i.e., speed of light) placed on causal action. Perhaps, it is just one more weird aspect of quantum theory to be tolerated. In any case, we have found it a useful tool for understanding intentional dynamics of any system – whether inanimate or animate.

It is important to note that Feynman's "mechanism" of phase correlation postulated to explain Hamilton's principle is not a causal principle. It operates through a kind of wave interference process across all possible paths at the same time. In fact, no one knows quite how to interpret the mathematics physically. There is agreement however that it works but it remains a mystery by what physical principle it does so. Could it be that this is just another case of intentionality in physics and that intentionality lies at the root of the mystery?

9   Ecosystems Have Current States Entangled with Goal-States

"There is no classsical analog for a system whose full state description contains no information about its individual subcomponents" (Susskind & Friedman [20], p. 231).

"Information about self accompanies information about the environment, and the two are inseparable . . . like the other side of a coin. Perception has two poles, the subjective and the objective, and information is available to specify both. One perceives the environment and co-perceives oneself." (Gibson [6], p. 126).

Consider a simple example. Certain pairs of systems are relational in the sense of being so inexorably related and mutually dependent that they can not be separated without losing something essential to their identity. For instance, one can not be a husband without having a wife. Mathematically, a variable cannot be a conjugate, x, without having a shared identity with another variable, y, such that together they are arguments of a conjugation operator, $(xy)^* = yx$. Here the $(xy)^*$ term is an operator that inverts the terms. More generally, the schema $(\ )^*$ can represent an abstract operator that inverts the order of any two things whatsoever (of the right kind) but with the caveat if and only if they have the same relation to the conjugacy operator. Consider the examples, $(AB)^* = BA$, or (up down)* = down up.

So it is with entangled pairs, there must be an entanglement-making operator that defines their shared identity. In quantum physics that operator is interference, or better, is *interferes with*. Remarkably, any two objects (of a certain kind) that were ever together will continue to be co-identified regardless of how much time or space separates them. With respect to ecosystems, in this context, *organism* (O)-*environment* (E) systems, the O and E components share a kind of conjugacy relation – E affords x for O if and only if O has the means for doing x. This is consistent with the Gibsonian concept of *affordance* (roughly, what use something has for an actor) and its dual *effectivity* (roughly, the actor's action of using it).

One of the chief characteristics of intentional dynamical systems that make them somewhat nonintuitive is their quantum-like inability to be broken down into smaller, more easily analyzable parts. Hence reductionism, a favorite and useful method for most sciences, especially classical physics, is inappropriate. Let's assume the subsystems, O (e.g., a particle, system, organism) and E (i.e., environmental context), are the entangled components of an ecosystem. Thus they can not stand alone because information about one is also information about the other, that is to say, they are contextually bound together because they have entangled states. They are distinct but inseparable. Mathematically speaking, such systems are said to be *non-factorizable*. The two subcomponents, O and E, are stuck together by shared interference terms. Let's take a moment to consider this claim in more detail. Specifically, in the next section, we consider the origins of entanglement.

10   Interference, Complex Numbers, and the Origins of Entanglement

What exactly makes quantum systems seem so weird as compared to the more intuitively comprehensible classical systems? Actually, the source of the weirdness is perfectly clear, so clear, in fact, that it is taught in every introductory course in quantum physics – even if the weird consequences may continue to boggle intuitive comprehension. The source resides in the difference between classical probability theory and quantum probability (amplitudes) theory. The main difference is that while classical probability theory is based on the familiar real numbers, quantum probability is instead based on complex numbers. In this matter, as Dr. Samuel Johnson admonished, although I can promise you an explanation, alas, I cannot promise you an understanding. For it is candidly admitted by experts in the field that they too find it difficult to understand.

> "Those who are not shocked when they first came across quantum theory cannot possibly have understood it." – Niels Bohr

> "I think I can safely say that nobody understands quantum mechanics" – Richard Feynman

Let A and B be mutually exclusive events, say, as observed with respect to the slits in the famous double slit experiment. In classical probability theory, they would have associated probabilities PA and PB, so that the total probability of them occurring is obtained through simple addition:

$$P_{A \cup B} = PA + PB.$$

Contrast this with quantum probability, where, instead, their complex number amplitudes add such that extra terms are produced:

$$P_{A \cup B} = PA + PB + (\Psi^* A \Psi B + \Psi A \Psi^* B) = |\Psi A + \Psi B|^2$$

There is an extra term, yielding physically different behavior. Also, for the right choices of ΨA and ΨB, you could end up with two events that have nonzero individual probabilities, but their probabilities sum to zero! Or, alternatively, they sum to a value higher than the individual probabilities.

To appreciate how the interference terms come about, consider the familiar example of squaring a two variable sum in simple algebra.

$(x + y)^2 = xx + \underline{xy} + \underline{yx} + yy$, where xy and yx are interference term analogs.

Notice how the squaring operation introduces, in addition to the self-multiplication of each variable separately, two mixed cross terms (underlined). If we are dealing with complex rather than real numbers, then the order of the variables in the cross terms cannot be inverted, i.e., $xy \neq yx$. However if we are dealing with real numbers, and since real numbers are their own conjugates, then $xy = yx$.

Probability amplitude for entangled events is:

$$p(S \text{ or } T) = |A(S) + A(T)|^2 = |A(S)|^2 + A(S)A^*(T) + A^*(S)A(T) + |A(T)|^2$$

Notice the formal analogy between the equation above for the quantum probability amplitudes of an entangled pair of systems, S and T, and the equation below for the quantum probability of the entangled subsystems of an intentional dynamical ecosystem, O and E. The analogy is made explicit by a one-to-one substitution of O for S and E for T, and noticing that the typographies of the two equations match perfectly.

$$p(O \text{ or } E) = |A(O) + A(E)|^2 = |A(O)|^2 + A(O)A^*(E) + A^*(E)A(O) + |A(E)|^2$$

To make the proposed analogy even clearer, we expand the squared terms to their product form:

$$|A(O) + A(E)|^2 = |A(O)A(O)| + A(O)A^*(E) + A^*(E)A(O) + |A(E)A(E)|$$

(Here * indicates conjugation so that the A and A^* are conjugates, in the usual way for complex numbers, i.e., $a + ix$ and $a - ix$.)

Figure 2 shows the interference equations in digraph form. The strongly connected pair of systems can be used to portray the mutual dependence of O and E during a "perceiving-acting" cycle where there is perceptual guidance of actions (e.g., One perceives in order to move, and moves in order to perceive). The perceiving-acting cycle, in the present context, plays the role of the goal-path propagator as in the Feynman's "sum of histories" path integral [3]. In Fig. 2, the arrows are given a dual interpretation; they represent the interplay of both information and control as conjugate operators. For simplicity, we show just one – the primal – of the two digraphs. The dual digraph is obtained by reversing the arrows on the primal digraph. (Elsewhere, we have discussed in detail this 'model' of an ecosystem under the auspices of Kalman's famous duality theorem [9] for adjoint systems [14] and, alternatively, as a Lie group [17].

11 Gauge Forces and Cascade of Entanglements

As mentioned earlier, widely separated pairs of particles (or systems) that initially interacted can become entangled. If so, they will exhibit what is called quantum correlation. Recall that this means they are no longer separate individuals but must be treated as different aspects of the same entity. Where ordinary correlation is linear, quantum correlation is nonlinear. The nonlinearity arises from the entangling process. And we saw how an ecosystem is also formed by the interaction of two systems, say, O and E, which coalesce into an inseparable whole, $O + E$, because they share states. When such coupling is strong, it is synonymous with being entangled – although we should bear in mind that there may be degrees of entanglement – a useful fact when dealing with learning or tuning. What is so interesting about entanglement? Here is the standard reply:

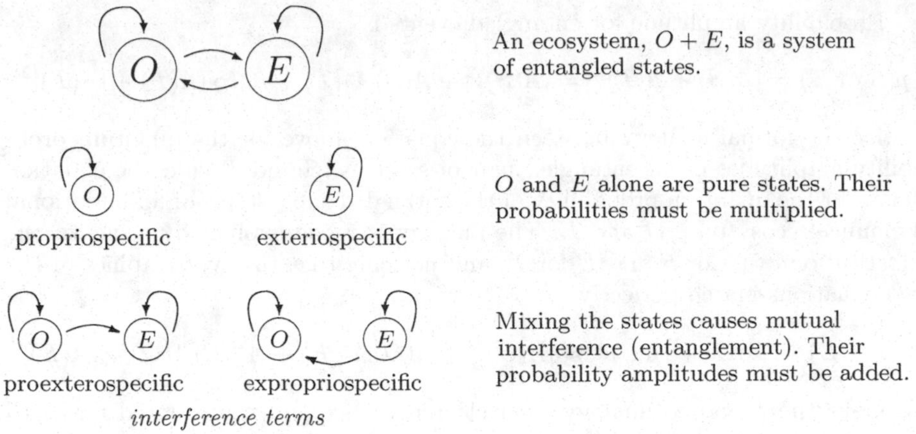

An ecosystem, $O + E$, is a system of entangled states.

propriospecific   exteriospecific

O and E alone are pure states. Their probabilities must be multiplied.

proexterospecific   expropriospecific

interference terms

Mixing the states causes mutual interference (entanglement). Their probability amplitudes must be added.

Fig. 2. Digraphs showing an ecosystem (top), the O and E subsystems (middle), and the interference terms (bottom). Terminology: *propriospecific* refers to information (or control) for an O independent of E; *exterospecific* refers to information (or control) for E independent of O; and *proexterospecific* and *exproexterospecific* refers to how O interacts with E and how E interacts with O, respectively. For our purposes here, the type of interaction is construed as interference. Again notice how the digraphs fit both interference equations by the simple substitution, as before, O for S and E for T. As stated earlier, the interference terms carry the entanglement of the two systems in both the physical and ecological case.

Being entangled bestows upon the system of compounded states a nonlinearity in phase correlation not previously there (hence the term "quantum" correlation). This added phase factor is conventionally called a "geometric" (or Berry) phase because it arises from a geometric property of the manifold (e.g., its curvature) on which the system's actions take place (such as moving from place to place). Since the added phase factor is *kinematic* in nature rather than kinetic, it leaves the energetics of a system untouched, and thus can be accrued by any system whatsoever.

Beginning with Einstein, the origin of the geometric phase factors is usually illustrated by showing how a frame-independent covariant derivative is needed to define a *connection* (a way of transporting in parallel fashion from one location to another on a manifold) that ordinary calculus cannot handle. The illustration, Fig. 3b, shows how a vector moved on a sphere through any closed triangular circuit (whose sides are portions of great circles) fails to return to its initial orientation. The lost orientability is the linear deficiency contributed by the acquired geometric phase and is usually represented as a *bracket product*, or commutator, whose value is other than zero (namely, $[A, B] = (AB - BA) \neq 0$). Moreover, this is also what it means to be *nonholonomic*.

Imagine a system moving along a goal-directed path (an intentional connection) accrues a geometric phase from the curvature of the manifold on which its actions are performed. Also, assume it appears to have rotated from its initial

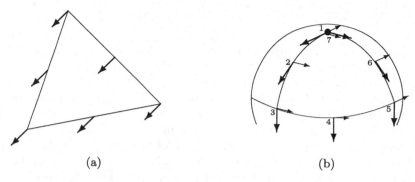

(a)   (b)

Fig. 3. Dynamic versus Geometric Phase. (a) A vector is parallel transported (without rotation) around the triangular circuit on a flat plane with no loss of orientation. But compare to (b). Here the spherical triangle consists of three arcs of great circles. A vector is also parallel transported (without rotation) around the circuit by a *covariant derivative* from position 1 to position 7 always pointing in the same direction – toward the South pole. But notice when it returns to the initial position (where 7 = 1) at the North pole, it has a different orientation although no forces have been applied to rotate it. Because its change in orientation is due only to the curvature of the spherical surface and not to forces, it is called a change in *geometric phase*. Here a very important concept is introduced into modern physics – that of *gauge force*.

goal-directed state. The goal-relevant information is a *global* variable while its apparent rotation (geometric phase change) is a *local* variable. To return to the intended goal direction (as globally specified) requires that the actor counter-rotate (locally) so as to cancel the effects of the geometric phase acquired globally. Since the actor has mass, to make the correction calls for application of a real torque force. Thus the corrective force was specified geometrically but applied kinetically. This is what is meant by a *gauge force*. In this way we see how information and control operators that define the perceiving-acting cycle, or propagator, are duals – as illustrated by the digraph earlier (Fig. 2).

The long range aim of our program will be to elaborate on the meaning of the following two general hypotheses and to justify their claims:

(*i*) *The actions of an ecosystem are controlled by gauge forces and specified by gauge information.*

(*ii*) *Intentional quantum dynamics is a positive process of entangling or negative process of disentangling states of O and E – all in the service of keeping to an intended goal-path.*

(NOTE: The loss of orientability is due to the system having moved along a *causal connection,* while the correction that cancels the geometric phase so accrued is a controlled, counter-directed torque force applied along an *intentional connection,* i.e., goal-path, intended to remove the accrued phase.)

12   A Peroration

Note again how the four information-control forms look analogous to the interference equations (Fig. 2). This should mean that they are also, formally speaking, evidence that O and E interfere with each other – evidence that they are generally quantum correlated, and therefore entangled. This means they are inseparable subcomponents of the unfactorizable ecosystem to which they belong. The ecosystem also comprises a set of superposed dual states – the affordances of E that O may choose as goals to realize and the effectivities of O that produce the actions, or means, to realize them. In the past [18], we have stressed that ecosystems are coalitions of dual pairs of dual operations, symbolized by '$<>$', at various scales:

$E <> O \supset affordances <> effectivities \supset perceptions <> actions \supset information <> control$

Now we want to amend that formal description by recognizing that the dualities that tied these items together are actually just examples of entanglements, at different scales, from most inclusive, to the least inclusive, that bind E and O together as an ecosystem.

(a) $E <> O$:   *system* entanglement
(b) effectivity $<>$ affordance: *function* entanglement
(c) perception $<>$ action: *process* entanglement
(d) information $<>$ control: *state* entanglement

These are the potential levels of entanglements that make an ecosystem a quantum dynamical system.

In bringing macroscale intentional dynamics into microscale quantum theory, have we jumped too many scales? Is there a danger that entanglements, even if they existed, might be destroyed? The entanglements postulated here however are not among massive objects or even ordinary states of such, but between intentions, information, and control state influences. The strength of these influences could be very, very small – perhaps, even Planckian scale. And might not the brain-cns processes involved in intentional dynamics be quantum scale as well (say, as argued by quantum brain dynamicists Jibu & Yasue [7])? If so, then the problem that might arise when skipping scales does not even arise. Also, in the theory and practice of quantum computation, all the qubit states are instantiated on macro-scale machines – so why not on the brain-cns system as well? Another example of the play of quantum dynamics at the macroscale is revealed in contemporary theories of friction – especially in the case of miniaturization.

Finally, to make the system capable of intended goal-directed behaviors, that is to say, to make it an intentional quantum dynamical system – we must also give it the freedom to make (creation operator) and break (annihilation operator) entanglements. Intentions, goals, and goal-paths are derivative of the entanglement possibilities already mentioned. Potentially, we see in this strategy a way to redress the long-standing conundrum of temporally "backward" causality in accounts of goal-directed behavior that rely on both local classical mechanism (i.e., causal connections) and nonlocal gauge mechanism (i.e., intentional connections). Correspondingly, we see in the move to a quantum intentional dynamics better prospects for a physically lawful account of goal-directed behavior at all scales of nature.

References

1. Dewey, J.: The reflex arc concept in psychology. Psychol. Rev. **3**, 357–370 (1896)
2. Dyson, F.: Disturbing the Universe. Basic Books, New York (1979)
3. Feynman, R., Hibbs, A.: Quantum Mechanics and Path Integrals. McGraw-Hill, New York (1965)
4. Flascher, I., Shaw, R., Michaels, C., Flascher, O.: A primer on the use of intentional dynamics measures and methods in applied research. Ecol. Psychol. **18**(4), 257–281 (2006)
5. Fodor, J., Pylyshyn, Z.: How direct is visual perception? Some reflections on Gibson's 'ecological approach'. Cognition **9**, 139–196 (1981)
6. Gibson, J.J.: The Ecological Approach to Visual Perception. Houghton Mifflin, Boston (1979)
7. Jibu, M., Yasue, K.: Quantum Brain Dynamics and Consciousness: An Introduction. John Benjamins Publisher, Philadelphia (1995)
8. Kadar, E., Shaw, R., Turvey, M.: Path space integrals for modeling experimental measurements of cerebellar functioning. Behav. Brain Sci. **20**, 253 (1997b)
9. Kalman, R.: On the general theory of control systems. In: Proceedings of First IFAC Congress, pp. 481–493 (1960)
10. Pattee, H.H.: Laws and constraints, symbols and languages. In: Pattee, H.H. (ed.) Laws. Language, and Life: Howard Pattee's Classic Papers on the Physics of Symbols with Contemporary Commentary. Springer, Netherlands (2012)
11. Poincaré, H.: Science and Hypothesis. Dover, New York (1952). (Original work published 1905)
12. Schwartz, J., Stapp, H., Beauregard, M.: Quantum physics in neuroscience and psychology: a neurophysical model of mindbrain interaction. Philos. Trans. R. Soc. B (2004). doi:10.1098/rstb.2004.1598
13. Shaw, R., Kadar, E., Kinsella-Shaw, J.: Modeling systems with intentional dynamics: a lesson from quantum mechanics. In: Pribram, K. (ed.) Appalacia II: Origins of Self-Organization. The Report of the Second Annual Appalachian Conference on Neurodynamics, pp. 53–101. Lawrence Erlbaum & Associates, Hillsdale (1995)
14. Shaw, R., Kadar, E., Sim, M., Repperger, D.: The intentional spring: a strategy for modeling systems that learn to perform intentional acts. J. Mot. Behav. **24**(1), 3–28 (1992)
15. Shaw, R., Kadar, E., Turvey, M.: The job description of the cerebellum and a candidate model of its "tidal wave" function. Behav. Brain Sci. **20**, 265 (1997a)
16. Shaw, R., Kinsella-Shaw, J.: Hints of intelligence from first principles. Ecol. Psychol. **24**(1), 60–93 (2012)
17. Shaw, R., Kugler, P., Kinsella-Shaw, J.: Reciprocities of intentional systems. In: Warren, R., Wertheim, A. (eds.) Control of Self-Motion. Lawrence Erlbaum & Associates, Hillsdale (1990)
18. Shaw, R., Turvey, M.: Coalitions as models for ecosystems: a realist perspective on perceptual organization. In: Kubovy, M., Pomerantz, J. (eds.) Perceptual organization. Lawrence Erlbaum Associates, Hillsdale (1981)

19. Skinner, B.: The Behavior of Organisms: An Experimental Analysis. Appleton-Century-Crofts, New York (1938)
20. Susskind, L., Friedman, A.: Quantum Mechanics: The Theoretical Minimum. Basic Books, New York (2014)
21. Thorne, K.: Black Holes and Time Warps: Einstein's Outrageous Legacy. W. W. Norton, New York (1994)
22. Turvey, M.: Affordances and prospective control: an outline of the ontology. Ecol. Psychol. 4(3), 173–187 (1992)
23. Wigner, E.: Symmetries and Reflections: Essays in Honor of Eugene P. Wigner. MIT Press, Cambridge (1967).

Note: After this paper was completed, we learned of work by Ken B. Wharton, Professor of Physics at San Jose State University. Here quantum theory is treated as involving two-point (time symmetric) boundary problems just as we do in framing intentional dynamics. A sample of his most relevant papers are:

24. Wharton, K., Miller, B., Price, H.: Action duality: a constructive principle for quantum foundations. Symmetry 3(3), 524–540 (2011)
25. Wharton, K.: Time-symmetric boundary conditions and quantum foundations. Symmetry 2(1), 272–283 (2010)

Towards an Empirical Test of Realism in Cognition

James M. Yearsley$^{(\boxtimes)}$ and Emmanuel M. Pothos

Department of Psychology, City University London, London EC1V 0HB, UK
james.yearsley.1@city.ac.uk

Abstract. We review recent progress in designing an empirical test of (temporal) realism in cognition. Realism in this context is the property that cognitive variables always have well defined (if possibly unknown) values at all times. We focus most of our attention in this contribution on discussing the exact notion of realism that is to be tested, as we feel this issue has not received enough attention to date. We also give a brief outline of the empirical test, including some comments on an experimental realisation, and we discuss what we should conclude from any purported experimental 'disproof' of realism. This contribution is based on Yearsley and Pothos (2014).

1 Introduction

Our aim in this contribution is to give an overview of recent work that seeks to address the question of whether models of cognitive processes can be (temporally) realist. We will define exactly what we mean by realist below, but the key finding is that given a suitable definition this question can be empirically answered by simple experiments. This contribution is based on Yearsley and Pothos (2014), but instead of simply summarising this paper we will instead focus on two of the most important issues and discuss them in depth. The two issues we shall focus our attention on are firstly the exact notion of 'realism' which is to be empirically tested, and secondly the possibilities open to us should experiments rule out this particular notion of realism. We feel these are important topics to address because the empirical test we shall propose, which has been discussed before (Attmanspacher and Filk (2010)), is borrowed from the physics literature, and it is far from clear how this test is to be derived or interpreted in the context of cognitive models. We shall take advantage of the fact that this contribution is based on an existing paper to skip much of the technical detail; interested readers are invited to consult Yearsley and Pothos (2014).

The rest of this contribution is structured as follows; in Sect. 2 we discuss the notion of realism in cognitive models in a general way and in Sects. 2 and 3 we introduce the two smaller assumptions that together make up the assumption of realism proper. In Sect. 4 we make some very brief comments on the empirical test of realism we propose. In Sect. 5 we then discuss the options for cognitive modelling should our empirical test rule out realism. We conclude in Sect. 6.

© Springer International Publishing Switzerland 2015
H. Atmanspacher et al. (Eds.): QI 2014, LNCS 8951, pp. 271–282, 2015.
DOI: 10.1007/978-3-319-15931-7_21

2   Realism in Cognitive Models

Every thought, feeling and memory that we have ultimately arises from, is processed by or is stored in the physical matter of our brains. Thus, in principle, if it were possible to know exactly the physical specification of a subject's brain at any moment of time, we should be able to know that subject's feelings and predict their judgments. Of course, such a scenario is the stuff of science fiction rather than current psychology, but the fundamental principle behind it, that the behaviour of cognitive variables such as feelings and judgments can be reduced to the physical specification of our neurophysical states does manifest itself in an important way in current cognitive models. In brief, most current cognitive models have a property that we might term 'realism,' that is, it is an implicit assumption of these models that all the cognitive variables whose values are described by a given model have definite values at all times (cf Raijmakers and Molenaar (2004)).

This assumption arises in a natural way when we consider the link between cognitive processes at the level of thoughts and feelings, and the underlying neurophysiology of the brain which is assumed to give rise to these thoughts and feelings. For the purposes of this contribution we assume the most fundamental processes in the brain relevant for cognition may be described by classical physics (the alternative hypothesis, that brain function at the neuro level is non-classical, is very controversial (beim Graben and Atmanspacher (2009))). It is a key feature of classical physics that the positions, electric charges, etc. of all classical particles are definite at all times, that is, whilst the values of these quantities may be *subjectively* uncertain (since we have only limited knowledge of them) they are nevertheless *objectively* certain. Thus, one might reasonably argue, if cognition is ultimately determined by brain neurophysiology, and if the most fundamental variables at the neurophysiological level have definite but unknown values, then presumably all cognitive variables must also have definite if unknown values. We will argue that this assumption is in fact highly questionable.

To make the argument more concrete consider a simple example; the first author of this contribution enjoys crisps, and he also enjoys chocolate. At any given moment of time he will have a preference for either crisps over chocolate, or vice versa. Let us denote this cognitive variable by the function $C(t)$, which may take values between $+1$ (definitely prefer crisps) and -1 (definitely prefer chocolate.) If we desire we could measure this variable crudely by asking the author which snack he would prefer, or we could measure it more precisely by asking him to make some trade off between various quantities of crisps and chocolate. The key assumption of classical models of cognition is that this variable $C(t)$ always has a well defined value between ± 1 at all times. This may seem reasonable over the course of some short lab experiment, but does it really make sense over longer periods of time? What happens when the author is distracted by writing a conference contribution? Or what if he has just sated his appetite with a bag of jelly beans? Does this cognitive variable nevertheless still exist, tirelessly winding some intricate path between ± 1 which only the gods, or possibly the advertising executives, can trace?

The alternative to a realist account of cognitive variables is one wherein such variables do not possess values until they are measured, that is, measuring such variables is a *constructive* process. The idea that measuring the value of a cognitive variable can change that value has been considered before, and can be easily incorporated within classical models of cognition. However what we are suggesting here is slightly different, it is not a question of measurements changing the values of *existing* quantities, rather the process of measurement *creates* those values, where previously there were none. This idea may sound familiar to anyone who has come across quantum theory before (see e.g. Jammer (1966)), and we will have more to say on this connection below. For now note that in the example we gave above it is not so hard to imagine that the author's preference for crisps over chocolate simply isn't *defined* at time when he is not, consciously or unconsciously, thinking about eating.

Why should we care whether our cognitive theories are realist or not? Well there are two main reasons; the first is that there are certain types of behaviour that are possible in non-realist models that are impossible in realist ones. This means that there may be limits on the type of cognitive processes realist theories are able to describe. The second reason seems to the authors more important; the ultimate aim of constructing cognitive models is not simply to describe or even predict cognitive processes, but at some level to understand them. For this reason it is important to have some confidence that the structural features of our models match or map in some sense the way cognition happens in the brain. Although our understanding of the physiology of cognition is currently far too limited to be used to impose detailed constraints on cognitive models, there are nevertheless some basic constraints that we can impose that do limit the classes of cognitive models we should consider acceptable. One of these concerns the idea of 'bounded cognition'; we would argue a second one concerns realism (for some work in this direction see Jones and Love (2011)).

So how are we to tell whether cognition is realist or not? We hinted at the answer earlier; there are some types of behaviour that are impossible to reproduce within a realist cognitive model. Our task therefore is to produce a test which will allow us to determine whether a given set of judgments can be described by a realist cognitive model, and to suggest some possible cognitive variables which may fail this test. We will do this below, but first we need to be clearer on exactly what we mean by realism in cognitive models.

In the next two sections we will discus two reasonable assumptions which together we claim form the assumption of 'realism' in cognitive models. We will spend some time discussing these assumptions in depth, because they are really the most important part of this work. Obviously since our test of 'realism' is really a joint test of these assumptions its significance depends entirely on whether one believes these assumptions really capture the correct notion of realism in cognition. But as well as this because there are two separate assumptions any purported failure of 'realism' leaves us the option of retaining one of the assumptions, and if we want to be clear about which one (if either) we should retain we need first be clear on their meaning. Once we have done this our empirical test of realism follows by some elementary algebra, which we shall skip, and the task of choosing a likely cognitive variable is an exercise in experimental cunning rather than intellectual vigour.

3   Realism Part 1: Cognitive Realism

Let us set out our first assumption which, together with the assumption discussed in the next section, together define 'realism' in cognitive models.

Cognitive Realism: This is the assumption that the reason for any judgement at the cognitive level is ultimately (in principle, if not in practice) reducible to processes at the neurophysiological level.

This assumption is perhaps what one might think of if one is asked to characterise realism. In fact it might seem like no further assumptions are needed, we will explain why this is not the case below. For now let us instead introduce some notation to help us make this assumption more precise, and to put it on the required mathematical footing needed for our empirical test. Consider again our example cognitive variable $C(t)$. Let us denote the complete neurophysiological state of a given subject as λ. Cognitive Realism means that there is a function which, given that the neurophysiological state of the subject is initially λ, will tell us the value of $C(t)$, let us denote this by $C(\lambda, t)$. This is what we meant in the introduction when we said that realism means that, in principle, were we to know the physical state of a subject's brain we would know all their feelings and be able to predict their judgments. However in practice of course we cannot know a subject's exact neurophysiological state, the best we can do is give some probability distribution based on the limited knowledge we do have. Let us denote the probability distribution representing our knowledge of a subject's λ as $\rho(\lambda)$. Then our best guess about the value of $C(t)$ given our knowledge of the neurophysiological state is,

$$\langle C(t) \rangle = \sum_{\lambda} C(\lambda, t) \rho(\lambda), \tag{1}$$

that is, the expected value of $C(t)$ is just the expectation value of $C(\lambda, t)$, given the probability distribution $\rho(\lambda)$.

Let us make few comments about this assumption, and its mathematical consequence Eq. (1).

- The observant reader may find the time dependence in Eq. (1) rather odd, in that is contained in the cognitive variable rather than in the distribution over neurophysiological states. This is purely notational, the current notation fits present purposes better.
- Let us stress that there is no expectation that we know the subject's λ, and also no requirement that we know the function $C(\lambda, t)$. Even if Cognitive Realism is true a subject's λ need not be knowable even in principle, but the λ's should be well defined and $C(\lambda, t)$ must exist.

- The assumption of cognitive realism may also be expressed in the following important way: for any set of judgements, and at all times, a subject has a definite opinion about all judgements.
- It is very difficult to see how this assumption could fail to be valid at some level. After all, if the values of cognitive variables are not determined by the brain, what are they determined by?
- The previous point notwithstanding, for the derivation of our empirical test to hold the λ need only be some variables which by assumption always have well defined values, it is not strictly necessary that they be neurophysiological. For more on this point see Yearsley and Pothos (2014).

Cognitive Realism may seem to totally capture the notion of realism we had in mind in the introduction. However there are two important missing ingredients in the discussion in this section. The first is a description of how measurement of a cognitive variable works. This may seem somewhat pedantic, but it is important to establish whether one can carry out reliable measurements of these variables, and to see how this fits in with realism. The second ingredient is some kind of assurance that we can take finite collections of cognitive variables and embed them into a cognitive model in a self-consistent way. In other words, Cognitive Realism is the assumption that the cognitive level can be connected to the neurophysiological level; what we also need is an assumption that the cognitive level can be *disconnected* from the neurophysiological level, and modelled on its own. That is the content of our second assumption.

4   Realism Part 2: Cognitive Completeness

Our second assumption is harder to state than our first. It concerns the cognitive state of subjects. This is defined to be the object that captures all the information needed to make predictions about a subject's judgments in the context of a particular cognitive model. It is therefore equivalent to an exhaustive set of probabilities for future measurement outcomes[1]. The exact form the cognitive state takes will depend on the model, and we want to state our assumption without reference to any particular form.

Cognitive Completeness: This is the assumption that the cognitive state of a person responding to such a set of judgements can be entirely determined by the probabilities for the judgement outcomes.

That is, observing participant behaviour can fully determine the underlying cognitive state, without the need to invoke neurophysiological variables. The reason this assumption is more vague than the first is that we have not defined exactly what the cognitive state is supposed to be. Generally this will depend on the model and we cannot assume, for example, that the cognitive state is a probability distribution over thoughts or judgments. However whatever the form

---

[1] The idea of defining the state of a system in this way occurs frequently in physics, see e.g. Hardy (2001).

of the cognitive state, if this is the object that allows us to predict judgment outcomes then it is important that it can be determined entirely in terms of them, otherwise it is not possible to establish this state empirically, making prediction impossible.

This assumption has an important consequence. Consider any measurement made on a group of participants that does not change the probabilities for the outcomes of any future judgement in the relevant cognitive model. Let us call such measurements non-disturbing. Whether or not a measurement is non-disturbing can be established empirically.

Cognitive completeness means that, as long as a measurement is non-disturbing, it can be assumed to have no effect on the neurophysiological state of a participant. This is because cognitive completeness tells us that the cognitive state of the participants may be fully determined by knowledge of the outcomes of all judgements in the relevant cognitive model. Thus, at most, a non-disturbing measurement may change the underlying neurophysiological state in a way that gives rise to the same cognitive state. However, any such change is undetectable by any measurement relevant to the cognitive model, and thus we can simply assume that no change in the neurophysiological state occurred.

It is useful to express this in a more mathematical way. Cognitive Completeness means that every cognitive model defines a set of similarity classes on the set of all probability distributions over the neuropsychological variables, with two distributions $\rho(\lambda)$ and $\rho'(\lambda)$ being similar, $\rho(\lambda) \sim \rho'(\lambda)$, if they lead to the same predictions for all judgements contained in the cognitive model. In general measurement of the cognitive variable $C(t_1)$ at t_1 will change the distribution of neurophysiological variables so that a subsequent measurement of, e.g. $C(t_2)$ with $t_2 > t_1$, will depend on whether or not the first measurement was made. Denote the new distribution over the λ after measurement at t_1 as $\rho(\lambda; t_1)$. Then joint measurement of $C(t_1)$ and $C(t_2)$ yields,

$$\langle C(t_1)C(t_2)\rangle = \sum_\lambda C(\lambda, t_1)C(\lambda, t_2)\rho(\lambda; t_1) \tag{2}$$

However if the measurement at t_1 was non-disturbing this is equal to

$$\langle C(t_1)C(t_2)\rangle = \sum_\lambda C(\lambda, t_1)C(\lambda, t_2)\rho(\lambda). \tag{3}$$

This is the mathematical result used in the derivation of our empirical test.

As a mathematical aside, we now sketch how Cognitive Realism and Cognitive Completeness may be used to derive the existence of a probability distribution over the cognitive variables[2]. We will assume that we are measuring the value of a cognitive variable $C(t)$ which may take a finite number of possible

---

[2] The existence of such a probability distribution in fact follows directly if our empirical test is satisfied, this is the cognitive analogue of Fine's theorem (Fine (1982), Halliwell (in press)). For a further discussion of the conditions under which such probability distributions may be defined, see Bruza et al. (2013).

values, which we will denote $\{c_i\}^3$. We begin with the generalisation of Eq. (2) for a series of measurements of $C(t)$ at a number of times,

$$\langle C(t_1)C(t_2)...C(t_n)\rangle = \sum_\lambda C(\lambda, t_1)C(\lambda, t_2)...C(\lambda, t_n)\rho(\lambda; t_1, t_2, ...t_n) \qquad (4)$$

For each measurement the set of possible λ may be split into subsets $\Lambda_i(t)$ according to the value of $C(\lambda, t)$. Denote the function which is 1 if $\lambda \in \Lambda_i(t)$ and 0 otherwise by $\chi_i(\lambda, t)$ This can be done for every measurement, so we can write,

$$\langle C(t_1)C(t_2)...C(t_n)\rangle = \sum_\lambda \sum_i c_i\chi_i(\lambda, t_1) \sum_j c_j\chi_j(\lambda, t_2)... \sum_k c_k\chi(\lambda, t_n)\rho(\lambda; t_1, t_2, ...t_n)$$

$$= \sum_{i,j...k} c_i, c_j...c_k P(i, t_1; j, t_2; ...k, t_3), \qquad (5)$$

where

$$P(i, t_1; j, t_2; ...k, t_3) = \sum_\lambda \chi_i(\lambda, t_1)\chi_j(\lambda, t_2)...\chi(\lambda, t_n)\rho(\lambda; t_1, t_2, ...t_n). \qquad (6)$$

Because $P(i, t_1; j, t_2; ...k, t_n)$ is just a coarse-graining of the original $\rho(\lambda; t_1, t_2...t_n)$ it is guaranteed to be a probability distribution on the set of measurement outcomes. However because $\rho(\lambda; t_1, t_2...t_n)$ depends on whether or not the measurements are performed this probability does not obey the correct sum rules when one or more measurements are summed out. However if we use the assumption of Cognitive Completeness we can drop the dependence of ρ on the measurements provided they are non-disturbing, in which case $P(i, t_1, j, t_2...k, t_n)$ becomes independent of whether the measurements are performed or not and therefore obeys the correct sum rules. This is the way in which Cognitive Realism and Cognitive Completeness imply the existence of a probability distribution over the cognitive variables.

5   Interlude: The Empirical Test and Some Experimental Considerations

Now that we have our two assumptions we can discuss the empirical test of realism that is the main achievement of this work. The test takes the form of a set of inequalities satisfied by realist systems but which may be violated by general systems. These inequalities may be easily derived from the mathematical expressions of Cognitive Realism and Cognitive Completeness, however rather than take up space in this contribution repeating algebra, we instead refer the interested reader to the appendix of Yearsley and Pothos (2014). We shall simply

---

[3] The extension to a cognitive variable with a continuous range of values is simple, but unenlightening.

quote the result, again in terms of our example variable $C(t)$ which recall takes values ± 1.

$$|\langle C(t_1)C(t_2)\rangle + \langle C(t_2)C(t_3)\rangle + \langle C(t_3)C(t_4)\rangle - \langle C(t_1)C(t_4)\rangle| \leq 2 \qquad (7)$$

Equation (7) is one of a collection of inequalities known as the temporal Bell[4], or Leggett-Garg inequalities, first derived as constraints on physical systems by Leggett and Garg (1985). Their significance in physics is much debated (see e.g. Ballentine (1987), Palacios-Laloy et al. (2010), Wilde (2012), George et al. (2013) and Yearsley (2013), and references therein), but note that the assumptions leading to their derivation in cognition are relatively uncontroversial. We will have nothing further to say about the use of these inequalities outside of cognition.

What would a concrete experimental set up to test these inequalities look like? Well we need four ingredients; the first is a cognitive variable which we are sure has two distinct values. There are many possible examples. The second is some way to manipulate the expected value of that variable, this could be through presentation of stimuli over which the experimenter does not have direct control, but which happen at regular time intervals, or it could be through presentation of stimuli over which the experimenter has direct control, in which case the frequency and order of presentation of the stimuli is not fixed in time, and the 't' variable in Eq. (7) is better thought of as a parameter rather than as a physical time. Again it is not hard to think of good examples.

The third ingredient is a reliably non-disturbing measurement process, in the sense outlined above. This might be hard to invent in general, but it is easy to establish whether a given measurement process is non-disturbing, so it presents no problem in principle. We mention in passing that it is not necessary that the measurement process be completely non-disturbing, being able to bound the disturbance to some low level is sufficient (Yearsley and Pothos (in preparation)). What might make a good non-disturbing measurement? In physics attention has focussed on so-called 'ideal negative measurements.' The idea is roughly that a particle which is not detected should not be disturbed by the detector (Leggett and Garg, 1985). One can therefore use an ideal negative measurement of whether a particle is in, say, $x < 0$ to establish that the particle is definitely in $x > 0$, but without causing any disturbance. It is not immediately clear whether these ideas can be translated to psychology.

However there may be another possibility available in psychology which is not available in physics. In psychology the extent to which a given judgment causes a change in the knowledge state of the subject can be influenced by details of the experimental design (e.g. White et al. (2014)). The psychological idea behind non-disturbing measurements would be to avoid a subject feeling as though they had made a strong commitment to a particular choice, and it is possible that this

---

[4] This term comes from the fact they these inequalities have a similar form to the standard Bell inequalities (see e.g. Bell (2004), for their significance in psychology see Conte et al. (2008) and Aerts et al. (2000). However beyond structural similarity the two sets of inequalities have little in common, and this terminology can sometimes lead to more confusion than clarity.

could be achieved through a sufficiently clever experimental design. Note that the question of whether or not this is possible is deeply connected to the issue of whether cognition is really 'quantum' (or possibly 'quantum-like'), so that fundamental limits such as the uncertainty principle always hold, or whether cognition merely has 'quantum features', in which case it may sometimes be possible to break what in physics are fundamental quantum limits.

What of the final ingredient? Well this is simply the expectation that the cognitive variable in question does behave in a non-classical way. This is in some sense the most simple and the most difficult property to establish. It may be possible to use variables which have previously been shown to behave in non-classical ways (see e.g. Busemeyer et al. (2011), Pothos and Busemeyer (2009), Trueblood and Busemeyer (2011), Wang and Busemeyer (2013), Wang et al. (in press)), otherwise some experiential cunning will be needed to choose an appropriate set of judgments.

6   What Should We Conclude if 'Realism' Fails?

Suppose we find an appropriate experimental set up, conduct a test of realism in the way outlined above, and find a convincing violation of Eq. (7). What should we conclude? Assuming one agrees with the arguments which lead to Eq. (7) then the only conclusion is that one or both of our assumptions, Cognitive Realism and Cognitive Completeness, must be incorrect. But which one?

If one is committed to realism one might be tempted to drop Cognitive Completeness. The problem is that it is Cognitive Completeness that ensures that the cognitive state can be empirically determined, and since the cognitive state is the object which determines the probabilities for the outcomes of judgments, Cognitive Completeness ensures that any model has genuine predictive power.

Nevertheless one might argue that this problem can be circumvented. If we cannot fix the cognitive state in terms of the outcomes of judgments contained in our cognitive model, can we not simply add more judgments, the probabilities for which *would* be enough to fix the cognitive state? The answer is that we cannot. The full argument is given in Yearsley and Pothos (2014), but the essence is that adding any cognitive variables which can be measured in a non-disturbing way simply gives an extended cognitive model from which the original one can be recovered by coarse-graining, but since the original model isn't realist the extended one cannot be either. Adding in cognitive variables which cannot be measured in a non-disturbing way solves this problem, but having cognitive variables which cannot *in principle* be measured in a non-disturbing way means the new model still lacks predictive power. In summary, Cognitive Completeness is possibly even more central to cognitive modelling than realism.

So if we cannot drop Cognitive Completeness, can we drop Cognitive Realism? The answer is we can, we can model cognition with non-realist theories like quantum probability theory that include a constructive role for judgment. Quantum probability theory is often described as quantum theory without the physics (see e.g. Aerts and Aerts (1995), Atmanspacher et al. (2006)), and is potentially applicable in any situation where there is a need to quantify uncertainty (see e.g. beam Graben and Atmanspacher (2009)). Indeed there has been no small measure of success modelling some aspects of cognition in this way (e.g. Aerts and Gabora (2005), Busemeyer et al. (2011), Pothos and Busemeyer (2009), Trueblood and Busemeyer (2011), Wang and Busemeyer (2013), Wang et al. (in press), Bruza et al. (2009). For an overview see Busemeyer and Bruza (2011), Pothos and Busemeyer (2013)).

However we need to be cautious. Realism imposes a bound on the right hand side of Eq. (7) equal to 2, but quantum theory also implies a non-trivial bound on Eq. (7) of $2\sqrt{2}$ (Tsirelson (1980)). Since the logical bound is 4 we could well find that our experimental test of realism rules out not just realist theories of cognition but also quantum ones! Even if the evidence doesn't directly rule out quantum theory there are possibilities for non-realist theories other than quantum theory. In other words, our test of realism may rule out realist models of cognition, but it cannot 'rule in' quantum models. We need to search elsewhere for convincing evidence for the correctness of quantum approaches to cognition.

Finally we should mention that a failure of realism in cognition could have great significance for models of memory. If judgment is a constructive process then it is easy to imagine that memory retrieval may also be modelled constructively in a similar way (this has been suggested before, e.g. Howe and Courage (1997)). This could open up exciting new possibilities for modelling memories.

7   Conclusion

In this contribution we discussed some of the key issues involved in recent work on the question of realism in cognitive models. We have focussed on what we believe are the key conceptual issues, readers desiring the full technical details are again invited to consult Yearsley and Pothos (2014).

What can we conclude from this discussion? Well firstly we have argued that the standard notion of realism in cognition might be well motivated, but it is open to empirical challenge. The successes of the quantum cognition programme to date suggest, although do not prove, that realism may have to be abandoned as an assumption in models of cognition. The proposed empirical test of realism will hopefully settle the issue. This test is tricky to implement, but should be possible with the right choice of cognitive variable and measurement.

If our tests do rule out realism, this is not by itself reason to adopt quantum models of cognition. However such models can give valuable insight into what non-realist approaches may look like. In particular contextually and constructive judgments are central parts of quantum theory (Kitto (2008), Busemeyer and Bruza (2011), White et al. (2014)) and these will also be key features of any non-realist theory.

We wish to conclude by saying that an experimental realisation of this test is currently underway (Yearsley and Pothos (in preparation)). We await the results with considerable interest.

Acknowledgments. E.M.P. and J.M.Y. were supported by Leverhulme Trust grant no. RPG-2013-00. Further, E.M.P. was supported by Air Force Office of Scientific Research (AFOSR), Air Force Material Command, USAF, grants no. FA 8655-13-1-3044. The US Government is authorized to reproduce and distribute reprints for Governmental purpose notwithstanding any copyright notation thereon.

References

Aerts, D., Aerts, S.: Applications of quantum statistics in psychological studies of decision processes. Found. Sci. **1**, 85–97 (1995)

Aerts, D., Aerts, S., Broekaert, J., Gabora, L.: The violation of Bell inequalities in the macroworld. Found. Phys. **30**(9), 1387–1414 (2000)

Aerts, D., Gabora, L.: A theory of concepts and their combinations II: a hilbert space representation. Kybernetes **34**, 192–221 (2005)

Atmanspacher, H., Romer, H., Wallach, H.: Weak quantum theory: formal framework and selected applications. Weak quantum theory: complementarity and entanglement in physics and beyond. Found. Phys. **32**, 379–406 (2006)

Atmanspacher, H., Filk, T.: A proposed test of temporal nonlocality in bistable perception. J. Math. Psychol. **54**, 314–321 (2010)

Ballentine, L.E.: Phys. Rev. Lett. **59**, 1493 (1987)

Bell, J.S.: Speakable and Unspeakable in Quantum Mechanics. Cambridge University Press, Cambridge (2004)

Bruza, P.D., Kitto, K., Nelson, D., McEvoy, C.L.: Is there something quantum-like about the human mental lexicon? J. Math. Psychol. **53**, 362–377 (2009)

Bruza, P.D., Kitto, K., Ramm, J.R., Sitbon, L.: A probabilistic framework for analysing the compositionality of conceptual combinations (2013). arXiv preprint arXiv:1305.5753

Busemeyer, J.R., Bruza, P.: Quantum Models of Cognition and Decision. Cambridge University Press, Cambridge (2011)

Busemeyer, J.R., Pothos, E.M., Franco, R., Trueblood, J.: A quantum theoretical explanation for probability judgment errors. Psychol. Rev. **118**, 193–218 (2011)

Conte, E., Khrennikov, A.Y., Todarello, O., De Robertis, R., Federici, A., Zbilut, J.P.: A preliminary experimental verification on the possibility of bell inequality violation in mental states. NeuroQuantology **6**(3), 214–221 (2008)

Fine, A.: Joint distributions, quantum correlations, and commuting observables. J. Math. Phys. **23**, 1306–1310 (1982)

George, R., Robledo, L., Maroney, O., Blok, M., Bernien, H., Markham, M., Twitchen, D., Morton, J., Briggs, A., Hanson, R.: Proc. Natl. Acad. Sci. **110**, 3777–3781 (2013)

Halliwell, J.J.: Two proofs of Fine's theorem. Phys. Lett. A **378**, 2945–2950 (2014)

Graben, P.B., Atmanspacher, H.: Extending the philosophical significance of the idea of complementarity. In: Atmanspacher, H., Primas, H. (eds.) Recasting Reality. Wolfgang Pauli's Philosophical Ideas and Contemporary Science, pp. 99–113. Springer, Heidelberg (2009)

Hardy, L.: Quantum theory from five reasonable axioms (2001). arXiv preprint arXiv:quant-ph/0101012

Howe, M.L., Courage, M.L.: The emergence and early development of autobiographical memory. Psychol. Rev. **104**, 499–523 (1997)

Jammer, M.: The Conceptual Development of Quantum Mechanics. McGraw Hill, New York (1966)

Jones, M., Love, B.C.: Bayesian fundamentalism or enlightenment? On the explanatory status and theoretical contributions of Bayesian models of cognition. Behav. Brain Sci. **34**(169), 231 (2011)

Kitto, K.: Why quantum theory? In: Proceedings of the Second Quantum Interaction Symposium, pp. 11–18. College Publications (2008)

Leggett, A.J., Garg, A.: Quantum mechanics versus macroscopic realism: is the flux there when nobody looks? Phys. Rev. Lett. **54**, 857–860 (1985)

Palacios-Laloy, A., Mallet, F., Nugyen, F., Bernet, P., Vion, D., Esteve, D., Korotkov, A.N.: Experimental violation of a Bell's inequality in time with weak measurement. Nat. Phys. **6**, 442 (2010)

Pothos, E.M., Busemeyer, J.R.: A quantum probability explanation for violations of 'rational' decision theory. Proc. R. Soc. B **276**, 2171–2178 (2009)

Pothos, E.M., Busemeyer, J.R.: Can quantum probability provide a new direction for cognitive modelling? Behav. Brain Sci. **36**, 255–327 (2013)

Raijmakers, M.E.J., Molenaar, P.C.M.: Modelling developmental transitions in adaptive resonance theory. Dev. Sci. **7**, 149–157 (2004)

Trueblood, J.S., Busemeyer, J.R.: A comparison of the belief-adjustment model and the quantum inference model as explanations of order effects in human inference. Cogn. Sci. **35**, 1518–1552 (2011)

Tsirelson, B.S.: Quantum generalizations of Bell's inequality. Lett. Math. Phys. **4**, 93 (1980)

Wang, Z., Busemeyer, J.R.: A quantum question order model supported by empirical tests of an a priori and precise prediction. TICS **5**, 689–710 (2013)

Wang, Z., Solloway, T., Shiffrin, R.M., Busemeyer, J.: Context effects produced by question orders reveal quantum nature of human judgments. PNAS **111**(26), 9431–9436 (2014)

White, L.C., Pothos, E.M., Busemeyer, J.R.: Sometimes it does hurt to ask: the constructive role of articulating impressions. Cognition **133**(1), 48–64 (2014)

Wilde, M.M., Mizel, A.: Addressing the clumsiness loophole in a Leggett-Garg test of macrorealism. Found. Phys. **42**, 256–265 (2012)

Yearsley, J.M.: The Leggett-Garg inequalities and non-invasive measurability (2013). Pre-print arXiv.org/abs/1310.2149

Yearsley, J.M., Pothos, E.M.: Challenging the classical notion of time in cognition: a quantum perspective. Proc. R. Soc. B **281**(1781), 20133056 (2014)

Yearsley, J.M., Pothos, E.M.: An Empirical Test of Temporal Realism in Cognition (in preparation)

Author Index

Printed in the United States
by Bookmasters

Printed in the United States
By Bookmasters